Lecture Notes in Educational Technology

Series Editors

Ronghuai Huang, Smart Learning Institute, Beijing Normal University, Beijing, China

Kinshuk, College of Information, University of North Texas, Denton, TX, USA

Mohamed Jemni, University of Tunis, Tunis, Tunisia

Nian-Shing Chen, National Yunlin University of Science and Technology, Douliu, Taiwan

J. Michael Spector, University of North Texas, Denton, TX, USA

D1827166

The series Lecture Notes in Educational Technology (LNET), has established itself as a medium for the publication of new developments in the research and practice of educational policy, pedagogy, learning science, learning environment, learning resources etc. in information and knowledge age, – quickly, informally, and at a high level.

Abstracted/Indexed in:

Scopus, Web of Science Book Citation Index

More information about this series at http://www.springer.com/series/11777

Daniel Burgos · Jako Olivier

Editors

Radical Solutions for Education in Africa

Open Education and Self-directed Learning in the Continent

 Springer

Editors
Daniel Burgos
Universidad Internacional de La Rioja
Logroño, Spain

Jako Olivier
North-West University
Mahikeng, South Africa

ISSN 2196-4963   ISSN 2196-4971   (electronic)
Lecture Notes in Educational Technology
ISBN 978-981-16-4101-5   ISBN 978-981-16-4099-5   (eBook)
https://doi.org/10.1007/978-981-16-4099-5

This Springer imprint is published by the registered company Springer Nature Singapore Pte Ltd.
The registered company address is: 152 Beach Road, #21-01/04 Gateway East, Singapore 189721,
Singapore

Foreword

Radical Solutions for Education in Africa explores the implications and the affordances of technology and specifically open educational resources, together with self-directed learning as a particularly enabling and empowering method within the African context, where access to and success in education remains a critical challenge. Critical in many of the chapters is the recognition that the transformative potential of education can be enhanced through a properly contextualised approach to technology and a sensitivity towards the learners' interests, capabilities, experiences and motivation levels. This is not the journey of the individual since self-directed learning entails reaching out to and working with peers in ways that learning is enhanced. Johnson and Johnson (2019, p. 47) list five conditions entailed in collaborative learning "positive interdependence, individual accountability, promotive interaction, social skills and group processing", themes which emerge throughout the chapters as the reader transverses school as well as higher education contexts.

Higher education institutions are key enablers in terms of not only providing access to technology, or online presence with a view to communication, learning and collaboration, but access to learning support, how technology enables such support and how learning can be enhanced through technology. Trustworthiness of access routes as well as trustworthiness of knowledge itself is important in terms of being properly contextualised and sufficiently diverse.

Also touched on in terms of access is how access is configured, and then how it comes to be experienced as accessible, relevant and engaging entails a pedagogic focus on the nature of the learner's direction in seeking, obtaining and utilising such access. Self-direction is a key consideration when considering access to, as well as use of technology. It is thus unsurprising that most of the research conducted in Africa pertaining to SDL is qualitative in nature, involving academics and university students, with overall trends concerning the need to develop teachers (and thus focusing on teacher education and health sciences education) to understand not only how to develop and facilitate the adoption of skills associated with SDL, but also to engender motivation among both educators and learners.

Chapters additionally explore the relationship between pedagogy and skills which are associated with SDL, and it is possible to create a supportive online learning environment through more conventional and established notions such as the flipped classrooms, which through their formulation engage students with the possibility of discovering how pacing affects their learning and how self-direction can be stimulated not only through technology and devices, but also through the environment. Alignment between environment creation, technology use and associated and conducive pedagogy makes for a compelling proposition in which benefits are evident in terms of memory enhancement, the capacity to self-regulation as well as self-directed discovery and new learning.

The book considers open educational resources (and development) and the fit between OER conceptualisation and the principles associated with SDL. This is motivated by the potential OERs represented in terms of enhanced access and the fact that such resources can be modified to suit different learning contexts. International research on OERs reveals that there is an explicit referencing to self-regulation as well as direction in which these resources are developed and the levels of collaboration and cooperation entailed. Thus, the methodology associated with OER creation itself entails pedagogy such that the learning process and experience take the form of evidence in terms of the design intentions as well as outcomes. In this regard, assessment becomes especially important from a design as well as experience perspective especially in the context of testing for progression and how this is approached. It has been noted the higher education institutions are "slow to evolve" in relation to the design of online assessment that not only reveals evidence of (self-directed) learning, but also encourages the explicit referencing of such, rather than knowledge store. Human difference (or variance) is important to allow for in such assessment design. Importantly, SDL should not be conflated with individualistic or isolated learning, and that it is possible to engage in community-based self-direction described in the literature as collaborative and cooperative learning in which networking and working together is part of the learning design.

The research described in Radical Solutions for Education in Africa shows that open educational resources lend themselves also to different modalities including distance learning. Self-directed learning in the online learning environment offers many affordances for the learner, but it has to be recognised that perceptions as regards access barriers, or anxiety about technology can play a role in limiting a learner's experience, suggesting that there is a need for mentoring and induction that enables the learner to explore with guidance the affordances of online learning using SDL. How to mentor or coach a learner effectively in the online or distance environment is thus an important part of an educator's development. That noted, there are power asymmetries inherent in the relationship between mentor and mentee. A focus on the development of softer skills as well as pedagogic approaches is thus necessary when mentoring is entailed: thus, for example, collaborative learning in which a problem is entailed in the learning experience allows for the development of sophisticated and nuanced communication skills between a mentor and mentee.

Readers are invited to consider also the applications of self-directed learning and OER development as a means of enriching adult learning in an African context, especially in the context of vocational training and education. In particular is explored the theorisation of cognitive apprenticeship and SDL in the context of workplace learning and the development of learner portfolios. The many themes explored in the text provide scholarly insights not only about research conducted concerning self-directed learning and OER development in Africa, but also emerging from the survey of such research.

Robert J. Balfour, Ph.D. (Cantab), FCCS
Deputy Vice-Chancellor (Teaching and Learning)
North-West University
Potchefstroom, South Africa

Preface

In Africa, open education and the use of open educational resources (OERs) have become increasingly prominent. Consequently, this has also made the associated open pedagogy and open educational practices relevant research foci. However, in order to prepare students for the needs of a twenty-first-century society and the challenges of the impending Fourth Industrial Revolution, students will have to be self-directed learners. Therefore, a need exists for research on how open education could be supportive to fostering self-directed learning (SDL).

Indeed, there are three main reasons behind this book. On the one side, Africa is in need for a new wave of innovation and practical solutions in education. Open education and SDL have become key for successful education across the continent. Further, SDL is now, with the global crisis in the context of the COVID-19 pandemic, a reasonable and doable aim and learning strategies supporting this characteristic should be encouraged towards greater student agency. Strategies to support SDL will become practical resources to learn and grow, no matter the restrictions linked to this or any other crisis. Finally, open education is proven to provide learners of any age with access to a limitless pool of resources and practices, ready to be used, reused, created and shared, with the proper licence. The combination of open education and SDL means a powerful framework, easy to implement and solid enough to last and make a significant impact.

The book is structured in three clusters: (1) focused on SDL, from Chaps. 1 to 5, with contributions from Olivier, Elsafi and Gunness. This section provides an overall outlook on SDL in general and specifically in the African context; (2) focused on open education, OERs and open educational practices, from Chaps. 6 to 10, with contributions from Shikalepo, Simui, Ferreira-Meyers, Seeletso and Tarling. This section explains openness as an integral part of education in many approaches: adult education, vocational education, science, educators and others; and (3) focused on practical case studies on textbooks, mathematics, secondary education and online courses, applied to Mauritius, Morocco and South Africa. It goes from Chaps. 11 to 14, supported by Sapire, El Kharki, Gooria and Ngimwa, as first and/or corresponding authors.

To this extent, this publication explores the state of open education in terms of self-directed learning on the African continent. Through a combination of conceptual, systematic literature review and empirical chapters, readers will get a research-based impression of these aspects in this area. Besides presenting existing wider trends regarding open education, this book also reports on effective open practices in support of self-directed learning.

Guest Editors
Daniel Burgos
Director UNIR iTED
Vice-rector for International Research
Universidad Internacional de La Rioja (UNIR)
Logroño, Spain

Extra-ordinary Professor
Research Unit Self-Directed Learning
Faculty of Education
North-West University
Potchefstroom, South Africa

Jako Olivier
Professor in Multimodal Learning
UNESCO Chair on Multimodal Learning
and OER
North-West University
Mahikeng, South Africa

Contents

Chapter 1
Online Access and Resources for Open Self-directed Learning in Africa

Jako Olivier

Abstract Learning online has grown significantly in the African context, and hence access and the nature of resources in this area have become more important. This chapter explores the context of online access and resources on the continent as contextualisation for open education and self-directed learning in Africa. This conceptual chapter provides an overview of the relevant scholarship on the nature of online access and resources in this context. To this end, published statistics and research were critically analysed. Successful online access does not only imply formal access to resources, but also require epistemic, demiurgic as well as axiopistical access. Consequently, these issues are also regarded in terms of what is required from students to reach all these levels of access. Furthermore, this chapter considers resources in terms of it being either material or human within the self-directed learning context and this chapter also focuses on how this concept is viewed within open education. The chapter concludes with a discussion and overview of how online access and resources and its role in education should be viewed within the African context and in terms of the concept of ubuntu where communal aspects of learning are highlighted.

Keywords Online access · Online resources · Open educational resources · Self-directed learning · Africa

1.1 Introduction

This chapter explores the nature of online access and resources in terms of open education and self-directed learning (SDL) in the African context. To this end, the wider African context is described after which access and resources for open SDL are considered. An overview of online in access in Africa is provided after which the nature of educational resources in this context is covered. Finally, the different levels of access to resources are discussed before some concluding recommendations and remarks are presented.

J. Olivier (✉)
Research Unit Self-Directed Learning, Faculty of Education, North-West University, Private Bag X2046, Mmabatho 2735, South Africa
e-mail: jako.olivier@nwu.ac.za

© The Author(s), under exclusive license to Springer Nature Singapore Pte Ltd. 2021
D. Burgos and J. Olivier (eds.), *Radical Solutions for Education in Africa*, Lecture Notes in Educational Technology, https://doi.org/10.1007/978-981-16-4099-5_1

It is clear that the concept of *access* has many different meanings within the educational context as it can pertain to physical access, but also be extended to other meanings (Du Plooy & Zilindile, 2014) and hence also relate to functioning, understanding and creating as part of obtaining access (Olivier, 2020). Access to education in the wider sense is also relevant to this discussion, and it is embedded in international guiding documents such as the Universal Declaration of Human Rights (UN, 2002b) as well as the Dakar Framework for Action (UNESCO, 2000).

The United Nations Sustainable Development Goal (SDG) 4 for Quality Education (UN, 2020a) highlights the importance of access to education at all levels. Within this context, the aims of the Global Education Coalition (UN, 2020a) should also be considered as they intend to:

- Help countries in mobilising resources and implementing innovative and context-appropriate solutions to provide education remotely, leveraging hi-tech, low-tech and no-tech approaches;
- Seek equitable solutions and universal access;
- Ensure coordinated responses and avoid overlapping efforts;
- Facilitate the return of students to school when they reopen to avoid an upsurge in dropout rates.

An important philosophical aspect to consider within the African context is the individual as seen as being an integral part of and from the community. This aspect is termed *ubuntu* within the South African context. The term also has equivalents in other African languages such as *botho* in the Sotho languages and *ukama* in Shona (Le Grange, 2019). For Letseka (2012), ubuntu is an African approach in which "a human being is a human being because of other human beings" (p. 57). Furthermore, according to Takyi-Amoako and Assié-Lumumba (2018) "[u]buntu as a distinctive African philosophy, history, culture, identity, and value of common humanity holds humanness as critical to human development into all its systems, particularly, its formal education systems" (p. 10). In addition, Lumumba-Kasongo (2018) highlights that ubuntu is not just an approach or even methodology but an African social value. Ubuntu has also been approached in the context of online learning (Kemeh, 2018) and is also relevant for this chapter. Kemeh (2018) interprets the SDGs in terms of ubuntu and concludes that "the UN sustainable development goal framework resonates with the Ubuntu framework in that what underpins both frameworks is making equal opportunities seamlessly available to all" (p. 189).

The relevance of online access and resources is evident from the literature. It is also clear that enhanced access to education supports economic growth through access to the Internet (Donou-Adonsou, 2019). Within the context of the Fourth Industrial Revolution, access to technology and specifically the Internet is also essential (Ayentimi & Burgess, 2019) especially in terms of education. In general, access to the Internet is linked to economic growth (Aikins, 2019; Gillwald, 2017) and specifically in research done on Sub-Saharan Africa[1] (Ayentimi & Burgess, 2019; Tripathi & Inani, 2016). The presence of fast Internet connections has had a positive impact on employment in the African context especially with regard to higher-skill occupations (Hjort & Poulsen, 2019). Yet, the affordances of technology for the African continent's educational context should be considered seriously and in this regard Waghid (2019, p. 140) proposes that:

> …the innovative use of educational technology as a means to flatten hierarchical control, whereby we are able to move away from teacher-centred approaches towards more democratic, inclusive forms of teaching and learning in the main, establishing communities of inquiry.

Consequently, not only does technology open up possibilities regarding access, but also allows for a more student-centred approach which is a requirement for SDL.

The issue of access has been a major topic of investigation in the literature and is often regarded within the context of the digital divide (Kuika Watat & Jonathan, 2020; Peroni & Bartolo, 2018; Wasserman, 2017). The *digital divide* is defined as "the gap between households with effective access to computers and the Internet and those with very limited or no access" (Aikins, 2019, p. 64). Overall, there still seems to be a digital divide between the rest of the world and Africa (Peroni & Bartolo, 2018), but there are also wide divides within the continent itself as well. Importantly, Wasserman (2017) asserts that "[s]tudies of the Internet in African societies consequently tend to foreground questions of access, development and democratic 'deepening', in other words, positioning digital technologies in the first instance as solutions to problems" (p. 3) and that in itself this access can lead to development. Hence, the issue of access—especially in the context of the African continent—should be considered in terms of historical but also current socio-economic factors and the realities of the ongoing digital divides between countries and communities.

A physical and policy context conducive to sufficient online access and availability to resources must be considered. According to Asongu and Le Roux (2017) as well as Ayentimi and Burgess (2019) policies that support information and communication technologies (ICTs), penetration could increase human development in Sub-Saharan Africa. However, Friederici et al. (2017) question the wide-scale impact of providing access and they contend that "the Internet and other ICTs have not had any undisputed transformational impact on economic development" and that "the evidence is inconclusive, and positive impacts appear to be idiosyncratic, contingent and variegated" (p. 15). Hence, access in itself might not be sufficient and hence the discussion on access should be considered in terms of wider empowerment and, as stated in this chapter, within the context of open education and SDL.

The African continent is very diverse, and while it is the second highest populated and second largest continent in the world, it also shows great divides in terms of access and resources. The next section provides an overview of the wider African context.

---

[1] Despite the vagueness and negative associations with the term "Sub-Saharan Africa", it is used in this chapter only in relation to published works where the term was used. As such, this chapter does not condone the usage of the term.

1.2   African Context

As this chapter relates to online access and resources on the African continent, it is imperative to provide a brief introduction to this context. The continent has 54 countries and is the second biggest in terms of size and population in comparison with other continents (Ayentimi & Burgess, 2019). Accordingly, it is essential to acknowledge that Africa is a very diverse and heterogenous continent (Takyi-Amoako & Assié-Lumumba, 2018) and that access to education, online or otherwise, differs between countries, regions and even at a local level. Hence, the wider African population is not just diverse, but their needs in terms of online access and resources are also very diverse.

The population of Africa is very young with 41% of the population being below the age of 15 in 2017, and for most countries on the continent between 60 and 70 per cent of the population is younger than 30 years (Takyi-Amoako & Assié-Lumumba, 2018). In research conducted by the UNESCO Institute for Statistics (2016), it was found that many children in Africa are not attending school and that in primary schools in a third of the countries researched, class sizes were more than 50 students per class. In addition, it is common for textbooks to be shared; for instance, in one country on average 14 students have to share the same mathematics textbook (UNESCO Institute for Statistics, 2016). The challenges in terms of access to schools and learning in general also seem to be highly problematic. Importantly, the majority of schools, regardless of level, do not have access to electricity (UNESCO Institute for Statistics, 2016). These circumstances make the need for online access and resources problematic as the infrastructure limits Internet access.

Two main barriers to infuse ICT into schools in the African context seem to be access to electricity and teacher preparedness; conversely, it seems that mobile devices show a lot of promise in this context (Samarakoon et al., 2017). This is especially relevant as mobile devices require less specialised skills as with computer-based Internet access (Gillwald, 2017).

According to the International Telecommunication Union (ITU) (2020), in Africa 44.3% of the population has access to 4G, while 33.1% has 3G and 11% has 2G mobile coverage; however, 23% of the population has no access to mobile Internet. Yet, there are some challenges regarding access to sufficient infrastructure and devices, while wide-scale research on the use of mobile devices in the African context is lacking (Kaliisa & Picard, 2017). In this regard, the ITU (2020) found that coverage is good in urban areas but is not sufficient in rural areas as 4G coverage is 77% and 22%, respectively. Due to lack of copper cable infrastructure, investment is often rather made to develop wireless technologies (Peroni & Bartolo, 2018).

It is also problematic if provision of technology for education becomes an aim in itself without consideration of how teaching and learning will benefit from such technologies. In this regard, Read (2015) notes that within Sub-Saharan Africa "[t]he educational benefits of ICT provision are usually expressed as generalities and there is a very widespread lack of a clear vision as to how ICT will actually be used in schools and the precise educational benefits that will accrue from it" (p. 199).

In their research on the impact of digital technology usage regarding economic growth in Africa, Solomon and Van Klyton (2020) recommend that a skilled labour force and enabling policy environment are essential and that digitalisation can be driven by individual users. Similarly, this approach has definitive implications for the online education context as digital skills, favourable policies and a focus on student and teacher agency are important. These digital skills are highly relevant, as according to Aikins (2019), "the lower the digital skills of African household members, the more likely of higher percentage of those households not using the Internet" (p. 69). However, in terms of policies it is important to note that Africa has the lowest average Affordability Drivers Index and this index is used to measure government policies that have an impact on Internet affordability (Alliance for Affordable Internet, 2020).

As this chapter approaches online access and resources in terms of open education and SDL, the latter two concepts are explored in the next section.

1.3   Access and Resources for Open Self-directed Learning

As stated at the start of this chapter, the nature of online access and resources is explored in terms of open education and SDL specifically in the African continent.

1.3.1   Access and Resources for Open Education

Open education is considered in this chapter specifically in terms of access and resources. Access to learning content is considered as being openly licensed, while in terms of resources the use of open educational resources (OER) is relevant. At the General Conference meeting in Paris in November 2019, OER were defined by UNESCO (2019) as:

> … learning, teaching and research materials in any format and medium that reside in the public domain or are under copyright that have been released under an open license, that permit no-cost access, re-use, re-purpose, adaptation and redistribution by others.

Importantly, this definition highlights that OER can be found in different formats. In the African context, the use of different formats is quite useful as content can be shared digitally and then downloaded and printed if needed in cases where continued Internet access is not possible. Read (2015) also notes how technology has made digital printing on demand (DPOD) possible in order to lower costs. Consequently, when considering OER in this context, appropriate formats should be considered where continuous Internet access might not be a requirement.

Despite an increase in use and research on OER in the African context, Mays (2017) notes that "much of the literature available in the African context comprises descriptive case studies rather than theoretical analyses, reflecting the emergent nature of engagement with OER in this context" (p. 387–388). Hence, there is also a need for further theoretical research-driven engagement in terms of OER.

Within the open education context, the concept of Massive Open Online Courses (MOOCs) is relevant. However, despite MOOCs being considered as ways through which education can be disrupted and democratised, Rambe and Moeti (2017), however, make the following statement regarding MOOCs in the African context:

> …the emergent, slow uptake of MOOCs in Africa higher education could be pointing to the inherent challenges in the philosophy and operationalization of MOOCs as well as African higher educational administrators' uncertainty about the transformative potential of MOOCs for their educational systems (p. 648).

Hence, the use and advantages of MOOCs—as is seen elsewhere in the world—should not be considered similar in terms of Africa. Yet, OER in general still hold promise for Africa.

OER are considered relevant for the African educational context due to cost and revisability. In terms of cost, it has been found that OER can be considered cheaper resources than commercial resources (Hilton et al., 2014; Ikahihifo et al., 2017; Miao, Mishra & McGreal, 2016). This is especially apt in an African context where the price textbooks, at school level, for example, vary a lot between countries and are often inadequately funded by governments or development partners (Read, 2015).

Furthermore, revisability is a very important aspect as for effective learning and especially in addressing the need for relevant and even decolonised content, resources need to be localised. In this regard, OER allow for localisation (Wolfenden & Adinolfi, 2019) and even translation into the many different languages used within the continent. Localisation efforts are essential as OER tend to be in English and come from the Global North (McGreal, 2017). Localisation also implies collaborative efforts through which OER can be customised to students' contextualised needs. Importantly, Casserly and Smith (2008) are of the opinion that OER allow "for the localization of the materials, where users tailor materials according to their language and culture, and for personalization, where materials can be adapted and modified for individual learners" (p. 263). Consequently, African teachers need to be empowered in order to be able to localise OER to make them appropriate and relevant for learning in specific learning contexts.

Throughout this process, it is sensible to promote SDL in order to ensure lifelong learning for African students and to this end adequate access and resources are necessary.

1.3.2 Access and Resources for Self-directed Learning

This chapter considers the intersections between online access and resources in terms of SDL. SDL is defined by Knowles (1975) as:

a process in which individuals take the initiative, with or without the help of others, in diagnosing their learning needs, formulating learning goals, identifying human and material resources for learning, choosing and implementing appropriate learning strategies and evaluating learning outcomes (p. 18).

Clearly, SDL implies access to human but also specifically material resources. Increased availability of online resources has opened up opportunities for SDL (Song & Bonk, 2016). However, as stated before in the African context access to such resources still remains a challenge. Hence within the continent, limitations in choices of resources need to be considered in order to support SDL-related initiatives.

SDL, which can be considered a student characteristic and a learning process (Brockett & Hiemstra, 2019; Curran et al., 2019; Knowles, 1975; Sumuer, 2018), involves many different aspects of learning. In this context, Hiemstra and Brockett (2012) emphasise the following three elements:

- Person: This includes characteristics of the individual, such as creativity, critical reflection, enthusiasm, life experience, life satisfaction, motivation, previous education, resilience and self-concept.
- Process: This involves the teaching–learning transaction, including facilitation, learning skills, learning styles, planning, organising and evaluating abilities, teaching styles and technological skills.
- Context: This encompasses the environmental and sociopolitical climate, such as culture, power, learning environment, finances, gender, learning climate, organisational policies, political milieu, race and sexual orientation. (p. 158).

In order to foster lifelong learning—a very necessary characteristic for the growing African population—SDL can be supportive in this regard (Bolhuis, 2003; Salleh et al., 2019; Sumuer, 2018). Motivation to learn is key to SDL, and in this regard Song and Bonk (2016) highlight, in their case specifically in terms of informal learning, the importance of freedom and choice, control, as well as interest and engagement for SDL.

However, in general SDL can benefit from students being presented with choices in terms of content and processes, control of their own learning path as well as being interested in the topic and wanting to engage with it. Despite the focus on the individual student taking charged in SDL, the process also involves an important communal aspect as learning is regarded as a social activity through which peers and teachers as facilitators can play integral roles.

Consequently, the concept of interdependence is highly relevant for SDL. Technology has contributed to support collaboration in the SDL context (Curran et al., 2019). As learning is considered a social phenomenon, so positive interdependence is also pertinent (Bolhuis, 2003). Towards effective cooperation in learning, Johnson and Johnson (2019, p. 47) list five conditions: "positive interdependence, individual accountability, promotive interaction, social skills and group processing".

In terms of ubuntu, Kemeh (2018) notes that "Ubuntu also espouses the value of interdependence; it encourages members of the university community to be mutually reliant on each other" (p. 188). In this regard, Kemeh (2018) adds that both students and teachers would be learning from each other in e-learning contexts infused with elements of ubuntu-related interdependence. Similarly, Rambe and Moeti (2017), in reference to MOOCs, also advocate for infusing ubuntu in online learning contexts to foster legitimate participation.

As stated in the introduction, Waghid (2019) asserts that educational technologies can be supportive of flattening the hierarchical relationships that might exist between students and teachers and allow for contributions to the learning process in a collective manner. In this context, using flipped classroom strategies, where content is handled outside of the classroom and application is facilitated by the teacher, the use of audience response systems to gauge feedback from students throughout a lesson or even the use of social networking sites is proposed as relevant options by Waghid (2019).

Yet in all these cases, a key requirement is online access. Moreover, the realities of online access in Africa are considered in the next section.

1.4 Online Access in Africa

Internet access is not common in Africa, and there are great divides in terms of access and literacies relevant to functioning effectively online within the continent. Despite a need for increased access through the provision of more opportunities to connect to the Internet, some African governments ultimately move towards taxing Internet data and consequently working against access (Bergère, 2019). Before 2000, Internet access was even more limited in Africa and was only extended further with the installation of submarine Internet cables linked to Europe in the 2000s with connections being available through copper cables, fibre, cell tower wireless connections and satellites (Hjort & Poulsen, 2019; Peroni & Bartolo, 2018).

Access to the Internet is limited due to lack of infrastructure and high costs, and it is also significant that limited local content is available online (Calandro, Chavula & Phokeer, 2019). The ITU (2020) notes how the costs of mobile Internet in Africa are far higher in terms of the gross national income per capita as compared with the rest of the world. In addition, Aikins (2019) states that "the percentage of African households not using the Internet is significantly influenced by affordability, digital skills, the population ages 15–64 as well as mobile phone subscriptions" (p. 75).

Furthermore, having access to the Internet does not imply having access to all relevant resources that are available. In this regard, Counted and Arawole (2015) note that "the challenge for a huge percentage of Africa's millennials is the lack of meaningful usage access to opportunities and resources on the Internet, specifically created for users in the global North and countries in the West" (p. 19). Consequently, there is need for resources created in Africa for Africa, but also bidirectional interaction in terms of resources.

Libraries can act as effective access points to online content; however, within the South African context it was found that despite providing access libraries do not necessarily address the needs of indigenous communities and support access to indigenous knowledge (Mhlongo & Ngulube, 2020). However, it has been found that

Multipurpose Community Telecenters (MCT) that provide basic digital services can also be of support in providing Internet access especially in rural areas (Kuika Watat & Jonathan, 2020).

Different statistics are reported in terms of Internet access for this continent. In this regard, according to the Internet World Stats (2020) 39.3% of the population of Africa has Internet access while the ITU (2020) puts this percentage at 29%. Despite the low numbers, it is clear that Internet access is increasing in the African context (Gillwald, 2017; Gueye et al., 2016). Interestingly, in terms of households in Africa, in urban areas 28% have access to Internet, while in rural areas only 6% has access (ITU, 2020). Consequently, improving access not only in urban areas but especially also in rural areas of Africa must be a priority.

An important aspect for Internet access in Africa is connecting by means of mobile devices. In an article in the *Economist*, it was stated that access to mobile phones is more common than access to electricity in Sub-Saharan Africa (Data Team, 2017). Furthermore, many sources emphasise the importance of mobile devices in Africa in terms of ICT in general (Solomon & Van Klyton, 2020) as well as for education (Samarakoon et al., 2017). But challenges regarding devices, support and platforms are also recognised in terms of the use of mobile devices in Africa (Kaliisa & Picard, 2017).

Apart from online access, online resources are also relevant to this chapter.

1.5   Educational Resources in Africa

This chapter considers the nature of access and resources for open education and SDL in the African continent. The focus of this chapter is not just on access to online resources, but also specifically resources for learning.

In terms of general learning and teaching support materials, access has been a constant problem on the continent. In reference to Sub-Saharan Africa, Read (2015) found that "despite decades of funding by governments and [development partners], few low-income [Sub-Saharan Africa] countries have been able to establish sustainable systems for providing textbooks and other essential [teaching and learning materials] on a regular basis" (p. 3).

Access to textbooks has been a priority for many governments; however, delivery of textbooks to schools does not imply that they will be used, textbooks should be written in appropriate languages and students might require some basic literacies before being able to effectively use textbooks (Read, 2015). At school level, in most countries in Sub-Saharan Africa, textbooks are chosen based on governmentally approved lists with the focus in Anglophone countries on local commercial publishers while Francophone countries tend to use works published externally (Read, 2015).

In Africa, there has been limited uptake of e-learning approaches in higher education (Kemeh, 2018). This situation is ascribed to insufficient infrastructure, digital literacy levels of both staff and students, limited training opportunities, lack of integration of online systems and a resistance to change (Kemeh, 2018).

It is essential that educational resources cannot merely be reused within the African context. In this regard, resources need to be adapted and localised. Rambe and Moeti (2017) even go as far as noting that "the exportation of MOOCs whole sale without any adaption to African conditions can also be interpreted less as a genuine effort to advance affordable, quality education to Africans and more as a subtle from of academic neocolonialism".

In this chapter, in considering the preceding discussion, the concept of access needs to be approached at different levels.

1.6 Levels of Access to Resources

This chapter considers the nature of access and resources for open education and SDL in the African continent. Consequently, the needs in terms of access and resources for both open education and SDL are contemplated. There seems to be a move away from considering providing access but also what happens once access is gained (Wasserman, 2017). Hence, it is proposed in this chapter that access relates to it being formal, epistemological, axiopistical and demiurgic.

The levels in Fig. 1.1 draw on the work by Morrow (2007) in terms of formal and epistemological access and Olivier (2020) on demiurgic access. Epistemological access has not been researched extensively but has been approached in contexts other than just higher education, in which it was originally considered in terms of the democratisation of access (Du Plooy & Zilindile, 2014). In this regard, formal access relates to being able to access learning institutions (Morrow, 2007) and in

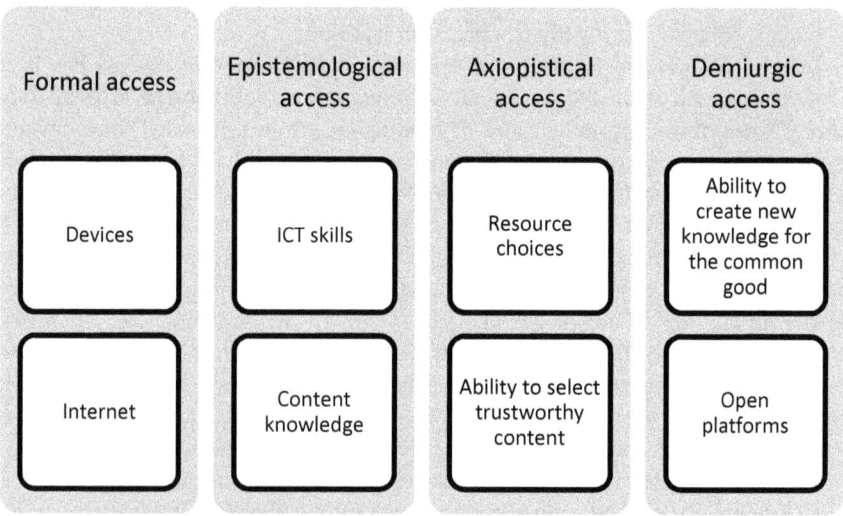

Fig. 1.1 Levels of access for online resources

this chapter we extend this view to having access to devices in order to make use of online resources.

Furthermore, epistemological access relates to being able to access knowledge. Consequently, in this chapter's context this implies accessing knowledge in order to use devices and then accessing online learning content itself. Furthermore, Morrow emphasised the important role of individual students' role in ensuring epistemological access through systematic learning (Du Plooy & Zilindile, 2014) In addition to Olivier's (2020) concept of demiurgic access—which pertains to be able to contribute to knowledge creation for the greater good of the community—this chapter proposes the addition of axiopistical access.

This axiopistical access, derived from αξιόπιστος or being trustworthy, relates to having access to variety resources and having the skills to determine the trustworthiness or reliability of a specific online resource. The needs for axiopistical access would imply fostering metaliteracy. Mackey and Jacobson (2011) expanded the concept of information literacy to metaliteracy, and they distinguish between these concepts as follows: "While information literacy prepares individuals to access, evaluate, and analyze information, metaliteracy prepares individuals to actively produce and share content through social media and online communities" (p. 76). Importantly, for Mackey (2019: 1) a "metaliterate learner is a critical consumer of information, continuously developing effective questions, verifying sources of information including authorship, and always challenging his or her own biases through metacognitive thinking". Four goals of metaliteracy are set by Jacobson et al. (2019: 6–7):

- Actively evaluate content while also evaluating one's own biases.
- Engage with all intellectual property ethically and responsibly.
- Produce and share information in collaborative and participatory environments.
- Develop learning strategies to meet lifelong personal and professional goals.

Therefore, access and specifically axiopistical access can effectively draw on the emerging developments on metaliteracy. Considering the levels of access discussed above, some further recommendations can also be made.

1.7 Discussion and Recommendations

A key requirement for effective online access and use of online resources for open SDL would be to foster the relevant literacies. A number of literacies have been identified as being relevant for SDL within an open context (Olivier, 2019). However, from the discussion in this chapter the need for specific digital literacies is evident in addition to basic literacy especially in a diverse context in terms of academic performance and multilingualism. In addition, the importance of metaliteracy was also noted in the previous section.

It is essential that a conducive policy context is created to support cheap and reliable Internet access (Gillwald, 2017), but also support online educational and resource-related activities in African countries (Aikins, 2019; Alliance for Affordable Internet, 2020; Solomon & Van Klyton, 2020). Read (2015) also notes the need for ICT policies from parents, students and teachers and that hardware provision should be supplemented with adequate support mechanisms.

In order to promote further online access, national policies should also be supportive of access and local content. Calandro et al. (2019) also note how policies should not just focus on skills and local content in local languages, but also supporting local online content hosting infrastructure. Moreover, it is essential for online services that might be relevant for students to not be biased in terms of access based on geographical location (Counted & Arawole, 2015). In this context, Counted and Arawole (2015) make the following observation:

> Africa's ongoing internet-fuelled developments lie in the creative hands of Africa's millennials as they exchange ideas and engage the rest of the world online without undue restrictions to participate in online communities, contribute to the internet technology, add to the positive stories about Africa, and benefit from the bottomless opportunities that abound in the internet ecosystem (p. 19).

In considering ubuntu, as noted at the start of the chapter, it is essential to contemplate how this can have an impact in terms of access and use of online educational resources. To this end, this chapter links up with Kemeh (2018), who considered ubuntu in terms of adoption of e-learning in Ghana, who states:

> The strengths of the values of communalism, interdependence, caring and sharing, and openness as espoused within Ubuntu all point to the facts that the adoption, use, and integration of e-learning systems will create access to affordable and quality higher educational opportunities…

Towards SDL in online context, access to a variety of online resources is essential. Moreover, as was also found by Sumuer (2018), students should be supported through scaffolding to support skills for SDL and using technology and environments be created to be supportive of SDL. But for SDL access to technology is regarded as being essential (Curran et al., 2019).

As important as alignment with the curriculum is for textbooks (Read, 2015) and more traditional learning and teaching resource materials, so should online material and OER also be created or adapted with consideration for the diverse curriculum and student needs.

Finally, access should extend beyond devices and availability of the Internet to ultimately also allow for formal, epistemological, axiopistical and demiurgic access.

1.8   Conclusion

In this chapter, the nature of online access and resources in terms of open education and SDL was considered in terms of the African context. The concept of access is complex, but it can be considered within the wider concept of educational access. Access for African students should be regarded within the concept of ubuntu where the individual within and as part of the community is considered. In this regard, technology provides opportunities for communal interaction and democratisation.

The African context is very diverse, and there are different needs for this mainly young population. In this context, the digital divide is prominent as access to technologies is unevenly spread. Furthermore, access to educational resources is limited especially in certain areas. In addition, there are also challenges in terms of sufficient skills and support towards effective online access and resource use.

Open education is highly relevant as OER provide cost-effective solutions for the different resource needs in the African context. Importantly, OER also allow for localisation and the accommodation of different languages and needs. In this context, lifelong learning is essential and consequently the fostering of SDL is relevant. Key to effective SDL is being able to access and then select appropriate resources. This, in turn, requires expansion of online access and resources relevant to the different African contexts.

Online access is limited in certain areas in the African milieu; however, especially mobile technologies hold a lot of promise for future developments. Problems around textbooks can also be potentially addressed through expanding on relevant open online resources. Different levels of access are implied for effective use of resources. Hence, formal, epistemological, axiopistical and demiurgic access would mean that not only do students have physical access and knowledge to use technologies, and select appropriate resources, but also create ones themselves.

Finally, online access and resources for open education and SDL imply not only increased availability of technologies but also supporting a number of relevant literacies, adequate policies, localisation and sufficient scaffolded support.

References

Aikins, S. K. (2019). Determinants of digital divide in Africa and policy implications. *International Journal of Public Administration in the Digital Age (IJPADA), 6*(1), 64–79.

Alliance for Affordable Internet. (2020). 2020 *Affordability Report*. Retrieved 13 November 2020, from https://a4ai.org/affordability-report/report/2020/

Asongu, S. A., & Le Roux, S. (2017). Enhancing ICT for inclusive human development in Sub-Saharan Africa. *Technological Forecasting and Social Change, 118*, 44–54.

Ayentimi, D. T., & Burgess, J. (2019). Is the fourth industrial revolution relevant to sub-Sahara Africa? *Technology Analysis & Strategic Management, 31*(6), 641–652.

Bergère, C. (2019). Don't tax my megabytes: Digital infrastructure and the regulation of citizenship in Africa. *International Journal of Communication, 13*(2019), 4309–4326.

Bolhuis, S. (2003). Towards process-oriented teaching for self-directed lifelong learning: A multidimensional perspective. *Learning and Instruction, 13*(3), 327–347.

Brockett, R. G., & Hiemstra, R. (2019). *Self-direction in adult learning: Perspectives on theory, research, and practice.* Routledge.

Calandro E., Chavula J., & Phokeer A. (2019). Internet development in Africa: A content use, hosting and distribution perspective. In G. Mendy, S. Ouya, I. Dioum, & O. Thiaré (Eds.). *e-Infrastructure and e-Services for Developing Countries. AFRICOMM 2018.* Lecture Notes of the Institute for Computer Sciences, Social Informatics and Telecommunications Engineering, 275. Springer. https://doi.org/10.1007/978-3-030-16042-5_13

Casserly, C. M., & Smith, M. S. (2008). Revolutionizing education through innovation: Can openness transform teaching and learning? In T. Iiyoshi & M. S. V. Kumar (Eds.), *Opening up education: The collective advancement of education through open technology, open content, and open knowledge* (pp. 261–276). MIT Press.

Counted, A. V., & Arawole, J. O. (2015). We are connected, but constrained: Internet inequality and the challenges of millennials in Africa as actors in innovation. *Journal of Innovation and Entrepreneurship, 5*(1), 1–21.

Curran, V., Gustafson, D. L., Simmons, K., Lannon, H., Wang, C., Garmsiri, M., Fleet, L., & Wetsch, L. (2019). Adult learners' perceptions of self-directed learning and digital technology usage in continuing professional education: An update for the digital age. *Journal of Adult and Continuing Education, 25*(1), 74–93.

Data Team. (2017). *In much of sub-Saharan Africa, mobile phones are more common than access to electricity.* The Economist. Retrieved 13 November 2020, from https://www.economist.com/graphic-detail/2017/11/08/in-much-of-sub-saharan-africa-mobile-phones-are-more-common-than-access-to-electricity

Donou-Adonsou, F. (2019). Technology, education, and economic growth in Sub-Saharan Africa. *Telecommunications Policy, 43*(4), 353–360.

Du Plooy, L., & Zilindile, M. (2014). Problematising the concept epistemological access with regard to foundation phase education towards quality schooling. *South African Journal of Childhood Education, 4*(1), 187–201.

Friederici, N., Ojanperä, S., & Graham, M. (2017). The impact of connectivity in Africa: Grand visions and the mirage of inclusive digital development. *The Electronic Journal of Information Systems in Developing Countries, 79*(1), 1–20.

Gillwald, A. (2017). *Beyond Access: Addressing Digital Inequality in Africa.* GCIG Paper No. 48, March 10, 2017. Waterloo, Canada/London: Centre for International Governance Innovation (CIGI)/Chatham House: Royal Institute of International Affairs. Retrieved 16 November 2020, from https://www.cigionline.org/sites/default/files/documents/GCIG%20no.48_0.pdf

Gueye, A., Mell, P., Banse, D., & Congo, F. Y. (2016). On the Internet Connectivity in Africa. In R. Glitho, M. Zennaro, F. Belqasmi, & M. Agueh (Eds.), *e-Infrastructure and e-Services: 7th International Conference, AFRICOMM 2015, Cotonou, Benin, December 15–16, 2015, Revised Selected Papers* (pp. 70–77). Springer.

Hiemstra, R., & Brockett, R. G. (2012). Reframing the meaning of self-directed learning: An updated model. *Adult Education Research Conference.* Retrieved 5 December 2020, from https://newpra iriepress.org/aerc/2012/papers/22

Hilton, J. L., Robinson, T. J., Wiley, D., & Ackerman, J. D. (2014). Cost-savings achieved in two semesters through the adoption of open educational resources. *International Review of Research in Open and Distributed Learning, 15*(2), 67–84.

Hjort, J., & Poulsen, J. (2019). The arrival of fast internet and employment in Africa. *American Economic Review, 109*(3), 1032–1079.

Ikahihifo, T. K., Spring, K. J., Rosecrans, J., & Watson, J. (2017). Assessing the savings from open educational resources on student academic goals. *International Review of Research in Open and Distributed Learning, 18*(7), 126–140.

International Telecommunication Union (ITU). (2020). *Measuring digital development: Facts and figures 2020.* Retrieved 5 December 2020, from https://www.itu.int/en/ITU-D/Statistics/Docume nts/facts/FactsFigures2020.pdf

Internet World Stats. (2020). Africa Internet Users, 2020 Population and Facebook Statistics. Retrieved 18 November 2020, from https://www.internetworldstats.com/stats1.htm

Jacobson, T. E., Mackey, T. P. & O'Brien, K. L. (2019). Developing metaliterate citizens: Designing and delivering enhanced global learning opportunities. University Libraries Faculty Scholarship, 129. Retrieved 18 November 2020, from https://scholarsarchive.library.albany.edu/ulib_fac_sch olar/129

Johnson, D. W., & Johnson, R. T. (2019). The impact of cooperative learning on self-directed learning. In E. Mentz, J. de Beer, & R. Bailey, (Eds.), *Self-directed learning for the 21st century: Implications for higher education* (pp. 37–66). Cape Town: AOSIS.

Kaliisa, R., & Picard, M. (2017). A systematic review on mobile learning in higher education: The African perspective. *TOJET: The Turkish Online Journal of Educational Technology, 16*(1), 1–18.

Kemeh E. (2018) Ubuntu as a Framework for the Adoption and Use of E-Learning in Ghanaian Public Universities. In: E. J. Takyi-Amoako & N. T. Assié-Lumumba (Eds.). *Re-visioning education in Africa. Ubuntu-inspired education for humanity.* (pp. 175–192). Palgrave Macmillan. https://doi.org/10.1007/978-3-319-70043-4_10

Knowles, M. S. (1975). *Self-directed learning: A guide for learners and teachers.* Follett.

Kuika Watat, J., & Jonathan, G. M. (2020). Breaking the digital divide in rural Africa. *AMCIS 2020 Proceedings, 2.* Retrieved 5 December 2020, from https://aisel.aisnet.org/amcis2020/global_dev/global_dev/2

Le Grange, L. (2019). Currere's active force and the concept of Ubuntu. In C. Hébert, N. Ng-A-Fook, A. Ibrahim & B. Smith (Eds.). *Internationalizing Curriculum Studies.* (pp. 207–226). Palgrave Macmillan. https://doi.org/10.1007/978-3-030-01352-3_13

Letseka, M. (2012). In defence of Ubuntu. *Studies in Philosophy and Education, 31*(1), 47–60.

Lumumba-Kasongo T. (2018). Ubuntu and Pan-Africanism: The Dialectics of learning about Africa. In: E. Takyi-Amoako & N. Assié-Lumumba (Eds.). *Re-Visioning Education in Africa.* (pp. 35–54). Palgrave Macmillan. https://doi.org/10.1007/978-3-319-70043-4_3

Mackey, T.P. (2019). Empowering Metaliterate learners for the post-truth world. In: Mackey, T. P. & T. E. Jacobson (Eds.), *Metaliterate Learning for the Post-Truth World.* (pp. 1–32). Neal-Schuman.

Mackey, T. P., & Jacobson, T. E. (2011). Reframing information literacy as a metaliteracy. *College and Research Libraries, 72*(1), 62–78. https://doi.org/10.5860/crl-76r1

Mays, T. J. (2017). Mainstreaming use of open educational resources (OER) in an African context. *Open Praxis, 9*(4), 387–401.

McGreal, R. (2017). Special report on the role of open educational resources in supporting the sustainable development goal 4: Quality education challenges and opportunities. *International Review of Research in Open and Distributed Learning, 18*(7), 292–305.

Mhlongo, M., & Ngulube, P. (2020). Resource provision and access to indigenous knowledge in public libraries in South Africa. *Information Development, 36*(2), 271–287.

Miao, F., Mishra, S., & McGreal, R. (Eds.). (2016). *Open educational resources: Policy, costs and transformation.* UNESCO and Commonwealth of Learning. Retrieved 16 November 2020, from http://oasis.col.org/handle/11599/2306

Morrow, W. (2007). *Learning to teach in South Africa.* HSRC Press.

Olivier, J. (2019). Towards a multiliteracies framework in support of self-directed learning through open educational resources. In: E. Mentz, J. de Beer, & R. Bailey, (Eds.), *Self-Directed Learning for the 21st Century: Implications for Higher Education.* (pp. 167–201). AOSIS.

Olivier, J. (2020). Self-directed multimodal learning to support demiurgic access. In D. Burgos (Ed.), *Radical Solutions and eLearning.* (pp. 117–130). Springer Nature.

Peroni, M., & Bartolo, M. (2018). The Digital Divide. In M. Bartolo & F. Ferrari (Eds.), *Multidisciplinary Teleconsultation in Developing Countries* (pp. 101–109). Springer.

Rambe, P., & Moeti, M. (2017). Disrupting and democratising higher education provision or entrenching academic elitism: Towards a model of MOOCs adoption at African universities. *Educational Technology Research and Development, 65*(3), 631–651.

Read, T. (2015). Where have all the textbooks gone? Toward sustainable provision of teaching and learning materials in Sub-Saharan Africa. The World Bank. Retrieved 16 November 2020, from https://elibrary.worldbank.org/doi/abs/10.1596/978-1-4648-0572-1

Salleh, U. K. M., Zulnaidi, H., Rahim, S. S. A., Bin Zakaria, A. R., & Hidayat, R. (2019). Roles of self-directed learning and social networking sites in lifelong learning. *International Journal of Instruction, 12*(4), 167–182.

Samarakoon, S., Christiansen, A., & Munro, P. G. (2017). Equitable and quality education for all of Africa? The challenges of using ICT in education. *Perspectives on Global Development and Technology, 16*(6), 645–665.

Solomon, E. M., & Van Klyton, A. (2020). The impact of digital technology usage on economic growth in Africa. *Utilities Policy, 67*, 101104.

Song, D., & Bonk, C. J. (2016). Motivational factors in self-directed informal learning from online learning resources. *Cogent Education, 3*(1), 1205838, 1–11.

Sumuer, E. (2018). Factors related to college students' self-directed learning with technology. *Australasian Journal of Educational Technology, 34*(4), 29–43.

Takyi-Amoako, E. J. & Assié-Lumumba, N. T. (2018). Introduction: Re-visioning education in Africa—Ubuntu-inspired education for humanity. In: E. J. Takyi-Amoako & N. T. Assié-Lumumba (Eds.), *Re-visioning education in Africa. Ubuntu-inspired education for humanity*. (pp. 1–18). Palgrave Macmillan. https://doi.org/10.1007/978-3-319-70043-4_1

Tripathi, M., & Inani, S. K. (2016). Does internet affect economic growth in sub-Saharan Africa? *Economics Bulletin, 36*(4), 1993–2002.

UNESCO. (2000). *Recommendation on Open Educational Resources (OER)*. Paris: UNESCO. Retrieved 15 November 2020, from https://sustainabledevelopment.un.org/content/documents/1681Dakar%20Framework%20for%20Action.pdf

UNESCO. (2019). *Recommendation on Open Educational Resources (OER)*. Paris: UNESCO. Retrieved 15 November 2020, from https://unesdoc.unesco.org/ark:/48223/pf0000373755/PDF/373755eng.pdf.multi.page=3

UNESCO Institute for Statistics. (2016). *School resources and learning environment in Africa: Key results from a regional survey on factors affecting quality of education (August 2016)*. Retrieved 16 November 2020, from http://uis.unesco.org/sites/default/files/school-resources-and-learning-environment-in-africa-2016-en/school-resources-and-learning-environment-in-africa-2016-en.pdf

United Nations (UN). (2020a). *Education—United Nations Sustainable Development*. Retrieved 16 November 2020, from http://www.un.org/sustainabledevelopment/education/

United Nations (UN). (2020b). *Universal Declaration of Human Rights*. Retrieved 16 November 2020, from https://www.un.org/en/universal-declaration-human-rights/

Waghid, F. (2019) Towards Decolonisation Within University Education: On the Innovative Application of Educational Technology. In: C. Manthalu C. & Y. Waghid (Eds.). *Education for Decoloniality and Decolonisation in Africa*. (pp. 139–153). Cham: Palgrave Macmillam. https://doi.org/10.1007/978-3-030-15689-3_8

Wasserman, H. (2017). African histories of the Internet. *Internet Histories, 1*(1–2), 129–137. https://doi.org/10.1080/24701475.2017.1308198

Wolfenden, F., & Adinolfi, L. (2019). An exploration of agency in the localisation of open educational resources for teacher development. *Learning, Media and Technology, 44*(3), 327–344.

Jako Olivier is the holder of the UNESCO Chair in Multimodal Learning and Open Educational Resources and is a professor of Multimodal Learning in the Faculty of Education at North-West University. His research, within the Research Unit Self-Directed Learning, focuses on self-directed multimodal learning, open educational resources, multiliteracies, blended and e-learning in language classrooms as well as multilingualism in education. He currently holds a Y rating from the National Research Foundation and was awarded the Education Association of South Africa's Emerging Researcher Medal in 2018. In addition to recently editing a book on self-directed multimodal learning, he has published numerous articles and book chapters at the national and international levels, and he also acts as a supervisor for postgraduate students.

Chapter 2
Self-Directed Learning at School and in Higher Education in Africa

Jako Olivier and Antoinette Wentworth

Abstract The changing educational context and dynamic needs around increasing online learning at all education levels highlight the importance of self-directed learning. In this regard, self-directed learning, which involves both a process and student characteristic, relates to the students taking charge of their learning in terms of setting aims, choosing material or human resources, choosing appropriate learning strategies and evaluating their learning. This chapter involves a systematic literature review that explores research on self-directed learning at school and higher education within the African context. This concept, despite the origins of the scholarship of self-directed learning being from the Global North and the West, is more expansive and, this chapter specifically aims to give an overview of the current discourses around self-directed learning in Africa. This chapter critically examined key literature regarding self-directed learning in this milieu and inductively identified general trends. Despite self-directed learning's focus on the individual, it seems to be a very appropriate learning process towards communal learning utilising cooperative learning strategies that support self-directed learning. Finally, the chapter provides a synthesis of the main trends around self-directed learning in Africa while identifying certain areas for future research.

Keywords Africa · Self-directed learning · University · Higher education · Schools · Systematic literature review

J. Olivier (✉)
Research Unit Self-Directed Learning, Faculty of Education, North-West University, Private Bag X2046, Mmabatho 2735, South Africa
e-mail: jako.olivier@nwu.ac.za

A. Wentworth
Centre for Open and Lifelong Learning at the Namibia University of Science and Technology, Private Bag 1338, Windhoek, Namibia
e-mail: awentworth@nust.na

D. Burgos and J. Olivier (eds.), *Radical Solutions for Education in Africa*, Lecture Notes in Educational Technology, https://doi.org/10.1007/978-981-16-4099-5_2

2.1 Introduction

This chapter explores the nature of self-directed learning (SDL) research within the African continent within the past 20 years (1990–2020). To this end, the researchers conducted a systematic literature review of relevant journal articles and book chapters found in selected databases.

The concept of SDL is understood in this chapter in terms of the classical definition by Malcolm Knowles. According to Knowles (1975, p. 18), SDL is "a process in which individuals take the initiative, with or without the help of others, in diagnosing their learning needs, formulating learning goals, identifying human and material resources for learning, choosing and implementing appropriate learning strategies and evaluating learning outcomes". Furthermore, SDL is conceptualised as being both a student characteristic and process.

The following research question served as the impetus for this research: *what is the nature of SDL research on the African continent between 1990 and 2020?*

In the next section, SDL is further unpacked, after which the methodology and findings of the systematic literature review are presented.

2.2 Self-Directed Learning (SDL)

2.2.1 Background

The origins of research on SDL can be traced to research on andragogy or adult learning in the 1960s and 1970s (Brockett & Hiemstra, 2019; Knowles, 1975). However, the phenomenon has been relevant in learning contexts for ages, and different terms have been used to describe it (Brockett & Hiemstra, 2019).

More recently, SDL has been researched wider with a focus not only on andragogy anymore but also with research being done at school level (Van Deur, 2017). In addition, despite an initial focus of SDL research within the Global North, this topic has since been explored by researchers on the African continent as well. In this regard, this research will aim to provide a snapshot of the research done regarding SDL in this milieu.

In terms of learning theories, SDL is closely aligned with constructivism, especially in terms of related social-cultural models (Van Deur, 2017). In this context, active inquiry and independence are highly relevant.

Despite the close association and interchangeable use between SDL and self-regulated learning (SRL) in some contexts, these concepts are not the same (Garrison, 1997; Robinson & Persky, 2020; Van Deur, 2017). Therefore, it is considered that SRL relates more to internal influences of students versus SDL's focus on both internal and external influences (Van Deur, 2017).

The research in this chapter considers what has been done on and related to SDL in Africa. This research ties in with a very strong focus on SDL within educational research on the continent. In this regard, the notable key publications from authors from the North-West University in South Africa, show how the exponential growth of scholarship on SDL in this context (cf. De Beer, 2019a; De Beer et al., 2020; Mentz & Bailey, 2020; Mentz et al., 2019; Mentz & Oosthuizen, 2016; Olivier, 2020).

2.2.2 Implementation of SDL

Researchers have proposed many different models in terms of describing and operationalising SDL (Bosch et al., 2019). Garrison (1997) proposed a model for SDL in which the self-management (contextual control), self-monitoring (cognitive responsibility), and motivational (entering and task) dimensions are integrated.

Furthermore, Robinson and Persky (2020: 293) identified six steps to develop SDL among students:

- developing goals for study;
- outlining assessment with respect to how the learner will know when they achieve those goals;
- identify the structure and sequence of activities;
- layout a timeline to complete activities;
- identify resources to achieve each goal; and
- locate a mentor/faculty member to provide feedback on the plan.

Moreover, specific strategies have also been proven to support SDL, and this includes active learning, cooperative learning, problem-based learning and process-oriented learning (Bosch et al., 2019). Therefore, strategies such as these were considered in the analysis of the identified sources in the corpus.

2.3 Research Design and Methodology

This chapter takes the form of a systematic review. Review research aims to evaluate sets of research adhering to specific inclusion criteria to provide an overall impression of a set topic. Review research can be presented as narrative or systematic reviews (Gülpınar & Güçlü, 2013). As for this chapter, the need was to provide a comprehensive and detailed review to generate an empirical, robust answer to the research question (Mallett et al., 2012). Hence, we conducted a systematic review.

For the purposes of this chapter, both quantitative and qualitative data was generated. However, the main focus was on qualitative data as the aim was to determine the nature of SDL research that has been conducted within the context of the African continent.

2.3.1 Data Collection and Inclusion Criteria

The first step in the data collection was to determine the relevant inclusion criteria to obtain data sources relevant to the identified topic. To this end, the following elements made up the inclusion criteria:

- the sources had to be published between 1990 and 2020;
- the focus of the sources had to be on an African country or countries; and
- SDL should be central to the research.

Therefore, the date limit was used as parameters for the literature search. In contrast "SDL", "Africa" and the names of the 54 African states recognised by the United Nations and the African Union, were used as keywords.

The data searches were conducted by searching for these keywords in the Sabinet African Journals database as well as Academic Search Complete and the Education Resource Information Center (ERIC) accessed through EBSCOhost. The first phase of searching resulted in 566 publications adhering to the criteria. However, after preliminary screening, these sources were reduced to 74 journal articles and chapters. From the analysis, any irrelevant publications—where SDL was only mentioned in a cursory manner or which did not adhere to the requirement of being an African publication—were eliminated. Consequently, the final corpus consisted of 54 publications.

The PRISMA (Preferred Reporting Items for Systematic Reviews and Meta-Analyses) study flow diagram (Čablová et al., 2017) in Fig. 2.1 illustrates the process followed for this research.

2.3.2 Data Analysis

The data analysis was approached with a combination of inductive and deductive approaches as certain aspects related to SDL were explicitly looked for in terms of the publications' aims, geographical location, and discipline. However, as the analysis commenced, other foci were added, such as the nature of the sample, sample level, thematic focus, discipline, and main findings.

The researchers used a Google Sheets document to systematise the findings and allow for inter-evaluator checks to ensure the trustworthiness of the analysis as well as the accuracy in which the research was conducted as reflected in the correctness of the research findings (Jane & Jane, 2003: 273), of the analysis.

Fig. 2.1 PRISMA study
flow diagram for this study

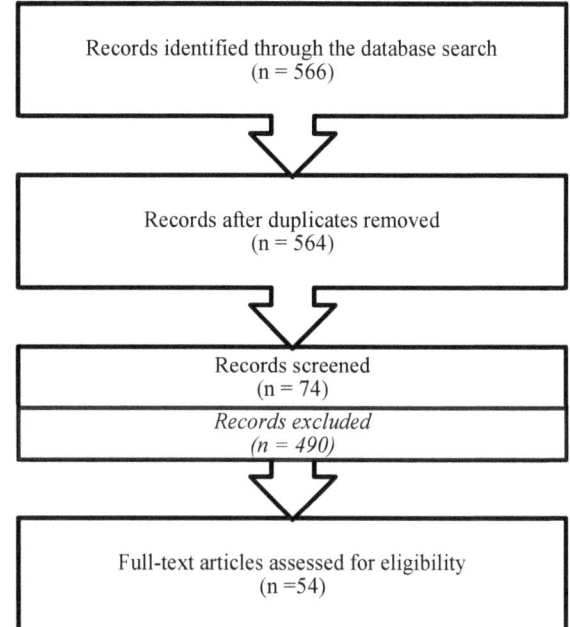

Records identified through the database search
(n = 566)

Records after duplicates removed
(n = 564)

Records screened
(n = 74)

Records excluded
(n = 490)

Full-text articles assessed for eligibility
(n =54)

2.4 Discussion

2.4.1 Geographical and Publication Date Spread

From the analysis, it was evident that most of the SDL research in Africa is based or focused on South Africa. However, there were some exceptions, such as Ethiopia (Shishigu et al., 2019), Ghana (Aheto et al., 2017), Namibia (Iiyambo & Geduld, 2019), and Nigeria (Abubakar & Arshad, 2015; Fakolade & Adeniyi, 2010; Mbagwu et al., 2020; Nottidge & Louw, 2017; Ottu, 2017).

The majority of the publications in this corpus was published between 2014 and 2020. It seems that there is a steady growth in publications, as is evident from Fig. 2.2. The low number for 2020 could be because data was collected only up to October 2020.

The next section deals with the disciplines in which the SDL research was conducted.

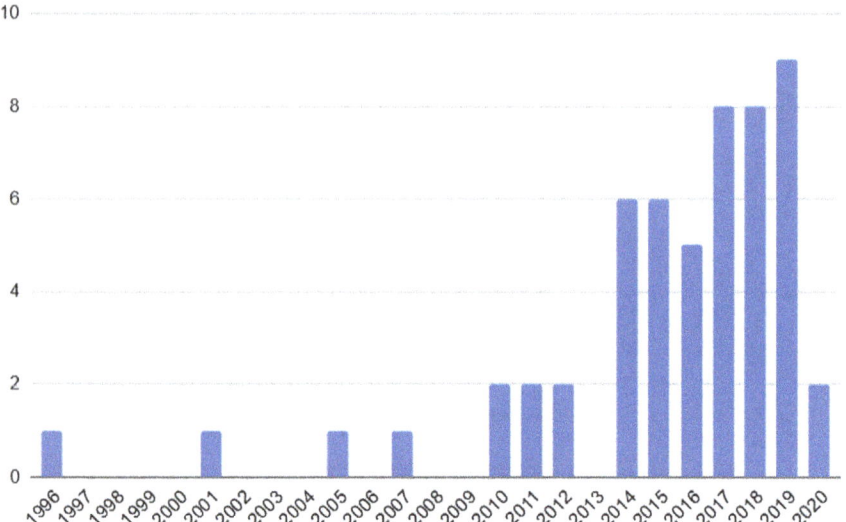

Fig. 2.2 Publication date spread

2.4.2 Disciplines

The majority of research done on SDL in this corpus was situated within the educational context. However, there were also sources focusing on SDL within the workplace (De Bruin & De Bruin, 2011; De Klerk & Fourie, 2017; Van Rensburg & Botma, 2015; Visser, 2018; Wittmann & Olivier, 2019).

The broad disciplines covered in the corpus are summarised in Table 2.1. In some cases, the publications met the criteria to fall into more than one discipline and were then repeated in the table.

A wide variety of disciplines were covered within the corpus. However, various fields within teacher education as well as health sciences were the most prominent. Furthermore, the research also probed the thematic focus and aims present in the corpus.

2.4.3 Thematic Focus and Aims

In addition to the sources in the corpus relating to SDL, they had different thematic foci and aims. In Table 2.2, the discernible foci of the items from the corpus are summarised.

The majority of studies in the corpus approached SDL in terms of specific contexts or variables. These variables are evident from the summary of foci and aims. Assessment as a focus and open distance learning as a context was quite prominent and as expected strategies such as cooperative learning, PBL and project-based learning were also represented.

Table 2.1 Disciplines represented in the corpus

Disciplines	Subdisciplines	Sources
Arts and humanities	General	De Bruin and Cornelius (2011)
	Languages	Sujee et al. (2015)
	Communication science	Terblanché (2010)
Economic and management sciences	Accounting	Stegmann and Malan (2016)
	Business	Aheto et al. (2017)
General education		Fakolade and Adeniyi (2010), Iiyambo and Geduld (2019), Jacobs and Van Loggerenberg(1996), Shishigu et al. (2019)
Teacher education	General	Du Toit-Brits (2018a, 2018b, 2019), Du Toit-Brits & Blignaut, 2019 Du Toit-Brits and Van Zyl (2017), Greyling et al. (2002) Mthethwa (2018), Setlhodi (2019)
	Chemistry	Abubakar and Arshad (2015)
	Computer applications technology	Breed and Bailey (2018), Lubbe (2017)
	Consumer studies	Du Toit et al. (2016)
	Economics	Maistry (2009), Van Wyk (2017)
	Foundation phase	Kruger et al. (2015)
	Information Technology	Breed (2016)
	Language	Olivier (2016), Olivier (2018), Vos and Van Oort (2018)
	Life Sciences	Petersen (2018)
	Life and Natural Sciences	De Beer (2016), De Beer and Mentz (2017)
	Mathematics	Van der Walt (2014)
	Mathematics and Physical Science	Malan et al. (2014)
Health sciences	Clinical medical practice	Hugo et al. (2012)
	Medicine	Nottidge and Louw (2017)
	Nursing	Lekalakala-Mokgele and Caka (2015), Mulube and Jooste (2014), Orton and Nokes (2012), Van Rensburg and Botma (2015)
	Physiotherapy	Statham et al. (2014)
Information Sciences	cataloguing	De Klerk and Fourie (2017)

(continued)

Table 2.1 (continued)

Disciplines	Subdisciplines	Sources
Law		Lumina (2005)
Natural Sciences	Consumer Sciences	Havenga and De Beer (2016)
No specific discipline		De Bruin et al. (2001), De Bruin (2007)
Vocational training		Mbagwu et al. (2020)
Workplace or professional development	Professional cataloguers	De Klerk and Fourie (2017)
	Teachers	Ajani (2019) De Beer (2019b) Wittmann and Olivier (2019)
	Various contexts	De Bruin and De Bruin (2011), Visser (2018)

2.4.4   Methodology and Instruments

2.4.4.1   Research Approaches and Designs

This section provides an overview of the trends regarding the research approaches, whether quantitative, qualitative or mixed method, as well as the various designs (Cohen et al., 2018) employed in the corpus.

Most of the research was empirical in nature; however, some exceptions were noted. One editorial article was observed (Visser, 2018) focusing on agile learners in terms of SDL within the workforce context. Furthermore, some conceptual articles were also identified (Ajani, 2019; Du Toit-Brits, 2015, 2018a, 2018b, 2020; Du Toit-Brits & Blignaut, 2019; Hugo et al., 2012; Olivier, 2018; Ottu, 2017; Wittmann & Olivier, 2019). One source in the corpus also provided a new view on previously collected empirical data (De Beer, 2016). In some cases, these conceptual works related to SDL in a generic sense and not necessarily specifically on SDL in the African context. The identified research approaches and designs from the corpus are summarised in Table 2.3.

Most of the research done on SDL in Africa, within this corpus, was qualitative in nature, this was followed by mixed-method research and then quantitative studies. Despite, a good spread, there seems to be a need for more quantitative work being done in this field.

In Table 2.3, the research designs were listed as they were named in the sources themselves. Alternatively, it was described in terms of what was done; hence, not all descriptions relate necessarily to a recognised research design. A trend was observed that in some studies the third-generation cultural-historical activity theory (Engeström, 1987) is used as an analytic lens (De Beer, 2016; De Beer & Mentz, 2017; Petersen, 2018).

Table 2.2 Foci and aims represented in the corpus

Foci	Sources
Applied competence	Kruger et al. (2015)
Assessment	Aheto et al. (2017), Lumina (2005) Stegmann and Malan (2016), Terblanché (2010), Van Wyk (2017)
Blended learning	Orton and Nokes (2012)
Cooperative learning	Breed (2016), Breed and Bailey (2018), Petersen (2018)
Computer-based tutoring	Mthethwa (2018)
Career decision-making	De Bruin and Cornelius (2011)
Developing SDL instruments	De Bruin et al. (2001)
Educators' expectations	Du Toit-Brits (2019)
Facilitative and obstructive factors in the learning environment	Lekalakala-Mokgele and Caka (2015)
Gifted students	Fakolade and Adeniyi (2010)
Indigenous knowledge and sciences	De Beer (2016), De Beer and Mentz (2017)
Information literacy self-efficacy	Mbagwu et al. (2020)
Learner agility	Visser (2018)
Lifelong learning	De Klerk and Fourie (2017)
Materials	Greyling et al. (2016)
Metacognition	Breed and Bailey (2018), Van der Walt (2014)
Motivation	Du Toit-Brits and Van Zyl (2017), Mulube and Jooste (2014)
Open Distance Learning	Aheto et al. (2017), Greyling et al. (2016), Iiyambo and Geduld (2019), Maistry (2009) Setlhodi (2019), Shishigu et al. (2019), Terblanché (2010), Van Wyk (2017)
Pacing	Setlhodi (2019)
Personality traits	De Bruin (2007)
Problem-based learning (PBL)	Abubakar and Arshad (2015), Maistry (2009), Malan et al. (2014), Orton and Nokes (2012), Statham et al. (2014)
Project-based learning	De Beer (2019b), Du Toit et al. (2016), Havenga and De Beer (2016)
SDL readiness	Lubbe (2017)
SDL status	Nottidge and Louw (2017)
Self-directed reading	Vos and Van Oort (2018)
Self-directed writing	Olivier (2016), Sujee et al. (2015)
Self-study	Jacobs and Van Loggerenberg (1996)
SRL	Iiyambo and Geduld (2019), Shishigu et al. (2019)
Student support	Van Rensburg and Botma (2015)

Table 2.3 Research approaches and designs represented in the corpus

Research approaches	Research designs	Sources
Qualitative	Action research	De Beer (2019b)
	Basic qualitative study	Aheto et al. (2017), De Beer and Mentz (2017), Du Toit-Brits (2019), Iiyambo and Geduld (2019), Jacobs and Van Loggerenberg (1996), Kruger et al. (2015), Lekalakala-Mokgele and Caka (2015), Lumina (2005), Sujee et al. (2015)
	Bricolage	Setlhodi (2019), Van Wyk (2017)
	Case study	Du Toit et al. (2016), Maistry (2009), Malan et al. (2014), Orton and Nokes (2012), Terblanché (2010)
	Design-based research	De Beer (2019b)
	Explanatory design	Abubakar and Arshad (2015)
	Instrumental case study	Du Toit-Brits and Van Zyl (2017) Van Rensburg and Botma (2015)
	Text analysis	Vos and Van Oort (2018)
Quantitative	Cross-sectional survey	De Bruin and Cornelius (2011)
	Exploratory descriptive design	Mulube and Jooste (2014)
	Quasi-experimental	Fakolade and Adeniyi (2010), Mbagwu et al. (2020), Shishigu et al. (2019)
	Survey	De Bruin et al. (2001), De Bruin (2007), Van der Walt (2014)
	Nonexperimental psychometric study	De Bruin and De Bruin (2011)
	Within-participants design	Lubbe (2017)
Mixed method	Concurrent triangulation approach	Stegmann and Malan (2016)
	One-group pre-test post-test experiment Basic qualitative approach	Breed (2016), Breed and Bailey (2018)
	Survey	De Klerk and Fourie (2017)
		Petersen (2018)
	Survey Document analysis	Greyling et al. (2016)
	Survey, test and project content	Havenga and De Beer (2016)
	Survey Basic qualitative approach	Mthethwa (2018), Nottidge and Louw (2017), Olivier (2016)
	Theory-based evaluation	Statham et al. (2014)

2.4.4.2 Sampling and Level

Although not all the published research in the corpus related to research participants, this section provides an overview of the nature of the different samples used in cases where participants were involved. In Table 2.4, an overview is provided of the type of samples involved in SDL research within this corpus.

From the overview of the sampling in the corpus, it is clear that most research is done with university students and lecturers with samples of varying sizes. However, it is evident that more research is necessary on SDL at school and vocational education level as well as how it functions within the work environment in terms of professional development, for example.

2.4.4.3 Instruments

A number of standardised instruments are used to gauge different aspects of stay away from the malls please SDL. Most notably the SDLRS by Lucy Guglielmino (1977), the Self-Directed Learning Perception Scale (SDLP) by Pilling-Cormick(1996), the Self-Rating Scale of Self-Directed Learning (SRSSDL) from Williamson (2007), the Self-Directed Learning Instrument (SDLI) by Cheng et al. (2010) as well as the Self-directed learning skill scale (Ayyildiz & Tarhan, 2015).

In some cases, the researchers from the studies in the corpus made use of questionnaires developed by themselves (De Bruin & Cornelius, 2011; De Bruin & De Bruin, 2011; Petersen, 2018; Stegmann & Malan, 2016).

A summary of the instruments used in the data is provided in Table 2.5, despite additional other instruments being used in some research. This chapter reports on the instruments specifically relating to SDL.

In the qualitative research, other techniques were also employed to generate data, and this included:

- document analysis (De Beer, 2019b; Du Toit et al., 2016; Greyling et al., 2016; Havenga & De Beer, 2016; Olivier, 2016; Setlhodi, 2019; Terblanché, 2010; Vos & Van Oort, 2018);
- focus-group interviews (Abubakar & Arshad, 2015; De Klerk & Fourie, 2017; Lekalakala-Mokgele & Caka, 2015; Maistry, 2009; Malan et al., 2014; Nottidge & Louw, 2017; Statham et al., 2014);
- individual interviews (Breed & Bailey, 2018; De Beer, 2019b; De Beer & Mentz, 2017; Du Toit et al., 2016; Du Toit-Brits, 2019; Du Toit-Brits & Van Zyl, 2017; Iiyambo & Geduld, 2019; Jacobs & Van Loggerenberg, 1996; Maistry, 2009);
- interactive interviews (Setlhodi, 2019);
- netnography (Sujee et al., 2015);
- observations (Abubakar & Arshad, 2015; Lumina, 2005; Malan et al., 2014);
- open-ended questionnaires (Aheto et al., 2017; Breed, 2016; Du Toit et al., 2016; Jacobs & Van Loggerenberg, 1996; Maistry, 2009; Mthethwa, 2018; Olivier, 2016; Petersen, 2018; Stegmann & Malan, 2016);

Table 2.4 Overview of the samples

Sample types	Level	Number of participants	Sources
College tutors		6	Iiyambo and Geduld (2019)
Indigenous knowledge holders	Various individuals aged between 9 and 66	16	De Beer and Mentz (2017)
Nurse educators	Professional	9	Van Rensburg and Botma (2015)
Pupil enrolled nurses	Second years	19	Lekalakala-Mokgele and Caka (2015)
School/college learners	Grade 10	15	Iiyambo and Geduld (2019)
	Grade 11	19	Sujee et al. (2015)
	No grade indicated	15	Abubakar and Arshad (2015)
	Various grades	75	Fakolade and Adeniyi (2010)
School teachers		18 (portfolios) 5 (interviews)	De Beer (2019b)
		1	Abubakar and Arshad (2015)
University students	Preparatory bridging programme	35	Malan et al. (2014)
	Final year	40	Nottidge and Louw (2017)
	First year	10	Breed (2016)
	First year	267	De Bruin and Cornelius (2011)
	First year[a]	1 585	De Bruin et al. (2001), De Bruin (2007)
	First year	12	Du Toit-Brits (2019)
	First year	17	Du Toit-Brits and Van Zyl (2017)
	First year	104	Havenga and De Beer (2016)
	First year	43	Lubbe (2017)
	First year	480	Mthethwa (2018)
	First year	168	Mulube and Jooste (2014)
	Second year	6	Aheto et al. (2017)
	Second year	33	Breed and Bailey (2018)

(continued)

Table 2.4 (continued)

Sample types	Level	Number of participants	Sources
	Second year	Not stated	Lumina (2005)
	Second year	85	Petersen (2018)
	Second year	257	Stegmann and Malan (2016)
	Second and third year	77	Van der Walt (2014)
	Third year	87 (surveys) 23 (interviews)	Maistry (2009)
	Third year	16	Olivier (2016)
	Third year	37	Statham et al. (2014)
	Unnamed postgraduate qualification	Not indicated	Greyling et al. (2016)
	Postgraduate Certificate in Education	5	Du Toit et al. (2016)
	Postgraduate Certificate in Education	367	Van Wyk (2017)
	Not stated	3 800 (Feedback) 11 000 (Surveys)	Jacobs and Van Loggerenberg(1996)
	Not stated	Not stated	Orton and Nokes (2012)
	Not stated	57	Setlhodi (2019)
University lecturers		4	Du Toit-Brits and Van Zyl (2017)
		3	Malan et al. (2014)
		2	Mthethwa (2018)
		9	Nottidge and Louw (2017)
		11	Statham et al. (2014)
Vocational training	Fourth years	153	Mbagwu et al. (2020)
Working adults		519	De Bruin and De Bruin (2011)
		59 (Questionnaires) 17 (Focus-group interviews)	De Klerk and Fourie (2017)

The same group of research participants were used for both studies noted here

Table 2.5 Overview of instruments used

Instruments	Sources
Learner Self-Directedness in the Workplace Scale	De Bruin and De Bruin (2011)
Self-Directed Learning Readiness Scale (SDLRS)	De Bruin (2007) De Bruin et al. (2001) Greyling et al. (2016)
Self-directed learning skill scale	Mbagwu et al. (2020)
Self-Rating Scale of Self-Directed Learning (SRSSDL)	Breed (2014), Breed (2016), Breed and Bailey (2018), Havenga and De Beer (2016), Lubbe (2017), Nottidge and Louw (2017), Olivier (2016), Van der Walt (2014)
Student Self-Directed Learning Questionnaire (SSDLQ)	De Bruin and Cornelius (2011)
Unnamed self-generated questionnaire	Mulube and Jooste (2014), Petersen (2018), Stegmann and Malan (2016)

- researcher reflections (Lumina, 2005);
- a bricolage of different artefacts and documents (Van Wyk, 2017); and
- the critical incident technique (Van Rensburg & Botma, 2015);

In terms of quantitative data, the SRSSDL by Williamson (2007) seems to be the most common instrument used. Interestingly, neither the SDLP nor the SDLI was used at all. Despite some work towards creating context-specific instruments and some being translated into local languages, there seems to be a need for the development of instruments to gauge SDL in the varied African contexts.

Within the qualitative context, many strategies were followed with document analyses, different types of interviews and open-ended questionnaires being the most common. However, it is evident that more observation research might be necessary to understand the SDL context in African classrooms.

2.4.5 Main Trends from the Corpus

In terms of broad trends from the corpus, the relevance of SDL is evident from all the sources part of this corpus used in this chapter. SDL is also considered an essential twenty-first-century skill (Du Toit-Brits & Blignaut, 2019). However, it is clear that in many cases, formal education in schools and even in higher education is teacher-centred (De Beer & Mentz, 2017; Iiyambo & Geduld, 2019). Furthermore, there is a need for teachers to be empowered to use strategies such as collaborative learning and others to foster SDL (De Beer, 2016; De Beer & Mentz, 2017).

Some of the sources relate to the role or impact of SDL on other constructs. In this regard, it was found that students measuring a high SDL would find career decision-making easier as there are correlations between SDL and career decision-making self-efficacy (De Bruin & Cornelius, 2011). Lubbe (2017) established that keyboarding skills of students increased for students with an average or high level of SDL readiness. Moreover, existing scholarship on SDL informed several interventions (Fakolade & Adeniyi, 2010; Mbagwu et al., 2020).

Limited studies explicitly focused on the SDL instruments alone, and the overall trend was on research in exploring or measuring SDL. A unique case was the study by De Bruin et al. (2001) in which the psychometric properties Self-Directed Learning Readiness Scale (SDLRS) were explored. They empirically determined the following factors "Openness to learning opportunities, Love of learning, Positive self-concept as an effective and independent learner, and Acceptance of responsibility for own learning" (De Bruin et al., 2001, p. 128).

On the side of teachers, despite the focus on the learner within SDL, specific actions can contribute to fostering SDL among students (Du Toit-Brits, 2018b). Du Toit-Brits (2019) found that educators' positive expectations can support SDL. The importance of motivation was also evident in terms of supporting SDL (Du Toit et al., 2016; Du Toit-Brits & Van Zyl, 2017; Mulube & Jooste, 2014). The need for teacher support for SRL and ultimately also SDL is evident (Iiyambo & Geduld, 2019; Shishigu et al., 2019). Interestingly, Greyling et al. (2016) explored how learning materials could be structured to create opportunities for the development of SDL.

Some studies showed how specific strategies such as cooperative learning, project-based learning and problem-based learning could be supportive of SDL. In this regard, cooperative learning can be supportive of SDL. Breed (2016) notes how incorporating "positive interdependence, individual accountability, promotive face-to-face interaction, appropriate social skills, and group processing" (p. 1) in group work can influence SDL. Petersen (2018) also concurs that cooperative learning can foster SDL. Malan et al. (2014) also agree that problem-based learning promotes significant learning patterns that positively contribute to the development of SDL skills.

In the study by Mbagwu et al. (2020), an intervention was constructed around the nine factors identified by Ayyildiz and Tarhan (2015) and this increased SDL skills:

- attitude towards learning,
- learning responsibility,
- motivation and self-confidence,
- ability to plan learning,
- ability to use learning opportunities,
- ability to manage information,
- ability to apply learning strategies,
- assessment of learning process, and
- evaluation of learning success/results.

Furthermore, metacognition is also regarded as an important factor in terms of SDL (Mariano & Batchelor, 2018). In the corpus, this was also evident, and Breed and Bailey (2018) found "that the use of the metacognitive self-questions during cooperative pair problem-solving, positively influenced the students' levels of self-directed learning" (p. 1). Van der Walt (2014) found correlations between dimensions of questionnaires for SDL and metacognition.

Other sources in the corpus also indicated the advantages of cooperative learning (De Beer & Mentz, 2017), project-based learning (De Beer, 2019b; Du Toit et al., 2016; Havenga & De Beer, 2016), problem-based learning (Abubakar & Arshad, 2015; De Beer & Mentz, 2017; Malan, Ndlovu & Engelbrecht, 2014; Statham et al., 2014) for SDL. Abubakar and Arshad (2015) noted the affordances of introducing real-life problems towards supporting SDL and Hugo et al. (2012) associate SDL with authentic learning. While Setlhodi (2019) advocated the use of a self-paced learning framework.

Malan et al. (2014) indicated that the introduction of problem-based learning promotes significant learning patterns, encourages SDL skills in students and ignites a "process of growth towards lifelong learning". This finding is echoed by Kidane et al. (2020) that SDL is "an appropriate and preferred learning process to prepare students for lifelong learning". Mbagwu et al. (2020) in their study to promote lifelong learning (LLL) in VET students, also found that SDL positively increases students' LLL tendencies.

It was found that certain personality traits are related to SDL readiness (De Bruin, 2007). In this regard, it was found that "students who are emotionally stable, trusting, well-controlled and relatively relaxed have good potential to be self-directed learners" and that in terms of the 16 Personality Factor Questionnaire (16PF), "Independence, Superego Strength and Sensitivity also seem to act as co-determinants of self-directedness" (De Bruin, 2007, p. 236).

Extrinsic motivation and positive influence contribute to students developing SDL. Du Toit-Brits (2019), found that educators' expectations in an SDL learning environment influence students to apply their SDL skills to direct their learning in class. The findings further showed that teachers who are confident in the delivery positively influence students and enhance their SDL readiness. In another study, Mulube and Jooste (2014) explored first year learner nurses' perceptions of SDL. It was found that students had a positive perception of their learning which revealed that they are driven to learn. Although their self-confidence lacked, SDL enhanced their clinical skills and better prepared them for assessment. On the other hand, Nottidge and Louw (2017) evaluated the perceptions of faculty leadership towards SDL in a Nigerian medical school. They found that this leadership believes that students need to be guided by teachers towards SDL.

Some studies focus on SDL and assessment. Aheto et al. (2017) described how the WikiEducator E-quiz platform could be used to support the self-assessment of students. Lumina (2005) found that the use of portfolios and peer marking supported student SDL according to the Law students in that research. Similarly, Van Wyk (2017) also observed that ePortfolios could be useful in fostering SDL. While with an overview of different studies on portfolios, De Beer (2019b), Kruger et al. (2015) and Terblanché (2010) found that portfolios can be used effectively to support SDL. Stegmann and Malan (2016) explored the role of detailed feedback and peer assessment, and they found despite some negativity towards peer assessment among students, changes in the way feedback were approached supported self-assessment and SDL.

There were also studies in the corpus exploring the role of technology in the process of promoting SDL. In this regard, there was research related to the use of Turnitin for writing instruction (Sujee et al., 2015) as well as the use of online assessment tools (Aheto et al., 2017). Orton and Nokes (2012) also reported on SDL within a blended learning context for an occupational health nursing course.

The affordances of SDL for professional development and within the workplace is evident. In this regard, Van Rensburg and Botma (2015) found that SDL can have a positive effect on forming life-long learners and on quality in practice within the professional environment. Similarly, Wittmann and Olivier (2019) also note the importance of SDL for the professional development of language teachers and De Klerk and Fourie (2017) for professional cataloguers. The study by De Bruin and De Bruin (2011) aimed to create an instrument to be used to gauge SDL in the work environment and found it to be a reliable measure for their research sample.

In the African context and recently specifically in the South African milieu (Le Grange, 2019), the issue of decolonisation of the curriculum is highly relevant. To this end, including indigenous knowledge (Ezeanya-Esiobu, 2019) in the curriculum is regarded as a suitable vehicle (Breidlid & Botha, 2015; De Beer & Mentz, 2019). In this regard, from the corpus, the work of De Beer (2016) and De Beer and Mentz (2017) is in support of this movement while considering the implications of SDL.

2.5 Findings

The overview of research from the created corpus of publications on SDL in Africa presented in this chapter has shown various trends as well as opportunities for future research. Steady growth in research on SDL is evident. Various disciplines and themes have been researched in terms of SDL; however, the majority of the works have focused on education and specifically teacher education as well as health sciences. Strategies that are in support of SDL have also been considered especially also in terms of open distance contexts. Methodologically most of the research is qualitative in nature and is, in most cases done with university students and to an extent, lecturers. Consequently, there is a need for increased school-based and vocational education level research. Certain instruments are commonly used, and this may provide opportunities for comparison; however, there is a need for additional instruments to be developed in and for African contexts.

In terms of the findings from the studies, overall, the need for SDL is clear. In many studies, the interaction between SDL and various variables was explored. The role of the teacher in terms of facilitating SDL was identified as significant in many studies. Cooperative learning, project-based learning and problem-based learning as strategies to foster SDL were also prominent. The role of metacognition, authentic real-life problems and motivation were also highlighted.

Interestingly quite a number of studies focused on assessment, and here, the role of portfolios was quite significant. Yet, the role of assessment with regard to SDL needs to be explored further. Finally, in terms of context, the increased importance of technology and situating learning as part of the decolonisation of the curriculum, were also noted.

2.6 Conclusion

At the start of the chapter, it was noted that this research aimed to determine the nature of SDL research on the African continent between 1990 and 2020 and this was done employing a systematic literature review.

This chapter explored the nature of SDL research within the context of Africa for the past 20 years. In this chapter, SDL was understood as both a learning process and learner characteristic. The 54 publications identified for analysis covered many disciplines and fields; however, most of the work was done within education and specifically teacher education and health sciences. The majority of research is done in and on South Africa, but there was also some research from Ethiopia, Ghana, Namibia and Nigeria. In terms of research methodologies, a lot of variety was observed, yet, most of the work is the research is qualitative and is done within university contexts.

Consequently, more research is needed at school, vocational education and professional development levels. Various standard SDL measuring instruments are used, but there is a need for the development of more instruments for the varied African contexts. Broadly the findings of the various SDL studies show how strategies like cooperative learning, project-based learning and problem-based learning can foster SDL. Also, variables such as metacognition, motivation, the teacher, the learning environment and unique African contexts are important.

Some limitations can be identified in terms of this research as the corpus was limited to specific criteria and databases. From the databases sources written in English and Afrikaans were identified from searches being done in English only. Hence, publications in other languages were not included in the analysis. In addition, the interpretations are based on the judgement of the two researchers. Thus, they are influenced by their approaches to SDL and their respective epistemological lenses inherent to their analyses. The findings from this research cannot be generalised to all research in Africa. But, it does provide an impression of what has been done.

References

Abubakar, A. B., & Arshad, M. Y. (2015). Self-directed learning and skills of problem-based learning: A case of Nigerian Secondary Schools Chemistry Students. *International Education Studies, 8*(12), 70–78.

Aheto, S. P. K., Ng'ambi, D., & Cronjé, J. C. (2017). An open source self-assessment platform as technological tool for distance and open education learners. *Progressio, 39*(1), 89–108.

Ajani, O. A. (2019). Understanding teachers as adult learners in professional development activities for enhanced classroom practices. *AFFRIKA Journal of Politics, Economics and Society, 9*(2), 195–208.

Ayyildiz, Y., & Tarhan, L. (2015). Development of the self-directed learning skills scale. *International Journal of Lifelong Education, 34*(6), 663–679.

Bosch, C., Mentz, E. & Goede, R. (2019) Self-directed learning: A conceptual overview. In E. Mentz, J. de Beer & R. Bailey (Eds.), *Self-Directed Learning for the 21st Century: Implications for Higher Education* (pp. 1–36). Cape Town: AOSIS.

Breed, B. (2016). Exploring a cooperative learning approach to improve self-directed learning in higher education. *Journal for New Generation Sciences, 14*(3), 1–21.

Breed, B., & Bailey, R. (2018). The influence of a metacognitive approach to cooperative pair problem-solving on self-direction in learning. *The Journal for Transdisciplinary Research in Southern Africa, 14*(1), 1–11.

Breidlid, A., & Botha, L. R. (2015). Indigenous Knowledges in Education: Anticolonial Struggles in a Monocultural Arena with Reference to Cases from the Global South. In W. J. Jacob, S. Y. Cheng, & M. K. Porter (Eds.), *Indigenous education: Language, Culture and Identity* (pp. 319–339). Springer.

Brockett, R. G., & Hiemstra, R. (2019). *Self-direction in adult learning: Perspectives on theory, research, and practice.* Routledge.

Čablová, L., Pates, R., Miovský, M. & Noel, J. (2017). How to Write a Systematic Review Article and Meta-Analysis. In T. F. Babor, K. Stenius, R. Pates, M. Miovský, J. O'Reilly & P. Candon (Eds.) *Publishing Addiction Science: A Guide for the Perplexed.* (pp. 173–189). London: Ubiquity Press. https://doi.org/10.5334/bbd.i.

Cheng, S. F., Kuo, C. L., Lin, K. C., & Lee-Hsieh, J. (2010). Development and preliminary testing of a self-rating instrument to measure self-directed learning ability of nursing students. *International Journal of Nursing Studies, 47*(9), 1152–1158.

Cohen, L., Manion, L., & Morrison, K. (2018). *Research methods in education* (8th ed.). Routledge.

De Beer, J. (2016). Re-imagining science education in South Africa: The affordances of indigenous knowledge for self-directed learning in the school curriculum. *Journal for New Generation Sciences, 14*(3), 34–53.

De Beer, J. (Ed.). (2019a). The decolonisation of the curriculum project: The affordances of indigenous knowledge for self-directed learning. NWU Self-Directed Learning Series Volume 2. (pp. 1–23). AOSIS.

De Beer, J. (2019). The affordances of project-based learning and classroom action research in the teaching and learning of Natural Sciences. *Perspectives in Education, 37*(2), 67–79.

De Beer, J. J., & Mentz, E. (2017). 'n Kultuurhistoriese aktiwiteitsteoretiese blik op die houers van inheemse kennis as selfgerigte leerders: Lesse vir onderwys in Suid-Afrikaanse skole: Navorsing. *Suid-Afrikaanse Tydskrif Vir Natuurwetenskap En Tegnologie, 36*(1), 1–11.

De Beer, J. & Mentz, E. (2019). The use of Cultural-Historical Activity Theory in researching the affordances of indigenous knowledge for self-directed learning. In J. De Beer (Ed.) *The decolonisation of the curriculum project: The affordances of indigenous knowledge for self-directed learning.* (pp. 87–116). Cape Town: AOSIS. https://doi.org/10.4102/aosis.2019.BK1 33.04

De Beer, J., Petersen, N. & Van Vuuren, H. J. (Eds.). (2020). *Becoming a teacher: Research on the work-integrated learning of student teachers.* NWU Self-Directed Learning Series Volume 4. AOSIS.

De Bruin, G. P., De Bruin, K., Jacobs, G. J., & Schoeman, W. J. (2001). The factor structure of the Self-directed Learning Readiness Scale. *South African Journal of Higher Education, 15*(3), 119–130.

De Bruin, K. (2007). The relationship between personality traits and self-directed learning readiness in higher education students. *South African Journal of Higher Education, 21*(2), 228–240.

De Bruin, K., & Cornelius, E. (2011). Self-directed learning and career decision-making. *Acta Academica, 43*(2), 214–235.

De Bruin, K., & De Bruin, G. P. (2011). Development of the learner self-directedness in the workplace scale. *SA Journal of Industrial Psychology, 37*(1), 01–10.

De Klerk, M. A. T., & Fourie, I. (2017). Facilitating the continuing Education needs of professional cataloguers in South Africa: A framework for self-directed learning. *Mousaion: South African Journal of Information Studies, 35*(1), 90–113.

Du Toit, A., Van der Walt, M., & Havenga, M. (2016). Verbruikerstudie-onderwysstudente se affektiewe ervarings tydens projekgebaseerde leer. *Suid-Afrikaanse Tydskrif vir Natuurwetenskap en Tegnologie, 35*(1), a1362, 1–9. https://doi.org/10.4102/satnt.v35i1.1362

Du Toit-Brits, C. (2015). Endowing self directed learning in learning environments: interrelated connection between students' environments and self directed preparedness. *Journal of Educational Studies,* (Special issue 1), 32–52.

Du Toit-Brits, C. (2018). Towards a transformative and holistic continuing self-directed learning theory. *South African Journal of Higher Education, 32*(4), 51–65.

Du Toit-Brits, C. (2018). Die onderwyser as beoefenaar en bemiddelaar van selfgerigte leer. *Tydskrif Vir Geesteswetenskappe, 58*(2), 376–386.

Du Toit-Brits, C. (2019). A focus on self-directed learning: The role that educators' expectations play in the enhancement of students' self-directedness. *South African Journal of Education, 39*(2), 1–11. https://doi.org/10.15700/saje.v39n2a1645

Du Toit-Brits, C. (2020). Unleashing the power of self-directed learning: Criteria for structuring self-directed learning within the learning environments of higher education institutions. *Africa Education Review, 17*(2), 20–32.

Du Toit-Brits, C., & Blignaut, H. (2019). Posisionering van voortgesette selfgerigte leervaardighede in een-en-twintigste-eeuse onderwys. *Tydskrif Vir Geesteswetenskappe, 59*(4), 512–529.

Du Toit-Brits, C., & Van Zyl, C.-M. (2017). Embedding motivation in the self-directedness of first-year teacher students. *South African Journal of Higher Education, 31*(1), 50–65.

Engeström, Y. (1987). *Learning by expanding: An activity-theoretical approach to developmental research.* Helsinki: Orienta-Konsultit.

Ezeanya-Esiobu, C. (2019). *Indigenous Knowledge and Education in Africa.* Springer Nature.

Fakolade, O. A., & Adeniyi, S. O. (2010). Efficacy of Enrichment Triad and Self-Direct Models on Academic Achievement of Gifted Students in Selected Secondary Schools in Nigeria. *International Journal of Special Education, 25*(1), 10–16.

Garrison, D. R. (1997). Self-directed learning: Toward a comprehensive model. *Adult Education Quarterly, 48*(1), 18–33.

Greyling, E. S. G., Geyser, H. C., & Fourie, C. M. (2002). Self-directed learning: Adult learners' perceptions and their study materials. *South African Journal of Higher Education, 16*(2), 112–121.

Guglielmino, L. M. (1977). *Development of the self-directed learning readiness scale.* (Unpublished doctoral dissertation). University of Georgia, Athens.

Gülpınar, Ö., & Güçlü, A. G. (2013). How to write a review article? *Turkish Journal of Urology, 39*(Suppl 1), 44–48.

Havenga, M., & De Beer, H. (2016). Project-based learning in consumer sciences: Enhancing students responsibility in learning. *Journal of Family Ecology and Consumer Sciences, 44*(1), 58–70.

Hugo, F. M., Slabbert, J., Louw, J. M., Marcus, T. S., Bac, M., Du Toit, P. H., & Sandars, J. E. (2012). The clinical associate curriculum. the learning theory underpinning the BCMP programme at the University of Pretoria. *African Journal of Health Professions Education, 4*(2), 128–131.

Iiyambo, S., & Geduld, B. (2019). Perceptions of Namibian College of Open Learning learners' self-regulated learning skills. *Progressio, 41*(1), 1–18.

Jacobs, C. M., & Loggerenberg, V. (1996). Transforming a project to a model: The guided self-study experience at the Rand Afrikaans University. *South African Journal of Higher Education, 10*(2), 138–143.

Jane, R., & Jane, L. (2003). *Qualitative research practice: A Guide for social science students and researchers*. Sage Publications.

Kidane, H. H., Roebertsen, H., & Van der Vleuten, C. P. (2020). Students' perceptions towards self-directed learning in Ethiopian medical schools with new innovative curriculum: A mixed-method study. *BMC Medical Education, 20*(1), 1–10.

Knowles, M. S. (1975). *Self-directed learning: A guide for learners and teachers*. Follett.

Kruger, C. G., Van Rensburg, J. J., & De Witt, M. W. (2015). The portfolio to support applied competency in a South African distance learning programme for foundation phase teachers-a case study. *Progressio, 37*(1), 154–171.

Le Grange, L. (2019). Different voices on decolonising of the curriculum. In J. De Beer (Ed.) *The decolonisation of the curriculum project: The affordances of indigenous knowledge for self-directed learning*. (pp. 25–47). AOSIS. https://doi.org/10.4102/aosis.2019.BK133.02

Lekalakala-Mokgele, E., & Caka, E. M. (2015). Facilitative and obstructive factors in the clinical learning environment: Experiences of pupil enrolled nurses. *Curationis, 38*(1), 1–7.

Lubbe, E. (2017). Die invloed van selfgerigteleergereedheid op die aanleer van die blindtiktegniek: Opvoedkunde. *Litnet Akademies, 14*(2), 627–649.

Lumina, C. (2005). Giving students greater responsibility for their own learning: Portfolio assessment and peer-marking as tools for promoting self-directed learning in a second-year law course. *South African Journal of Higher Education, 19*(3), 73–88.

Maistry, S. M. (2009). Applying a partial problem-based learning environment to a non-major economics course: A case of cognitive dissonance. *South African Journal of Higher Education, 23*(2), 329–339.

Malan, S. B., Ndlovu, M. & Engelbrecht, P. (2014). Introducing problem-based learning (PBL) into a foundation programme to develop self-directed learning skills. *South African Journal of Education, 34*(1).

Mallett, R., Hagen-Zanker, J., Slater, R., & Duvendack, M. (2012). The benefits and challenges of using systematic reviews in international development research. *Journal of Development Effectiveness, 4*(3), 445–455.

Mariano, G. J. & Batchelor, K. (2018). The Role of Metacognition and Knowledge Transfer in Self-Directed Learning. In F. G. Giuseffi (Ed.) *Emerging self-directed learning strategies in the digital age*. (pp. 141–159). IGI Global.

Mbagwu, F. O., Chukwuedo, S. O., & Ogbuanya, T. C. (2020). Promoting Lifelong Learning Propensity and Intentions for Vocational Training among Adult and Vocational Educational Undergraduates. *Vocations and Learning, 13*, 419–437. https://doi.org/10.1007/s12186-020-09245-1

Mentz, E. & Bailey, R. (Eds.). (2020). *Self-directed learning research and its impact on educational practice*. NWU Self-Directed Learning Series Volume 3. AOSIS.

Mentz, E. & Oosthuizen, I. (Eds.). (2016). *Self-directed learning research*. AOSIS.

Mentz, E., De Beer, J. & Bailey, R. (Eds.). (2019). *Self-directed learning for the 21st century: Implications for higher education*. NWU Self-Directed Learning Series Volume 1. AOSIS.

Mthethwa, L. C. (2018). Computer-based tutoring role in Inducting the first year's students at a previously disadvantaged university. *Gender and Behaviour, 16*(2), 11452–11464.

Mulube, S. M., & Jooste, K. (2014). First-year learner nurses' perceptions of learning motivation in self-directed learning in a simulated skills laboratory at a higher education institution. *South African Journal of Higher Education, 28*(6), 1776–1794.

Nottidge, T. E., & Louw, A. J. N. (2017). Self-directed learning: Status of final-year students and perceptions of selected faculty leadership in a Nigerian medical school–a mixed analysis study. *African Journal of Health Professions Education, 9*(1), 29–33.

Olivier, J. (2016). A journey towards self-directed writing: A longitudinal study of undergraduate language students' writing. *Per Linguam, 32*(3), 28–47.

Olivier, J. (2018). Van oplees na self ooplees: die moontlikhede wat selfgerigte leer met behulp van oop opvoedkundige hulpbronne die letterkundeklas bied. *Stilet: Tydskrif van die Afrikaanse Letterkundevereniging, 30*(1–2), 148–168.

Olivier, J. (Ed.). (2020). *Self-directed multimodal learning in higher education.* NWU Self-Directed Learning Series Volume 5. AOSIS.

Orton, P., & Nokes, K. M. (2012). Introduction of a blended teaching strategy in an Occupational Health Nursing Education programme. *Occupational Health Southern Africa, 18*(5), 23–25.

Ottu, I. F. (2017). Cooperative Stakeholding: Optimising Students' Educational Practice through Need-Centred Self-Determination, Connectedness with Learning Environment and Passion. *Journal of Education and Practice, 8*(4), 21–33.

Petersen, N. (2018). Selfgerigte leer: Die ervarings en menings van lewenswetenskappe-onderwysstudente tydens die gebruik van werkkaarte in 'n koöperatiewe onderrig-leer-omgewing. *Litnet Akademies, 15*(3), 1119–1142.

Pilling-Cormick, J. (1996). *Development of the self-directed learning perception scale.* (Unpublished doctoral dissertation). University of Toronto, Toronto.

Robinson, J. D., & Persky, A. M. (2020). Developing Self-Directed Learners. *American Journal of Pharmaceutical Education, 84*(3), 847512. https://doi.org/10.5688/ajpe847512

Setlhodi, I. I. (2019). The Value of Pacing in Promoting Self-Directed Learning. In Giuseffi, F. G. (Eds.), *Self-Directed Learning Strategies in Adult Educational Contexts* (pp. 1–22). IGI Global. https://doi.org/:10.4018/978-1-5225-8018-8.ch001

Shishigu, A., Michael, K., & Atnafu, M. (2019). Can Blended Learning Enhance Students' Tendency to Regulate Their Own Learning?: An Experience From Pedagogical Experiments. In Giuseffi, F. G. (Ed.), *Self-Directed Learning Strategies in Adult Educational Contexts* (pp. 44–70). IGI Global. https://doi.org/10.4018/978-1-5225-8018-8.ch003

Statham, S. B., Inglis-Jassiem, G., & Hanekom, S. D. (2014). Does a problem-based learning approach benefit students as they enter their clinical training years? Lecturers' and students' perceptions. *African Journal of Health Professions Education, 6*(2), 185–191.

Stegmann, N., & Malan, M. (2016). Accounting students' experience of an improved strategy of feedback on assessment. *Journal of Economic and Financial Sciences, 9*(3), 769–788.

Sujee, E., Engelbrecht, A., & Nagel, L. (2015). Effectively digitizing communication with Turnitin for improved writing in a multilingual classroom. *Journal for Language Teaching, 49*(2), 11–31.

Terblanché, E. J. (2010). Portfolios: An alternative to traditional assessment in ODL. *Progressio, 32*(2), 117–133.

Van der Walt, M. S. (2014). Metakognitiewe bewustheid, selfgerigtheid in leer en een leerprestasie van voornemende wiskundeonderwysers vir die intermediêre en senior fase. *Suid-Afrikaanse Tydskrif Vir Natuurwetenskap En Tegnologie, 33*(1), 1–9.

Van Deur, P. (2017). *Managing Self-Directed Learning in Primary School Education: Emerging Research and Opportunities: Emerging Research and Opportunities.* IGI Global.

Van Rensburg, G. H., & Botma, Y. (2015). Bridging the gap between self-directed learning of nurse educators and effective student support. *Curationis, 38*(2), 1–7. https://doi.org/10.4102/curationis.v38i2.1503

Van Wyk, M. M. (2017). An e-portfolio as empowering tool to enhance students' self-directed learning in a teacher education course: A case of a South African university. *South African Journal of Higher Education, 31*(3), 274–291.

Vos, E., & Van Oort, R. (2018). 'n Selfgerigte-lees-proses: Traumabelewing en-verwerking in die jeugroman Blou is nie 'n kleur nie deur Carin Krahtz. *Litnet Akademies, 15*(3), 826–962.

Visser, A. (2018). The agile learner and self-directed learning. *finweek*, 48–49.

Williamson, S. N. (2007). Development of a self-rating scale of self-directed learning. *Nurse Researcher, 14*(2), 66–83.

Wittmann, G., & Olivier, J. (2019). Professional Development in Fostering Self-Directed Learning in German Second Additional Language Teachers. *Per Linguam, 35*(3), 125–142. https://doi.org/10.5785/35-3-870

Jako Olivier is the holder of the UNESCO Chair in Multimodal Learning and Open Educational Resources and is a professor of Multimodal Learning in the Faculty of Education at North-West University. His research, within the Research Unit Self-Directed Learning, focuses on self-directed multimodal learning, open educational resources, multiliteracies, blended and e-learning in language classrooms as well as multilingualism in education. He currently holds a Y rating from the National Research Foundation and was awarded the Education Association of South Africa's Emerging Researcher Medal in 2018. In addition to recently editing a book on self-directed multimodal learning, he has published numerous articles and book chapters at the national and international levels, and he also acts as a supervisor for postgraduate students.

Antoinette Wentworth holds a Master's Degree in Educational Technology: Instructional Design and is currently the Manager of instructional material development, print and online, for Open and Distance Learning at the Namibia University of Science and Technology. She serves on the eLearning Standing Committee under the umbrella of the Namibia Open Learning Network Trust with a keen focus on the development of Open Education Resources. Her research interest involves re-thinking instructional design models to convert traditional face-to-face course material to a Technology Enhanced Learning Environment. Her newly found interest is in self-directed learning, specifically on what role self-directed learning play in online teaching and learning.

Chapter 3
Fostering Students' SRL in an Online Learning Environment

Abdelwahed Elsafi

Abstract Recent research suggests that emerging technologies such as mobile devices represent unprecedented opportunities for students to be self-regulated learners, to work independently, and leverage their ability of self-regulated learning (SRL) to acquire knowledge and therefore to take responsibility for their learning regardless of any circumstance concerning learning environments. Effective pedagogical approaches such as select, organize, associate, and regulate (SOAR) is mainly developed to be an efficient instructional method for fostering students' SRL skills. This study examined and compared the effectiveness of three mobile learning strategies: Mobile SOAR (M-SOAR), mobile SOAR with paper (M-SOAR-P), and mobile without SOAR (M-W-SOAR) to enhance students' SRL skills, promote motivation, and improve learning performance of a science topic in an online learning environment. This study was carried out in Khartoum city, Sudan. Three classes of Sudanese higher school students participated in the study. The students were assigned to the M-SOAR approach (experimental group A, $n = 34$), M-SOAR-P (experimental group B, $n = 32$), and M-W-SOAR (control group, $n = 33$) as three learning methods. The online self-regulated learning questionnaire (OSLQ) and elements of attention, relevance, confidence, and satisfaction (ARCS) motivation questionnaire as well as the performance test were accomplished. The findings yielded that SRL skills and motivation of experimental group A were more positive compared to the experimental group B and the control group. The performance test computed by SPSS yielded that there was a statistically significant difference between three groups, in favor of the experimental group A. The study recommends further research into the effectiveness of a pedagogical SOAR approach on fostering students' SRL in online learning environments.

Keywords Online learning environment · SOAR learning approach · Mobile learning · Self-regulated learning (SRL)

A. Elsafi (✉)
Department of Instructional Technology, Collage of Education, University of Bari, Bahri, Sudan

© The Author(s), under exclusive license to Springer Nature Singapore Pte Ltd. 2021   41
D. Burgos and J. Olivier (eds.), *Radical Solutions for Education in Africa*, Lecture Notes in Educational Technology, https://doi.org/10.1007/978-981-16-4099-5_3

3.1 Introduction

Fostering students' SRL and promoting motivation are core issues to be considered for science education while students are studying in online environments (Türel & Kilic, 2018; Cho & Castañeda, 2019). Previous studies in the domain of high schools science education (Alsalhi et al., 2019; Nikou & Economides, 2018) have demonstrated that using emerging technologies, for instance mobile devices with effective learning strategies could improve students' performance, promote motivation, and successfully develop SRL skills in both formal and informal educational contexts. Examples include physics courses (Alsalhi et al., 2019), problem-based learning activities (Mustafa & Tuncel, 2019), a context-aware ubiquitous learning environment (Chiang et al., 2014), and inquiry-based learning activities (Chang et al., 2016). Thus, educators need to cultivate students' skills of SRL for better engagement and communication in complex learning processes (Elsafi, 2020). As a result, developing students' self-directed skills is becoming more important than ever, self-directed learning is considered one of twenty-first-century skills that students' need to acquire however and participate effectively in a community of knowledge (Elsafi, 2020). Findings from a systematic review of science learning for k-12 students in online learning environments have shown that mobile-based learning approaches such as scaffolds, flipped classrooms are more beneficial to enhance students' ability of self-directed learning (Sletten, 2017; Zheng & Chen, 2016). However, it is necessary to leverage the advantages and potentials of mobile devices to help students engage in online learning environments.

Researchers have recommended that it is essential to incorporate effective SRL strategies to facilitate learning and improve performance and further lead to cultivate k-12 students' abilities to take charge of their learning regardless of any educational circumstances (Sampaio & Almeida, 2015). For better success in learning and for developing students' self-directed learning, educators should emphasize the integration of efficient and effective learning strategies to promote students' interaction and collaboration in online learning environments (MacCallum et al., 2014).

Kiewra (2009) developed four steps; select, organize, associate, and regulate (SOAR) as a cognitive and self-regulated learning strategy which acronym stands for four theoretically driven and empirically supported components. Each component of the SOAR strategy is based on the cognitive process of meaningful learning. This instructional strategy is relatively not explored into its effects on promoting students SRL skills in open and online learning environments. This study was done in Sudan. The study adapted the SOAR pedagogy to support students' SRL of factual, conceptual, and relationship knowledge of a science topic in an online learning environment using mobile devices. The study investigates the following question:

Do students who learn with a mobile SOAR learning intervention have better SRL skills, motivation and achievements, in terms of factual, conceptual, and relationship knowledge of a science topic than those who learn with mobile SOAR with paper and the mobile without SOAR strategy?

3.2 Background

3.2.1 Online Learning in Sudan

Sudan is one of the developing countries that realized the important role of Information and Communication Technology (ICT) implementation in the education system. The government launched the first initiative for ICT implementation in 1999, which emphasized the introduction of ICT into the secondary school curriculum (Nour, 2016). The national strategy has covered important points including; providing technology infrastructures, human resources development, supporting national software industries, etc. Furthermore, the ICT plan was launched in practice in 2002 and focused on aspects of the curriculum reform and development, teachers' preparation for ICT implementation in learning in schools across subjects as well as supporting the idea of lifelong learning (Nour, 2015). To achieve these goals, however, the Ministry of Education (MoE) has equipped some secondary schools with computers and preliminary ICT infrastructures such as scanners and printers to facilitate the technology integration in learning processes.

More precisely, the department of curriculum and training at MoE in Sudan is engaging in a variety of curriculum development and reform programs. The main purpose is to achieve the country's educational goals in light of ICT strategic plans. The engineering science curriculum of secondary schools is considered a modern curriculum that should align with a new life cycle of science learning. Thus, the department seeks to improve students' ability to be independent learners and drive learning with technology (e.g., ICT tools and mobile devices) as therefore teachers have to apply effective instructional strategies in teaching and learning processes.

Due to the poor ICT infrastructure in most Sudanese secondary schools learning environments and lack of teachers' pedagogical skills in which emerging technologies can successfully be incorporated across subjects, online learning is still not active as required. More recently, open education resource (OER) is becoming an important issue, not only because of rapid technological challenges but also because of other corresponding educational aspects such as challenges in teaching methods, curricula design, and the inclusion in education on a new generation.

In Sudan, the overall educational policies and curriculum reform were to improve the effective use of ICT in high schools or lower levels of education but no mention or focus to provide OER. Until now, there were no national strategies or even initiatives to offer OER at the level of K-12 education. Consequently, to startup and offer OER to be accessed and to increase learning opportunities, MoE in Sudan should formulate a clear strategy to successfully and efficiently provide OER. Capacity-building for stakeholders is also necessary; teachers need to be trained on how they can utilize online and open educational resources for teaching and learning purposes and other relevant coordinations with responsible bodies are important to reduce expected challenges while access to OER.

3.2.2 SRL in Online Learning Environments

Fostering students' self-regulated learning skills is a key aspect of learning, in particular when students work in online learning environments (Zheng & Chen, 2016). The ultimate goals of promoting a student's SRL skills are to make them engage in the learning process and rise ability to be responsible for their learning from digital repositories. Skills such as monitoring and regulating can be cultivated directly (in the classroom learning activities through effective learning strategies) or indirect while they are doing learning tasks outside a school environment (in a field or at home to accomplish learning activities). In this context, a large body of research has exposed to measure SRL in online learning environments and examined how learners work in such situations might affect in developing their SRL skills and improve their ability to be more independent learners (Zheng & Chen, 2016; Sha et al., 2011). The reason why SRL in an online learning environment is a critical matter and should be taken into consideration that is because educators and practitioners have realized, SRL has always been necessary for students to be acquired to enable them to participate actively in both formal and informal learning situations; however, they can manage, monitor and motivate themselves in different learning conditions (Cárdenas-Robledo & Peña-Ayala, 2018). At the same time, instructors did take into consideration the students' engagement strategically and efficiently using wireless technology devices such as mobile learning could help to avoid distraction and interference in learning (Elsafi, 2020).

In this respect, both theoretical and empirical researches have demonstrated that how emerging pedagogies could promote students' SRL skills in online learning environments. An earlier study that measured self-regulated learning skills for two science classes of students in Singaporean schools who spent 5 weeks studying magnet-scientific concepts was investigated by (Sha et al., 2011). The study was done based on a project of the mobilized curriculum of Singaporean schools. The authors developed a framework to analyze the processes of the mobile learning application "Go Know." The Go Know mobile learning application was selected to support mobilized curriculum and help students to engage meta-cognitively in learning processes. The study attempted to measure students' SRL in the terms of (behavioral, motivational, and meta-cognitive). Three types of measurements including motivated learning strategy questionnaire (MLSQ), parental autonomy support (PAS) survey (to measure students' perception when they interacted with their parents for learning science out of schools), and online behavioral data (OBD) to measure students' behavior engagement through answering a series of questions. Overall, the results gained from three types of SRL measurements (MLSQ, PAS, OBD) pointed out, students were reported positive SRL behaviors. The study concluded that this result explored patterns of behavior during learning using mobile devices. SRL strategies such as goal setting, monitoring, regulating, and reflecting are playing an important role in developing learners' cognitive skills (Bolaji & Fakomogbon, 2017).

Acquiring skills of these strategies could increase students' ability to take charge of the learning processes, particularly in mobile learning environments. Some studies have examined the impact of SRL in a mobile learning environment compared to the traditional learning environment for instance; Naemi and Naemi (2017) have conducted an empirical study to examine the effectiveness of smartphones training on self-efficacy and self-regulated learning in a science course. The participants were 56 and divided into two equal sizes (experimental and control groups), the study used to teach the experimental group by smartphones for studying a science course while the control group used traditional ones. Three measurements were administered the self-regulated questionnaire, the self-efficacy questionnaire, and the post-test. The results revealed that the experimental group was scored better than the control group in academic achievements. Moreover, the use of smartphones in the training process developed self-efficacy and self-regulation of the experimental group compared to the control group.

Lin et al. (2016) have articulated the processes of an online learning system to foster a mobile learning environment. The online learning system called (Self-Regulated Learning with Group Awareness and Peer Assistance -SRL-GAPA). The system has established many functions including students are being aware of learning activities that their peers involving to conduct, they are also able to see other group works, and they can ask for help collaboratively to overcome any expected challenges while conducting activities. Therefore, many opportunities can offer to learn in collaborative manners to promote their SRL. The participants were divided into two groups; the experimental group used Self-Regulated Learning with Group Awareness and Peer Assistance -SRL-GAPA while the control group used Self-Regulated Learning without Group Awareness and Peer Assistance-SRL-WGAPA. The results have yielded that the experimental group outperformed the control groups regarding learning achievements and SRL behaviors (Lin et al., 2016).

The components of SOAR were developed to be highly supported to help students being self-directed learners not only in a traditional classroom environment but also in assisted students to work effectively in online learning environments. There is a lack of research concerning exploring the impact of SOAR in promoting students' SRL skills; however, this study could add to the growing body of the literature review, that is, effective integration of mobile SOAR could improve students' SRL skills of a science topic. It offered empirical evidence, the mobile SOAR environment provided learning tools in which students have organized learning, and therefore, it supports them to be self-regulated learners.

3.3 Experiment Design

3.3.1 Participants

The participants were three classes of male students, 99 in total at a high school in Khartoum city. The average age of participants was 14. All students had already experienced using mobile devices for communication, web searching, and entertainment purposes, and sometimes for study support (e.g., searching and accessing online educational resources). The permission for conducting activities was obtained from parents and the higher school principal for recruitment students to be involved in the study. Before the experiment was conducted, each participant was asked to confirm their parents had signed the consent form and informed that they could withdraw from the study at any time. Additionally, the confidentiality of participation could be maintained and all data collected could be kept under secure conditions. Participants were randomly assigned to three groups. The first class ($n = 34$) was assigned to the experimental group A, the second class ($n = 32$) was assigned to the experimental group B, and the third class was assigned to the control group. Students in the experimental group A followed M-SOAR, students in the experimental group B followed M-SOAR-P, whereas students in the control group were used M-W-SOAR. In order to assess students learning outcomes, the system evaluated students after learning sessions.

3.3.2 Measurement Tools

The subject was electrical circuit components (ECC) which is covered in the Sudanese high school science curriculum. In order to evaluate students' knowledge of ECC such as the current, voltage, and resistance, a pretest was developed to evaluate students' prior knowledge regarding factual, conceptual, and relationship knowledge of ECC. It comprised 20 multiple-choice questions with total scores of 100 points. The pretest was intended to examine the students' prior understanding and to ensure that they have equivalent knowledge about the topic and further to participate effectively in learning activities. In order to assess students' levels of motivation, the ARCS questionnaire was administrated. The questionnaire consisted of 17 questions. Responses to all questions were based on a five-point Likert-scale ranging from 5 for "strongly agree" to 1 for "strongly disagree." After completing learning activities, the students filled out the questionnaire. Concerning the questionnaire reliability, the Cronbach's alpha (α) for the questionnaire was 0.91, and Cronbach's alpha (α) for sub-dimensions of the questionnaire (attention, relevance, confidence, and satisfaction) are 0.82, 0.75, 0.81, and 0.0.76 respectively. The post-achievement test was also conducted to determine which group of students under a specific learning strategy (M-SOAR, M-SOAR-P, and M-W-SOAR) could significantly achieve higher learning achievement than the other two groups. In sum, the one-way ANOVA analysis was performed. The independent variables were three abovementioned mobile learning strategies, the dependent variables were total achievement scores, and covariance was pretest scores. The total achievement test scores were 100 points generated from 20 multiple-choice questions. The analyses were done through two phases; in phase one, (ANOVA) was conducted to investigate whether a significant difference could exist between three groups in total academic achievement scores. In the second phase, the analyses of (ANCOVA) multiple comparison were calculated to compare and determine where high statistical significance could occur between three groups. The study was also used OSLQ. The questionnaire has 24 items self-report scale measured students' use of specific self-regulation strategies. It is designed to assess students' engagement in regulatory behaviors while studying and doing learning tasks in the online and blended learning environment (Martinez-Lopez et al., 2017). The questionnaire comprised six sub-scales including goal setting (5 items) environment structuring (4 items), time management (3 items) task strategies (4 items), and help seeking (4 items). The questions were followed a five-point Liker-scale ranging from 5 for strongly agree to 1 for strongly disagree.

3.3.3   System Description

This study used ClassFlow and Mindomo as two online learning platforms. These platforms have been developed to meet the modern teaching and learning styles and to offer ubiquity learning to serve a wide range of users and increase opportunities for accessing learning. The reasons for using these platforms were that participants have trained to use them for the purpose of this study. The ClassFlow and Mindomo are available online at http://classflow.com and https://www.mindomo.com respectively.

3.3.4   Experiment Procedure

The experiment procedure is shown in Fig. 3.1. In order to test the impact of proposed M-SOAR compared to the M-SOAR-P and M-W-SOAR strategies, a variety of learning activities were performed. The following stages illustrated the experimental procedures.

In the preparation stage, the teacher informed students in three groups about the subject matter (ECC) and instructed them strategically to learn about it. They provided handheld smartphone devices operating with the Android system and connected to the WiFi as well as they oriented to operate mobile devices to facilitate learning activities. According to the experiment procedures, the participants received training to perform three conditions (M-SOAR, M-SOAR-P, and M-W-SOAR). In the beginning, the experimental group A followed the M-SOAR approach as explained following:

Select: Before the classroom started, the instructor informed students of learning objectives for studying ECC. The instructor sent students video content which demonstrated the electrical circuit operation and recommended particular links for enhancing better understandings. In the classroom, the instructor illustrated how participants could successfully "select items" demonstrated by mobile devices to sort out ideas and sub-ideas behind each object by utilizing a note tool embedded in the system to enable them to report information. After students figured out the information concerning learning objects, the instructor provided them with corrected

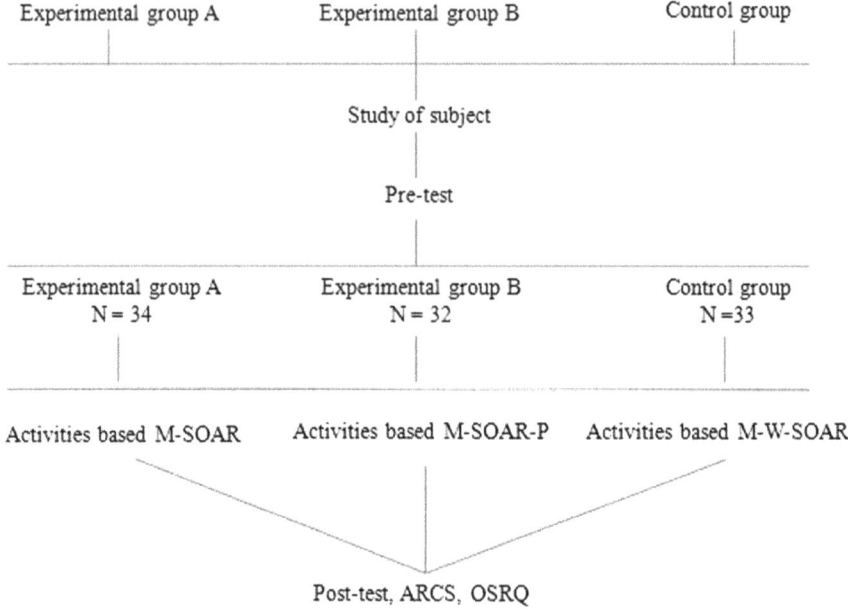

Fig. 3.1 Experiment procedures

feedback about the validity of those objects. The importance of this stage is to stimulate and grasps a student's attention to learn. The time spanned for this stage was 30 min.

Organize: In this stage, students were also trained to effectively organize selected information. The instructor continuously required students to work collaboratively by engaging in an online discussion to share and exchange ideas. Then each student individually could organize his graphic organizer/ table to develop a conceptual understanding of learning objects by utilizing existing tools that help students to organize selected ideas to create a coherent structure of learning; the time spanned for accomplished this activity was 30 min.

Associate: Once the students selected objects and organized them to facilitate conceptual understanding, the next stage is to create a conceptual knowledge framework to classify and relate the ideas between objects. Thus, students were followed the instructor in the processes of demonstrated concept maps. They worked individually to create a conceptual knowledge map and shared their maps via an online tool https://www.mindomo.com/; therefore, the ideas of the relationship between objects came together. The time spent for completing this activity was 30 min.

Regulate: When the students' associated objects, they need to examine their understanding of the learning objects. To achieve this purpose, the instructor guided them to assign the online (factual, conceptual, and relationship tests) presented by mobile devices; the time for achieving the online test was 20 min. Figure 3.2 presents the processes of SOAR learning activities.

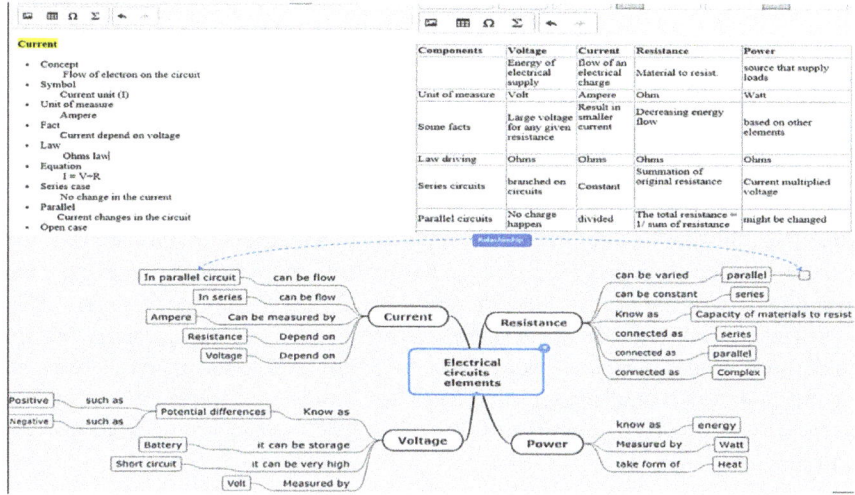

Fig. 3.2 Processes of learning activities

In the actual experiment, participants in the experimental group A oriented to the online learning materials and also asked to study learning materials (self-study) including watching video materials, conduct learning activities, and perform the assignment for assessing learning outcomes with given a specific time for achieving each learning task. Follow up the implementation of the M-SOAR approach that is to select important information as keywords and sub-ideas or information behind the keywords, for example, (voltage is a keyword, and sub-ideas are the concepts of voltage, its relationship with the current and resistance, its characteristics in series and parallel circuits, etc.). Therefore, participants individually can make an online note of important information comprised of facts and concepts about the electrical circuit elements.

After participants' cloudy noted selected information concern the electrical science subject, the second stage was to organize information to facilitate understanding, recall facts, and recognize concepts of the subject components. In this stage, the instructor encouraged participants to discuss online and share their ideas through online discussion to support social interaction and collaboration on how information could be organized in table formats. However, each student could create his own organizer/ table after having a viewpoint of other students. The time spent in achieving this activity was 30 min. The third stage of mobile SOAR learning was an association of selected and organized information about the electrical circuit topic. To associate information, participants asked to create concept maps to associate relationships between the circuit elements. For doing so, participants continued to discuss online about the key concepts and sub-concepts and how those elements can be related to creating maps that show the hierarchy of knowledge about the subject. After the end of the discussion, every participant could create his concept map by using the www.mindomo.com tool for map creation. The time dedicated to this activity was 40 min. The last stage of the M-SOAR learning strategy was the participants' regulation of information. Participants performed 20 min of the online achievement test to get feedback about their understanding.

The participants in the experimental group B employed M-SOAR-P; in this strategy, participants implemented the same stages that participants of the experimental group A were carried out in the training and experiment period; the differences were that when participants study the information about the electrical circuit topic from the learning platform, they reported information through the paper and discussed offline. For the participants in the control group in the training and study period, they were free to choose a preferred way to study learning materials. They instructed to watch the video content and supported online learning materials, making notes (on the system), exchange ideas through (online/ offline discussion), then create the individual conceptual maps using a free https://www.mindomo.com/ tool for map creation as well as taking online tests. Figure 3.2. Has shown processes of learning activities.

3.4   Results

Pretest

Prior to the actual experiment, the participants took the pretest to ensure that they had an entry level of knowledge about the subject being tough before doing the learning activities. One-way analysis of covariance (ANCOVA) was performed to allow differences between sets of means to be assessed. The result of the pretest is presented in Table 3.1.

Table 3.1 presents the results of the pretest including the number of students (N), Mean (M), Standard Deviation (SD), degree of freedom and P-value. From the results of assessing the homogeneity of variances, however, it can be concluded that three groups had an equivalent pre-require knowledge of ECC, which means no significant differences found between three groups $F\ (2.96) = 2.4, p > 0.05$.

Performance Tests

During the processes of learning activities, students' works were captured, analyzed, and scored by the teacher using two rubrics. Rubric one was developed by Daher and Kiewra (2014) and used to score students' learning activities results obtained from

Table 3.1 Presents results of the pretest for students in three groups

Variable	Groups	N	M	SD	F (2,96)	P-value
Pretest	Experiment group A	34	75.5	7.7	2.4	0.95
	Experiment group B	32	72.1	8.6		
	Control Group	33	71.4	8.1		

$^{*}P < 0.05$

the first and second phases of SOAR (selecting and organizing). The rubric scores students (selecting) idea units and the number of words used to describe those ideas concern ECC. The rubric also scores (organizing) tables based on the appearance of the tables and the total number of cells used to describe idea units. The results of students' achievements obtained from the scoring rubric of selecting and organizing are explained in the following:

Selecting: To assess students selected information, two criteria were specified; (a) a number of idea units which scored as (complete idea = 2 points, incomplete idea = 1 point and wrong idea = 0 point), (b) a number of words used to describe those idea units which scored as (counted total number of words then each word scores 1 point).

Idea units: From analysis results of the mean and standard deviation for three groups, the mean of the experimental group A ($M = 37.87$, SD $= 4.24$) was significantly ($p < 0.05$) greater than the mean of the experimental group B ($M = 34.45$, SD $= 5.48$) and the mean of the control group ($M = 31.27$, SD $= 4.43$). These results suggested that the participants of the experimental group A reported higher idea units about the electrical science topic than other two groups.

Number of words: From analysis results of the mean and standard deviation for three groups, the mean of the experimental group A ($M = 236.69$, SD $= 44.85$) was significantly ($p < 0.05$) higher than the mean of the experimental group B ($M = 211.03$, SD $= 51.82$) and the control group ($M = 197.39$, SD $= 33.41$). It found that participants of the experimental group A reported a greater number of words compared to the other two groups.

Organization results: Students created study learning materials were evaluated according to the appearance of the organizer/ table which means the total number of cells (filled by correct information within the organizer. According to the assessment rule, (a) each table having organized information of idea units could worth 1 point, (b) each cell on the table could worth 1 point.

Apparent of the organizer: The results have yielded that the means of the three groups were differed. The mean of the experimental group A ($M = 1.33$, SD $= 0.47$) was significantly ($p < 0.05$) higher than the mean of the experimental group B ($M = 1.03$, SD $= 0.17$) and the control group ($M = 0.09$, SD $= 0.29$). It seems that experimental group A created a higher number of organizers than the experimental group B and the control group.

Number of cells: The results suggested that the mean and standard deviation of the three groups were significantly different. That is the mean of the experimental group was greater than the mean of the experimental group B ($M = 33.30$, SD $= 7.81$) and the control group ($M = 2.93$, SD $= 9.57$). The results suggested that the participants of the experimental group A created a higher number of cells than participants of the experimental group B and the control group. From these results, it is clear that when ideas increased the words described, those ideas will also increase.

To assess students' knowledge of facts, concepts, and relationships of ECC, one-way ANOVA was conducted to determine the effect differences between three modes of mobile learning strategies on students' performances concerning three types of the tests.

For the fact test scores, SPSS statistical results revealed that the mean and standard deviation were 15.09 and 1.508 for the experimental group A and 14.20 and 2.027 for the experiment group B, and 13.98 and 1.611 for the control group F $(2.96) = 3.8, P < 0.05$) which means significant differences found between three groups of students in the facts test result.

For assessing the concepts test, the study adapted rubric two to score students concept mapping (Novak & Gowin, 1984). Analysis of variance (ANOVA) for students *concept mapping* revealed, there were no significant differences existed between three groups in *Concept relationship f* $(2.96) = 2.83, p > 0.05$) and *Hierarchy levels* f $(2.96) = 1.23, p > 0.05$). While, highly significant differences found between three groups in *Cross linkages f* $(2.96) = 13.3, p < 0.05$) and *Examples f* $(2.96) = 13.5, p < 0.05$).

For the relationship test, one-way ANOVA was also computed to show the differences in means between three groups. The result in Table 3.3 has shown that significant differences existed between three groups, f $(2.96) = 3.73, p < 0.05$), that is, the mean and standard deviation of the experimental group A $(M = 19.75, SD = 0.96)$ were higher than mean and standard deviation of the experimental group B $(M = 18.69, SD = 2.18)$ and the control group $(M = 18.24, SD = 3.21)$.

Post-Achievement Test

The post-achievement test was performed. The one-way analysis of covariance was done via two phases; in phase one, ANOVA was conducted to investigate whether a significant difference could exist between three groups in total academic achievement scores. In the second phase, the analyses of (ANCOVA) multiple comparison were calculated to compare and determine where high statistical significance could occur between three groups. Table 3.2 shows the post-achievement test results.

Table 3.2 presents phase one of ANOVA analysis; the mean and standard deviation of post-test achievement scores were 77.54 and 7.85 for the experimental group A and 73.50 and 9.52 for the experimental group B and 71.38 and 7.81 for the control group, respectively. From these results, however, there were significant differences between three groups in learning achievement, $(2.96) = 4.96, p < 0.05$.

In phase two, the post-hoc Turkey test for multiple comparison was performed to make a comparison between three groups and to find out which group of students could differ significantly from the other two groups. The next section provides a comparison between three groups.

Table 3.2 Mean and standard deviation for three groups

Group	N	Mean	SD	F (2.96)	Sig
Experiment A	34	77.54	7.85	4.96	0.01
Experiment B	32	73.50	9.52		
Control	33	71.38	7.81		

$^{*}P < 0.05, **P < 0.001$

Table 3.3 Comparison between three groups

(I) Group (J) Group	Mean Difference (I-J)	Std. Error	Sig	95% Confidence Interval	
				Lower Bound	Upper Bound
Experiment B	−4.84830	2.09465	0.05	−9.8348	0.1382
Experiment A	5. 97,219*	2.06314	0.01	1.0607	10.8837
Control					
Experiment A	4.84830	2.09465	0.05	−0.1382	9.8348
Experiment B	1.12390	2.07943	0.85	−3.8264	6.0742
Control					
Experiment A	−5.97219*	2.06314	0.01	−10.8837	−1.0607
Control	−1.12390	2.07943	0.85	−6.0742	3.8264
Experiment B					

The experimental group A and B: The results presented in Table 3.3 revealed that there were significant differences in achievement scores between the experimental group A and experimental B ($p = 0.05$). However, this result suggested that the M-SOAR approach was more effective in developing students' understanding of the ECC topic.

The experimental group A and control group: The results in Table 3.3 have shown that there were significant differences in achievement scores between the experimental group A and the control group ($p = 0.01$). However, it seems that, M-SOAR was more effective in developing students' understanding of the subject.

The experimental group B and control group: According to the results in Table 3.3, there were no statistically significant differences in achievement scores between the experimental group B and the control group ($p = 0.85$). However, this result suggested that both two groups were nearly had similar levels of understanding regarding ECC.

Learning motivation

For ANOVA analysis results of the ARCS questionnaire to the three groups, the results revealed that there were statistically significant differences in learning motivation between three groups, f (2.96) $= 8.52$, Sig $= 0.0001$, $p < 0.00$). The mean value of participants in the experimental group A (123.2) was higher than other two groups means; the experimental group B and the control group (121.6 and 111.6), respectively.

Self-regulation

After the experiment, participants were asked to take the OSLQ. A total of 99 students responded to a five-point Likert-scale ranging from strongly agree (5) to strongly disagree (1). ANCOVA was computed and the results revealed the mean values of sub-scales of OSLQ for the experimental group A were greater than the mean values of the experimental group B and the control group.

Goal setting was significantly ($p < 0.05$) higher for the experimental group A ($M = 21.00$, SD $= 1.87$) than those in the experimental group B ($M = 20.06$, SD $= 1.96$) and the control group ($M = 19.03$, SD $= 2.03$). *Environment structuring* was significantly ($p < 0.05$) higher for the experimental group A ($M = 16.12$, SD $= 1.94$) than the experimental group B ($M = 14.54$, SD $= 2.37$) and the control group ($M = 13.12$, SD $= 1.72$). *Task strategy* was significantly ($p < 0.05$) higher for the experimental group A ($M = 21.93$, SD $= 1.56$) than the experimental group B ($M = 15.48$, SD $= 2.23$) and the control group ($M = 14.21$, SD $= 2.52$). *Time management* was significantly ($p < 0.05$) higher for the experimental group A ($M = 12.12$, SD $= 1.67$) than the experimental group B (M $= 10.84$, SD $= 2.42$) and the control group (M $= 11.27$, SD $= 1.79$). Help seeking was significantly ($p < 0.05$) higher for the experimental group A ($M = 15.90$, SD $= 2.15$) than the experimental group B ($M = 14.15$, SD $= 2.48$) and the control group ($M = 13.06$, SD $= 1.56$). *Self-evaluation* was not differ significantly ($p > 0.05$), the experimental group A ($M = 15.78$, SD $= 2.05$) the experimental group B ($M = 15.03$, SD $= 2.59$) and the control group (M $= 14.84$, SD $= 2.57$).

3.5   Discussion and Conclusion

In this chapter the M-SOAR learning approach is proposed to improve students' learning achievements (in terms of factual, conceptual, and relationships knowledge) of the ECC topic and influence their motivation and foster SRL skills. More research is required to investigate the impact of M-SOAR on improving students' knowledge in science domains at the level of high schools' learning. Compared to M-SOAR-P and M-W-SOAR in the learning processes in which students could select, organize, and associate relationships of ECC, it is found that M-SOAR is more effective in improving students' learning performance.

In addition, M-SOAR is also positively impacting students' recall facts, recognize concepts and establish relationships knowledge of ECC. This result is consistent with a similar experimental study by Daher and Kiewra (2016) examined two groups (SOAR group vs preferred group strategy) on student's factual and conceptual knowledge of a natural science topic which demonstrated through an online learning environment. The SOAR group performed better on facts and concepts than their peers in the preferred learning strategy. These results could attribute to the effective integration of the mobile SOAR approach.

Regarding learning motivation, a considerable body of research confirmed that motivation is a key issue for students to be successful in science learning (Sari & Nurcahyo, 2018). Also, motivation is mainly focused to attract students' attention, introduce them relevant learning materials, improve their confidence and became more satisfied with their work (Keller, 2010). There is a lack of research emphasizing on the M-SOAR learning approach for measuring student's motivation; however, the current study contributes for mobile-based SOAR learning to promote students' motivation in science subjects. The other significant result of this study is increasing student's motivation scores given to the experimental group A. It seems the M-SOAR approach has a positive effect on promoting students' to participate effectively in online learning activities.

In this paper, the focus was to influence students' SRL skills as a condition for students' to be SDL learners. The M-SOAR approach was clearly instructed, well-organized learning materials, and clarified assessments to having participants perform SDL skills. The platform used for this study was worthy learning materials and OER that are most relevant and best quality to fulfill the study purpose.

For instance, in the ClassFlow platform, the participants could search and find useful OER that helps students carry out learning activities.

Higher levels of self-regulated learning indicate the positive impact of M-SOAR on students' learning in the online learning environment. In line with similar research (Barnard et al., 2009; Olakanmi & Gumbo, 2017), this study added to the growing body of the literature review, that is, effective integration of M-SOAR could improve students' SRL skills of ECC elements in the online learning environments. It offers empirical evidence; the M-SOAR environment provided learning tools in which students can organize learning and therefore it supports them to be more self-regulated learners. It is consistent with previous findings by (Mahmoodi et al., 2014). Generally, the experimental group A has significantly obtained higher self-regulated learning skills than the other two groups. The ability of the experimental group A to report higher SRL behaviors could refer to the effective engagement in the processes of learning from the online learning environment. This result informs that, students gaining a higher level of attention, and then it makes sense that students can develop a considerable level of SRL. Olakanmi and Gumbo (2017) have developed a mobile self-regulated learning system. The authors have used different characteristics compared to this study in the term of group numbers (two groups; the experimental group and the control group), the group size (30 per each group) the topic (English). In comparison with this study, the results are closely tied, and the experimental group has gained higher SRL skills than the control group.

More research is needed on investigating the impact of SOAR on fostering students' SRL in online learning environments. In addition, cultivate students' SRL skills based on the SOAR pedagogy with emerging technologies require more research to covers both formal and informal learning. Therefore, stakeholders (policymakers, administrators, school leaderships, parents and practitioners) have to take into consideration growing up students' abilities of self-directed learning is becoming more necessary than ever; this is because in the near future, learning with emerging technologies will be more outside than inside school learning environments.

Future research should focus on investigating effective pedagogical approaches to improving students' SRL skills in online learning environments; this will meet future generation needs, diversities, learning styles, and preferences. The combination of OER and online learning not only holds the promise for increasing opportunities to access learning but also help to expand opportunities for communication with experts, teachers, and access materials.

This research was done in the capital city of Sudan "Khartoum" while other Sudanese cities have different circumstances such as school environments and the level of technology awareness; therefore, conducting a comparison study perhaps may generate different results. More importantly, the SOAR learning approach needs to design a complementary system "as a tool" with functions to support full integration and take advantages for each stage of the SOAR method.

References

Alsalhi, N. R., Eltahir, M. E., & Al-Qatawneh, S. S. (2019). The effect of blended learning on the achievement of ninth grade students in science and their attitudes towards its use. *Heliyon, 5*(9), e02424. Retrieved from https://sci-hub.tw/10.1016/j.heliyon.2019.e02424

Barnard, L., Lan, W. Y., To, Y. M., Paton, V. O., & Lai, S.-L. (2009). Measuring self-regulation in online and blended learning environments. *The Internet and Higher Education, 12*(1), 1–6. https://doi.org/10.1016/j.iheduc.2008.10.005

Bolaji, H. O., & Fakomogbon, M. A. (2017). Effects of collaborative learning styles on performance of students in a ubiquitous collaborative mobile learning environment. *Contemporary Educational Technology, 8*(3), 268–279.

Chang, C., Chang, C.-K., & Shih, J.-L. (2016). Motivational strategies in a mobile inquiry-based language learning setting. *System, 59*(2016), 100–115. https://doi.org/10.1016/j.system.2016.04.013

Chiang, T.-H.-C., Yang, S.-J.-H., & Hwang, G.-J. (2014). An augmented reality-based mobile learning system to improve students' learning achievements and motivations in natural science inquiry activities. *Educational Technology & Society, 17*(4), 352–365.

Cho, M.-H., & Castañeda, D. (2019). Motivational and affective engagement in learning Spanish with a mobile application. *System.* https://doi.org/10.1016/j.system.2019.01.008

Daher, T., & Kiewra, K. (2016). An investigation of SOAR study strategies for learning from multiple online resources. *Contemporary Educational Psychology, 46*, 10–21. https://doi.org/10.1016/j.cedpsych.2015.12.004

Elsafi A. (2020). Augmented strategies for mobile and ubiquitous learning technologies. In S. Yu, M. Ally, & A. Tsinakos (Eds.), *Emerging Technologies and Pedagogies in the Curriculum. Bridging Human and Machine: Future Education with Intelligence* (pp. 245–260). Springer.

Keller, J. M. (2010). *Motivational design for learning and performance: The ARCS model approach.* Springer.

Kiewra, K. A. (2009). *Teaching how to learn.* Corwin Press.

Lin, J.-W., Lai, Y.-C., & Chang, L.-C. (2016). Fostering self-regulated learning in a blended environment using group awareness and peer assistance as external scaffolds. *Journal of Computer Assisted Learning, 32*(1), 77–93. https://doi.org/10.1111/jcal.12120

Lopez, R., Yot, C., Tuovila, I., & Perera-Rodríguez, V.-H. (2017). Online self-regulated learning questionnaire in a Russian MOOC. *Computers in Human Behavior, 75*, 966–974. https://doi.org/10.1016/j.chb.2017.06.015

Luo, L., Kiewra, K. A., Flanigan, A. E., & Peteranetz, M. S. (2018). Laptop versus longhand note taking: effects on lecture notes and achievement. *Instructional Science, 46*, 947–971. https://doi.org/10.1007/s11251-018-9458-0

MacCallum, K., Jeffrey, L., & Kinshuk. (2014). Factors impacting teachers' adoption of mobile learning. *Journal of Information Technology Education, 13*, 40–162. Retrieved from : http://www.jite.org/documents/Vol13/JITEv13ResearchP141-162MacCallum0455.pdf

Mahmoodi, M. H., Kalantari, B., & Ghaslani, R. (2014). Self-regulated learning (SRL), motivation and language achievement of Iranian EFL learners. *Procedia—Social and Behavioral Sciences, 98*, 1062–1068. https://doi.org/10.1016/j.sbspro.2014.03.517

Mustafa, F., & Tuncel, M. (2019). Integrating augmented reality into problem based learning: The effects on learning achievement and attitude in physics education. *Computers & Education*, 103635. https://doi.org/10.1016/j.compedu.2019.103635

Naemi, A. M., & Naemi, N. (2017). Effectiveness of smart training on self-efficacy and self-regulation in science course of fifth grade students of primary schools. *International Journal of Educational Psychology, 3*(1), 47–52.

Nikou, S. A., & Economides, A. A. (2018). Mobile-based micro learning and assessment: Impact on learning performance and motivation of high school students. *Journal of Computer Assisted Learning, 34*, 269–278. https://doi.org/10.1111/jcal.12240

Nour, S. S. O. M. (2015). Overview of technology transfer in the manufacturing industries in the Arab countries: The case of UAE and Sudan. *International Journal of Sudan Research, 5*(1), 03–24.

Nour, S. S. O. M. (2016). The impact of ICT in public and private universities in Sudan. *Journal of the Knowledge Economy*. https://doi.org/10.1007/s13132-016-0429-x

Novak, J. D., & Gowin, R. (1984). *Learning how to learn*. Cambridge University Press.

Olakanmi, E., & Gumbo, M. (2017). The effects of self-regulated learning training on Students' met cognition and achievement in chemistry. *International Journal of Innovation in Science and Mathematics Education, 25*(2), 34–48. Retrieved from https://openjournals.library.sydney.edu.au/index.php/CAL/article/view/11341/11123

Sampaio, D., & Almeida, P. (2015). Pedagogical strategies for the integration of augmented reality in ICT teaching and learning processes. *Procedia Computer Science, 100*(2016), 894–899. https://doi.org/10.1016/j.procs.2016.09.240

Sari, A.-M., & Nurcahyo, H. (2018). Improving students learning motivation through mobile learning. *Indonesian Journal of Biology Education., 4*(3), 271–276. https://doi.org/10.22219/jpbi.v4i3.6859

Sha, L., Looi, C.-K., Chen, W., Seow, P., & Wong, L.-H. (2011). Recognizing and measuring self-regulated learning in a mobile learning environment. *Computers in Human Behavior, 28*, 718–728. https://doi.org/10.1016/j.chb.2011.11.019

Sletten, S.R. (2017). Investigating Flipped Learning: Student Self-Regulated Learning, Perceptions, and Achievement in an Introductory Biology Course. *Journal of Science Education and Technology*, 347–358 (2017). https://doi.org/10.1007/s10956-016-9683-8

Turel, Y. K., & Sanal, S. O. (2018). The effects of an ARCS based e-book on student's achievement, motivation and anxiety. *Computers & Education, 127*(3), 130–140. https://doi.org/10.1016/j.compedu.2018.08.006

Zheng, X. L., & Chen, F. (2016). Effects of a mobile self-regulated learning approach on students' learning achievements and self-regulated learning skills. *Innovations in Education and Teaching International*. https://doi.org/10.1080/14703297.2016.1259080.02014.pdf

Dr. Abdelwahed Elsafi is assistant Professor at Department of Instructional Technology, Collage of Education, Bahri University, Sudan. He received his Ph.D. in Educational Technology from Beijing Normal University, China, and a Master in Computer Integrated Education from Sudan University of Science and Technology, Sudan. He has more than ten years of experience in higher education in Sudan. He has published 5 papers and book chapters. His major research interests include mobile learning, ubiquitous learning, ICT in education and learning strategies.

Chapter 4
Gathering Expert Opinions on Self-directed Learning and Online Assessment Using OER—A Delphi Approach for Redesigning Student Assessments

Sandhya Gunness, Isabel Tarling, and Erkkie Haipinge

Abstract Self-directed learning encourages students to take responsibility for their learning. This can be achieved through greater access to educational resources and providing students with necessary scaffolding to engage knowingly with the learning content and with facilitators. In the past, summative assessment approaches have not adequately supported the goals of self-directed learning. In contrast, continuous and/or formative assessment—that focuses on assessment *for* learning, assessing learning over time and provides the student with greater ownership and opportunity for demonstrating individual strengths. In parallel, over the past two decades, different global educational initiatives have broadcast widely about how and why educators should consider using and developing open educational resources but the uptake of these has remained sluggish. Instead, as we witnessed during the pandemic, education stakeholders remained majorly concerned with immediate access to online learning content and assessments, mainly in the form of high-stake summative tests and examinations. This study aimed at regrouping OER experts and champions of open educational practices (OEP) and garnered their views on how to address assessment in higher education institutions in future so that it better responds to the twenty-first-century workforce, while allowing for nurturing the individual strengths of the self-directed learner. Using a modified Delphi approach with 2 rounds of feedback, the study gathered consensus from the expert OER panel on (i) the educational changes required to promote and acknowledge self-directed learning, (ii) how to harness OER and OEP for bringing about this change and thus (iii) how to propose

S. Gunness (✉)
University of Mauritius, Moka, Mauritius
e-mail: s.gunness@uom.ac.mu

I. Tarling
Two Oceans Graduate Institute, Cape Town, South Africa
e-mail: isabel.tarling@togi.ac.za

E. Haipinge
Centre for Open, Distance and eLearning, University of Namibia, Windhoek, Namibia
e-mail: ehaipinge@unam.na
URL: http://www.unam.edu.na

© The Author(s), under exclusive license to Springer Nature Singapore Pte Ltd. 2021   59
D. Burgos and J. Olivier (eds.), *Radical Solutions for Education in Africa*, Lecture Notes in Educational Technology, https://doi.org/10.1007/978-981-16-4099-5_4

an assessment framework for self-directed learning using open pedagogies for higher education.

Keywords Self-directed learning · Online assessment · Open educational practices · Open educational resources · Twenty-first-century skills

4.1 Introduction

In the wake of the COVID-19 pandemic, teaching and learning briskly swung from face-to-face to an online mode, thereby requiring educational institutions to dispense teaching, learning and assessment through e-learning platforms, videoconferencing software and tele-learning. Global organisations and many educational institutions such as the World Bank, UNESCO and the OECD amongst others anticipated the long overdue adoption of educational innovation such as mobile learning, open education and open pedagogies as a new learning philosophy and eventually expected for an invigorated and more equitable education system.

However, as in the past two decades, the uptake of these has remained sluggish (Chesbrough, 2020). Instead, it seemed that education stakeholders were mainly concerned with the persistent issues of traditional access to online learning content and assessments, finding different formats like proctored examinations and timed assessments, intrusive gesture control and eye tracking software, to continue with high-stake summative tests and examinations (Daniel, 2020; UNESCO, 2020). This perennial focus on final examinations as an ultimate outcome of the higher education system needs a global rethink. During the confinement, learners were mostly on their own or with some support from online lecturers, either referring to their prescribed textbooks and class notes or searching for online resources to help them continue with their studies.

With all the OER available, how could these learners be inspired to become more self-directed? How could they be encouraged to tap into OER, demonstrate more agency within processes of learning and bolster competence in fields that were their forte? How could they take ownership of their learning and demonstrate the twenty-first-century skills that were the requirements of an era of constant change and disruption. There is an urgent need to reflect on ways to further promote OER and OEP for advancing self-directed learning and redesigning student assessment so that it could be more relevant for the current times of uncertainty. This study had the following objectives:

1. To determine the scope of changes needed to transform assessment modalities when shifting from a face-to-face to an online mode.
2. To gather expert consensus around changes needed in the way assessments are carried out to promote self-directed learning in online learning environments.
3. To investigate potential instances of OER in assessment for learning and propose an assessment framework for self-directed learning to be integrated within open pedagogy.

A review of related literature guided by the main concepts addressed in the chapter preceded a Delphi study with OER experts from the Global North and South, to garner consensus around self-directed learning and the coherence of current modes of assessment. This study presents policy-makers and educators with global OER expert recommendations for changes that are required in educational systems to boost self-directed learning and relevant assessment practices for twenty-first-century learning.

4.2 Literature Review

The concepts related to self-directed learning and online assessment using open educational resources are discussed within the wider framework of open education. This review also addresses open education and open learning, open educational practices, self-directed learning and open educational resources. The types of assessment that support or hinder self-directed learning, as well as how they can be delivered online in ways that make them open and reusable within the open education framework, are also discussed.

4.2.1 *Open Education and Open Educational Practices*

Open education, open learning and open educational practices (OEP) are interrelated concepts all of which refer to the notion of innovating through opening up education and expanding access. While open learning is the philosophical basis on which open institutions are founded and refers to "the removal of both administrative and educational constraints to learning", and wherever possible, reviewing and replacing restrictions that are placed on students (Bozkurt et al., 2019, p. 79), open education represents a discipline and area of study related to operational, legal and visionary aspects throughout the "analysis, design, realization and evaluation of learning experiences to facilitate high quality education meeting the given situation, needs and objectives" (Stracke, 2017, p. 286).

Cronin (2017) claims that OEP are collaborative acts of creating, using and reusing OER, whether for pedagogical goals or not, that specifically employ participatory technologies and social networks to foster interaction, shared engagement and knowledge creation which empowers learners and teachers. She further states that open educational practices "respect and empower learners as co-producers on their lifelong learning paths" (p. 3), thereby enhancing learner-centred practices and strengthening pedagogical methods aligned towards self-directed learning.

Open education and open educational practices thus empower learners to take charge of their learning by enhancing their access to both learning resources and others (peers or educators for instance) using a variety of platforms such as online learning technologies and social networks to enhance interaction and collaborative learning activities. It is this access to resources and others that paves way for learners to cultivate their self-directed learning capabilities.

4.2.2 Self-directed Learning

The subject of self-directed learning has been discussed by various scholars. SDL is often situated in the field of open and distance learning and associated with traditionally adult learners. The philosophical and theoretical orientation of different scholars has tended to shape different definitions, starting with an understanding of SDL as simply as "the ability to learn on one's own" (Knowles as cited in Garrison, 1997, p. 19). Garrison defines self-directed learning (SDL) as "an approach where learners are motivated to assume personal responsibility and collaborative control of the cognitive (self-monitoring) and contextual (self-management) processes in constructing and confirming meaningful and worthwhile learning outcomes" (Garrison, 1997, p. 18). Another comprehensive conceptualisation of SDL is offered by Knowles (as cited in Bosch et al., 2019, p. 2), defining it as

> A process in which individuals take the initiative, with or without the help of others, in diagnosing their learning needs, formulating learning goals, identifying human and material resources for learning, choosing and implementing appropriate learning strategies, and evaluating learning outcomes.

Taking the conceptualisation of SDL above on board, its key aspects that are relevant in the context of this study include the taking of personal responsibility of learning through self-monitoring and self-management of the cognitive and contextual dimensions, respectively. Furthermore, SDL requires learners to not only diagnose their learning needs, but also formulate learning goals and find the resources they need to achieve their learning outcomes by using suitable strategies, while able to evaluate their learning at the end. Given this context, one should then ask what should be the role of assessment in SDL? What kind of assessment approaches best fosters SDL and how can these approaches be implemented in an online learning environment? These questions are addressed next.

4.2.3 Assessment of Learning, Assessment for Learning and Open Assessment

Assessment and learning are intricately linked in that teaching does not automatically result in learning and it is assessment that helps educators to ascertain whether and to what extent learning has taken place. According to William (2011, p. 3), assessment is pivotal to effective teaching because it is "only through assessment that we can find out whether a particular sequence of instructional activities has resulted in the intended learning outcomes". However, not all types of assessment can provide this feedback to educators and learners and this is where the distinction between assessment of learning and assessment for learning needs to be made.

Baird et al. (2017, p. 335) state that assessment of learning entails "the summative use of assessment which primarily measures what has been learned" and whose function is to make judgements about learner progress within an education system. Assessment of learning is rooted in the instruction-centred educational approaches that see teaching as bereft of any weaknesses and the role of the student being that of receiving and grasping what is being taught. In cases where learners fail, "the causes of any failures to learn lay within the individual learner" (William, 2011, p. 3) and they would require to be remedied by the system.

Assessment of learning has relied on high-stake testing whose policies tend to focus on learner test scores rather than learning. Research evidence in the USA shows that as a result of high-stake tests "student learning is indeterminate, remains at the same level it was before the policy was implemented, or actually goes down when high-stakes testing policies are instituted" (Amrein & Berliner, 2002, p. 75). As far as learning is concerned, high-stake assessment has been found to be "limited to developing basic academic and cognitive skills" while neglecting "other major goals such as developing students' creativity, self-concept, interpersonal relations, ability to be self-directed" and others (Jones, 2007, pp. 69–70). Thus, assessment of learning, especially high-stake testing, takes away learner agency from their own learning processes, which is incompatible with self-directed learning where learners ought to regulate and take charge of their own learning.

Some of the unintended consequences of summative assessment which represents assessment of learning are that it may direct teaching and learning to the test where teachers and learners only, respectively, teach and learn items covered by the assessment and thereby neglect some areas of the curriculum or competencies important to the discipline (Bennett, 2010). This may have a detrimental effect on learner self-efficacy in taking charge of their own learning and setting learning goals because the learning goals are in fact determined by assessment policies.

Assessment for learning on the other hand refers to "the process of seeking and interpreting evidence for use by learners and their teachers to decide where the learners are in their learning, where they need to go and how best to get there" (Broadfoot et al., as cited in William, 2011, p. 10). In other words, assessment for learning is one "for which the first priority in its design and practice is to serve the purpose of promoting students' learning" (Black et al., as cited in William, 2011, p. 10). Assessment for learning is distinct from assessment of learning on the basis of purpose in that the former seeks to inform both learners and educators about their learning and teaching processes and how they can be improved. Assessment for learning tends to use formative assessment which provides "formative feedback, self and peer assessment [that] enhances student self-regulation on learning" (Weldmeskel & Michael, 2016, p. 104).

Comparing assessment of learning to assessment for learning, one can conclude that the latter is more oriented towards empowering learners to play an active role in their learning process, which is less so for the former. In fact, Kirkpatrick and Zang (2011) found that curriculum heavily based on examinations negatively affected students' motivation to learn, creativity as well as their self-efficacy, resulting in a detrimental effect on self-directed learning. Using assessment for learning is not the only way to enhance learner participation in the learning and assessment process. One other such method is Open Assessment of Learning (OAoL), which as an open educational practice is referring to a

> process of learning verification and feedback that takes place collaboratively, mediated by free access tools in which teachers produce or adapt assessment resources and students adapt and reshape these resources for the purpose of generating for themselves an assessment that meets their personal needs, learning styles and context. (Chiappe as cited in Chiappe et al., 2016, p. 45)

With the enhanced access to ICT and the Internet, a lot of assessment activities has adopted the use of ICTs in delivering assessment or creating assessment instruments. The next section focuses on the role of online tools in supporting assessment.

4.2.4 Online Assessment

Educational institutions continue to be slow in evolving from traditional teaching and assessment methods set in face-to-face four-walled classrooms to online and digital practices. Online assessment offers various advantages such as flexibility of assessment times, control over the method of question arrangement and delivery to learners, reusability and redistribution of questions, learner access to questions multiple times to enhance mastery, provision of prompts for scaffolding learning as well as feedback to learners (Spivey & McMillan, 2014). Some of these advantages offer opportunities for enhancing self-directed learning such as in cases where technology-enhanced assessment can help "produce digital feedback and increase the student's ability to regulate their performance" (Seifert & Feliks, 2019, p. 170).

Peer assessment and self-assessment that are suitable to the promotion of self-directed learning are best administered through online because technology provides degrees of anonymity which "increases students' willingness to assess their peers' performances" (Seifert & Feliks, 2019, p. 170). Another aspect of assessment that supports self-directed learning is feedback. According to Embo et al. (2010, p. e264), "feedback can facilitate reflection and self-assessment" by revealing to learners their strengths and weaknesses and providing them with opportunities to "evaluate whether they are achieving their learning goals, developing new goals or making plans to pursue those goals", all of which are features of self-directed learning. Technology through online assessment platforms makes it easier to provide feedback to learners in a timely manner as feedback can also be automated through e-learning systems, or it can be provided by peers facilitated by communication tools.

4.2.5   *Open Educational Resources and Open Assessment Resources*

Open education resources (OER) are "educational materials and resources that are offered freely, are openly available to anyone and, under some licences, allow others to reuse, adapt and redistribute them with few or no restrictions" (Hoosen et al., 2016, p. 2). OER include "teaching, learning, and research resources that reside in the public domain or have been released under an intellectual property license that permits their free use and re-purposing by others" (Biswas-Diener & Jhangiani, 2017, p. 12). OER complement open education, open learning and open educational practices in that the learning resources are central to enhancing learner access to learning. With greater access to these learning resources through the Internet, there is a greater need for learners to develop self-directed learning competencies to be able to take advantage of these resources on their own. But how do OER relate to assessment? To answer this question, one has to turn attention to open assessment resources.

According to Gibson et al. (2016, p. 5), resistance towards the use of OER by higher education institutions in particular could be attributed to the idea that institutions "focus on the problems of summative assessment, which prevents them from embracing their formative assessment possibilities". This is particularly because the "certification and accreditation" systems in higher education solely make use of high-stake summative assessment to measure academic achievements (Gibson et al., 2016, p. 260). One of the grounds for the distrust of formative assessment in favour of summative assessment is the focus on lower-level thinking and objectives such as remembering, understanding and applying knowledge.

Gibson et al. (2016, p. 261) explain that the open assessment resources (OAR) provide a framework that "is focused on a few high-level assessable outcomes" such as the twenty-first-century skills of problem-solving, innovation, collaboration and communication as well as the "feedback [involving] recommendations for improved performance, prompts for further elaboration of ideas, suggestions for alternatives that pertain to supporting and achieving these outcomes within a specific OER". By adding clarity about assessment purposes, OAR forms an assessment bridge between OER and self-directed learning.

In addition to OAR and what it offers to the adoption of OER, there is another concern with regard to institutional traditional practices. In research, universities have no issue with sharing and building on the ideas of others, yet in teaching there has been a perception that each institution must lock its teaching material behind restrictive copyright regimes that minimise sharing at the expense of learning (Macintosh et al., 2011). Using OER to enhance self-directed learning has been curtailed by the lack of accreditation of learning attained in this way. Initiatives such as the "OER for assessment and credit for students" aimed "to provide flexible pathways to ensure that OER learners can achieve credible qualifications" (p. 10) are crucial in legitimising OER and their formal use to support not only learning in general, but also SDL in particular.

The continuing challenge regarding OER in education may be the rate and levels of adoption. Stagg (2014) proposes a continuum of open practice that suggests five stages of OER adoption in a higher education context where the fifth state involves the use of OER by students. At this stage, "student use of OER is purposeful and aligned to course objectives and learning outcomes, appropriately and purposefully scaffolded within the course design, and the assessment reflects an engagement with open resources" (Stagg, 2014, p. 160). Considering that this is the stage of OER use where "student work could then be released into the open community to be reused and remixed by other practitioners", it is apparent that OER use is best placed to support self-directed learning when its use is at higher levels of maturity in educational institutions. It then follows that institutions need to deliberately institute policies that inform teaching practices reflective of mature use of OER or self-directed learning opportunities such as MOOCs.

Massive Open Online Courses (MOOCs) benefit learners better when their self-efficacy is well developed. Since there is limited direct teaching support for learners when using MOOCs, Wong et al. (2019, p. 52) argue that self-directed and self-regulated learning capacities such as "goal setting, strategic planning, self-evaluation, task strategy, elaboration, and help seeking" are crucial. It is in these learning environments where the open assessment resources framework that is geared towards generic high-level twenty-first-century-oriented assessable outcomes legitimises assessment for learning delivered through online tools with a higher potential for strengthening learners' self-directed learning.

4.3 Methodology

When other surveys identify "what is," the Delphi technique attempts to explore "what could/should be". (Miller, 2006)

The Delphi method (Dalkey & Helmer, 1963) is a formal data collection approach involving experts who, iteratively, provide insights for goal setting, policy investigation or eventual predicting of future events, through the expression of rational opinions in response to a questionnaire (Ludwig, 1997; Turoff & Hiltz, 1996; Ulschak, 1983). This analytical technique enables the exploration of underlying assumptions of the experts to "seek out information which may generate consensus on the part of the respondent group" (Hsu & Sandford, 2007, p. 1). For the present study, this entailed asking a series of questions to a panel of 22 geographically dispersed experts in open educational resources (OER) about their views on self-directed learning and assessments within their respective contexts. As Nworie (2011) posits, the strength of the Delphi method is fundamentally its consensus-building focus, and the responses that received the most "votes" were filtered out for deriving the required framework as per the objectives of this research. We accede to not having followed the pure Delphi format, and the findings should be further monitored for gathering the additional consensus with the panel again. However, there was agreement on a number of important issues which we present in the aim of continuing the discussion around OER and SDL, especially for policy-makers.

4.3.1 Research Design

The modified Delphi study (Johnston et al., 2014; Kearney et al., 2017; Mahawar et al., 2020) comprised 2 rounds preceded by a pretest with two OER consultants who vetted the questions and proposed modifications and suggestions to better orient the study for the African context. The panel of OER higher education experts for this study was selected utilising a purposive criterion sampling method (McMillan & Schumacher, 2010). The selection of our panel of experts followed closely that of Okoli and Wang (2015) (Table 4.1).

The experts were contacted by email (blind copied), and responses were compiled anonymously and presented back to the panel as shown in Fig. 4.1.

Twenty-two experts responded to the first round, whereby open- and closed-ended questions requiring respondents to justify or clarify their responses were included allowing to quickly address consensus-building components. Ten participants responded to the second round, and while this does limit the findings, the comprehensiveness of the first questionnaire as well as the confirmatory approach we adopted to explore the resultant tensions observed within the panel allowed us to make some well-guided conclusions.

As displayed in Fig. 4.2, the OER experts hailed from different geographical locations which allowed for a diverse range of perspectives and experiences (Hasson et al., 2000).

Table 4.1 Phase 1: selecting experts for the study

Steps	Activity
Step 1: prepare knowledge resource nomination worksheet (KRNW)	Recollection of OER experts whom the research team have working relationships Harness the OER expert networks to further recommend other relevant academics and practitioners in the OER field
Step 2: populate KRNW with names	Collect names of experts from different organisations and ensure gender and geographical balance
Step 3: invite experts to participate	A total of 44 experts from different global organisations and locations A total of 22 experts agreed to participate

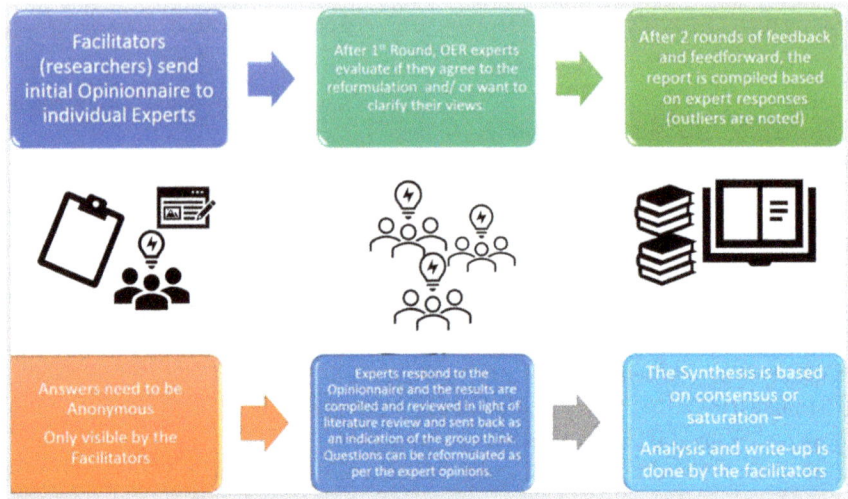

Fig. 4.1 Web-based Delphi survey and feedback process

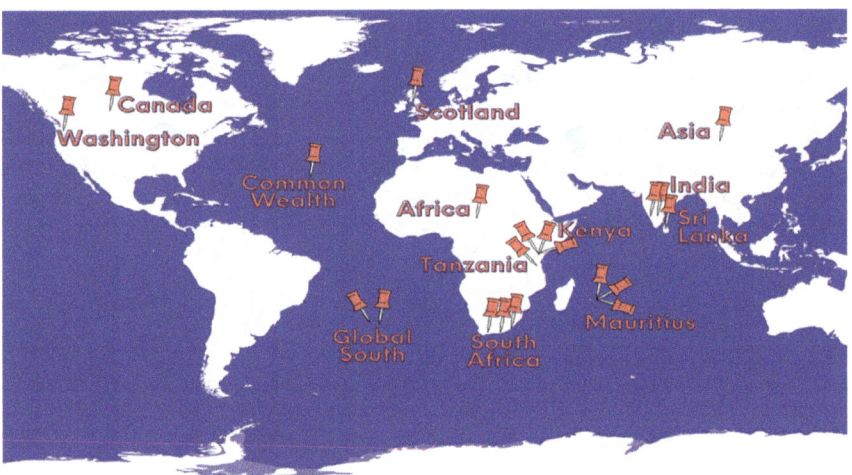

Fig. 4.2 Geographical dispersion and number of respondents per region

4.3.2 Ethical Clearance and Choice of OER Experts for Delphi Panel

Ethical clearance for the questionnaire was obtained from the Two Oceans Graduate Institute, South Africa. Throughout the study, anonymity was maintained for the 54% ($n = 12$) male and 46% ($n = 10$) female participants who were mostly early adopters, early majority and innovators (86%) in the OER field, and their job descriptions ranged from librarians to professors.

In Table 4.2, we acknowledge the OER experts who kindly consented to have their names published in the report after the two rounds. We also are very grateful to the seven other participants who preferred to remain anonymous and respect their decision, while acknowledging their precious contribution to this study.

Table 4.2 Delphi study participants

Names	Designation	Institution and Location
Mr. Parveen Sharma	Faculty	UniSkills India
Dr. Deepika Kohli	Assistant Professor	Khalsa College of Education, GT Road, Amritsar, Punjab, India
Ms. Rubina D. Rampersad	Educational Technologist	Centre for Innovative and Lifelong Learning, University of Mauritius
Dr. Kezia H. Mkwizu	Postdoctoral Scholar	The Open University of Tanzania under the Directorate of Research, Publications and Innovations, Tanzania
Mr. Senthil Kumar M. K.	Programme Manager	GESCI, an UN Founded Initiative, Kenya
Dr. Pauline Ngimwa	Programme Manager	Partnership for African Social and Governance Research (*PASGR*)—Kenya
Prof. Karen Ferreira-Meyers	Coordinator Linguistics and Modern Languages	Institute of Distance Education, University of Eswatini
Mr. Paul West	Senior Education Adviser and CEO	West and Associates South Africa
Prof. Romeela Mohee	Higher Education Commissioner	Mauritius
Dr. David Porter	Senior Adviser: Higher Education Commonwealth of Learning	Commonwealth of Learning, Canada
Dr. Cable Green	Director of Open Education	Creative Commons
Dr. Kaviraj Goodoory	Associate Professor	Mauritius Institute of Education
Professor Frank Rennie	Professor of Sustainable Rural Development and Head of Research and Postgraduate Development	Lews Castle College UHI (The University of the Highlands and Islands)
Prof. Shironica P. Karunanayaka	Professor in Educational Technology Dean/Faculty of Education	Open University of Sri Lanka

4.3.3 First Round

The scoping literature review allowed for the development of a framework which would encompass the questionnaire elements of self-directed learning, open educational resources and assessment. In contrast to the classic Delphi method (Hasson et al., 2000), we replaced open-ended questions, which are used to generate ideas, by a structured questionnaire using a Likert scale (Brill et al., 2006; Rajhans et al., 2020), devised from the scoping literature to gather information pertaining to the vision, definitions, changes in perception and academic competences that were most relevant for open educational practices and SDL in general. The resulting questionnaire comprised six sections (consent forms, overview of Delphi approach, OER expert demographics, OER and OEP integration, high-stake assessments and self-directed learning and OER) and was piloted, revised and uploaded as a Google form at https://forms.gle/AiHsfvdtEDX5AW9A9, and the link was emailed to the 22 OER experts. After the ethical and demographic sections, we provided the respondents with an overview of how the Delphi study would be carried out. The next three sections of the questionnaire are related to the actual survey of assessment practices and which skills and enablers would be more effective to support the goals of self-directed learning. Following the first-round responses, a first analysis using Wordcloud generators and Google form charts were presented using a PowerPoint to visually represent the responses obtained from all the participants. The responses that received greater than 75% agreement were highlighted and thematically regrouped as the main recommendations of the panel for mainstreaming OER, OEP and SDL. This allowed for accessible and timely assessment of the opinions of their academic counterparts and aimed at facilitating the second round of responses.

4.3.4 Second Round

Here, we made use of open-ended questions and elicited feedback from respondents towards consensus establishment. The second round of the Delphi was uploaded onto shared document at https://docs.google.com/document/d/1GPAUaWOMduL GCeHgLsubOH9XB_oOua4ar5ADYl5Szrk/edit?usp=sharing. All the participants from the first round were invited to view the consolidated responses from the 1st round and access the link to the second round for further confirmatory content analysis. We chose to have the second round in a more open format through a shared Google document which allowed the participants to input, view and modify their responses as desired. The OER experts were requested to use different colours to differentiate their entries and not to modify or edit other participants' responses. They were given 10 days for entering their responses, after which they could only view these and edits were not allowed anymore.

The versioning history functionality of the Google shared document allowed each panel member to read through the opinions of the other participants. Through the version history, we could also investigate whether they had modified their views as a result of reading through the other responses on that page through the text entry timestamps. There were no changes observed for the entries, from which we could infer that opinions had not been swayed by other participants' inputs.

The aim of the second round had two main goals: (1) identify the gaps in the responses as compared to the literature around OER, OEP and SDL and (2) probe into the tensions and dissonance that had been detected in the first round and allow the panel members to review, or eventually reiterate, their original responses in the light of the arguments from the other OER experts. Further to responses and constructive critiques from the panel, additional probing was deemed significant and pertained to:

1. Equity and care in the education system, in particular for assessments.
2. Ubuntu, OER and the concept of self-directed learning in the African context.
3. Rationales for shifting to assessment for learning rather than assessment of learning.
4. High-stake examinations for large cohorts.

The findings are presented and form the basis for developing an enabling framework for reuniting the main components of OER, assessments and self-directed learning.

4.4 Results

The combined results from the first and second rounds of the Delphi are presented below and form the main structural elements for a framework that can help policy-makers and tertiary education institutions design their programmes to integrate OER, OEP and SDL in a more coherent manner and eventually respond to the aims of this study.

4.4.1 Vision for Open Education

Opening the scene with the question about "how do you foresee open education in future?" engaged very mixed responses, but the panel was unanimously hopeful about the future of open education ranging from a very enthusiastic "default for educational content, practices and policy" to more realistic "Open education is slowly building momentum… I have been involved since the earliest stages (2001). Given this time span of almost 20 years, I am optimistic that OER will become mainstream, but also doubtful that it will achieve more than 30% penetration of the education resource market or mindset".

4.4.2 OER (Re)Definition

The panel favoured different definitions of OER, with an equal majority (22.7%) each referencing the UNESCO 2019 definition and Creative Commons definitions. Those who preferred the UNESCO definition broadly mentioned its comprehensiveness (covering most of the important issues, widely and officially recognised) for encompassing the public domain, while those for the Creative Commons (CC) detailed out their arguments mentioning the 5Rs ("Provides everyone with free and perpetual permission to engage in the 5R activities—retaining, remixing, revising, reusing and redistributing the resources"), the inadequacy of the UNESCO definition: "The CC definition avoids the pitfalls introduced by the 2019 UNESCO Recommendation and covers all requirements. Personally, I find that even ND materials are useful as part of the wider need for OER even though they may best be included as annexes because of the inability to remix and adapt them" and the need to distinguish between open education and OER "One of the issues with many definitions is the use of 'free of charge'. Open Education is not free of charge".

The commentaries showed deep-rooted beliefs about OER, but the divergence of opinion also pointed to what Mishra (2017) observed about the conflation of OER or OEP with open education and why it is important for educational stakeholders to understand the delineations, debate current practices and present more inclusive and flexible approaches for removing the barriers for OER to reach the people who need it the most.

4.4.3 What Should Change for OER to Be Mainstreamed and for OEP to Enhance Teaching and Learning?

The OER agenda has been taken up by many international organisations, and yet its mainstreaming within member state education systems has been quite slow. The panel members suggested improvements to this situation through:

1. Effective leadership and institutional recognition of the efforts required for developing and using OER, and eventually perpetuating open educational practices.
2. Addressing the incoherence between different educational policies and how existing educational policies were biased towards commercial resources, or OER-related policies were taking too long to be implemented.
3. Actively promoting awareness about OER and OEP—it was noted that there was still much groundwork to be done here.

Table 4.3 presents the verbatim responses obtained from the OER panel regrouped thematically.

The panel (22 responses) conceded almost unanimously (>75%) that:

Table 4.3 Thematic regrouping of responses to the question: what should change for OER to be mainstreamed and for OEP to enhance teaching and learning?

Theme	Individual comments from PANEL members
1. Leadership and recognition	– There needs to be champions for OER and examples of successful implementation or products that can be shared
	– There needs to be a mix of top-down policies (and rewards) and acknowledgement, praise, rewards for those champions
	– Building trust
	– Improved quality assurance and recognition of people's work in the field of OER
2. Tensions and dissonance in policy and implementation	– OER through creation of African journals by African universities so that research conducted in Africa be accessible easily within African journals
	– Competing interests: commercial publishers' models and the rewards that those carry in terms of academic recognition (Academic Promotion Criteria requiring publishing in high-impact factor journals)
	– Those with vested interests in current publishing models should be called out and confronted
	– We need government policy to steer education towards open education
	– Perceptions on the value and quality of commercially and openly published resources, policies and funding
	– Alternative funding
	– People give speeches on OER but then in their own institution do not create or promote OER
	– A change in attitude of teaching staff and top managers in institutions
	– OER needs to actually come out of the BIG HALLS of planning to implementation because there are masses who need it but the movement has been quite slow
	– It requires an advocacy to disseminate the OER for further customisation to the context of countries

(continued)

Table 4.3 (continued)

Theme	Individual comments from PANEL members
3. Enhance awareness and pedagogical approaches around OER and OEP	– We will need multiple options of quality OER in all grade levels, all subjects, all (major) languages – Understanding of basic concepts of OE, OER, copyright and of course OEP – Alternative assessment models – OEP to adopt new technologies for teaching and learning purposes – OEP still needs to be "presented" to the world, and a lot more awareness raising has to be done in that area – Stand-alone islands of excellence need to be consolidated

1. Traditional assessment methods do not cater enough for human variance (each learner has their own individual strengths) in learning ($n = 21$).
2. Education ministries needed to provide clear guidelines of how to operationalise the integration of OER within institutional copyright policies ($n = 19$).
3. Educators who know about and integrate OER are a minority of the education system ($n = 18$).
4. Education ministries needed to invest in the sustainable development and maintenance of national OER repositories to show their commitment to the OER movement ($n = 17$).
5. There needs to be more resources for assessments using OER ($n = 17$).

It was noted that there was a high level of agreement that the traditional approach of assessments prevented educators from innovating in their fields ($n = 16$) and that capacity building around OER is done at small scale and exists in "pockets of excellence". Members pointed to the lack of commitment from institutions who superficially agree to support OER, but do not implement any academic recognition system to encourage the use and development of OER, thus not genuinely promoting open educational practices (for detailed responses pertaining to OER, SDL and assessment, see Annex 1).

There was consensus around the leadership role that educational ministries should play. As mentioned by the panel members, there are many OER initiatives implemented at smaller scale (Weller, 2010) for teaching, SDL, remote learning and assessments and the capacity building efforts are at small-scale level. There is thus a need to implement stronger mechanisms to institutionalise and scale successful models using a top-down approach. Funding was seemingly not a major issue, while changing mindsets seemed to be predominantly an issue that needed more attention, while also being the hardest to achieve.

4.4.4 Which Assessment Methods Would Be Most Appropriate for Self-directed Assessments of/for Learning that Was Supported by OER

In response to assessment practices that would be appropriate for self-directed assessments, accreditation of prior learning and course-based portfolios scored the most as the panel's preferred mode of assessment for self-directed learning, followed by practicums and workplace assessments. As one member pointed out: "Assessments must be career and implementation focused. Theoretical, memory-based assessments are useless as is the practice of disposable assessments. Assessments must be created in collaboration with industry and employers and must be usable after being marked".

Given that this question was key to our study aims for the African context, we probed the panel further in the second round, adding the Ubuntu perspective which would also encompass the values of openness. The question was formulated as below:

The term self-directed learning focuses on the individual. Perhaps, this individualistic focus may be related to a Western outlook and understanding of the individual? In different contexts, such as those in African communities, the individual is seen as part of the community and there is a more community orientation—think, for example, of Ubuntu: I am because WE are.

With this in mind, how could we reimagine self-directed learning that is more community-orientated that could embrace a less individualistic approach, while at the same time harnessing the strengths of self-directed learning?

The panel was quick to respond to the fact that there is a potential danger in viewing SDL as an individualistic approach to learning that the group of experts addressed. They referred to Africa and Southern Asia, where the dominant cultural systems value community, and education systems often utilise community-based models of learning and collaborative knowledge building.

Designing learning from this perspective, one expert suggests, could be reframed as designing for "community-oriented self-directed learning". As such, the learning should be designed to target group learning, networking, collaboration and cooperation to achieve a common goal. In one example, especially during lockdowns, it was shown that younger students were able to access learning through SDL practices, which they then transferred to help other learners continue learning despite disruptions to their education. The current pandemic has in this sense accelerated SDL especially where learners could access relevant resources.

4.4.5 Skills and Attitudes Required for Academics to Engage with Open Education

The majority of respondents acclaimed collaboration, critical thinking ($n = 18$) and open licensing ($n = 17$) as extremely important skills for engaging with open education closely followed by creativity ($n = 16$). While collaboration and open licensing were the most obvious and expected responses, we thought that critical thinking was an interesting addition and was further elaborated in the comment "OER are a way of demonstrating one's social responsibility - making knowledge freely available, not behind paywalls. Critical thinking - using OER to teach those critical literacy thinking skills, but also using one's own in engaging with OER, and yes, engagement requires a huge dollop of creativity, not only for the end product but also in terms of attitude and approach".

4.4.6 Changes that Are Required in the Practices of Educators and Policy-Makers to Implement Assessment that Supports Self-directed Learning?

A change in mindset and attitudes was mostly quoted for supporting self-directed learning. It seems that learner-centredness is yet to be instilled in many higher educational institutions, that, time-bound, seated, one-size-fits-all, formal examination was perceived as superior to other forms of assessment and that institutions needed to "be openly courageous towards change in general". Professional development (digital fluency, more access to digital devices and connectivity) and training on innovative assessment to change perception that self-directed learning and its assessment is inferior, and development of clear transparent rubrics needed implementation.

4.4.7 Changes Required for More Self-directed Learning to Happen. (Question Reformulated to Emphasise the Focus on Students)

Panel members were of the opinion that self-discipline, critical thinking, discernment between different assessment possibilities and the students' ability to define short- and long-term objectives for themselves were important traits for SDL. Self-directed learners should be disciplined to commit to their study schedules and be able to access and select appropriate study resources through more agency and empowerment.

4.5 Discussion

The modified Delphi approach for this study allowed for a rapid appraisal of comprehensive viewpoints about SDL and changes in assessments required in the education system by influential OER practitioners. As advocates of "openness" in education, it was important to understand how they guide stakeholders and forecast the mainstreaming of OER—and what this would entail for the African region. Learner autonomy is key to SDL, and research in this area is increasingly important because of the rapidly changing education demands of current Volatile, Uncertain, Complex and Ambiguous (VUCA) world, which require learners to take responsibility for their own learning and to be equipped with lifelong learning skills.

Findings from the first round of this study show clearly that the educational system and its stakeholders need to be geared with the right mindset, technology and policies to encourage learner autonomy. Learners on the other side need to develop more self-discipline as well as critical thinking skills. The second round helped to confirm and corroborate this result. However, there were a few challenges and limitations owing to the short time frame that we had to collect the responses and the reduced possibility to have a greater number of responses during the 2nd round of the Delphi panel. In further iterations of this study, an online validation session on the derived framework (Fig. 4.1) with the panel would help to ease out any misconstrued concepts and also help to refine the components.

As already stated, the aims of this study were threefold:

- Determine the scope of changes needed to transform assessment modalities when shifting from a face-to-face to an online mode.
- Gather OER expert consensus around changes needed in the way assessments are carried out, and how to promote self-directed learning in online learning environments.
- Propose an assessment framework for self-directed learning to be integrated within open pedagogy.

4.5.1 Scope of Changes Needed to Transform Assessment Modalities When Shifting from a Face-To-Face to an Online Mode

Shifting assessments from face-to-face to an online mode requires a change in mindset, as the panel had duly observed, for institutions, policy-makers, educators and students alike. Research from Sub-Saharan Africa has shown that SDL practices have been used by indigenous knowledge holders for many generations, and there was a need to align SDL in the context of Ubuntu. In this respect, SDL is not learning in isolation but about becoming self-aware and self-motivated, to be learning-ready and develop agency. Also, agency is not intended to mean "I am an island", but to develop self-directedness to know when to learn in a community or individually. This aligns with Knowles' definition that includes the ability to choose and use material and human resources, in other words, learning to discern when to work on one's own or when to call in the help of others. Designing learning from this perspective, one expert suggests, could be reframed as designing for "community-oriented self-directed learning". As such, the learning should be designed to target group learning, networking, collaboration and cooperation to achieve a common goal.

The current pandemic has in this sense accelerated SDL especially where learners could access Internet platforms and share learning opportunities from those within their networks. In another example, OER was developed for children in refugee camps and specifically encouraged group learning. Thus, when SDL is effectively designed it can be a community-based approach to learning and assessment modalities would follow suit to encompass online group work, especially for large groups. The panel prescribed the use of learning analytics for identifying leadership qualities and eventually at-risk students.

4.5.2   Gather OER Expert Consensus Around Changes Needed in the Way Assessments Are Carried Out, and How to Promote Self-directed Learning in Online Learning Environments

The issue of equity and reusable assessment had been brought up in the first round, and we thought it judicious to close the gap in the second round by asking the panel about guiding principles they could proffer with respect to shareable and reusable assessments. Members opined that the key would be to involve students from the planning stages as they need to feel included in the process of setting assessments. Furthermore, equitable access also means localised assessments in languages understood by the students. Making assessments reusable implies lecturers planning for assessments themselves to become student-generated artefacts studied, critiqued and used in future classes. Assessments can, through this process, also be made to address real-world situations and problems and be authentic and not just disposable. The design and validation of effective assessment rubrics would also be crucial to ensure fairness, coherence and transparency in the evaluation of competencies and knowledge. Clearly, as mentioned by the panel, there are programmes of studies which need stringent validation (health professionals, engineering, electrical wiring, etc.), but which can still be accomplished by self-directed learners who would then need to validate their learning within well-defined organisational set-ups. The OER material would cover the main theoretical aspects, and the practical validation would then need to be within respected norms. Examples of SDL in the field of health professionals were presented by Murad and Varkey (2008, p. 588) who posited that there is increasing interest in SDL by educators and "SDL is a potential methodology to promote lifelong learning in medical education". With the explosion of new content, competency-based education requires SDL, e.g. the Practice-Based Learning and Improvement (PBLI) competency and the requirements for the Maintenance of Certification by the American Board Internal Medicine (ABIM).

4.5.3   An Assessment Framework for Self-directed Learning to Be Integrated Within Open Pedagogy

Drawing from the literature and panel discussions and findings, SDL as comprised of learner motivation, self-monitoring and self-management (Garrison, 1997) and an important tool for lifelong learning (Boyer et al., 2014), however, needs to be assessed and professionally supervised through effective quality assurance mechanisms.

Open pedagogy as conceptualised by Walz (2017) is teaching that "assign[s] students more agency, making a course more public, creating assignments [or assessments] which are meaningful or useful beyond the course, or considering other ways to make courses more open or accessible" (p. 158). As such, open pedagogy facilitates the link between theory and practice, what is learned in class and its real-world application—thereby enhancing its quality in terms of relevance, while opening up courses to the public fosters scrutiny that may lead to improvement in the quality of courses, such as what happens with course audits carried out by most MOOCs.

The findings suggest that SDL provides agentic influence on student self-awareness and self-motivation, which in turn enhances the ability to iterate between collaborative and networked learning within communities on the one hand and individual learning on the other. Additionally, student active involvement in the development of assessment artefacts may enhance transparency of assessment and its contextualisation to students' local settings and expand the pool of open assessment resources. Assessment rubrics (using criterion-based assessment) have been suggested as means for ensuring fairness and enabling students to validate their learning, while learning analytics can help students with self-monitoring, while identifying students at risk and thereby informing remedial interventions.

We therefore suggest an assessment framework for SDL informed by both literature and the findings of the study, comprising both self-directed learning and open assessment and open learning environment elements at macro-, meso- and micro-levels (see Fig. 4.3).

The framework consists of self-directed learning through attributes such as self-awareness, self-motivation and self-monitoring, which strengthens student agency to decide on self-directed learning approaches, whether collaborative/community-oriented or individualised. Through these learning approaches, students engage in open learning environments using networked learning or creating personal learning environments (PLEs). Through open pedagogies, students can actively be involved in the creation of assessment artefacts that are made open as open assessment resources (OAR) mainly using criterion-based assessment such as rubrics, thereby enabling

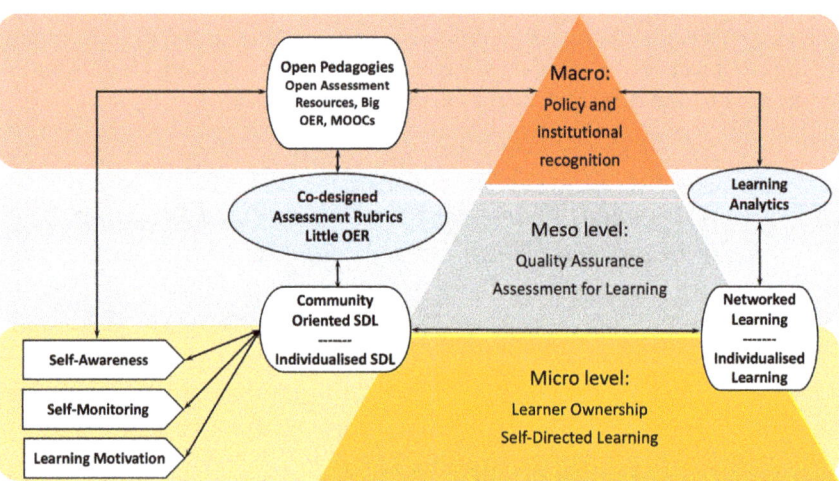

Fig. 4.3 Assessment framework for self-directed learning using open pedagogies

students to monitor their attainment of curricula goals and strengthening self-monitoring in particular and self-directed learning in general. OAR, being context-sensitive, would enhance student achievement while making learning more authentic. Data generated from the open learning environments feed learning analytics that help students to make decisions about how to learn, while also strengthening their self-awareness and monitoring, again resulting in enhanced self-directed learning. The framework, as an open tool, can be modified and adapted to suit different open learning contexts.

4.6 Conclusions

In pursuing openness in the form of OER, institutions may foresee a move to OER as a quick economic fix for reducing costs and increasing resource accessibility. However, such a transition can be accompanied by a variety of multi-layered challenges—for example, copyright and intellectual property issues, OER quality, relevance and applicability, resistance from faculty and the publishing industry, and institutional degrees of openness (D'Antoni & Savage, 2009; Wiley, 2010)—each of which needs to be addressed before successfully implementing a full-scale OER solution.

Self-directed learners—those who have the appropriate learning dispositions, tools and technologies—can only thrive through their engagement with open educational practices. As these learners exhibit criticality and discernment for their own capacities and eventually learning needs, having access to and creating resources which are unique to their own situation can only enhance the growing OER repositories throughout the world. However, these creative, personalised and incremental resources need to form part of a much bigger resource base which is much more formalised, peer acknowledged and recognised by relevant authorities and peer learners, much in the same way that many content-generated open-access sites operate (e.g. Flickr, Openclipart, OpenStreetMap, etc.). These specific skillsets, or what Olivier (2019) calls multiliteracies, need to be further supported.

The OER Delphi panel, in all their wisdom, has shared important insights for acknowledging and accrediting SDL, namely a much needed change in institutional policies for assessments and even access (equity) to these institutions. A change in mindset to rethink the raison d'être of formal examinations, recentre learning as a measure of what the learner excels at and how assessments can positively contribute back to society as a feed-forward can really change the way education is being carried out. This study has demonstrated that much of the onus for change is on the authorities, since SDL is already a reality and is increasingly being built through open educational practices.

Annex 1: Responses to Statements Regarding OER, Assessments and SDL

Legend

■ Agree ■ Disagree ■ I don't know ■ It depends

Rating of assessment practices to potentially support self-directed assessment

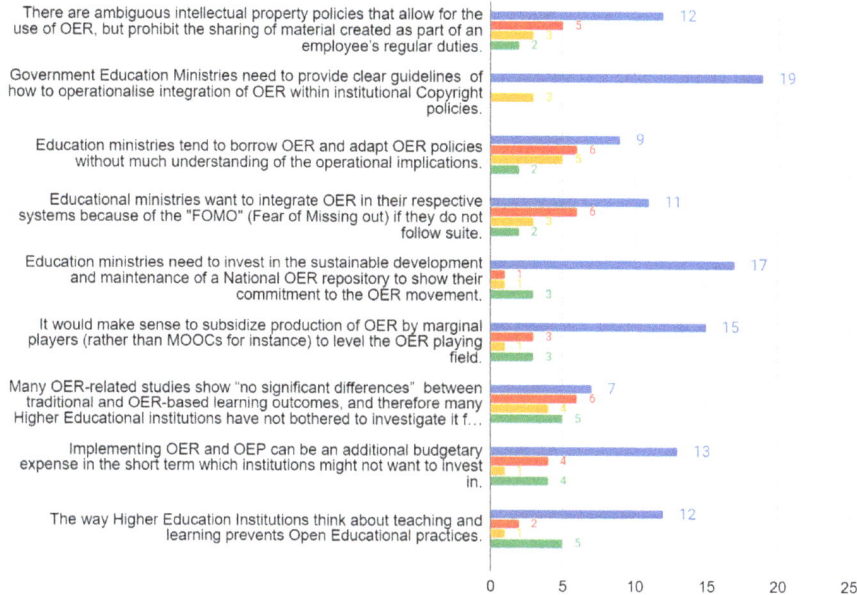

There are ambiguous intellectual property policies that allow for the use of OER, but prohibit the sharing of material created as part of an employee's regular duties.

Government Education Ministries need to provide clear guidelines of how to operationalise integration of OER within institutional Copyright policies.

Education ministries tend to borrow OER and adapt OER policies without much understanding of the operational implications.

Educational ministries want to integrate OER in their respective systems because of the "FOMO" (Fear of Missing out) if they do not follow suite.

Education ministries need to invest in the sustainable development and maintenance of a National OER repository to show their commitment to the OER movement.

It would make sense to subsidize production of OER by marginal players (rather than MOOCs for instance) to level the OER playing field.

Many OER-related studies show "no significant differences" between traditional and OER-based learning outcomes, and therefore many Higher Educational institutions have not bothered to investigate it f…

Implementing OER and OEP can be an additional budgetary expense in the short term which institutions might not want to invest in.

The way Higher Education Institutions think about teaching and learning prevents Open Educational practices.

Ranking skills and attitudes related to open education

References

Amrein, A. L., & Berliner, D. C. (2002). High-stakes testing & student learning. *Education Policy Analysis Archives, 10*, 18.

Baird, J. A., Andrich, D., Hopfenbeck, T. N., & Stobart, G. (2017). Assessment and learning: Fields apart? *Assessment in Education: Principles, Policy & Practice, 24*(3), 317–350. https://doi.org/10.1080/0969594X.2017.1319337

Bennett, R. E. (2010). Cognitively based assessment of, for, and as learning (CBAL): A preliminary theory of action for summative and formative assessment. *Measurement, 8*(2–3), 70–91.

Biswas-Diener, R., & Jhangiani, R. (2017). *Open: The philosophy and practices that are revolutionizing education and science* (p. 302). Ubiquity Press.

Bosch, C., Mentz, E., & Goede, R. (2019). Self-directed learning: A conceptual overview. In E. Mentz, J. De Beer, & R. Bailey (Eds.), *Self-directed learning for the 21st century: Implications for higher education*. NWU Self-Directed Learning Series (Vol. 1, pp. 1–36). AOSIS. https://doi.org/10.4102/aosis.2019.BK134.01

Boyer, S. L., Edmondson, D. R., Artis, A. B., & Fleming, D. (2014). Self-directed learning: A tool for lifelong learning. *Journal of Marketing Education, 36*(1), 20–32.

Bozkurt, A., Koseoglu, S., & Singh, L. (2019). An analysis of peer reviewed publications on openness in education in half a century: Trends and patterns in the open hemisphere. *Australasian Journal of Educational Technology, 35*(4), 78–97. https://doi.org/10.14742/ajet.4252

Brill, J. M., Bishop, M. J., & Walker, A. E. (2006). The competencies and characteristics required of an effective project manager: A web-based Delphi study. *Educational Technology Research and Development, 54*(2), 115–140.

Chesbrough, H. (2020). To recover faster from Covid-19, open up: Managerial implications from an open innovation perspective. *Industrial Marketing Management, 88*, 410–413.

Chiappe, A., Pinto, R., & Arias, V. (2016). Open assessment of learning: A meta-synthesis. *International Review of Research in Open and Distributed Learning: IRRODL, 17*(6), 44–61.

Cronin, C. (2017). Openness and praxis: Exploring the use of open educational practices in higher education. *International Review of Research in Open and Distributed Learning: IRRODL, 18*(5), 15–34.

Dalkey, N., & Helmer, O. (1963). An experimental application of the Delphi method to the use of experts. *Management Science, 9*(3), 458–467.

Daniel, J. (2020). Education and the COVID-19 pandemic. *Prospects, 49*(1), 91–96.

D'Antoni, S., & Savage, C. (2009). *Open educational resources: Conversations in cyberspace.* UNESCO.

Embo, M. P. C., Driessen, E. W., Valcke, M., & Van der Vleuten, C. P. M. (2010). Assessment and feedback to facilitate self-directed learning in clinical practice of Midwifery students. *Medical Teacher, 32*(7), e263–e269. https://doi.org/10.3109/0142159X.2010.490281

Garrison, D. R. (1997). Self-directed learning: Toward a comprehensive model. *Adult Education Quarterly, 48*(1), 18–33.

Gibson, D., Ifenthaler, D., & Orlic, D. (2016). 13. Open assessment resources for deeper learning. In *To access digital resources including: Blog posts videos online appendices* (p. 257). Retrieved from https://library.oapen.org/bitstream/handle/20.500.12657/31229/633870.pdf?sequence=1#page=280

Hasson, F., Keeney, S., & McKenna, H. (2000). Research guidelines for the Delphi survey technique. *Journal of Advanced Nursing, 32*(4), 1008–1015.

Hoosen, S., Moore, D., & Butcher, N. (2016). *Open educational resources (OER) guide for students in post-secondary and higher education.* Retrieved from http://oasis.col.org/handle/11599/2093

Hsu, C. C., & Sandford, B. A. (2007). The Delphi technique: Making sense of consensus. *Practical Assessment, Research, and Evaluation, 12*(1), 10.

Johnston, L. M., Wiedmann, M., Orta-Ramirez, A., Oliver, H. F., Nightingale, K. K., Moore, C. M., Stevenson, C. D., & Jaykus, L. A. (2014). Identification of core competencies for an undergraduate food safety curriculum using a modified Delphi approach. *Journal of Food Science Education, 13*(1), 12–21.

Jones, B. D. (2007). The unintended outcomes of high-stakes testing. *Journal of Applied School Psychology, 23*(2), 65–86. https://doi.org/10.1300/J370v23n02_05

Kearney, A., Williamson, P., Young, B., Bagley, H., Gamble, C., Denegri, S., & Woolfall, K. (2017). Priorities for methodological research on patient and public involvement in clinical trials: A modified Delphi process. *Health Expectations, 20*(6), 1401–1410.

Kirkpatrick, R., & Zang, Y. (2011). The negative influences of exam-oriented education on Chinese high school students: Backwash from classroom to child. *Language Testing in Asia, 1*, 36. https://doi.org/10.1186/2229-0443-1-3-36

Ludwig, B. (1997). Predicting the future: Have you considered using the Delphi methodology. *Journal of Extension, 35*(5), 1–4.

Macintosh, W., McGreal, R., & Taylor, J. (2011). *Open education resources (OER) for assessment and credit for students project: Towards a logic model and plan for action.* Athabasca University, Technology Enhanced Knowledge Research Institute. Retrieved from http://auspace.athabascau.ca/bitstream/2149/3039/1/Report_OACS-FinalVersion.pdf [Google Scholar].

Mahawar, K. K., Omar, I., Singhal, R., Aggarwal, S., Allouch, M. I., Alsabah, S. K., Angrisani, L., Badiuddin, F. M., Balibrea, J. M., Bashir, A., Behrens, E., Bhatia, K., Biertho, L., Biter, L. U., Dargent, J., De Luca, M., DeMaria, E., Elfawal, M. H., Fried, M., … Aminian, A. (2020). The first modified Delphi consensus statement on sleeve gastrectomy. *Surgical Endoscopy, 1*–7.

McMillan, J. H., & Schumacher, S. (2010). *Research in education: Evidence-based inquiry.* MyEducationLab Series. Pearson.

Mishra, S. (2017). Open educational resources: Removing barriers from within. *Distance Education, 38*(3), 369–380. https://doi.org/10.1080/01587919.2017.1369350

Murad, M. H., & Varkey, P. (2008). Self-directed learning in health professions education. *Annals Academy of Medicine Singapore, 37*(7), 580.

Nworie, J. (2011). Using the Delphi technique in educational technology research. *TechTrends, 55*(5), 24–30.

Okoli, C., & Wang, N. (2015, August). Business models for online education and open educational resources: Insights from a Delphi study. In *Proceedings of the 21st Americas Conference on Information Systems*, Puerto Rico.

Olivier, J. (2019). Towards a multiliteracies framework in support of self-directed learning through open educational resources. In E. Mentz, J. De Beer, & R. Bailey (Eds.), *Self-directed learning for the 21st century: Implications for higher education*. NWU Self-Directed Learning Series (Vol. 1, pp. 167–201). AOSIS. https://doi.org/10.4102/aosis.2019.BK134.06

Rajhans, V., Rege, S., Memon, U., & Shinde, A. (2020). Adopting a modified Delphi technique for revisiting the curriculum: A useful approach during the COVID-19 pandemic. *Qualitative Research Journal*.

Seifert, T., & Feliks, O. (2019). Online self-assessment and peer assessment as a tool to enhance student-teachers' assessment skills. *Assessment & Evaluation in Higher Education, 44*(2), 169–185. https://doi.org/10.1080/02602938.2018.1487023

Spivey, M. F., & McMillan, J. J. (2014). Classroom versus online assessment. *Journal of Education for Business, 89*(8), 450–456. https://doi.org/10.1080/08832323.2014.937676

Stagg, A. (2014). OER adoption: A continuum for practice. *International Journal of Educational Technology in Higher Education, 11*(3), 151–165. https://doi.org/10.7238/rusc.v11i3.2102

Stracke, C. M. (2017, July). The quality of MOOCs: How to improve the design of open education and online courses for learners? In *International Conference on Learning and Collaboration Technologies* (pp. 285–293). Springer. https://doi.org/10.1007/978-3-319-58509-3_23

Turoff, M., & Hiltz, S. R. (1996). Computer based Delphi processes. In *Gazing into the oracle: The Delphi method and its application to social policy and public health* (pp. 56–85).

Ulschak, F. (1983). *Human resource development: The theory and practice of needs assessment*. Reston.

UNESCO. (2020). *Exams and assessments in COVID-19 crisis: Fairness at the centre*. Retrieved from https://en.unesco.org/news/exams-and-assessments-covid-19-crisis-fairness-centre

Walz, A. (2017). A library viewpoint: Exploring open educational practices. In R. S. Jhangiani & R. Biswas-Diener (Eds.), *Open: The philosophy and practices that are revolutionizing education and science* (pp. 147–162). Ubiquity Press. https://doi.org/10.5334/bbc.l

Weldmeskel, F. M., & Michael, D. J. (2016). The impact of formative assessment on self-regulating learning in university classrooms. *Tuning Journal for Higher Education, 4*(1), 99–118. https://doi.org/10.18543/tjhe-4(1)-2016pp99-118

William, D. (2011). What is assessment for learning? *Studies in Educational Evaluation, 37*(1), 3–14. https://doi.org/10.1016/j.stueduc.2011.03.001

Wong, J., Baars, M., Davis, D., Van Der Zee, T., Houben, G. J., & Paas, F. (2019). Supporting self-regulated learning in online learning environments and MOOCs: A systematic review. *International Journal of Human-Computer Interaction, 35*(4–5), 356–373.

Sandhya Gunness is Senior Lecturer in open and online learning and Programme Coordinator for the MSc Educational Technologies and the MA Educational Leadership programmes at the University of Mauritius (UoM). She has conducted many workshops with COL, UNESCO, COMESA and the SADC on numerous e-learning projects and is currently pursuing her Ph.D. studies in the field of horizontal collaborative networks and development of T-shaped graduates. She was consulted by the Ministry of Education for conducting a national survey on the use of digital tablets in primary schools in Mauritius in collaboration with the World Bank and has contributed to the drafting of the National Open Educational Resources policy for Mauritius. Her research interests include open educational practices, transdisciplinary skills and collaborative networking.

Isabel Tarling is ICT Integration Specialist, holds a Ph.D. in Education Technologies and Teacher Professional Development from UCT and is director of Limina's learning design division. Her extensive experience working with teachers from all phases, subjects and backgrounds directly impacts the hands-on and change-driven teacher professional development courses she develops. In 2019, she was selected by the UNESCO chair at the Josef Stefan Institute, Slovenia, to create an online course for teachers as part of the Open Education for a Better World program. As Author, she is widely published and her research on teacher change is included in the National Professional Development Framework for Digital Learning. In July 2020, her adaption of the book, Teachers Discovering Computers: Integrating Technology in the South African Classroom, was published for teachers and teaching students. She passionately believes that the key to transforming teaching and learning lies in empowering all educators to create and innovate with technologies and to plan and manage change. This belief drives her to inspire all those in education to create and innovate with technologies and to inspire others to do the same. Her research interests focus on technology integration in discipline-specific areas, design thinking and developing socially embedded transformative programmes to support community-based innovation.

Erkkie Haipinge is Lecturer of Educational Technology and Project-Based Learning at the University of Namibia (UNAM). As Specialist in technology integration in teaching and learning, he also serves as Deputy Director for eLearning and Learning Design at the Centre for Innovation in Learning and Teaching (CILT) at UNAM. He coordinates the Centre's academic support services in areas of blended, online and remote learning, as well as online assessment. This involves development of relevant policies and guidelines, benchmarking and the implementing eLearning across the curriculum. He has provided consultation to COL in areas of training on digital assessment and development of rapid course development. He is a proponent of open education and open educational resources through open source technologies.

Chapter 5
Self-directed Learning, Online Mentoring and Online Coaching

Jako Olivier and Shikha Trivedi

Abstract The fourth industrial revolution has brought changes in current education systems. Many academic institutions are opting for open education throughout the working lives of individuals that led to a distinctive rise in e-learning; thus, a need is identified to explore the intersections between self-directed learning, online mentoring and online coaching. The aim of this chapter is to describe the main common trends on these topics and identify gaps in the scholarship that can serve as impetus for future research. Self-directed learning pertains to a process where students take responsibility for their own learning by setting outcomes, choosing material or human resources, selecting appropriate learning strategies and evaluating their learning. The online context brings specific opportunities for self-directed learning, but learners may require the support of others for mentoring (a long-term and relationship-based process) and coaching (limited to a specific task) at different levels of education, to instil learners with a love for open and distance learning. The chapter explores how self-directed learning could be supported by both approaches as well as can be fulfilled by peers or teachers. To this end, a systematic literature review was conducted of article publications related to self-directed learning, online mentoring and online coaching within the African continent between 2000 and 2020. It was found that limited research has been done in this context and that most works were focussed on South Africa and the education sector with some work in the health professions and other work contexts.

J. Olivier (✉)
Research Unit Self-Directed Learning, Faculty of Education, North-West University, Private Bag X2046, Mmabatho 2735, South Africa
e-mail: jako.olivier@nwu.ac.za
URL: http://www.jako.nom.za

S. Trivedi
Botswana Open University, Western Bye-Pass, Block 6, Plot 39972, Gaborone, Botswana

P.O. Box 26788, Gaborone, Botswana

S. Trivedi
e-mail: strivedi@staff.bou.ac.bw

© The Author(s), under exclusive license to Springer Nature Singapore Pte Ltd. 2021
D. Burgos and J. Olivier (eds.), *Radical Solutions for Education in Africa*, Lecture Notes in Educational Technology, https://doi.org/10.1007/978-981-16-4099-5_5

Keywords Self-directed learning · Mentoring · Coaching · Online learning ·
Multimodal learning

5.1 Introduction

The aim of this chapter is to explore trends regarding self-directed learning (SDL)
in research done on online mentoring and online coaching within the African continent for the past 20 years (2000–2020). Consequently, a systematic literature review
was conducted on relevant research articles related to online mentoring and online
coaching in order to determine whether aspects of SDL were included in the literature.

Central to this chapter is the concept of SDL and this is defined by Knowles (1975,
p. 18) SDL as "a process in which individuals take the initiative, with or without
the help of others, in diagnosing their learning needs, formulating learning goals,
identifying human and material resources for learning, choosing and implementing
appropriate learning strategies and evaluating learning outcomes". Furthermore, this
analysis drew on the extensive scholarship on SDL (Brockett & Hiemstra, 2019;
Garrison, 1992; Gibbons, 2002; Knowles, 1975; Morris, 2019; Saks & Leijen, 2014)
in order to determine whether aspects thereof could be found in the dataset.

For the purposes of this chapter, mentoring and coaching online are considered as
two related but separate concepts. From the literature, it is evident that the concepts
are sometimes used interchangeably or used in conjunction with each other (Connor
& Pokora, 2012; Garvey et al., 2017). In this regard, Pask and Joy (2007) use the
combined term *mentoring-coaching*. However, the terms are used separately in this
chapter.

Firstly, the term *mentoring* is derived from the noun *mentor* which refers to a
person acting in counselling capacity. The origin of the word can be traced back to
the Greek epic poem the *Odyssey*, where Méntōr or Μέντωρ, which in the poem
actually is the goddess Athena disguised as him, guides and mentors Telemachus,
Odysseus's son, in searching for his father (AHD, 2000; Eby et al., 2007; Pask & Joy,
2007). It is evident that mentoring as a concept has been extended beyond merely a
senior or experienced individual providing guidance and support to protégés (Ensher
et al., 2003). But the term remains poorly defined or delineated (Griffin et al., 2015).

For both mentoring and coaching, there are at least two individuals involved the
mentor or *coach* who guides and fulfils the facilitation and support role as well as the
mentee or *coachee*. Different terms are used in this regard such as *protégés* (Ensher
et al., 2003) or even the more generic *learner* (Parsloe & Leedham, 2009).

The relevance of mentoring and coaching for SDL is evident as within the context
of social cognitive theory as according to this theory learning takes place through
observation of others (Merriam & Bierema, 2014). Hence, the role that a mentor or
coach can play in this observation process is central to how individuals, or mentees,
can learn through the help of others in becoming self-directed themselves.

As this chapter focuses on mentoring and coaching within an online context, it is
also essential to take note that, especially in massive open online courses (MOOCs)

for example, feedback and monitoring might be difficult (Bonk et al., 2018) and this can be regarded as a disadvantage of online learning (Morris, 2019).

The focus on mentoring in the workplace as well as in literature is increasing with the lacuna around online mentoring is being addressed (Ensher et al., 2003). However, this chapter aims to specifically address the gap in this wider discourse in terms of the role of SDL in this context. The systematic literature review presented in this chapter is driven by the following research question: *What is the nature of SDL in research on online mentoring and online coaching in publications from the African continent for the past 20 years?*

5.2   Online Mentoring

This chapter focuses on online mentoring, but in order to provide a theoretical overview of this concept, it is essential to also understand how a mentor and mentorship in general is viewed in the literature.

Central to the concept of mentoring is the mentor or person providing the mentoring. Ensher et al. (2003) define a *mentor* as "one of a network of developers who provides instrumental, psychosocial, and/or role modelling support on an ongoing basis to a protégé" (p. 267). Furthermore, according to Ensher et al. (2003) mentors fulfil three roles:

- enhancing protégé's careers through providing support at vocational or instrumental levels;
- providing psychosocial support counselling and assistance; as well as
- modelling appropriate behaviour.

In discussing the definition of mentoring, Eby et al. (2007) state that this concept "reflects a unique relationship between individuals", "mentoring is a learning partnership", "mentoring is a process, defined by the types of support provided by the mentor to the protégé", "a mentoring relationship is reciprocal, yet asymmetrical" and "mentoring relationships are dynamic; the relationship changes over time" (p. 10). Furthermore, mentoring done online is also called e-mentoring in some literature (Rickard, 2004).

The scholarly tradition around mentoring can be traced back to the work by Levinson on mentoring in terms of adult development (Eby et al., 2007). But since, mentoring and its related research has been expanded to various other fields and contexts. Theoretically mentoring can be approached in terms of theories of expertise, human and social capital theories (Laverick, 2016).

Mentoring generally takes place in formal work or educational settings, but research has shown that it at times also occurs spontaneously or informally (Eby et al., 2007; Ensher et al., 2003). In this context, SDL is also relevant for both formal and informal contexts (Morris, 2019). The importance of mentoring in the wider higher education context is evident (Laverick, 2016). In this context, peers, more senior students or even university staff can act in a mentoring capacity. Furthermore, from the literature it is evident that most of the research on mentoring has focussed on "mentoring of youth, student–faculty mentoring relationships, and mentoring within the workplace" (Allen & Eby, 2007, p. 3).

Merriam and Bierema (2014) regard cognitive apprenticeships as being a form of mentoring, and for them, this refers to a process where a mentor models the way a mentee should think about what is learned. Furthermore, it is essential for mentors to adapt their mentoring to the different needs of the individual mentees (Griffin et al., 2015).

Online mentoring is highly relevant in a context where education and work are increasingly impacted by technology and access to the Internet. However, it is evident that there are also negative aspects of online mentoring, "including misunderstandings, flaming, and coldness of the medium" which can be countered by training (Ensher et al., 2003, p. 283).

5.3 Online Coaching

The origin of the word *coach* relates to a vehicle used to get from one place to another and the etymology of the term is actually related to the Hungarian village, Kocsi, which was famous as a place where coaches were built during the middle ages (Pask & Joy, 2007). Coaching is even traced back to being a form of Socratic dialogues (Garvey et al., 2017). Hence, within the context of this chapter a coach is also someone who helps another person to get to a specific goal through an online medium. Coaching is also associated with an informal process, rather than the more formal long-term approach associated with mentoring, as the need for coaching may arise at any point (Parsloe & Leedham, 2009).

The focus of mentoring is on developing at a personal, professional or career level and usually for a longer term (Connor & Pokora, 2012). Coaching, on the other hand, is more structured, for a shorter period and the emphasis is on changing (Connor & Pokora, 2012). Connor and Pokora (2012) present a view where the two concepts are regarded as complementary activities and they define this combined phenomenon as follows: "Coaching and mentoring are learning relationships which help people to take charge of their own development, to release their potential and to achieve results which they value" (p. 6). Importantly, this definition relates to SDL as it emphasises learners taking charge of their learning and setting goals they choose.

The trends observed by Garvey et al. (2017) regarding existing coaching literature included case studies related to coachee experiences often from the perspective of the coach and often this research is actually insider accounts. However, there seems to be less research on coaching than mentoring (Garvey et al., 2017).

It is important that a coach does not make decisions on behalf of who is being coached but rather, in the words of Pask and Joy (2007) helps the person to think in order to reach identified goals. Four stages can be identified for the generic coach-mentoring process (Parsloe & Leedham, 2009, p. 21):

- Analysing for awareness of need, desire and self.
- Planning for self-responsibility.
- Implementing using styles, techniques and skills.
- Evaluating for success and learning.

These stages show the prominence of the self and coachee-centredness or by implication learner-centredness, which is also associated with SDL. In addition to coachee agency, there are also elements that reflect the SDL definition of Knowles (1975) as the coachee takes charge and that there are steps related to the planning, implementation and evaluation. The role of SDL in the online mentoring and coaching contexts is explored in the next section.

5.4 SDL and Online Mentoring and Coaching

The importance of a mentor or coach for SDL is clear in the literature. Even in the definition of SDL by Malcolm Knowles, stated at the beginning of this chapter, the prominent role of help by others and human resources was evident. Exploring the role of online mentoring and coaching in terms of SDL is also relevant as fostering SDL "seems fundamental for empowering learners to deal with a world that is becoming ever more complex and changeable" (Morris, 2019, p. 648).

The role of a mentor or coach is important for SDL. Due to the fourth industrial revolution, the focus of research shifted on the interplay of self-directed learning with technology (Brown & Duguid, 2017; Herrington, 2013). In the process of SDL, students need support to overcome their challenges as well as timely feedback which calls the attention for coaching or mentoring. In this regard, Merriam and Bierema (2014) observe that "[l]earners exhibit varying degrees of self-directedness along a continuum from high dependency on the instructor to independent SDL that may rely on the instructor as a consultant or mentor" (p. 80). An advantage for SDL in formal educational settings is the fact that learners may have access to experts to support their learning process (Morris, 2019) and as such mentors and coaches can also fulfil this role.

It is problematic if mentoring is described as a "role model–observer relationship" (Eby et al., 2007) as this might imply a more passive role on the side of the student. Consequently, the dynamic aspect of mentoring might be more relevant within the context of SDL where the student should take an active role in the process.

As important as student agency is for SDL, within the literature of mentoring the agency and uniqueness of the mentee are also evident (Pask & Joy, 2007). Furthermore, the relevance of coaching for SDL is evident. In a study focussed on medical trainees Wolff et al. (2020) found that coaching facilitated SDL behaviour and that feedback is an essential component within the coaching process.

5.5   Research Design and Methodology

This section presents the research design and methodology followed in this systematic literature review. Initially, the data collection process and the inclusion criteria used are presented. Thereafter the way in which the data analysis was conducted is explained.

5.5.1   Data Collection and Inclusion Criteria

In order to explore trends regarding SDL in research done on online mentoring and online coaching within the African continent for the past 20 years, specific inclusion criteria had to be set. In this regard, the following criteria were used in the searches in the identified databases:

- the sources had to be published between 2000 and 2020;
- the focus of the sources had to be on an African country or countries;
- the sources had to relate to online mentoring and online coaching; and
- the sources had to refer to SDL.

However, even with preliminary investigative searches it was evident that no sources—regardless of the time of publication—contained online mentoring, online coaching and SDL with a focus on an African country. Hence, SDL was removed from the search criteria and elements related to SDL were rather specifically searched for in the articles that adhered to the criteria set.

In the search process, *Sabinet African Journals* database as well as *Academic Search Complete* and the *Education Resource Information Center (ERIC)* accessed through *EBSCOhost* were consulted. For the search itself, the date range was used as stated above and "online mentoring", "online coaching", "Africa" and the names of the 54 African states as recognised by the United Nations and the African Union, were employed as keywords.

In total, 51 articles from the identified databases were listed, and from the initial screening, this was reduced to 27 articles that adhered to the set inclusion criteria. The analysis involved two phases: an initial phase during which the identified articles were read by both researchers independently during which irrelevant articles were removed as well as a second phase where the articles were analysed in-depth. If mentoring or coaching were only referred to in a cursory manner then such articles were discarded. Hence, only articles researching either mentoring or coaching specifically or where these issues were also handled within the empirical part of the article were included. Finally, only 14 articles were relevant for this study.

To ensure trustworthiness, the initial screening and two phases of the analysis were done independently and then checked until consensus was reached regarding the process and findings.

5.5.2 Data Analysis

5.5.2.1 General Profile of the Article Corpus

The majority of the articles related to the South African context with most authors also coming from this country. Exceptions were research done within the wider sub-Saharan context (McGuire et al., 2020) or research done with participants from Malawi (Smith et al., 2018) and Namibia (Wilder et al., 2010). Albert et al. (2017) report on research done in many different countries including Cameroon, Ethiopia, Lesotho and Tanzania.

The focus of this research was on articles published between 2000 and 2020, but there were some years of which no articles adhered to the inclusion criteria and most of the publications in the corpus were published in 2017 or 2018.

The spread of the different articles in terms of year of publication is presented in Fig. 5.1.

A variety of methodologies were employed within the corpus of studies analysed in this chapter. A number of studies followed a quantitative design (Albert et al., 2017; Kunaka & Moos, 2019). But qualitative studies were also conducted (Arend et al., 2017; McGuire et al., 2020; Ndlela & Brysiewicz, 2018; Wilder et al., 2010). Mixed-method studies were also observed (Foulds, 2003; Smith et al., 2018; Takavarasha et al., 2018; Van Staden, 2018). While there were also studies focussing on a document analysis (Linnegar, 2015) or a more conceptual approach to research (Baijnath, 2014; Deyzel & Faris, 2010; Marsh, 2017).

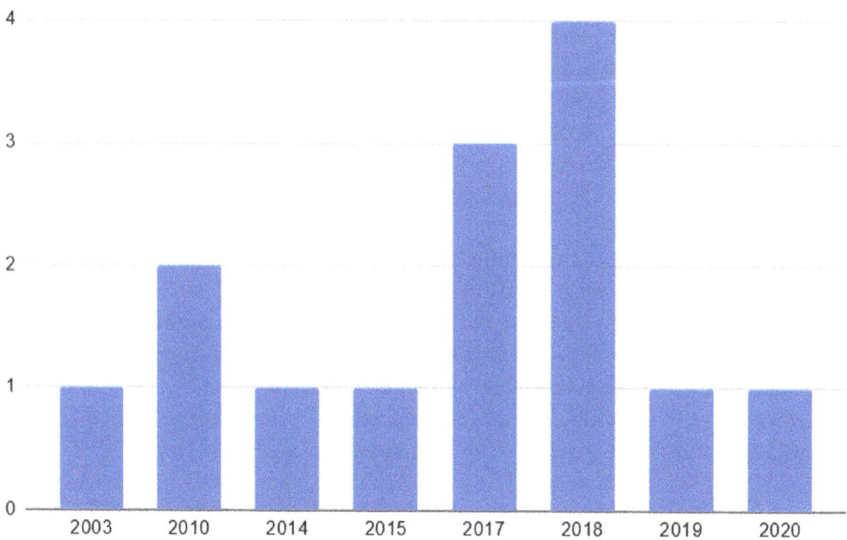

Fig. 5.1 Number of publications per year

Table 5.1 Types of participants or focus

Participants or focus	Article in the corpus
University students	Arend et al. (2017) Baijnath (2014) Deyzel and Faris (2010) McGuire et al. (2020) Ndlela and Brysiewicz (2018) Smith et al. (2018) Takavarasha et al. (2018) Van Staden (2018)
University lecturers	Baijnath (2014) McGuire et al. (2020)
School teachers	Foulds (2003) Wilder et al. (2010)
Civil engineers	Marsh (2017)
Entrepreneurs and small business owners	Kunaka and Moos (2019)
Text editors	Linnegar (2015)
Healthcare professionals	Albert et al. (2017) McGuire et al. (2020)

A clear distinction between mentoring and coaching literature focussing on the educational and professional contexts was evident. In Table 5.1, an overview of the nature of the participants or focus is provided.

In terms of disciplinary focus, mentoring and coaching were approached within the educational context. In higher education, at undergraduate level, this involved online mentoring for academic literacy (Arend et al., 2017), a focus on peer mentoring for nursing students (Ndlela & Brysiewicz, 2018), university student digital citizenship (Takavarasha et al., 2018) and mentoring through WhatsApp for a module on adult education (Van Staden, 2018). Or for more senior students as part of an online learning and collaboration space for psychology postgraduate students (Deyzel & Faris, 2010) or for online learning for master's students in surgical sciences (Smith et al., 2018).

In terms of professional contexts, one article focussed on mentoring for entrepreneurs and small business owners (Kunaka & Moos, 2019), teachers (Foulds, 2003), family medicine (McGuire et al., 2020), tuberculosis laboratory specialists (Albert et al., 2017), civil engineers (Marsh, 2017) and mentoring for text editors (Linnegar, 2015) as well as teachers (Wilder et al., 2010).

A wide range of individually used or combinations of instruments were used. This included questionnaires generated by researchers (Kunaka & Moos, 2019; Smith et al., 2018; Takavarasha et al., 2018) with both closed and open questions. Wilder et al. (2010) made use of surveys and content analysis of online discussions and reflections. Furthermore, interviews were also employed by certain studies in the corpus (Ndlela & Brysiewicz, 2018; Takavarasha et al., 2018). In the research by

McGuire et al. (2020) and Albert et al. (2017), data was generated through conducting workshops. Van Staden (2018) made use of netnography and social network analysis.

Overall from the discussion below, it is evident that the majority of works within the corpus focus on mentoring and not coaching. However, Linnegar (2015) refers to coaching, but also indicates that the focus in that article is on mentoring as a more holistic approach while coaching is limited to improving a specific skill or improving performance. For text editors, as is the case in Linnegar (2015), the need is for them to enter into a mentoring relationship in order to improve text editing practices in a self-directed manner through engagement with a mentor.

5.5.2.2 Approaches to Online Mentoring and Coaching in the Corpus

While some of the articles approach mentoring generically (Kunaka & Moos, 2019), there are also articles that focus specifically on online mentoring specifically (e.g. Arend et al., 2017; Baijnath, 2014; Deyzel & Faris, 2010; Foulds, 2003; Linnegar, 2015; McGuire et al., 2020; Smith et al., 2018; Van Staden, 2018; Wilder et al., 2010).

The need for mentors was consistently expressed in the corpus. For example, Takavarasha et al. (2018) noted how students can attain digital literacy themselves but struggle to reach digital citizenship without having mentors. While McGuire et al. (2020) explored research mentorship for family physicians and note how mentorship can be a driver for research engagement. In the case of Van Staden (2018), the researcher was invited by students to become a mentor herself after which one of the students started to fulfil that role.

Interestingly, Foulds (2003) interprets the use of mentors in an online training programme for teachers in terms of communities of practice (Wenger, 1999). For Foulds (2003), in this context the brokering (Hefetz & Ben-Zvi, 2020; Henry & Mackenzie, 2012) role of mentors was quite significant. Deyzel and Faris (2010) also note the important role of mentors within communities of practice in the higher education context.

Marsh (2017) highlighted the affordances of online and specifically mobile technologies in opening up access to mentoring. In the mentoring through WhatsApp, Van Staden (2018) highlights the researcher's role that is not to "provide all the information, but rather to shine a light on the road ahead, to identify dangers and to facilitate learning" (p. 352). Arend et al. (2017) describe how they made use of online mentoring to support university students acquire academic literacy. Within this context Arend et al. (2017) found that online mentoring became "an invaluable tool for helping students to grapple with the application of theory to their own lives, so as to allow them to move beyond the abstractions that so often undermine meaningful learning" (p. 92).

In some cases, mentors are considered part of a wider approach to improving a system. In research on improving a quality management system, Albert et al. (2017) explained how mentors are used in the tuberculosis laboratory context and how mentors are trained. In this research, there is a distinction made between more long-term embedded mentors and short-term mentoring conducted over two to three days. Such a short-term mentoring is considered by Albert et al. (2017) as being "cost-effective, scalable and sustainable, and is well suited to the workshop approach of implementation" (p. 7). To an extent, this short-term approach may possibly be considered coaching as it has a specific set short-term goal.

5.5.2.3 Peer Online Mentoring and Coaching in the Corpus

The issue of peer mentoring or coaching was also noted in the corpus (McGuire et al., 2020; Ndlela & Brysiewicz, 2018; Takavarasha et al., 2018; Van Staden, 2018). In this regard, Ndlela and Brysiewicz (2018) reached the following conclusion regarding peer mentoring:

> The peer mentoring programme enabled students to access information, to have unlimited support and to feel empowered by the process. As mentees, students could access from their mentors any kind of information valuable to them at any time; therefore, they experienced unlimited support, both with academic matters and in the clinical setting. (p. 7)

Similarly, peer mentoring or coaching can also be done online through using former students as e-tutors (Smith et al., 2018) and it can also happen spontaneously (Van Staden, 2018). Such interactions can also be done in person as Takavarasha et al. (2018) notes that their research prompted a "need to change teaching strategies by using learners to support other millennials in the communities of both the university and the home activity systems" (p. 14). McGuire et al. (2020) refer to e-mentorship or virtual mentorship in this context and notes how online mentorship groups and social media platforms could be useful mediums to facilitate such work.

Online peer mentoring or coaching can also be realised across geographical borders. In this regard, Wilder et al. (2010) report on peer mentoring between teachers from the USA and teachers from Namibia. This project proved to be successful in establishing a relationship between mentors and mentees and that both sides benefited from the interactions.

Smith et al. (2018) note the importance of the Community of Inquiry (CoI) (Garrison, 2016) framework for their medical training as this is used to inform e-tutor's practices. Garrison et al. (1999) are of the opinion that "a worthwhile educational experience is embedded within a Community of Inquiry that is composed of teachers and students–the key participants in the educational process" (p. 88).

Different roles for mentors or coaches were identified in the corpus. This included providing academic as well as pastoral support (Smith et al., 2018). Baijnath (2014) also concludes that students found in selected signature online courses where students allocated mentors that it leads to "removing the distance from distance education".

5.5.2.4   Barriers to Online Mentoring and Coaching in the Corpus

Some barriers to establishing mentorship were identified. According to McGuire et al. (2020), power differences between mentees and potential mentors might act as a barrier to establishing such a relationship. In addition, unclear expectations, a shortage of mentors as well as there not being a culture of mentorship were also identified as possible challenges (McGuire et al., 2020).

In online contexts, the issues of access to technology and associated costs were also mentioned as variables that need to be considered within the African milieu (Foulds, 2003; Smith et al., 2018; Takavarasha et al., 2018). In this regard, in peer mentoring by teachers from the USA with teacher mentees from Namibia it was found that "[t]he constrained time period of the collaboration, acerbated by the technology problems, made it harder for the US and Namibian participants to really connect until the very end" (Wilder et al., 2010, p. 40).

5.5.2.5   Recommendations for Online Mentoring and Coaching in the Corpus

Apart from some of the elements discussed above which may also prompt good practices in terms of online mentoring and coaching some sources in the corpus also overtly presented recommendations towards effective mentoring and coaching.

McGuire et al. (2020) mention the need for policies supporting mentoring as well as explicit mentorship training for both mentors and mentees as early as possible not only when, in this case family physicians, are in practice. Such training should also include interpersonal communication strategies as well as other skills related to research which was specifically relevant for this context (McGuire et al., 2020).

It is recommended that teachers be actively involved and be visible in online environments when acting as a mentor (Van Staden, 2018). In this research, it was found that WhatsApp can act as a useful medium within the South African highest education context; however, it might not be useful for very large groups or in cases where earlier posts need to be accessed easily.

Structured mentoring is proposed by Albert et al. (2017) as a way in which, in their case, quality management systems can be supported in laboratories. In addition, in this article the importance of mentor training is also noted. Another approach to online mentoring, within the context of academic literacy (Arend et al., 2017), involved a specific focus on feedback. This feedback was often done collaboratively and not necessarily individually. In this case, mentors regarded themselves as both responders and designers to the learning situation.

In the conceptual article by Marsh (2017), the following recommendations are made for mentoring, which in this case related to supporting civil engineers towards professional registration:

- Develop a compelling professional registration support mentoring purpose
- Empower and enable all the participants

- Ensure a win-win approach for long-term sustainability
- Cater for multiple journeys and multiple agendas
- Develop the wisdom of the collaborative
- Provide an appropriate level of structure and systemisation
- Ensure scalability and sustainability
- Provide the best combination of integrated tools and technologies
- Enhance the knowledge exchange and experiential wisdom with value-add contributors at regular intervals
- Professional development is more important than professional registration.

From this list and the discussion by Marsh (2017), the dynamic and purpose-driven role of a mentor is evident. In the next section, the focus turns more specifically to aspects related to SDL as was found in the corpus.

5.5.2.6   Elements of Self-directed Learning in the Corpus

As stated earlier, SDL was removed as part of the search criteria as this resulted in no relevant hits in the searched databases. However, it was decided to inductively search for elements of and related to SDL in the texts.

Central to SDL is that it is learner-centred (Knowles, 1975). Within the corpus, Linnegar (2015) also refers to the need for a mentee-driven approach to the mentoring of text editors while in this case, mentors provide guidance. Arend et al. (2017) acknowledge the importance of individual agency and ownership within the learning process in terms of online mentoring for academic literacy at university level. Baijnath (2014) also notes the importance of learner-centred teaching and learning. Mentees' needs might vary and that they might be at different levels of development (Marsh, 2017). Wilder et al. (2010) discussed how their approach, using WebQuests, was a learner-centred strategy that was employed with teachers who mainly functioned within a teacher-centred context.

However, contrary to SDL's learner-centred focus in some instances articles from the corpus showed a tendency towards a teacher or rather mentor/coach-centeredness. In this regard, Kunaka and Moos's (2019) focus on "skills transfer outcomes" and "knowledge transfer outcomes" emphasise the mentor's transfer of these two outcomes rather than facilitating construction of knowledge by the mentee.

Smith et al. (2018) also noted the importance of SDL in imparting lifelong learning skills and highlighted how students were encouraged to continue with continuing professional development, peer interaction and self-reflection. In addition, the need for students to acquire soft skills, in terms of digital literacy, by themselves is highlighted in research by Takavarasha et al. (2018). Van Staden (2018) emphasised the importance of learner-centredness and individual responsibility in mentored online learning in a higher education context.

An important recommendation made in terms of mentoring that also has implications for SDL is that Van Staden (2018) found that in that research it was concluded that "WhatsApp groups provide a key to student success in distance education if the mentor is present to structure a cooperative learning process and to facilitate the development of self-regulating skills" (p. 353). The concepts of SDL and self-regulated learning (SRL), as noted here, are related but are considered distinct concepts (Loyens et al., 2008; Saks & Leijen, 2014; Zimmerman & Lebeau, 2000).

An aspect that relates to SDL as well as mentoring and coaching is the importance of collaboration. This collaboration should be interpreted in terms of the approach to SDL by Knowles (1975) where individuals take charge of their own learning "with or without the help of others" and also make use of human resources for learning (p. 18). In educational contexts, the affordances of cooperative learning strategies for SDL have been evident (Mentz & Van Zyl, 2018). In terms of collaboration and mentoring, the issue of peer mentoring also seemed to be highly relevant in the higher education context (Ndlela & Brysiewicz, 2018).

The online environment can also through discussion boards create an interactive collaborative space that can work against isolation and, therefore, motivate students (Smith et al., 2018). Conversely, Takavarasha et al. (2018) found that collaboration was negatively affected when students had to work at distance from home in contrast to the interactions on campus. Baijnath (2014) describes students as becoming "self-organised and participatory learners" in a mentor-supported online distance learning context.

Within this context, Kunaka and Moos (2019) relate how entrepreneurs and small business owners occasionally "engage in more than one mentoring relationships" (p. 7). Linnegar (2015) also highlights the importance of SDL and collaborative rather than didactic learning in terms of the mentoring of text editors. Foulds (2003) also notes this aspect in terms of teacher professional development where the relevance of "effective brokering practices on the part of mentors, and/or communal learning support from fellow participants" (p. 62) was noted. Furthermore, it was significant that "teachers identified by their mentors as participating in group interaction completed their modules more successfully than those identified as non-participants" (Foulds, 2003, p. 62). Marsh (2017) refers to collective wisdom in this regard as mentees, mentors and experts interact.

Problem-based learning (PBL) is also closely associated with SDL as it is a strategy that can foster SDL among students (Breed & Bailey, 2018; Loyens et al., 2008; Zimmerman & Lebeau, 2000). The relevance of PBL within the mentoring context is noted by Linnegar (2015).

Motivation and effectual issues were also prominent in the corpus. In terms of SDL, it is notable that motivation is part of Garrison's (1992) Comprehensive model of SDL and in this regard, he notes that "[m]otivation plays a very significant role in the initiation and maintenance of effort towards learning and the achievement of cognitive goals" (p. 26). In this context, the issue of motivation was noted in the corpus. Kunaka and Moos (2019) noted the importance of entrepreneur resilience outcomes in terms of mentoring with entrepreneurs and small business owners. Furthermore, McGuire et al. (2020) referred to "the development of a positive research culture" (p. 3) which pertains to creating a context which would be conducive to research mentorship.

Within the online context, it was evident that learning had to be situated. This aspect ties in with the research done within the South African context where in terms of self-directed multimodal learning in a South African university Olivier (2020) found that learning was situated in terms of specific vocation but not necessarily in terms of student context or culture. The importance of a person's situation or context in terms of an individual's learning needs is clear in the SDL literature (Morris, 2019). In Smith et al. (2018), it was evident that students "were interested to learn about clinical practice in other parts of the world, but they sometimes found it difficult to relate to clinical guidelines for surgical procedures they are not familiar with" (p. 162). McGuire et al. (2020) also emphasised that "[s]uccessful mentorship programmes must be contextual and recognise diversity" (p. 3). Hence, in online approaches to mentoring and coaching there should be room to acknowledge and adapt to local needs and contexts.

An important recommendation made in the corpus in terms of mentoring is that it can be realised through peer mentoring supported by formalised policies in higher education (Ndlela & Brysiewicz, 2018).

SDL's foundation on constructivism prompts the need for authentic and real-life situations within the learning process (Morris, 2019). In this regard, the majority of articles related to mentoring towards a specific vocation or skills used within the world of work. Hence, through mentoring individuals can be capacitated as entrepreneurs and small business owners (Kunaka & Moos, 2019), teachers (Foulds, 2003), healthcare professionals (McGuire et al., 2020; Ndlela & Brysiewicz, 2018) and text editors (Linnegar, 2015) for example.

5.6 Discussion

Overall, it seems limited research has been done on SDL in terms of online mentoring and coaching within the context of the African continent for the past 20 years. The majority of the research was done in and focussed on South Africa. The focus in the corpus was also mainly on mentoring and not coaching; however, other terms were used in the texts in reference to what could be considered coaching.

Methodologically, most of the research seems to be qualitative in nature, while there were also some quantitative and mixed-method studies. Apart from some empirical work, some conceptual articles were also identified. Different instruments and approaches were followed in terms of data generation but there was a distinct gap in using a single mentoring- or coaching-focussed questionnaire or standardised instrument.

The most prominent focus was on educational contexts especially higher education followed by a number of mentoring or coaching aspects within professions such as teaching, engineering, business, text editing as well as healthcare professionals.

It is clear that in the different educational and professional contexts mentorship is needed. The prominence of online mentorship was evident, and it was often regarded as a means to improving practices within the work environment. A prominent feature was peer online mentoring and coaching where individuals with similar profiles may act as mentors.

A number of barriers were identified for online mentoring and coaching. Firstly, this related to relationships between mentors and mentees with regard to established power relationships. Furthermore, access to technology and associated costs seem to be a recurring theme that has an effect on online mentoring and coaching.

Some appropriate recommendations could be drawn from the corpus. This included a need for policies that support mentoring and coaching; online mentors and coaches having a sustained online presence; there needs to be structure to the mentoring; mentors need to be trained and be able to effectively provide feedback. The approach by mentors and coaches should be broad and flexible meeting the individual needs of all the mentees, while being collaborative and sustainable.

Finally, it is evident that although not always overtly stated SDL is significant in any online mentoring or coaching. Online mentoring or coaching requires a mentor-centred approach in which mentor agency is important. The SRL skills of mentees also need to be addressed within an SDL context. Collaboration between mentees is essential especially in learning contexts. In such a context, PBL also seems to be relevant in terms of mentoring. Motivation underlies the whole online mentoring or coaching process and is as important here as it is for fostering SDL. The mentoring situation also needs to be situated in terms of the wider context of the mentees.

5.7 Conclusion

This chapter explored the nature of SDL in research on online mentoring and online coaching in publications from the African continent for the past 20 years. An extensive scholarship exists on mentoring and coaching internationally and these concepts are often used in conjunction. In this chapter, the focus was also specifically on the intersections between the online mentoring, online coaching and SDL, and hence, all three concepts had to be delineated.

Certain limitations were pertinent to this research. Due to the low number of articles available, it might be necessary in future studies to include more databases, also focus on books and book chapters as well as including text from languages other than just English.

The chapter involved a systematic literature review of journal articles on and from the African continent for the past 20 years. Overall, more research articles within the African context and adhering to the set inclusion criteria related to mentoring than coaching. This fact corresponds with the literature reviews conducted by Garvey et al. (2017) which also showed a similar trend. A variety of methodologies were used, but there seems to be a need for bigger quantitative studies in this context. A variety of professions and educational contexts were represented, but there are clear gaps in terms of underrepresented disciplines. Within the African context issues around online access and the nature of relationships between mentors or coaches and mentees or coachees need to be addressed. In the majority of texts, elements of SDL were present especially in terms of mentee/coachee agency and the importance of collaboration. However, it is clear that more research is needed in terms of SDL and actual mentoring and coaching practices within the continent.

References

AHD (American Heritage Dictionary). (2000). *The American Heritage Dictionary of the English language* (4th ed.). Houghton Mifflin Harcourt.

Albert, H., Trollip, A., Erni, D., & Kao, K. (2017). Developing a customised approach for strengthening tuberculosis laboratory quality management systems toward accreditation. *African Journal of Laboratory Medicine, 6*(2), 1–8.

Allen, T. D., & Eby, L. T. (2007). Overview and introduction. In T. D. Allen & L. T. Eby (Eds.), *The Blackwell handbook of mentoring: A multiple perspectives approach* (pp. 3–6). Blackwell.

Arend, M., Hunma, A., Hutchings, C., & Nomdo, G. (2017). The messiness of meaning making: Examining the affordances of the digital space as a mentoring and tutoring space for the acquisition of academic literacy. *Journal of Student Affairs in Africa, 5*(2), 89–111.

Baijnath, N. (2014). Curricular innovation and digitisation at a mega university in the developing world—The UNISA "signature course" project. *Journal of Learning for Development-JL4D, 1*(1). Retrieved December 10, 2020, from https://jl4d.org/index.php/ejl4d/article/view/36

Bonk, C. J., Zhu, M., Kim, M., Xu, S., Sabir, N., & Sari, A. R. (2018). Pushing toward a more personalized MOOC: Exploring instructor selected activities, resources, and technologies for MOOC design and implementation. *International Review of Research in Open and Distributed Learning, 19*(4), 92–115.

Breed, B., & Bailey, R. (2018). The influence of a metacognitive approach to cooperative pair problem-solving on self-direction in learning. *The Journal for Transdisciplinary Research in Southern Africa, 14*(1), 1–11.

Brockett, R. G., & Hiemstra, R. (2019). *Self-direction in adult learning: Perspectives on theory, research, and practice.* Routledge.

Brown, J. S., & Duguid, P. (2017). *The social life of information: Updated, with a new preface.* Harvard Business Review Press.

Connor, M., & Pokora, J. (2012). *Coaching and mentoring at work: Developing effective practice.* McGraw-Hill Education.

Deyzel, L., & Faris, L. (2010). The development of an online learning and collaboration space for postgraduate students. *New Voices in Psychology, 6*(2), 64–75.

Eby, L. T., Rhodes, J. E., & Allen, T. D. (2007). Definition and evolution of mentoring. In T. D. Allen & L. T. Eby (Eds.), *The Blackwell handbook of mentoring: A multiple perspectives approach* (pp. 7–20). Blackwell.

Ensher, E. A., Heun, C., & Blanchard, A. (2003). Online mentoring and computer-mediated communication: New directions in research. *Journal of Vocational Behavior, 63*(2), 264–288.

Foulds, S. (2003). Internet-based teacher development in the context of curricular change: A South African case study. *Education as Change, 7*(2), 46–68.

Garrison, D. R. (1992). Critical thinking and self-directed learning in adult education: An analysis of responsibility and control issues. *Adult Education Quarterly, 42*(3), 136–148.

Garrison, D. R. (2016). *E-learning in the 21st century: A community of inquiry framework for research and practice.* Routledge.

Garrison, D. R., Anderson, T., & Archer, W. (1999). Critical inquiry in a text-based environment: Computer conferencing in higher education. *The Internet and Higher Education, 2*(2–3), 87–105.

Garvey, B., Stokes, P., & Megginson, D. (2017). *Coaching and mentoring: Theory and practice.* Sage.

Gibbons, M. (2002). *The self-directed learning handbook: Challenging adolescent students to excel.* Jossey-Bass.

Griffin, K. A., Eury, J. L., Gaffney, M. E., York, T., Bennett, J., Cunningham, E., & Griffin, A. (2015). Digging deeper: Exploring the relationship between mentoring, developmental interactions, and student agency. *New Directions for Higher Education, 2015*(171), 13–22.

Hefetz, G., & Ben-Zvi, D. (2020). How do communities of practice transform their practices? *Learning, Culture and Social Interaction, 26,* 100410.

Henry, A., & Mackenzie, S. (2012). Brokering communities of practice: A model of knowledge exchange and academic-practitioner collaboration developed in the context of community policing. *Police Practice and Research, 13*(4), 315–328.

Herrington, A. (2013). *Rethinking education: Self-directed learning fits the digital age.* Retrieved December 10, 2020, from https://www.wired.com/insights/2013/12/rethinking-education-self-directed-learning-fits-the-digital-age/

Knowles, M. S. (1975). *Self-directed learning: A guide for learners and teachers.* Follett.

Kunaka, C., & Moos, M. N. (2019). Evaluating mentoring outcomes from the perspective of entrepreneurs and small business owners. *The Southern African Journal of Entrepreneurship and Small Business Management, 11*(1), 1–11.

Laverick, D. M. (2016). *Mentoring processes in higher education.* Springer.

Linnegar, J. (2015). Mentoring for text editors: Fit for purpose in the era of freelancing, more so than alternative development strategies. *Stellenbosch Papers in Linguistics, 44,* 81–103.

Loyens, S. M., Magda, J., & Rikers, R. M. (2008). Self-directed learning in problem-based learning and its relationships with self-regulated learning. *Educational Psychology Review, 20*(4), 411–427.

Marsh, P. (2017). Professional registration support mentoring and the emergence of the professional cyber-sage. *Civil Engineering, 2017*(v25i1), 55–58.

McGuire, C. M., Yakubu, K., Ayisi-Boateng, N. K., Motlhatlhedi, K., Ameh, P., Fatusin, B. B., Makwero, M., & Jenkins, L. S. (2020). Exploring gaps, strategies and solutions for primary care research mentorship in the African context: A workshop report. *African Journal of Primary Health Care & Family Medicine, 12*(1), a2320. https://doi.org/10.4102/phcfm.v12i1.2320

Mentz, E., & Van Zyl, S. (2018). The impact of cooperative learning on self-directed learning abilities in the computer applications technology class. *International Journal of Lifelong Education, 37*(4), 482–494. https://doi.org/10.1080/02601370.2018.1513426

Merriam, S. B., & Bierema, L. L. (2014). *Adult learning: Linking theory and practice.* Jossey-Bass.

Morris, T. H. (2019). Self-directed learning: A fundamental competence in a rapidly changing world. *International Review of Education, 65*(4), 633–653.

Ndlela, N. T., & Brysiewicz, P. (2018). Students' perceptions of student support services at a nursing campus. *Africa Journal of Nursing and Midwifery, 20*(2), 1–14.

Olivier, J. (2020). Situated and culturally appropriate self-directed multimodal learning. In J. Olivier (Ed.), *Self-directed multimodal learning in higher education* (pp. 235–284). AOSIS.

Parsloe, E., & Leedham, M. (2009). *Coaching and mentoring: Practical conversations to improve learning.* Kogan Page Publishers.

Pask, R., & Joy, B. (2007). *Mentoring-coaching: A guide for education professionals.* McGraw-Hill Education.

Rickard, K. (2004). E-mentoring and pedagogy: A useful nexus for evaluating online mentoring programs for small business? *Mentoring & Tutoring: Partnership in Learning, 12*(3), 383–401.

Saks, K., & Leijen, Ä. (2014). Distinguishing self-directed and self-regulated learning and measuring them in the e-learning context. *Procedia-Social and Behavioral Sciences, 112,* 190–198.

Smith, P. J. W., Garden, O. J., Wigmore, S. J., Borgstein, E., & Dewhurst, D. (2018). The effectiveness of an online, distance-learning Master's in Surgical Sciences programme in Malawi. *African Journal of Health Professions Education, 10*(3), 159–165.

Takavarasha, S., Cilliers, L., & Chinyamurindi, W. (2018). Navigating the unbeaten track from digital literacy to digital citizenship: A case of university students in South Africa's Eastern Cape province. *Reading & Writing, 9*(1), 1–15.

Van Staden, C. (2018). WhatsApp? Die ontwikkeling van 'n positief-interafhanklike e-praktyknetwerk tydens die samestelling van e-portefeuljes in afstandhoëronderwys. *Litnet Akademies, 15*(2), 350–396.

Wenger, E. (1999). *Communities of practice: Learning, meaning, and identity.* Cambridge University Press.

Wilder, H., Ferris, S. P., & An, H. (2010). Exploring international multicultural field experiences in educational technology. *Multicultural Education & Technology Journal, 4*(1), 30–42.

Wolff, M., Stojan, J., Buckler, S., Cranford, J., Whitman, L., Gruppen, L., & Santen, S. (2020). Coaching to improve self-directed learning. *The Clinical Teacher, 17*(4), 408–412.

Zimmerman, B. J., & Lebeau, R. B. (2000). A commentary on self-directed learning. In D. Evensen & C. E. Hmelo (Eds.), *Problem-based learning: A research perspective on learning interactions* (pp. 299–313). Erlbaum.

Jako Olivier is the holder of the UNESCO Chair in Multimodal Learning and Open Educational Resources and is a professor of Multimodal Learning in the Faculty of Education at North-West University. His research, within the Research Unit Self-Directed Learning, focuses on self-directed multimodal learning, open educational resources, multiliteracies, blended and e-learning in language classrooms as well as multilingualism in education. He currently holds a Y rating from the National Research Foundation and was awarded the Education Association of South Africa's Emerging Researcher Medal in 2018. In addition to recently editing a book on self-directed multimodal learning, he has published numerous articles and book chapters at the national and international levels, and he also acts as a supervisor for postgraduate students.

Shikha Trivedi area of specialisation is family relations and early childhood. She pioneered the Department of Early Childhood at BA ISAGO University and is currently a lecturer at the Botswana Open University coordinating online teaching programmes. She has been involved in developing programmes for early childhood at various levels. She was involved in the adjudication exercise for the material selection for the Ministry of Basic Education. She was a member of a UNICEF consultancy to analyse the impact of the Reception Class Programme in Botswana. She has published in peer-reviewed journals and her area of research interest are emergent literacy, child and family relation, and child advocacy.

Chapter 6
Open Education and Self-directed Learning in Adult, Professional and Vocational Education in Africa

Elock Emvula Shikalepo and Aletta Mweneni Hautemo

Abstract Open education and self-directed learning are increasingly becoming the preferred modes of learning worldwide. The Fourth Industrial Revolution requires flexible learning opportunities for adults and professionals intending to access life-long educational opportunities. Open education and self-directed learning also suit technical and vocational fields, where the modes are not gaining momentum owing to the practical nature of the field. Despite the significance of self-directed learning, the mode is not fully embraced in fostering lifelong learning opportunities due to adherence to traditional ways of learning. Yet, traditional ways of learning are not compatible with current learning dispensation. This chapter discusses the application of self-directed learning in adult, professional and vocational education settings from an African perspective. A systematic desktop review of existing literature findings related to self-directed learning in Africa underpins the discussions, revolving around thematic areas for the multiple facets related to self-directed learning on the African continent. The chapter motivates the necessity of self-directed learning in Africa, by modelling how African education institutions can capitalise on self-directed learning for course delivery.

Keywords Open education · Self-directed learning · Life-long learning · Adult education · Vocational education and training

6.1 Introduction

The advent of advanced technology demands educators and students to become proficient in the application of various technologies to teaching and learning. As technologies provide opportunities for students to learn on their own, the concept of "self-directed learning" comes into being (Malison, 2018). Self-directed learning is a process in which a student takes initiative, with or without the help of others, in

E. E. Shikalepo (✉) · A. M. Hautemo
Namibia University of Science and Technology, Windhoek, Namibia

A. M. Hautemo
e-mail: alettanghelo@gmail.com

diagnosing their learning needs, formulating learning goals, identifying human and material resources for learning, choosing and implementing appropriate learning strategies and evaluating mastery of learning outcomes (Jossberger et al., 2010). The process involves a multiplicity of learning activities directed by students themselves. Brookfield (2009) defines self-directed learning as a system of learning in which the conceptualisation, design, conduct and evaluation of a learning process are directed by the students. The instructional method requires an individual to plan their learning activities, implement them and evaluate own progress in mastering learning outcomes.

Self-directed learning does not necessarily imply that learning is individualised and happens in isolation, but the practice implies that students learn on their own, by directing their learning, alongside engaging in group learning settings with their peers and tutors for expert guidance. Garrison (1997) asserts the phrase "self-directed learning" raises both social and cognitive issues, namely self-direction and self-learning, respectively. Students are subjected to self-management of the learning tasks by taking own responsibility to manage and satisfy learning outcomes with minimum guidance from teachers.

Self-directed learning is not only necessitated by technological innovation, but the practice is also necessitated by numerous professional and occupational challenges as highlighted below (Tripon, 2015):

(a)   The number of adults whether unemployed or employed continues to increase in higher education institutions, requiring higher education institutions to design appropriate educational strategies to contain the increasing number of adult students, in addition to students admitted from high schools.

(b)   Limited funding experienced by institutions of higher learning prompted institutions to find new conduits of transmitting knowledge efficiently.

(c)   Requests by the community for educational institutions to design efficient course delivery methods for students of different categories.

(d)   Dynamism of the labour market and the increasing number of responsibilities related to management skills and employment, requiring people to be able to learn on their own and from their own experience and setting, with minimum guidance from institutions.

Self-directed learning is thus a necessity that should be embraced by institutions to cater for the learning needs of all students admitted, regardless of their social or professional characteristics.

6.2   Overview of Self-directed Learning in Africa

Self-directed learning is an emerging practice, especially in African literature. Learning in Africa has been conducted through traditional classroom attendance presided over by teachers and lecturers. The inclination of African education systems to traditional ways of teaching and learning can be attributed to shortcomings related to technological advancement and human resource capabilities to effectively inno-vate and apply innovation in their teaching and learning processes. As a new concept in Africa, self-directed learning is enabled by technological innovations and the adoption of open and lifelong learning (ODL) on the continent. As population of Africa continues to increase rapidly, so does the admission in educational institu-tions. Consequently, the capacity of the available educational institutions is insuf-ficient to accommodate increasing admission rates, comprising of adult population and learners from high schools (Musingafi et al., 2015). In addition to inadequate infrastructures, the human resource capacity in the existing institution is unable to provide the required teaching and learning to increased enrolment rates. Hence, a need for African educational authorities to embrace new conduits of transmitting knowledge to students at existing educational institutions, as the growing student enrolment figure can no longer be satisfied using traditional means of instruction.

Self-directed learning can help educational institutions in Africa to confront the challenges related to course delivery, as these challenges relate to limited infrastruc-tures, shortage of human resource capacity, limited funding and limited instructional resources. A high percentages of the African adult population and other profes-sionals have taken up studying through open and lifelong learning programmes to keep abreast with knowledge systems and remain competitive in the labour market. Besides, considerable enrolment figures have been recorded in the field of technical, vocational education and training fields, which figures have outnumbered the avail-able vocational institutions and manpower. These trends require African institutions to embrace self-directed learning as a method of instruction.

6.3   Theoretical Perspective

Two common theories underpinning self-directed are explained next.

6.3.1   Andragogy

Knowles (1980) is accredited for having popularised the theory of andragogy, as the art and science of helping adults learn. The theory acknowledges that adults cannot learn in the same way as learners in schools due to their differentiated roles and responsibilities. This acknowledgement birthed a theory of learning that considers adults' typical characteristics and occupational requirements in the provisioning of education.

Andragogy is made up of the following key learning assumptions (TEAL Centre Staff, 2011):

1. Adults consider themselves independent and capable of being in charge of their own learning. Being an adult means maturity to direct own learning needs with minimal guidance.
2. Adult learners have accumulated a wealth of experiences over a period of time. The experiences are significant as students can draw insights from their previous experiences to better inform their current learning. Prior learning experiences justify parents to direct own learning as their prior experiences can serve as guiding posts.
3. Adults have differentiated roles which often compromise with their learning schedules. The different roles require an adult-tailored learning model that allows adults to learn whenever and wherever they are, and regardless of their social roles.
4. Adults are problem-centred in their roles. Adult try to fix problems in their setting. Learning should allow adults to acquire practical solutions that they can implement to resolve problems and achieve immediate results. Traditional learning models focus more on the acquisition of knowledge by learners, which knowledge learners can apply to other contexts once they have left schools. This is, however, not the same with adults as they are already in problem-laden settings and need learning methods that allow them to learn solutions and apply them instantly to solve problems.

Even though andragogy seeks to promote the learning interests of adult learners, the theory has attracted criticism. Brookfield (2009) called the theory "culture blind," arguing that the theory of andragogy could undermine the traditional view of learning that regards teachers as experts who should direct learning and not students themselves. Some cultural values and positivists regard teachers as custodians of learning and should be responsible for learning activities regarding the age of their students. However, this criticism may not be applicable to current practices where curriculum and instructions have shifted from teacher-centred to learner-centred education, making it possible for students to direct their own learning with minimum facilitation from teachers. It becomes clear that andragogy offers convenience to adults. The theory is considerate of adults' differentiated roles, which consideration would have been difficult to achieve if adults were to learn through traditional ways of instruction.

6.3.2   Transformational Learning

Transformative learning is often described as learning that changes the way individuals think about themselves and their world (TEAL Centre Staff, 2011). It is a learning framework that transforms learning from being conducted in traditional ways to modern ways. Freire (2000) regards transformational learning as an emancipating type of learning. It emancipates students from learning within the confines of the classrooms to learning independently in their own settings and convenience. Mezirow

(2000) regards transformational learning as a rational process, where students reflect and discuss their assumptions about the world around them.

For transformative learning to take place, educators should consider the following aspects to in facilitating self-directed learning to adults (TEAL Centre Staff, 2011):

1. Educators should create a climate that supports transformative learning. Taylor (2000, p. 313) suggests that educators need to be "trusting, empathetic, caring, authentic, sincere and demonstrative of high integrity". Educators need to provide students with immediate and helpful feedback, employ activities that promote student autonomy, participation and collaboration, thereby helping them to explore alternative views and engage in problem-solving and critical reflection (Taylor, 1998).

2. Educators should know the characteristics of their students and their learning styles to design appropriate assessment activities for their students as a way of assisting them to master their self-directed learning outcomes. Some students are logical in their learning and would appreciate critical debates and scenario questions, whereas some students enjoy learning in groups and experiments (Cranton, 2002).

3. Educators should provide students with learning activities that promote self-reflection. As students direct own learning, they need to reflect on their own learning to establish how well they are progressing. An educator can give students activities that require them to make personal reflections about learning (Cranton, 2002). Critical reflections help to establish good learning practices and fill any gaps that may be present in the self-directed learning process.

Transformational learning is criticised for not considering the individual's race, class, gender or the historical context in which learning occurs (Corley & Tinker, 2003; Sheared et al., 2010). The theory has also been criticised as hyper-rational, ignoring feelings, relationships, context and culture of the individual involved in learning (Silver-Pacuilla, 2003). Despite the criticism, transformational learning is relevant to self-directed learning because it enables students to transform their thinking capacity and learning patterns from the traditional way of learning such as physical classroom attendance under teacher's guidance, to contemporary ways of learning such as self-directed learning, where students are in charge of their own learning.

6.4 Significance of Self-directed Learning

Self-directed learning is beneficial for various reasons, including the following:

1. Students can structure their own study programmes according to their work or personal schedule. Students are not compelled to classroom teaching as is the case with the traditional way of teaching. Instead, all students require is the course outcomes and a list of possible study materials useful for attaining course

outcomes, and students make their own time to study and meet expectations without traditional classroom bureaucracies. Authors have discovered that once people start seeing themselves as adults, they develop expectations of being independent in decision-making (Jossberger et al., 2010).

2. Self-directed learning requires students to access and read different materials for scholarly inquiry and a deepened understanding of course content. Reading different materials comes with an enriched understanding of the course content as absorbed from multiple sources, which understanding would not have been attained if students were confined to classroom teaching under teachers' guidance. Self-directed learning broadens students' understanding of course content as students learn various content from different sources (Blaschke, 2014).

3. Self-directed learning does not mean that learning is exclusively self-oriented. Students can interact with each other for guidance about course content. Such a working relationship culminates in a network of learning and intellectual formations lasting for a longer period even after the academic programme is completed.

4. Self-directed learning is necessitated by a shortage of resources in their multiplicity, both on the students' side and at the institutions' side. Adults would have travelled long distances to attend lessons at institutions, incurring multiple costs in the process. The convenience that comes with self-directed learning includes the benefit of having to cut costs related to travelling for school attendance. As institutions, self-directed learning cuts the costs related to the provision of operational expenses. Students studying on their own can use own internet and other instructional resources and technologies, saving institutions from incurring exorbitant expenses.

It becomes evident that self-directed learning is crucial, requiring adults, professional and vocational students to embrace the practice as an emerging learning mode in Africa.

6.5   Methodology

The chapter contains empirical evidence related to open and self-directed learning on the African continent. A desktop review was carried out to identify key trends and prospects related to open and self-directed learning in Africa. Desktop review involves reviewing available findings of previous studies and accessing different data sources to retrieve information relevant to the subject of current focus. The empirical content of multiple facets as contained in this chapter was mainly collected through a desktop review of literature evidence by prior researchers, as well as reviewing recent accounts of experiences of students who completed studies through self-directed mode. Existing related literature evidence by authors who have published about open and self-directed learning were reviewed and provided insights about current trends of open and self-directed learning in Africa. The documents that were reviewed relate to the reflections made by students who completed learning programmes offered through self-directed mode at African institutions. The documents were reviewed, and the findings were analysed and used to justify the discussion, and as case studies demonstrating current developments of self-directed learning on the Africa continent.

The experiences presented as case studies have been captured with pseudonyms to protect the sources. In addition, a range of additional sources of information including scientific reports and policy briefs were also reviewed for enriched data gathering. Reviewing multiple sources of information was useful in minimising bias by cross-checking between case studies and literature evidence of informants from different open and lifelong learning institutions. The collation of all the findings from the multiple sources as reviewed enabled a richer thematic presentation of content and case studies for increased understanding of the multiple facets of open and self-directed learning in Africa.

6.6 Trends of Self-directed Learning in Africa: Case Studies

This section discusses the current developments in the implementation of self-directed learning in the provision of adult, professional and vocational education in African context. The discussion starts with the prevalent nature of Open and Distance Education (ODL) in the adult and professional education sector and its roles in the effective integration of self-directed learning. The section ends with a detailed discussion on the provision of self-directed learning in the vocational education and training (VET) sector. The section includes case studies drawn from students' experiences in the programmes delivered through self-directed methodologies.

6.6.1 Self-directed Learning in Adult and Professional Education

The higher education landscape has changed significantly over the years due to the impact of innovation and the embracing of online learning technologies. Mitchell (2015) states that the notion that education is a human right has led to concerted efforts to bring equitable education closer to the people in this global village. The notion has led to the adoption of the concepts of, firstly, "open education", which is described as "an educational policy that states that no one is denied access to an open educational program" (Bates, 2015, p. 341) and secondly, "open schooling", which is described as "the physical separation of school-level learners from the teacher" through an open system which does not consider age, prerequisite, economic status, educational background (Mitchell, 2015, p. 69). Open schooling is being embraced in Africa whereby national institutions such as Botswana Open University

(BOU), University of South Africa (UNISA) and Namibian College of Open Learning (NAMCOL) are fostering the adoption of "openness", in their tertiary education level programmes. According to Mitchell (2015), the word "openness" is used in distance education to refer to the application of freedom and rights to learn, by providing students with the freedom of choice and autonomy to control what and how to learn it. Openness gives students a chance to learn in a self-directed manner, which increased demands for higher education qualifications, address the provision of skills for employment to the employed and cater learning needs for students who are willing to study independently. The adoption of open schooling can assist African educational institutions to contain infrastructural challenges that are threatening course content delivery.

The next section exemplifies the application of self-directed learning in professional education.

The Case Study of Namibian College of Open Learning

Open and Distance Learning (ODL) institutions continue to embrace lifelong learning by introducing online and technology-enhanced learning programmes. In Namibia, the Namibian College of Open Learning (NAMCOL) in coalition with the Commonwealth of Learning (COL) has introduced the Post-graduate Diploma in Open School Operation and Management (PDOSOM) in 2018. The main purpose of this fully fledged online programme is to prepare administrators, support staff and faculty to effectively plan and manage the day-to-day operations of an open school using various delivery technologies and pedagogical methods (Hautemo & Uunona, 2018).

The PDOSOM is a two-year post-graduate programme pitched at NQF Level 8, developed for ODL practitioners. The PDOSOM students were asked to reflect on how the institution and structure of the programme assisted them to become self-directed learners and also to reflect on the challenges of the programmes. Participants stressed the importance of developing autonomy and ownership of student's own learning by studying through self-directed mode. Students cited self-disciplined as requirement for identifying their own learning goals, monitoring the learning process and deciding the pace of learning. Students commended on the facilitator's role in guiding students throughout the learning process, in addition to the flexibility of working on a Moodle platform. Below is one of the reflections.

VA—Aged 50—Distance Education Coordinator

The institution and programme assisted me to become a self-directed student in two ways. Firstly, the programme was accessible on the Moodle Platform. As a result, I was able to log onto the platform and review notes. I was able to decide when to go through the study materials, as long as I met deadlines set for activities. With each module, I had a facilitator who provided guidance although I retained ownership of learning. Secondly, the programme was designed in such a way that it required me as a student to apply theory to practice. I work in the ODL environment, and most of the concepts were fairly new to me because

I don't have a formal qualification in Open and Distance Learning. However, they were very much related to the type of work I do. The activities of the programme allowed me to freely respond based on my personal experience.

The structure of the course motivates students to learn in a self-directed manner. This means that the structure of an online learning course needs to be designed in a way that the content is divided into manageable chunks that students can do on weekly basis. The learning content should be facilitated through relevant pedagogies which are interactive, to fill the gap between the students and the lecturers. Collaborative activities should be promoted through online group works, e-portfolio reflections, peer reviews and wikis that allow collaborative writing and reflections on the course work. Self-directed learning needs to be fostered right from the beginning of the course whereby students should be provided with sufficient information, course orientation and training on the learning strategies and assessment expectation.

Next is another reflection from one of the participants in the PDOSOM programme:

TN—Age 29—VE Standards Coordinator

The orientation resources were provided, that directed me on how to navigate the Moodle page, and this includes; where to find the readings, assignment, and feedback forms and how to interact with the tutor and peers. The programme was designed in a way that it was flexible, it allowed students to submit work if they missed the set due dates. It was a challenge to study because one needs to balance between work and school, time was not enough for a person to understand the content before submitting the assignment. Assignment due dates for different modules were set close to each other, which made it difficult for intensive research. Lack of access to technologies and failing internet connectivity were some of the challenges that delayed submission of assessment activities on time.

To enable students to learn in a self-directed manner, the outcomes for courses should be SMART (Specific, Measurable, Attainable, Reliable and Time-bound) for effectiveness (Muñoz & Jojoa, 2014). This enables the students to connect easily with the content presented and assessment criteria which encourages them to do proper research and submit well-written assignments. The course activities and assignments should be time-bound, whereby a proper module schedule is presented outlining the expectations and the time period of task completion. Read the reflection below in this respect:

LN—36 Years Old—Community Liaison Officer

The PDOSOM is a course I took online for the first time. NAMCOL helped me to be self-directed. It has provided me with all the modules that I needed to study, links that directed me to further readings, and an Online instructor for guidance. Course development and design is very SMART and is always rejuvenate me to quest for more learning, it seems to me that there is always a voice of hope in the design which says "come on" and activities such as discussion has always created a room of learning from others and opportunity to teach others too. The biggest challenge I experienced was the time which was not always enough, and the other thing was the nature of my employment which required me to work in far deep remote areas, this led me to come to my study too late and it has contributed to poor results sometimes. Another challenge was the poor network reception. To assist students who are 100% fully online should be provided with portable learning devices with certain limited free data.

Time constraints and lack of Internet facilities remain the biggest challenge against self-directed learning in a professional education online programme. Students who are employed on a full-time basis can become overwhelmed with striking a balance between work, studies and life commitments. Institutions should create opportunities for self-managing, self-monitoring and self-modifying in the course structure. On lack of Internet infrastructure, another PDOSOM student reflected:

SE—46—Adult and Distance Education Officer

NAMCOL as an institution has assisted me to be a self-directed student as I have just studied with my own time and at my own pace. The programme has assisted me as it was designed in the manner that it has no specific hour during the day in which to start classes. The nature of my work as a full-time employee was not compatible with my studies as there was no public network connectivity where I can access internet to study at work. Limited technologies such as laptops also posed threat to my study. I want to advise NAMCOL as an ODL institution to come up with different registration packages inclusive of a computer and internet devices such as pocket Wi-Fi.

Openness provides students with an opportunity to have access to courses with a global concepts of open educational resources (OERs), open textbooks, conduct open research, and use open data. Openness brings flexibility which helps students to learn what they want, how they want to learn and where they want to learn it. The provision of the e-learning platform is essential to the removal of barriers towards access to adult and professional educational programmes.

The next section discusses the roles and application of self-directed learning in the vocational education and training (VET) sector.

6.6.2   Self-directed Learning in VET

This section discusses the background of VET in general, then proceeds to deliberate the models for self-directed learning and assessment in VET. Moreover, the section debates cognitive apprenticeship as a model for integrating self-directed learning and its applicability in the sector.

6.6.2.1   Background of VET in Africa

Vocational education and training has faced challenges more than any other educational system in Africa. One of the main challenges had been the perception that it is the last minute stop centre for students who could not make it to the universities. According to Shindi (2017), VET programmes in Africa are viewed as "a carrier path for those who do not qualify to go to universities", and thus they are often offered admissions at vocational training centres. Further, Subasubani (2017) observed that the VET sector in Africa specifically in Namibia is faced with problems of attitude and lack of technical skills. Another reality observed on the ground were the lack of work placements and a lack of access to centralised workshops at training centres. Lack of financial resources to roll out technological programmes and procure resources to the vocational centres threatens students' learning and self-development in the Fourth Industrial Revolution (4IR). This trend demands a shift of the pedagogical approaches in VET, to pedagogies that provide enough pre- and in-service training opportunities and self-directed learning to facilitate a smooth transition into the employment terrain.

VET has seen an emergence of new innovative learning paradigm shifts over the recent years. In Africa, the VET sector in countries like Namibia, Kenya, Uganda, South Africa and Ghana, has widely adopted the use of the competency-based education (CBE) paradigm in their vocational training mainstreams. The CBE model offers an opportunity for VET students to access training through the Recognition of Prior Learning (RPL) and the provision of industry-linkage training. Afunde (2010) postulates that RPL widens capacity to provide access to training and education for adults and youth who were historically disadvantaged. The RPL programme is a beneficial approach to most developing countries especially in Africa, which are looking at growing their economies by investing in training which is located within the workplace environment and offered through a decentralised competency-based assessment system (Said, 2018).

6.6.2.2 Self-directed Learning Through CBE Model

The CBE model was first introduced by Wesselink et al. (2007) to define the competencies relevant to the vocational courses by organising and redesigning units for learning and assessment. One of its tenets is to introduce authentic learning activities that enable students to take the autonomy of their learning. Said (2018, p. 47) asserts that authentic learning is considered to be effective in VET because the "assignments given to students are taken from vocational practice". Trainees are provided with an opportunity for flexible learning in which they can adjust their learning according to their own needs. Wesselink et al. (2007) believed that through CBE, vocational education trainees are given a chance to reflect on their learning which is seen as a basis for lifelong learning attitude for the students.

Self-reflection on learning equates well to self-directed, as prevalent in adult education (Knowles, 1975) and self-regulated learning as used in educational psychology (Zimmerman, 2013). Therefore, self-directed learning is applicable in all learning situations and contexts in which students find themselves, be it in higher education, adult education and/or vocational education. In this section, the focus is on the applicability of self-directed learning in vocational education and training.

It is imperative to unpack the roles of self-directed learning on VET and discuss how it can be fostered in the vocational education settings. According to Knowles (1975, p. 17), the central focus of self-directed learning is on the "ability for a human being to learn on his or her own". Knowles (1975) suggested that through self-directed learning, students are involved in a process where they plan for conducting and reviewing own learning. Garrison (1997, pp. 23–26) explained that self-directed learning can be promoted through the motivation of students to initiate a task, take responsibility for own learning, address metacognitive and cognitive learning development processes and self-manage. Students need to develop a sense of self-control, which is often realised through collaboration with teachers, mentors and peers. This means that self-directed learning is still facilitated in a formal setting to set up enabling learning conditions that enhance the achievement of learning objectives.

Rogers (1969) cited in Morris (2018a) explicated three learning conditions that are effective for self-directed learning, which applies to the VET sector. These are:

1. The importance of the educators to set the initial mood or climate of learning experience for the students;
2. Enabling the collaborative setting of learning objectives with learners;
3. Providing access to a range of resources for learning, including availing themselves as resources;
4. Working toward a share of control of achieving the learning objective without imposing learning on students.

These conditions portray self-directed learning as a collaborative effort between the institution and students. Tan (2017, p. 250) maintains that self-directed learning is a "shared moral vision between the individual (the learner) and the collective (the learning community)". Therefore, students need to appreciate self-directed learning to develop internal motivation and the urge to compete and succeed in their training.

VET trainees need to develop the ability to associate with fellow trainees in their community of practice so that they can transform themselves into cognitive apprentices. This then turns TVET trainees into skilful learners who possess a great intrinsic interest in their learning and exhibit greater self-efficacy that they are motivated from within to persist through challenges (Müller & Seufert, 2018).

6.6.2.3 Cognitive Apprenticeships as a Model for Self-regulated Learning in TVET

Cognitive apprenticeship is a model introduced through the situated learning theory (Collins et al., 1990; Lave, 1988; Lave & Wenger, 1991). Situated learning theory focuses on creating a learning context that reflects on the application of knowledge in everyday situation, encompassed by physical, social and cultural environmental aspects and communication with peers (Hautemo & Dalvit, 2016). Situated learning enables the use of cognitive apprenticeship model which is designed to acculturate students into authentic practices by practitioners in their everyday work (Collins et al., 1990). In the case of VET in Namibia, student apprentices are linked to industries through an apprenticeship programme agreements between the training institutions and the employers with a purpose of mentoring and inducting the trainees to workplace learning, so that trainees become employable at the end of their training period. According to Lave (1988, p. 25), through apprenticeship, the novice can interact, think, act and interact with a more knowledgeable peer or expert who assists him/her to be a member of that community of practice. Although Lave and Wenger (1991) argue that learning through cognitive apprenticeship is a social activity rather than an individual phenomenon, it is this learning that develops a student to become an individual part of that community of practice, who can develop and use their metacognitive knowledge to contribute equally in a self-directed manner towards the full participation and success of the community.

The following case study deliberates the apprenticeship programme in the VET sector in Namibia.

Case Study: Apprenticeship Programme at the Namibia Training Authority (NTA)
The development of knowledge, skills and attitudes has been a critical factor in theory development for VET. As such, vocational education and training (VET) is considered as an education that ought to develop autonomous students to become employable and entrepreneurs. In Southern Africa, countries like Namibia have observed a drastic need for an effective relationship between industries and training institutions (Subasubani, 2017). This need led to the formation of the Namibia Training Authority (NTA) which is mandated to facilitate effective regulation of the provision of VET in the country through a promulgated Vocational Education Training Act (Act 1 of 2008). This Act

empowers NTA, which serves as a linkage between the industry and the VET training institutions, to collect the vocational education and training levy (VET Levy), from industry to support the training of the student and reimburse money to empower the industry to procure enough equipment and tools that support on-job training. Since its implementation, NTA has introduced different programmes aimed at developing VET students into self-directed trainees, who are attached to the industry while still on-training to develop relevant and appropriate work-based skills. One of those is the apprenticeship programme introduced in 2014. The apprenticeship programme was defined by the Global Apprenticeship Network (GAN) in Namibia (2018, p. 2), as the "training programmes that combine vocational education with work-based learning for intermediate occupational skills and that are subjected to externally impose training standard". Through the apprenticeship programme, the trainees are attached to a company for the duration of their training in which a mentor is prepared on basic training to mentor the apprentice effectively.

In 2019, the NTA and the Bank of Namibia signed a Memorandum of Understanding (MoU) on the apprenticeship programme in which the national bank agreed to support trainees from the agriculture, tourism and Auto-mechanic fields for over three-years, by locating them within the companies or participating employers who will, induct, mentor and train trainees on-the-job training in the area of specialisation (The Namibia Newspaper, 28.03.2019). According to Jerry Beukes,

> Apprenticeship is a powerful vehicle for developing skills of potential employees and existing employees, improving production and profitability…it creates an ideal opportunity for employers to inculcate a work ethic, the right attitude and a productivity mindset, which cannot be easily acquired at a training institution. (Jerry Beukes, at the MOU signing between BON and NTA, 2019)

Since its inception, the NTA has gone into several MoUs with the industries focussing on apprenticeship programme that enables the VET trainees to receive workplace training opportunities which are supported, inducted and mentored by both the adopting employer and theoretically, by the training institution. This means that the trainees are allowed to use self-directed learning opportunities, by scheduling their learning at work and at the same time receive competency-based assessment opportunities.

Jossberger et al. (2017, p. 134) maintained that "VET is supposed to equip and empower young people with the knowledge and skills needed to learn and work autonomously to become employed in today's dynamically changing world". This is an indication that self-directed learning plays a significant role in VET in which training is deeply intertwined with and mediated by workplace practical training and interaction with people in the industry. Through this students are empowered to become actively involved in their work, by being reflective as they construct meaning and using materials and resources optimally to learn effectively.

Application of cognitive apprenticeship model in VET for self-directed learning

As seen in the case study of the Namibia Training Authority, the apprenticeship programme is offered as a three-way system that involved the trainee, the institution, and the industry (employer). According to Hartmann (2017, p. 105), "enterprises need workers to perform their work responsibly and self-directed since the tasks are complex and instructions cannot be given to every detail". To promote self-directed learning, training should be based on authentic contexts in which students are urged to use authentic tools. The VET institutions, the employee (including the mentor) and the trainee (who is the apprentice) need to develop a Community of Practice (CoP) (Lave & Wenger, 1991) in which multiple perspectives on the learning matter are shared and expert assistance and scaffolding are offered to the trainee.

There should also be collaboration among the parts concerned in which articulation of skill and reflection on learning needs to take place on both the side of the learner and the mentor.

Cognitive apprenticeship should be used to assist the students to become self-directed. This can be done in three ways as depicted by Fig. 6.1.

The three concepts are interlinked in a way that they provide broader access to an authentic learning environment that is collaborative. This allows the mentor to use concepts that resemble the real-life tools and artefacts used in the industry to induct the trainee to practical training. This in turn assists the trainee to become self-directed and self-regulated in ensuring that they develop the ability to record, use and reflect on the knowledge gained during the apprenticeship period and can apply theory into practice. The experts can demonstrate certain skills applicable to their job by scaffolding and modifying learning to fit the context and the background theoretical knowledge of the students. In training the apprentice, the mentor begins by modelling the expert-like strategies on how the task should be performed, through scaffolding to give hints that encourage the trainee to move a step ahead or to proceed to the next step until they can perform the task independently.

Fig. 6.1 Application of self-directed learning through cognitive apprenticeship

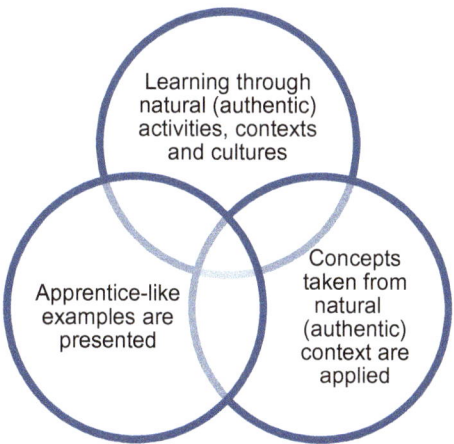

According to Bockarie (2002), the mentoring process is considered to be an interpersonal process by which a senior person assists a junior to learn new skills in a trusted manner. The scaffolding process may also lead to coaching which is often directed by the employee deficiencies, and it involves one-on-one guidance and instruction to improve the knowledge, skills and work performance of the apprentice (ibid.). The fading process enables the trainee to take ownership and autonomy of the work and in a way becomes self-directed by adapting to the work with little or no assistance. After developing self-control over the task, the trainee should be able to evaluate learning by discussing and making relations and references to realise—thereby generalising facts. This process is illustrated by Fig. 6.2.

By offering gradual support to the trainees, the trainees become more articulate in developing their competencies and in a long run develop self-reflective abilities that enable them to become self-directed in performing the task, as they have developed the ability to relate and refer to what happened in real life. According to De Bruijn and Leeman (2011, p. 695), cognitive apprenticeship stresses "both learnings to perform in practice and going beyond the learning context to acquire understanding, metacognitive skills, and flexibility". Thus, the five elements of cognitive apprenticeship presented in Fig. 6.2 assist VET trainees who learn through competency-based education (CBE) to become active and reflective thinkers. When trainees learn to reflect on their learning, they become innovative as they can think critically and

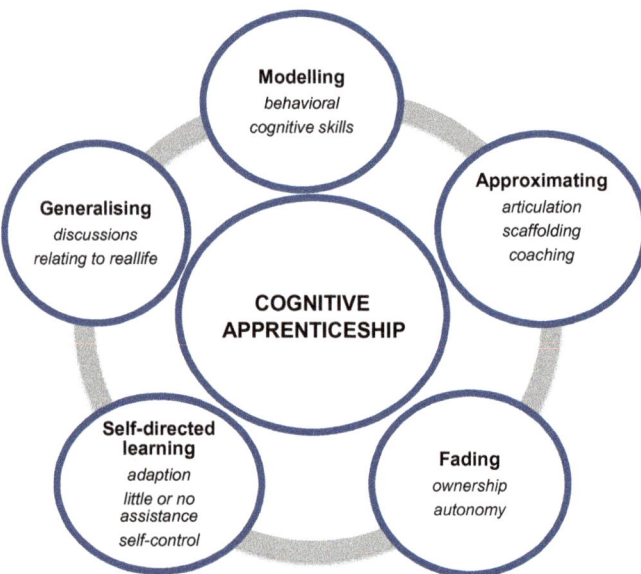

Fig. 6.2 Cognitive apprenticeship model for self-directed learning. *Source* Hautemo and Dalvit (2016, p. 60)

experiment with different ways to produce different solutions. Students can articulate new knowledge and skills that can be used to execute the tasks effectively during the assessment and evaluation of learning.

6.7 Challenges for Self-directed Learning in Adult, Professional and Vocational Education

Self-directed learning is faced by numerous challenges. Knowing the challenges enables educators and students to design better interventions for dealing with them and ensure that successful self-directed learning takes place. The common limitations relate to the one described below:

1. Due to a limited understanding of the concept, students have not yet recognised that self-directed learning requires them to depend on their abilities and create learning opportunities independently, concerning what to learn and how to learn it. To deal with these challenges, students should have better insight into their learning processes so that they can plan, monitor and evaluate their learning performance (Ericsson, 2006; Kicken et al., 2008). Self-directed learning method requires students to take primary responsibility of being in charge of their learning with minimal external support and not many students are prepared for this responsibility.

2. Self-directed learning does not imply that learning is entirely upon the students to make sure that it does happen, but assistance is required to enable students to direct their learning. Much-needed support from teachers is required to guide students in diagnosing their learning needs, formulating realistic goals and implementing their learning activities (Timmins, 2008). As seen in the case studies, self-directed learning has become a challenge to many students due to limited administrative and academic support provisions. Limited communication between students and lecturers, clarity of assessment instructions, timing and scheduling of assessment activities are some of the areas that self-directed students require much-needed assistance.

3. Planning learning resources is very important to self-directed students and requires both the institution and the students to trace appropriate instructional resources from which to study relevant information to satisfy their learning needs. Resources related to reading materials and digital literature are often not available or difficult to access. Students need Internet connectivity to search for learning resources with useful information about their learning needs. Without internet connectivity, the self-directed learning capabilities of students are inhibited.

6.8 Prospects of Self-directed Learning in VET

Notwithstanding the challenges associated with the provision of self-directed learning, the hopes of realising a functional self-directed learning are promising, depending on how well African countries attend to the essentials. To facilitate self-directed learning, holistic strategies are proposed.

1. According to Filipatali (2013), ICT provides powerful tools to support cognitive apprenticeships and enable students to share online information and suggestions to enhance collaborative teaching and learning. This can be done through the use of open educational resources (OERs) that enable training institutions to curb the lack of materials. OERs have gained momentum in education sector, in which teachers and students could acquire learning materials freely. By using OERs, the training institution could use the enabling didactics that allows facilitators and industry mentors to assist their students to develop the autonomy to plan, undertake and evaluate their learning, independently (Arnold, 2017; Morris, 2018b). In giving them autonomy, students can be oriented on the use of OERs and how to adopt, reuse and redistribute them effective learning.

2. Jossberger et al. (2017) proposed the use of simulations for practical training and assessment. The use of simulation is increasingly gaining appreciation in the Fourth Industrial Revolution whereby technical institutions are encouraged to use artificial intelligence (AI) and augmented reality (AR) programmes to authentic activities and materials to reality. This allows lifelong learners to access learning on their electronic devices wherever they are, be it at the workplace or home and partake in practical assessment activities without actually coming to the training centre. This gives a chance to the training institutions to easily move away from theoretical domain-specific knowledge offered at the institutions to the domain-specific practical transfer of knowledge and skills that students can acquire through a self-directed process. Simulations enable educational institutions to keep abreast of newly development that correspond with those in the industry.

3. The introduction of the Learning Management Systems (LMS) was made to facilitate learning. Currently, in countries like Namibia and Botswana, vocational training institutions are not offering fully fledged VET courses online. The lack of provision of ICT infrastructures such as Internet connectivity at the training institutions in rural areas, lack of bandwidth and lack of technical support for quality system administration and to train students on online pedagogical skills threaten self-directed learning. These trends calls for the provision of hybrid or blended learning, which is the fusion of classical face to face and online learning experiences. This requires the redesigning and restructuring of learning activities to self-paced learning and live e-learning presentations. Availing these opportunities allows students the flexibility of access to learning, removing barriers caused by financial implications to procure instructional materials, and also access to well-designed programmes and online packages. Through LMS, students could easily organise their training records in

the e-portfolios and share ideas with peers and trainers. The e-portfolios can also be used to share videos of practical experiences with the class group and instructors, and it can also be used as an assessment or grading tool.

4. There is a need for an e-apprenticeship model to be developed. The preliminary findings of the literature study on the background revealed the lack of industry-linkage opportunities and support to both the VET training centre and the trainees. This is also influenced by the fact that Africa's economy is still very low, hence lack big industries with advanced technological equipment and tools. E-apprenticeship gives opportunities for the VET trainees to use technological tools to facilitate practical training, which is linked to the newly innovated ideas only available to industrialised nations.

For all these opportunities to be realised, the professional and vocational education institutions need to enforce capacity-building opportunities for the facilitators and trainers/instructors to strengthen their level of understanding, application and integration of self-directed learning.

6.9 Requirements for Successful Integration of Self-directed Learning

In addition to the prospects discussed above, Cottrell (2017) asserts that an effective self-directed learning system is mainly determined by two determinants, the student and the course, in addition to teachers. The specific requirements in respect of each determinant as applicable in Namibian and any given ODL setting are discussed.

6.9.1 Student Requirements for Self-directed Learning

Different authors have summarised the characteristics of a skilful self-directed student, as related to the ability to learn at one's own pace, personal responsibility for the internal cognitive and motivational aspects of learning, independence, autonomy and the ability to control own affairs (Jossberger et al., 2010; Levett-Jones, 2005). The following characteristics are very essential to students if self-directed learning is to be realised effectively:

1. Self-directed learning requires students who can set realistic learning goals for themselves and manage their learning tasks efficiently and effectively. In the traditional way of teaching, it would have been the teacher's task to set the learning goals that should be attained by learners within a specific time frame. Self-directed learning requires the opposite of the traditional way of teaching and learning.

2. The process of mastering the learning goals should be monitored continuously as self-directed learning carries on. Students should be able to take on their assessment to test themselves how well they are mastering the learning outcomes. Traditionally, it would have been a teacher who sets up assessment activities and requires students to attempt them. With self-directed learning, students are in charge of their learning.

3. Self-directed learning makes the course outcomes available to students, and the tasks rest with the students to trace resources useful for mastering learning outcomes. Unlike in the traditional set-up where students are provided with study materials, self-directed learning requires students to search for relevant materials to fulfil the course outcomes.

4. There are various learning strategies such as case studies, summarising and experimenting, among others. Self-directed learning requires that each student maps out appropriate learning strategies that best suits them. Hence, self-directed learning requires students to map out learning strategies that best suit their learning needs and personal uniqueness.

5. Even though students are studying on their own and scheduling their study time, students should be very careful with how they manage their time, so that the available time is used meaningfully for studying and cover all the content that needed to be covered within the required time frame.

6. Self-directed learning requires that students should be able to make self-introspection about how they study to detect areas of improvement. Without self-reflection, students may not establish how effective their learning is, which may ultimately compromise the quality of self-directed learning.

6.9.2 Programme Requirements for Self-directed Learning

Courses that require to be studied through self-directed learning should cater for the following features:

1. The course outlines should be very clear in terms of expectations. By reading the course syllabi and course outline on their own, students should be able to notice with ease, trace and access useful materials for understanding the course outcomes.

2. Assignments given to students should be very clear and relevant to the course. Instructions should not be vague and ambiguous as they will confuse students, given the fact that students will attempt the assignment instructions in the absence of the teachers to clarify the questions and clear any vagueness.

3. Most of the students who endeavours to study through self-directed mode are adults who have multiple responsibilities. The scheduling of the assessment tasks should consider the tight schedule of the students and provide enough time for attempting the assignments and submitting them.

4. Even though students are studying on their own, effective academic and administrative support should be provided. Institutions should provide student support

officers to attend to students' inquiries. Besides, tutors should be provided to students so that students can engage them on content areas.

5. The course should provide periodical assessment means to monitor the effectiveness of self-directed learning on the side of the students. Assessing the effectiveness of self-directed learning helps to ensure that students are engaged with their learning content and provided with feedback. Feedback is essential to motivate good performance and enable students to change practices that are not supportive to their learning.

6. Staff development interventions such as training and workshops should be organised to capacitate teachers on how to facilitate self-directed learning. In addition, workshops and working sessions should be conducted with students to help them successfully carry out self-directed learning.

6.9.3 Faculty Requirements for Self-directed Learning

For self-directed learning to be implemented efficiently and effectively, educators should commit to the following functions (Knowles, 1980; TEAL Center Staff, 2011):

1. Conduct a self-assessment of skill levels and needs to determine adults' specific learning needs and interests;
2. Match appropriate resources (books, articles, content experts) and methods (Internet searches, lectures, electronic discussion groups) to the learning goal;
3. Develop positive attitudes and independence relative to self-directed learning and self-reflection of the student in relation to what the student is learning;
4. Encourage and support students throughout the process, helping them recognise their own growing thought processes and strategies;
5. Educators should set a cooperative climate for learning in the learning platform;
6. Educators should evaluate the quality of learning by adult students and make necessary adjustments as required for improvement.

The above requirements in their multiplicity can ensure a successful application of self-directed learning in African institutions.

6.10 Conclusion

The chapter discussed the benefits for self-directed learning in adult, professional and vocational education, which relates to increased provision of transferable knowledge and the fostering of lifelong learning opportunities. The case studies analysed, served as evidence that self-directed learning is an emerging practice, especially in an African context. Most African educational institutions are still inclined to the traditional ways of classroom teaching and learning due to limited understanding of the practice and the resources required to render self-directed learning effective. Countries such as Namibia have started to implement self-directed learning, but the implementation is characterised by challenges related to students resisting self-directed learning and cancelling courses, limited human resources capacity to facilitate self-directed learning and limited supply of modern infrastructures such as the Internet to assist with facilitation. In some countries, some universities are planning to implement self-directed learning by improving practices used by institutions that are currently using the learning mode.

References

Afunde, N. (2010). *Access to ODL programmes at NAMCOL through recognition of prior learning.* Windhoek.

Arnold, R. (2017). *The power of personal mastery: Continual improvement for school leaders and students.* Rowman & Littlefield.

Bates, A. W. (2015). *Teaching in a digital age* (Chap. 10). Available at: http://opentextbc.ca/teachinginadigitalage/

Blaschke, L. M. (2014). Using social media to engage and develop the online learner in self-determined learning. *Research in Learning Technology, 22*, 1–23.

Bockarie, A. (2002). The potential of Vygotsky's contributions to our understanding of cognitive apprenticeship as a process of development in adult vocational and technical education. *Journal of Career and Technical Education, 19*(1), 47–66.

Brookfield, S. D. (2009). Self-directed learning. In R. Maclean & D. Wilson (Eds.), *International handbook of education for the changing world of work.* Springer.

Collins, A., Brown, J. S., & Newman, S. E. (1990). Cognitive apprenticeship: Teaching the crafts of reading, writing, and mathematics. In L. B. Resnick (Ed.), *Knowing, learning and instruction: Essays in honour of Robert Glaser* (pp. 453–494). Lawrence Erlbaum.

Corley, R. H. V., & Tinker, P. B. (2003). *The oil palm* (4th ed.). Wiley.

Cottrell, S. (2017). *Critical thinking skills: Effective analysis, argument and reflection.* Macmillan International Higher Education.

Cranton, P. (2002). Teaching for transformation. *New Directions for Adult and Continuing Education, 93*, 63–72.

De Bruijn, E., & Leeman, Y. (2011). Authentic and self-directed learning in vocational education. Challenges to vocational educators. *Teaching and Teacher Education, 27*, 694–702.

Ericsson, K. (2006). *The Cambridge handbook of expertise and expert performance.* Cambridge University Press.

Filipatali, T. (2013). *Learning theories. Their influence on teaching methods.* Retrieved from https://www.grin.com/document/293498

Freire, P. (2000). *Pedagogy of the oppressed.* Continuum International Publishing Group.

Garrison, D. R. (1997). Self-directed learning: Toward a comprehensive model. *Adult Education Quarterly, 48*(1), 18–33.

Global Apprenticeships Network. (2018). *Toolkit for employers.* Namibia Employers' Federation.

Hartmann, M. D. (2017). Theory and methods of reflection levels—Its use in vocational education and training. In F. Eiker, G. Haseloff, & B. Lennartz (Eds.), *Vocational education and training in sub-Saharan Africa: Current situation and development* (pp. 104 –111).

Hautemo, A. M., & Dalvit, L. (2016). Situated learning: A theoretical base for online learning: Wikipedia translation into Oshikwanyama at a Namibian school. Paper presented at the eLmL 2016: The Eighth International Conference on Mobile, Hybrid, and On-Line Learning, Venice, Italy, April 24–28, 2016.

Hautemo, A. M., & Uunona, D. N. (2018). Knowledge society for Africa: ICT development in the education sector in Namibia. In P. Cunningham & M. Cunningham (Eds.), *International information management corporation* (pp. 1–9). ISBN: 978-1-905824-60-1.

Jossberger, H., Brand-Gruwel, S., van de Wiel, M. W., & Boshuizen, H. (2017). Learning in workplace simulations in vocational education: A student perspective. *Vocations & Learning, 11*, 179–204.

Jossberger, H., Brand-Gruwel, S. B., Boshuizen, H., & van de Wiel, M. (2010). The challenge of self-directed and self-regulated learning in vocational education: A theoretical analysis and synthesis of requirements. *Journal of Vocational Education and Training.* https://doi.org/10.1080/13636820.2010.523479

Kicken, W., Brand-Gruwel, S., Merrienboer, J. J. G., & Slot, W. (2008). The effects of portfolio-based advice on the development of self-directed learning skills in secondary vocational education. *Educational Technology Research and Development, 57*(4), 439–460.

Knowles, M. S. (1975). *Self-directed learning: A guide for learners and teachers.* Follett.

Knowles, M. S. (1980). *The modern practice of adult education: From pedagogy to andragogy.* Cambridge Adult Education.

Lave, J. (1988). *Cognition in practice: Mind, mathematics and culture in everyday life.* Cambridge University Press.

Lave, J., & Wenger, E. (1991). *Situated learning: Legitimate peripheral participation.* Cambridge University Press.

Levett-Jones, T. (2005). Self-directed learning: Implications and limitations for undergraduate nursing education. *Nurse Education Today, 25*(5), 363–368.

Malison, K. (2018). An exploratory study of self-directed learning: The differences between it and non-it employees in Thailand. *Journal of Entrepreneurship Education, 21*(3), 1–16.

Mezirow, J. (2000). Learning to think like an adult. Core concepts of transformation theory. In J. Mezirow & Associates (Eds.), *Learning as transformation. Critical perspectives on a theory in progress* (pp. 3–33). Jossey-Bass.

Mitchell, J. (2015). *Foundations and evolution of ODL and open schooling.* Commonwealth of Learning.

Morris, T. H. (2018a). Adaptivity through self-directed learning to meet the challenges of our ever-changing world. *Adult Learning.* Advance online publication. https://doi.org/10.1177/1045159518814486

Morris, T. H. (2018b). Vocational education of young adults in England: A systemic analysis of teaching–learning transactions that facilitate self-directed learning. *Journal of Vocational Education & Training, 70*, 619–643.

Müller, N. M., & Seufert, T. (2018). Effects of self-regulation prompts in hypermedia learning on learning performance and self-efficacy. *Learning and Instruction, 58*, 1–11.

Muñoz, L. B., & Jojoa, S. T. (2014). How setting goals enhances learners' self-efficacy beliefs in listening comprehension. *HOW Journal, 21*(1), 42–61.

Musingafi, M. C. C., Mapuranga, B., Chiwanza, K., & Zebron, S. (2015). Challenges for open and distance learning (ODL) students: Experiences from students of the Zimbabwe Open University. *Journal of Education and Practice, 6*(18), 59–66.

Said, A. (2018). Vocational teaching-learning through the eyes of undergraduate vocational students in Malta: A qualitative exploratory study. *International Journal for Research in Vocational Education and Training, 5*(1), 42–63.

Sheared, V., Johnson-Bailey, J., Colin III, S. A. J., Peterson, E., & Brookfield, S. D. (2010). *The handbook of race and adult education: A resource for dialogue on racism.* Jossey-Bass.

Shindi, A. (2017). Presentation of ideas on the motivation and establishment of a further education system, especially in universities in sub-Saharan Africa. In F. Eiker, G. Haseloff, & B. Lennartz (Eds.), *Vocational education and training in sub-Sahara Africa: Current situation and development* (pp. 205–211).

Silver-Pacuilla, H. (2003). Transgressing transformation theory. In *Proceedings of 52nd National Reading Conference Yearbook* (pp. 356–368).

Subasubani, J. K. (2017). Situation and development of vocational education and training (VT) and VT science in Namibia. In F. Eiker, G. Haseloff, & B. Lennartz (Eds.), *Vocational education and training in sub-Sahara Africa: Current situation and development* (pp. 152–157).

Tan, C. (2017). *Teaching critical thinking: Cultural challenges and strategies in Singapore*. British Educational Research Association.

Taylor, E. (1998). *The theory and practice of transformative learning: A critical review*. Center on Education and Training for Employment.

Taylor, E. (2000). Analyzing research on transformative learning theory. In J. Mezirow & Associates (Eds.), *Learning as transformation: Critical perspectives on a theory in progress* (pp. 285–328). Jossey-Bass.

TEAL Centre Staff. (2011). *TEAL center fact sheet no. 11: Adult learning theories*. U.S. Department of Education.

Timmins, F. (2008). *Making sense of portfolios. A guide for nursing students*. Open University Press.

Tripon, C. (2015). *Importance of self-directed learning*. Lumen Publishing House.

Wesselink, R., Harm, J. A., Biemans, H. J. A., Mulder, M., & Elsen, E. R. V. (2007). Competence-based VET as seen by Dutch researchers. *European Journal of Vocational Training, 40*(1), 38–51.

Zimmerman, B. J. (2013). From cognitive modeling to self-regulation: A social cognitive career path. *Educational Psychologist, 48*(3), 135–147.

Elock Emvula Shikalepo is a Namibian academic and researcher, currently practising instructional design and technology at the Namibia University of Science and Technology. He holds graduate and post-graduate qualifications in teaching, education law, education systems and education management, obtained with Namibian, Zimbabwean and South African universities. He obtained his Doctor of Philosophy from the University of South Africa, with a focus on staff motivation and performance in the education sector. His thesis evaluated the influence of financial incentive on teacher motivation and learner performance in Namibian rural schools. He has presented at conferences, researched widely and published extensively in peer-reviewed journals on the areas of technical, vocational education and training, open and lifelong learning, education legislations, teaching and learning, management and leadership, Information and Communication Technologies and research methods. He has vast experiences in instructional design, blended learning, online course development, online course delivery, research supervision and external examination of masters and Ph.D.'s dissertations and theses.

Aletta Mweneni Hautemo is the Coordinator for Instructional Design and Technology at the Namibia University of Science and Technology in Windhoek, Namibia. She obtained her Ph.D. in 2019 at Stellenbosch University (SA) in which she researched on the use of Wikipedia Translation as a task-based language teaching and learning task in a multilingual tertiary education teaching programme. She has a Master in ICT in education from Rhodes University, a post-graduate diploma in ICT Leadership in the Knowledge Society from Dublin City University Ireland) and a BEd (Honours) in education from Rhodes University (SA). Having started off her career as a professional teacher in 2007, she has gained broader experience in general education, vocational education and training—as an Assessment Officer and later a Curriculum Implementation coordinator at Namibia Training Authority; and Language education Lecturer at the University of Namibia. She is well versatile in Instructional design, e-learning course development and online teaching in ODL. She is a certified RPL Assessor and Curriculum Developer. She has published more than ten articles in accredited journals and has presented papers at various local and international conferences. She is an active member of the Namibian Open Learning Network Trust (NOLNet). Her research interest includes technology-enhanced language learning, online translation and localisation of indigenous languages, ICT integration in education, multimodal learning and Open and Distance Education.

Chapter 7
Open Education, Open Learning and Open Teaching at the African University

Francis Simui and Karen Ferreira-Meyers

Abstract In this chapter, we focus on three purposively selected African universities that have embraced open education, open learning and open teaching, and discuss possible reasons why others have only partially or not at all taken the "open" route. Evidence on the status of Open Education is generated using a non-obtrusive methodology embedded within social media. Official Facebook sites for three universities in Eswatini, South Africa and Zambia are purposively selected and further interrogated retrospectively for a period of 12 months to elicit discussion from the posts of staff and students on the phenomenon under study. Given the prevailing Covid-19 pandemic, it becomes imperative that we take a closer look at Higher Education and how it has responded to the demands of the "new normal" which have compelled nearly all institutions to adopt open teaching and open learning approaches to survive. In the first instance, definitions of the concept of open education and its "relatives", open teaching and open learning, are considered. Consensus on the meaning and depth of these notions is important for wider roll-out. The chapter then goes on to describe some enablers and disablers that make teaching and learning more "open" to achieve the sustainable development goals related to education.

Keywords Africa · Open education · Open teaching · Open learning policy and implementation · University

7.1 Introduction

Although the term Open Education is not new, there have been multiple interpretations and, as we will see below, the Open Education movement has several dimensions. At the end of the 1960s-early 1970s, discussions on opening up education and classrooms were initiated in the UK and the USA. In the documents from those days, the focus is on "opening possibilities and responsibilities to teachers as well

F. Simui (✉)
University of Zambia, Lusaka, Zambia

K. Ferreira-Meyers
Institute of Distance Education, University of Eswatini, Kwaluseni, Swaziland

as to children" (Bussis & Chittenden, 1970). The principles associated with open education then include respect, honesty and warmth (Bussis & Chittenden, 1970), trust, choice and flexibility (Evans, 1971). Walberg and Thomas (1971) identified several characteristics of open education: attention to children's thinking processes, more individual attention, less focus on goals, growth opportunities for all stakeholders. It is also noteworthy that, at that point in time, "open" was often equated to "informal" (Katz, 1972). However, a commonly accepted definition of open education was sorely lacking as, apart from vague statements like "open education is a way of thinking about" (idem), nothing much was available. Walberg and Thomas (1972, p. 97) defined Open Education as "a chance for real attention to individual learning, respect for the child, authentic relationships, and opportunities for both teacher and child to participate in significant learning". In 1975, Don Tunnell was one of the first to look into the definition and concept of Open Education. Over the years, Open Education has been characterised as learning by doing, informal learning, a holistic approach, real-world learning ("authentic learning"), etc.

Today, a definition such as Walker's (in Iiyoshi and Kumar, p. 77) shows how far the concept has come: Open Education is "education that is available to virtually any learner, is within his or her means, and results in meeting his or her learning objectives". Openness also refers to transparency of practice and activity, to inclusiveness, to personalised learning, among other qualities. In this chapter, we examine some of the Open Education dimensions, in particular those of Open Teaching and Open Learning, in view of finding out which situations and contexts are enablers to the Open Education movement and which ones form barriers to a wider acceptance of the main principles of Open Education. Iiyoshi and Kumar noted, as the key tenet of the movement, that "education can be improved by making educational assets visible and accessible and by harnessing the collective wisdom of a community of practice and reflection" (2008, p. 2). This refers to Open Access mainly, but other important principles include agency, ownership, participation, inclusion, equity and experience.

7.2 Context

This chapter was written against the background of the importance and urgency of Open Education, Open Teaching and Open Learning within the ambit of the United Nations' Sustainable Development Goals. The 2030 Agenda for Sustainable Development and committed to 17 Sustainable Development Goals (SDGs). (https://sustainabledevelopment.un.org/sdgs). SDG4 is about "Education: Ensure inclusive and equitable quality education and promote lifelong learning opportunities for all". Open Education, in the form of open resources (Open Textbooks, Open Educational Resources and Open Licensing) and practices (including Open Pedagogy and Open Educational Practices such as Open Teaching and Open Learning and related Open Assessment and Open Badges as well as Open Standards), was explicitly linked to SDG4 by various authors and international declarations (e.g. the Ljubljana OER Action Plan 2017).

Seen as an overall philosophy, Open Education deals with the way people produce, share and build on knowledge, which is a basic human right. Proponents of Open Education work towards eliminating barriers to this goal, such as prohibitive monetary costs, outdated or obsolete materials, or legislation that prevents or inhibits collaboration among stakeholders in the educational realm. Open Education presents a number of important advantages for different stakeholders in education. For learners, these are, among others, the fact that the knowledge they acquire is applied to a wide context; learning opportunities can be accessed anywhere, at any time; learning materials are centred on the learners, respond to learners' needs and social/collaborative/active learning (socio-constructivist and connectivist) approaches are used. The advantages of Open Education for teachers include that users of OER and Open Textbooks can give feedback and this can lead to continuous revision and updating of the teaching and learning materials and practices. The open sharing of ideas, information, data, practices and strategies is beneficial to all involved. Specifically looking at Open Educational Resources and Open Content, their transformative educational potential can be described as follows: the increased availability of high quality, relevant learning materials will contribute to better performing learners and teachers, and make it possible to adapt existing materials through a collaborative approach. This way of working can give both learners and educators an opportunity, as active participants, to learn by doing and creating, one of the main skills necessary in the twenty-first century.

Open Education also includes the opening up of the teaching process: in Open Teaching, teachers "are able to share and participate in the trials and successes of their fellow educators as they tweet and blog about their work. This process can be as simple as posting ideas for the classroom or as profound as posting daily reflections on the successes and failures of different approaches" (Cormier & Siemens, 2018, pp. 34–35). Before listing our research questions, it is essential to briefly examine who are the main open education stakeholders, apart from the obvious ones—already included above—learners and educators.

Who could have a particular interest in Open Education, Open Learning and Open Teaching? Librarians, textbook publishers, but also ministries, inspectors and education administrators alike. With Open Education, teachers and lecturers get assigned at least one new role, that of "scholar-curators associated with data and primary content information resources serving as guides and teachers to individuals and learning communities wanting to directly engage these resources in cyberspace" (Iiyoshi and Kumar, p. 115). Laurillard (2008) stated, based on Dalziel's (2005) definition of "open source teaching" as what happens in an environment in which "educators can freely and openly share best practice teaching", that Open Teaching combines the following four characteristics: (1) support for some personal development in how to teach; (2) the means to build on the work of others to design their approach; (3) the means to experiment and reflect on what the results imply for their design and their understanding; and (4) the means to articulate and disseminate their contribution.

7.3 Research Questions

To explore the Open Education, Open Learning and Open Teaching phenomenon in selected African universities, the following research questions guided the study:

1. What is the current status of Open Education, Open Learning and Open Teaching?
2. What are the enablers to Open Education, Open Learning and Open Teaching?
3. What are the disablers to Open Education, Open Learning and Open Teaching?

7.4 Methodology

In order to explore Open Education, Open Learning and Open Teaching at selected African universities, we adopted an unobtrusive method with a focus on document review on the phenomenon under study. According to Rathje (1979) and Babbie (1989) (in Simui et al., 2018c), an unobtrusive approach studies the actual rather than reported behaviour. This approach could be repeated as it is non-disruptive, non-reactive, easily accessible, inexpensive and a good source of longitudinal data. In addition, unobtrusive research methods offer a strong critique of positivism, the concept that truths about the social world can be determined through scientific measurement. Instead, these methods belong to the epistemological theory of interpretivism which is that the social sciences are fundamentally different from natural sciences; therefore, they require researchers to reject empiricism and grasp subjective meaning of social action (Bryman, 2004). In terms of ontological considerations, unobtrusive methods fit into the constructionism theory whereby social phenomena and their meanings are continually accomplished and revised by social actors (Bryman, 2004). The unobtrusive approach was well suited for this particular study as it relied on social media (Facebook) and website sources on Open Education, Open Learning and Open Teaching about selected African universities which could be extrapolated into longitudinal data in a non-reactive and non-disruptive environment. This is consistent with the ideas of the founders of the unobtrusive method, Webb et al. (1966) who argued that unobtrusive research methods are presumed to avoid the problems caused by the researcher's presence. In addition, unobtrusive methods, because they do not disrupt research participants, are easily repeatable.

7.5 Sample Size

The sample had a double layer from participating universities with the first layer consisting of 11 universities selected among institutions practising Open Education while the second layer included only 3 universities whose participants shared in-depth views on the phenomenon under study. Both the first and second layers of sampled universities contributed to the discourse via their official Facebook sites available to the public. A purposive sample was used in this study (Kemper et al., 2003). It was chosen to address qualitative demands such as the need for reflexivity, fit for purpose, availability and accessibility. In carrying out this study, we used Official Blue Button Facebook sites available and accessible to the public to construct impressions on Open Education, Open Learning and Open Teaching in purposively selected universities across Africa, namely the University of Cape Town, Cairo University, Marsoura University, University of Ibadan, University of Ghana, University of Nairobi, Open University of Tanzania, Zimbabwe Open University, University of South Africa, University of Zambia and University of Eswatini.

The second layer had the following universities that participated, namely (Pseudonyms) Saniso, Zamisa and Eswoni. The universities were selected on the basis of their active involvement in Open and Distance Education as single or dual-mode institutions as well as their being lead universities in their respective countries. The elicited information was cross-checked by insider informants to avoid the usual emic/etic problems. This means that interpretation of physical traces or observations may be from the point of view of the stranger or outsider (etic) and, therefore, may fail to grasp important in-group meanings (emic).

Table 7.1 shows the pseudonyms used of the key participating countries and universities involved in Open Education, Open Learning and Open Teaching within Africa as elicited through the document review research process, their countries, university, mode of delivery of services to their learners.

7.6 Data Generation Procedure

In carrying out this study, we used official Facebook sites with blue button focused on African higher education institutions purposively selected where Open Education, Open Learning and Open Teaching was practised. Emergent from the literature review on Open Education, Teaching and Learning is a checklist with key pointers to open education which we used as a guide to explore the Open Education, Open Learning and Open Teaching phenomena. An online WordArt generator was applied to generate the checklist (see Fig. 7.1).

To examine the phenomenon of "openness" being the critical feature, we used social media, in particular Facebook, and other official platforms openly and widely used by universities for communication purposes. Evidence on the universities' views of Open Education, Open Learning and Open Teaching was generated from these online environments. We applied non-participant observer techniques to enlist student members on official institutional Facebook platforms and then conducted a review for a period of 6 months to 1 year retrospectively for each institution to unearth-related issues to Open Education, Open Learning and Open Teaching. The researchers took time to get immersed into student and staff teaching–learning cultures ethnographically and to identify enablers and disablers to the learning experiences within the framework of Open Education.

Table 7.1 Key participating universities

	Participants (Pseudonym)	University (Pseudonym)	Country
1	AAunisa	Saniso	South Africa
2	AAunza	Zamisa	Zambia
3	BOunisa	Saniso	South Africa
4	BZuneswa	Eswoni	Eswatini
5	CKunza	Zamisa	Zambia
6	DFunisa	Saniso	South Africa
7	ENunisa	Saniso	South Africa
8	FLunza	Zamisa	Zambia
9	GHunisa	Saniso	South Africa
10	GMuneswa	Eswoni	Eswatini
11	HJunisa	Saniso	South Africa
12	JKunisa	Saniso	South Africa
13	JMunza	Zamisa	Zambia
14	JOunisa	Saniso	South Africa
15	JPunisa	Saniso	South Africa
16	KKunza	Zamisa	Zambia
17	KLuneswa	Eswoni	Eswatini
18	KMunisa	Saniso	South Africa
19	LMunza	Zamisa	Zambia
20	LNunisa	Saniso	South Africa
21	MFuneswa	Eswoni	Eswatini
22	MKuneswa	Eswoni	Eswatini
23	MMuneswa	Eswoni	Eswatini
24	MTunisa	Saniso	South Africa
25	MWunisa	Saniso	South Africa
26	NJuneswa	Eswoni	Eswatini
27	NSunisa	Saniso	South Africa
28	NZunisa	Saniso	South Africa
29	OPunisa	Saniso	South Africa
30	PKunisa	Saniso	South Africa
31	PMunisa	Saniso	South Africa
32	SLunisa	Saniso	South Africa
33	SSuneswa	Eswoni	Eswatini
34	XKunsa	Zamisa	Zambia
35	YJunisa	Saniso	South Africa
36	YLunisa	Saniso	South Africa
37	YYunisa	Saniso	South Africa

Fig. 7.1 Pointers to open education

7.7 Trustworthiness

In this study, Guba's (1981) four criteria on trustworthiness were applied. They are credibility, transferability, dependability and confirmability. The data generation process was triangulated using observation, document review and individual interviews. The researchers used a reflexivity approach to decipher meaning from generated data. In addition, the researchers had early familiarity with the culture of the participants prior to data generation. The data generation procedure and boundaries were documented for the purposes of ensuring transferability of the study findings to different settings. Further, the elicited information was cross-checked by participants to avoid the usual emic/etic problems. This means that interpretation of physical traces or observations may be from the point of view of the stranger, or outsider (etic), and therefore may fail to grasp important in-group meanings (emic) (Berry, 1989). Given that the findings were presented verbatim, coupled with participant checks on the research, the study meets the dependability and confirmability criteria as well.

7.8 Findings and Discussion

Emergent from the data mined on institutional platforms and through Facebook was the engagement of learners through social media as noted in Fig. 7.2:

Status on Open knowledge sharing via Facebook.

The descriptive statistics above suggest that UNISA had the largest following of 896,264 as at 24 September 2020 and their services were liked by 841,484 users of the page. UNISA's Facebook has been in existence since 20 May 2009. Second position was Cairo University in Egypt with 606,551 followers and 602,888 Likes. This

Facebook Followers and Likes as at 24th Sept, 2020

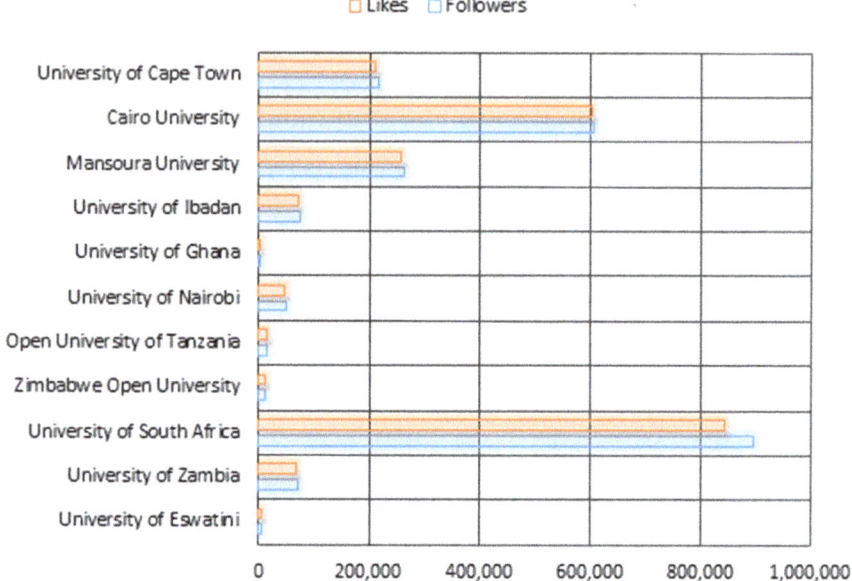

Fig. 7.2 Status on open knowledge sharing via Facebook

university's Facebook page was created on 20 February 2011. Mansoura University in Egypt created its Facebook page on 9 March 2011 and was in third place with 262,534 followers and 256,456 Likes. Mansoura University was closely followed by the University of Cape Town with 218,224 followers and 209,018 Likes on a Facebook page created on 13 January 2010. The rest of the universities selected recorded below 74,000 followers with the University of Ibadan in Nigeria recording 72,778 Followers and 70,501 Likes on a Facebook page created on 27 November 2011, while the University of Ghana had the least number of followers at 367 and Likes at 355 recorded on its official Facebook page created on 4 April 2013. Simui et al. (2018b) observe that social media such as Facebook and WhatsApp are critical ingredients for effective learner support services for distance education. Thus, given the important numbers of learners using social media, open information sharing is enhanced. However, not all learners and learning facilitators are comfortable with use of ICTs for teaching–learning purposes due to what some refer to as the digital immigrants syndrome (Mwewa & Namangala, 2019). Muleya et al. (2019).

In addition, the following emerged as themes to explain the status of Open Learning, Open Teaching and Open education within Higher Education in Africa: Peer support, Staff support, Equity, Cost, Communication, Application of ICTs and Assessment among others. We organised these emergent themes according to whether they can be seen as enablers or disablers of Open Education, as identified in student and staff discourse published on social media and online communication (official university websites).

7.8.1 Enablers to Open Education

A number of enablers to Open Education were established such as peer support, staff support and inclusion of diversity as catalysts for innovation among others.

7.8.1.1 Peer Support

The link between OER and peer support has been noted by Fetter et al. (2012), and Seely Brown and Adler (2008), among others. This is what students had to say on their institutional Facebook pages: *I'm doing HC Financial Accounting this year and want to do a degree next year. My question is, do I apply or automatically I'm depending on whether I pass or not this year?* (DFunisa, 2020).

In turn, DFunisa's question was responded to by MTunisa, a fellow student who gave the following advice: *Apply because they don't know your plans about your certificate whether you just want to use it as a bridge or for looking for a job* (MTunisa, 2020). Equally, JOunisa wanted to know the quality of services for undergraduate students in comparison with postgraduate services. He noted,

> If I may ask, is [Saniso]'s postgrad services as bad as undergrad? My question is based on the fact that during registrations, you will find that postgrad students are given some well deserved preferential treatment. They don't stand on those long lines the whole day. (JOunisa, 2020)

It is clear from JOunisa's submission that undergraduate students were not pleased with the quality of support during the registration period. In addition, YYunisa posed a question to fellow peers,

> Greetings guys. My question is, if you are a final year student and you want to do a postgraduate qualification next year do you apply now? Or wait for your results in December?.coz I've been trying to apply and the system wants me to attach completed qualification. (YYunisa, 2020)

While peer support proved to be a critical positive ingredient in Open Learning, there were moments when learner-to-learner misinformation was noted. For instance, LNunisa was confronted by PKunisa, a peer, for having misinformed other learners as noted below. LNunisa noted that,

> Did you know that Unisa is Capitec registered beneficiary? I mean you can pay your application fee or study fee, using the Capitec App. You just have to use the correct allocation reference. (LNunisa, 2020)

The above claim by LNunisa was corrected by PKunisa as follows:

No. It is not capitec my sister, stop misleading us, it was standard bank and now fnb, so wena what u doing is cellphone banking, you are using capitec app to transfer your money to [Saniso] fnb account, obviously u have to put ur ref n student no to show what is that money for, [Saniso] doesn't have capitec bank account, u can do transfer with any bank to any bank. (PKunisa, 2020)

The active peer engagement above (relating to various study-related matters) appears to have enabled learners to succeed in their academic enterprise as supported by Sinclair (2017). Accordingly to Sinclair, peer support for e-learners is vital to their academic success. In her study, she noted that students placed great emphasis on the importance of peer support, with more than half of the respondents explicitly stating that their peers were helpful to them regarding educational needs, such as finishing their degree and passing their courses (Sinclair, 2017).

7.8.1.2 Staff Support

While in a study in the UK, staff did not understand the meaning of Open Education and their role within it (e.g. Harold & Rolfe, 2019), in the selected African universities under study staff seemed to comprehend the vital role a learning facilitator plays. For instance, FLunza noted that,

Thanks to our dedicated lecturers. The knowledge you imparted in us meets the demands of the current educational management systems. May God bless you as u serve our great nation Zambia. (FLunza, 2020)

While the role played by learning facilitators in the Open Education enterprise cannot be overemphasised, *AAunisa* noted the complementary input that learners needed to contribute. He noted that,

A residential school is usually for students to interact with lecturers and highlights grey areas picked from your course modules [in an Open Education setting online] Lecturers let you run the show and they provide guidelines. The programme is fully self-study. (AAunisa, 2020)

In addition, the need for a responsive school calendar that takes the concerns of learners on board was stressed as a vital ingredient to the academic success of learners. Staff have an important role to play in crafting a responsive school calendar. For instance, WJunza noted the following: *my humble request to the management is that you may make residential periods during school holidays so that it is easy to get permission* (WJunza, 2020).

In line with FLunza, AAunisa and WJunza, Ouma and Nkuyubwatsi (2019) advocate for transformation of university learner support in open and distance education. In their study, it was noted that inadequate faculty support from university management and limited distance learners' representation in their leadership and governance was rampant in Uganda (Ouma & Nkuyubwatsi, 2019).

7.8.1.3 Inclusion and Diversity

Open Education is expected to be open to all learners. However, learners across the universities practising Open Education reported experiences where learners with disabilities were marginalised and excluded. For instance, at Saniso, YLunisa noted that,

> Students leaving [sic] with disabilities were neglected totally during May/June 2020 examinations and are neglected once more during semester 2 registrations and as we approach October/November 2020 Examinations, they never received their promised devices which have different specifications to level with their respective disabilities. (YLunisa, 2020)

Supposedly, ICTs are enablers to effective inclusive education (Simui, 2018). However, negative attitudes and practices as cited above are a major barrier to effective inclusive education (Simui, 2018; Simui et al., 2018a). Thus, inclusion and diversity should be viewed as catalysts for creativity and innovation among learners and learning facilitators.

7.8.2 Disablers to Open Education

While enablers were noted above, disablers to successful application of Open Education were voiced out by learners. Disablers included the negative side effects of ICTs on the health of the learners, cost of open education, Inaccessible free Data Bundles, Open Cheating in formative Assessment and Covid-19 Effects on Open Education among others.

7.8.2.1 Negative Effects of ICT on Learners' Health

Whereas ICTs are highly appreciated for serving as catalysts to Open Education, there are negative side effects associated with their continuous use, especially on the sight of users. For instance, HJunisa retorted:

> By the time i graduate, my eyesight would be bad news. This thing of reading on a laptop is straining me. I have been hoping that my study material would be delivered by now. (HJunisa, 2020)

Equally, HJunisa noted that *reading from the laptop is damaging my eyesight, when is* [Saniso] *mailing the study material?* (HJunisa, 2020). Woo et al. (2016) observe that information and communication technology has harmful effects on the health of learners. For example, according to the American Optometric Association, a person who exceeds 2 h of computer use per day is at risk of computer vision syndrome (CVS) (Woo et al., 2016).

7.8.2.2 High Cost of Open Education

Open Education is often equated, in popular parlance, to free education. However, there exist prohibitive tuition fees in some learning institutions as observed by MMunza, *consider reducing the fees for PHD. Too expensive* (MMunza, 2020). Most consumers of Open Education goods and services do not appreciate upward adjustments to tuition fees, as observed by AAunza, *Hello. I am in the process of registering for my courses for the 2017/2 academic year MBA Year 2 and I've noticed that the amount is K2000 per course. Have the prices* (AAunza, 2020).

The cost of education was compounded by the effects of Covid-19 as observed in Eswatini. For example, MMuneswa argued that,

> our economic situation and the University's I guess, is also struggling to the core. We wish to engage in this initiative but it is not possible because of the limitations that have been caused by this pandemic. I personally don't even have the requested gadgets. I borrowed the phone from a neighbour. I lost my job and life is difficult. (MMuneswa, 2020)

While the cost of Open Education was noted to be high in the three studied universities, it has to be highlighted as well that Open Educational Resources should make it possible to lower textbook costs. Clinton (2018) advocates for the adoption of Open Educational Resources (OER) developed to free students from the expense and instructors from the restrictions of commercial materials. A study on a Cost, Outcomes, Usage, and Perceptions framework indicates that OER adoption yielded cost savings while generally having similar or better outcomes in terms of grades (Clinton, 2018).

Flexibility and user-friendly fees play a critical role in the successful implementation of Online Distance learning as noted by MWunisa, *Hi there. [Saniso] is a distance learning university for those of us that work. And it is the cheapest for people who pay their own* (MWunisa, 2020). Huang et al. (2020) advocate for the presence of the following five conditions, namely OER, Open Teaching, Open Collaboration, Open Assessment and enabling technology, for any meaningful Open Education Practices can take place. Huang et al. (2020) emphasised that, in OEP, students are encouraged to carry on with flexible learning.

7.8.2.3 Inaccessible Free Data Bundles

ICTs were noted to be vital tools for effective Open Teaching–Learning processes to take root. For instance, Eswoni reported the availability of free data bundles to assist with online learning as noted by KLuneswa,

> All our students are requested to ensure that they have the correct MTN mobile number submitted with their Faculty Administrator to ensure they receive a 3GB data bundle to assist with online learning. The bundles can be used to visit websites belonging to Regent, Moodle, Exams council of Eswatini, Eswoni …. (KLuneswa, 2020)

However, ICTs availability and accessibility among learners appears to have been a challenge as noted in the response of one of the staff members at Eswoni:

Your concerns have been noted and will be forwarded to the relevant Department. Eswoni cares about the utmost well-being of all students and will do whatever it takes to take care of your needs. (BZuneswa, 2020)

7.8.2.4   Inappropriate Pedagogy of Open Teaching

Open Teaching and Open Learning call for the appropriate pedagogy in the use of online resources as noted by MFuneswa, 2020. The student advocated for the following:

Please record the lecturer delivering their lessons. Make them into short 5 mins to 15 mins videos for each topic or section. Then we will download those videos and watch them then ask questions and do the assignment later. We all know that streaming through Zoom or Google Classroom will take more data than what MTN provides at cheap prices. By the way, that is how I take my lessons at an online university I am currently enrolled in…. (MFuneswa, 2020)

This indicates the need for training of both students and staff, management included.

7.8.2.5   Inaccessible Internet Facilities

Inevitably, ICTs are a catalyst to Open Education. As noted in Fig. 7.1, higher education institutions were riding on ICTs platforms to communicate with their learners during the Covid-19 pandemic, as conventional approaches, which include face-to-face interactions, could not be of assistance. In some institutions, even examinations were administered through online platforms. This was the case with Saniso and Eswoni universities as observed by PMunisa, NJuneswa and KMunisa,

when results came out the three multiple choice exams were fine but the other 2 they said absent from examination, I have sent proof of submission hundred times and have been sent from pillar to post. Right now I'm frustrated because I studied and wrote the exams but now I have no results….I wonder whether it's worth it for me to study and write them at this point in time. I am frustrated with online exams. (PMunisa, 2020)

It is true that not all students are set up for online learning and students who are from poor families, especially in Africa, have less access to key tools. Covid-19 has exposed the technological divide that exists in our society. You might have a laptop, access to Wifi at home or you can afford to purchase data bundles to learn online. But what about the student who does not have access to all this? (NJuneswa, 2020)

Guys I didn't submit any assignment, because I had no access to the Internet until last week so some of them have closed already, which means I won't be able to write some of the modules even if I wanted to. (KMunisa, 2020)

Students' reactions indicate the level of frustration with some of the online delivery modes and requirements. Rahman (2014) observes that Open and Distance Learning is getting more dependent on Information and Communication Technology (ICT) and now plays an important role in the delivery strategies of distance learning. Educational technologies are replacing direct teacher-student interaction. Anything that helps distance learners communicate—learner with instructor, learner with learner and learner with the learning materials—may be labelled as educational technology. Similarly, Ali (2020) observes that, in the light of the rising concerns about the spread of Covid-19 and calls to contain the pandemic, a growing number of tertiary institutions around the world have shut down their face-to-face classes. The coronavirus has revealed emerging vulnerabilities in education systems globally. It is now clear that society needs flexible and resilient education systems as we face unpredictable futures. Inevitably, universities worldwide are moving more and more towards online learning or E-Learning. Apart from resources, staff readiness and confidence, accessibility and motivation play important functions in ICT-integrated learning. For example, SLunisa noted this: *In the online examination, I had to apply what I learned, and it was tough. But still, I prefer online examination, because it doesn't make me feel anxious* (SLunisa, 2020).

7.8.2.6   Negative Attitude

Negative attitude was yet another disabler to academic success in the Open Education space. For example, SSuneswa lamented the negative attitude from staff and/or management experienced at the University of Eswoni. The student stated:

> What's with this appalling attitude of making the students feel like this arrangement is being gifted to them? Start addressing the students like stakeholders, not like beneficiaries of some benevolence by the university. They have earned their place there. Please. (SSuneswa, 2020)

Another student reported her frustration with online registration processes: *Student registrations to date are still being finalised and assignments have been postponed more than 2 times while we count only days to October/November Examinations* (GHunisa, 2020).

7.8.2.7   Poor Communication

Communication between learners and their respective institutions was noted to be ineffective in some instances such as the one reported by SAunisa,

> Does anyone know if there are any staff working at [Saniso]? I have been emailing remarks and the finance department since October 2019 and from then till now I have received no correspondence from them, but they have received my funds and provide me with no service that I paid for. I even sent a mail to say fine if you don't want to remark then refund me. But still nothing. They don't respond but they can send statements every month. Hai. Nonsense. (SAunisa, 2020)

Equally, ENunisa re-echoed SAunisa's observations as well. She retorted that she was…

> so worried that till this day I haven't received any timetable and exams will commence next month. So when are we going to get the dates and time? This you will be informed thing is

making me sick (ENunisa, 2020). I am also still waiting. I have a 4th year module. Submitted in June and have been waiting for 3 months. (BOunisa, 2020)

BOunisa's concerns are similar to what Musingafi et al. (2015) reported at the Zimbabwe Open University. They noted that ODL learners were challenged by a range of obstacles in their course of studies. The most reported challenges were lack of sufficient time for study, difficulties in access and use of ICT, ineffective feedback and lack of study materials (Musingafi et al., 2015).

Despite the reported challenges in communication between learners and their respective universities, our study participants noted a significant number of announcements which were meant to convey messages from the university side. For instance, at the University of Zamisa, the marketing officer posted announcements on the Facebook platform on several occasions, as noted:

To all graduands participating in the Virtual Graduation Ceremony on 31st July 2020, kindly note that you can have your portrait taken at [Zamisa] Customer Service Centre on the following dates: Saturday 27.06.2020 9-13hrs...Kindly deposit K50 in any of the following bank accounts for the service …. (CKunza, 2020)

7.8.2.8 Open Cheating in Assessments

"Open Cheating" was noted to be a barrier to successful Open Education implementation. We use this terminology to describe the advertising of unlawful means and ways to obtain grades. Students are addressed directly, online, with proposals of "assistance": outsiders indicate that they are willing, for a fee, to do the students' assignments, etc. The challenge of Open Cheating was reported by the University of Zamisa. For example, *L*Munza,

Are you a Postgraduate (Phd, Masters) or undergraduate student having difficulties/problems in Research, proposal Writings or assignments/projects. Call or whatsapp this line for help *097822XXXX*. (LMunza, 2020)

Similarly, at Saniso, Open Cheating was noted as NZunisa, among others, advertised the following services: *If you need help with assignments, solutions all modules whatsapp at 072076XXXX or call 071722XXXX or portfolio or exam packs or exam preparation* (NZunisa, 2020). Another instance of such encouragement of Open Cheating, was noted here: *If you need any assistance regarding any Assignments, Portfolio and online sessions, please kindly inbox or text me on WhatsApp 065517XXXX. Graduate easily with distinctions* (NSunisa, 2020).

Open Cheating was also initiated by the learners themselves as noted by *GMuneswa*: *Please anyone who is willing to help me with assignment 2 SEPT1501 … I can't take it anymore* (GMuneswa, 2020). And, again:

Please help. I am confused. I don't know how to go about with assignments. I have all the data but the assignments have no guide except for the long paper. There is no number of pages, specified citation and I am being referred to the tutorial letter which I have not received...Please I am in issues here help out please.. My email address is. (OPunisa, 2020)

7.8.2.9 Covid-19 Effects on Open Education

The impact of the Covid-19 pandemic cannot be minimised. The consequences of the brutal transition from face-to-face (however limited it was before the pandemic) and distance to full online teaching and learning will be felt for a long time, even post-pandemic. It is therefore understandable that student reactions were shared on social media. For example, MKuneswa noted this:

> What about us Nursing students at Eswoni who are expected to attend clinicals in the wards and various health facilities across Eswatini this semester without proper protective gear (PPE). We feel very much exposed and the university is not saying or doing anything even when we highlight this to the respective channels. Is the degree worth our lives? Can Clinicals be postponed till the dust settles as well please. (MKuneswa, 2020)

In addition, BZuneswa stated: *Please tell the lecturers to stop giving us assignments without teaching us anything. We are still traumatised by this situation. We will get back to class and hurry as if we will die if we pause learning due to this pandemic* (BZuneswa, 2020). Equally, Covid-19 had other effects on the nature of examinations prepared for and administered to learners. In the name of observing social distance to limit the spread of Covid-19, e-examinations were advocated for. At Saniso, some learners found Open Examinations challenging, as noted by JPunisa:

> Some of you are complaining about online exams but can I just point out that exams are about to get worse. Guys the online exams I wrote were tough. There were no answers in the textbook or Google. It will be impossible to copy or find answers in the textbook or Google. (JPunisa, 2020)

Educational activities made possible in open educational environments are characterised by the opportunities for collaborative participation and creative exchange. Open Education, Open Content, and Open Source as a collective idea are often discussed as a means to liberation (Unsworth, 2004), empowerment, and democratisation (Vest, 2006). Equal access to current knowledge and a standing invitation to everyone to participate in advancing new ideas are common themes of the Open Education movement. Open Education is an attitude, a practice, a philosophy that goes beyond a mere approach to teaching and learning. Ideally, Open Education will bring about a more equitable access to course materials—and thus knowledge—through the sharing of lessons and materials with the wider community.

Bonk (2009) observes that the World is now Open with the aid of Web technology. Concomitantly, Institutions in developed countries are beginning to grapple with how the open education movement can bring vitality and relevance to curricula through new models of learner participation, and through cross-disciplinary and global perspectives. These institutions have begun to rethink their educational infrastructure in order to better support open education. However, the question remains how far African countries have come in implementing the basic principles of Open Education, Open Learning and Open Teaching at higher education levels.

There remain important obstacles. We note a few of them here (in line with the ones proposed by our study participants). The first one is that of negative attitudes towards sharing. However, studies have shown that there is an ongoing shift as some

"Academics are willing to release their material if they are (a) protected from litiga-
tion; (b) protected from criticism; (c) given an incentive to do so; and (d) furthering
their discipline" (Lee in Iiyoshi & Kumar, 2008, p. 57). Additionally, literature indicates the lack of meaningful methods of assessing and validating what someone has
learned, as well as the failure to integrate Open Education initiatives into other institutional approaches to enhance faculty development. Finally, and this echoes what
was noted by our study participants, there is reluctance to participate in Open Education because of financial, sustainability, and preservation concerns (the generalised
idea that "open" means "free" is definitely a contributing factor to the continued
existence of these concerns).

These points were not directly brought to the surface by our study participants,
but they have a bearing on the issues raised. In the next section, we propose some
recommendations.

7.9   Recommendations

1.   There is a need to cultivate peer support structures within the Open Education
     space to maximise social capital within the Open Teaching and Open Learning
     processes.
2.   There is a need for free data bundles to assist with online learning seeing that
     its cost serves as a barrier to effective use of online Open Education Resources
     and broader acceptance of Open Education.
3.   While the cost of Open Education was noted to be high in the targeted univer-
     sities, more generalised application of Open Educational Resources is recom-
     mended to free students from the expense and instructors from the restrictions
     of commercial materials.
4.   In view of the potential negative effects on ICTs users such as students and
     teaching staff, there is a need to embed ergonometric principles in the engi-
     neering of ICT products, processes and systems, and in the design of computer
     workstations in schools, colleges and universities. This is a sure way of averting
     potential health challenges.
5.   Considering the challenges associated with poor Internet infrastructure and
     limited ICT skills, there is a need to give students a choice whether to write
     examinations online or at a physical venue. Open Education should go hand in
     hand with the principle of flexibility.

7.10   Conclusion

Open Education is an attitude, a practice, a philosophy that goes beyond a mere
approach to teaching and learning. Ideally, Open Education will bring about a more
equitable access to course materials through the sharing of lessons and materials

with the wider community. In this chapter, we set out to analyse feedback from staff and students shared with the world via social media (Facebook pages of selected universities). This had the main objective of finding out what some of the enablers and disablers of Open Education, Open Teaching and Open Learning are in the opinions of major educational stakeholders.

As enablers, the following themes stood out: peer and staff support. However, without adequate training, these types of support could easily turn into disablers. On the disabler side, our study participants noted negative attitudes towards Open Education, Open Learning and Open Teaching as well as poor communication. Both of these disablers can be counteracted with specific initiatives to enhance communication and interaction. An additional side effect is that of Open Cheating. Further research into this unlawful behaviour is warranted. Finally, we note the impact of the Covid-19 pandemic. Here too, further research is needed to find out whether the long-term impact of the "forced" transition to online learning (we can call it emergency learning in many situations in the Southern African region) is a positive or a negative one.

References

Ali, W. (2020). Online and remote learning in higher education institutes: A necessity in light of COVID-19 Pandemic. *Higher Education Studies, 10*(3). https://doi.org/10.5539/hes.v10n3p16.

Bonk, J. C. (2009). *The world is open: How web technology is revolutionizing education.* Jossy-Bass.

Bryman, A. (2004). *Social research methods.* Oxford University Press.

Bussis, A. M., & Chittenden, E. M. (1970). *An analysis of open education.* Educational Testing Service.

Clinton, V. (2018). Cost, outcomes, use, and perceptions of open educational resources in psychology: A narrative review of literature. *Psychology Learning and Teaching, 18*(1), 4–20. https://doi.org/10.1177/1475725718799511

Fetter, S., Berlanga, A. J., & Sloep, P. B. (2012). Peer-support and open educational resources. In *Collaborative Learning 2.0: Open Educational Resources* (pp. 253–271). IGI Global.

Harold, S., & Rolfe, V. (2019). "I find the whole enterprise daunting": Staff understanding of Open Education initiatives within a UK university. *Open Praxis, 11*(1), 71–83.

Huang, R., Liu, D., Tlili, A., Knyazeva, S., Chang, T. W., Zhang, X., Burgos, D., Jemni, M., Zhang, M., Zhuang, R., & Holotescu, C. (2020). *Guidance on open educational practices during school closures: Utilizing OER under COVID-19 Pandemic in line with UNESCO OER recommendation.* Smart Learning Institute of Beijing Normal University.

Hülsmann, T. (2000). The cost of open learning: A handbook. Bibliotheks-und Informationssystem der Universität Oldenburg.

Iiyoshi, T., & Kumar, M. S. V. (Eds.). (2008). *Opening up education: The collective advancement of education through open technology, open content, and open knowledge* (pp. 47–59). MIT Press.

Lambert, S. R. (2018). Changing our (dis)course: A distinctive social justice aligned definition of open education. *Journal of Learning for Development, 5*(3).

Laurillard, D. (2008). Open teaching: The key to sustainable and effective open education. In T. Iiyoshi and M. S. V. Kumar (Eds.), *Opening up education: The collective advancement of education through open technology, open content, and open knowledge* (pp. 319–335). MIT Press. https://jl4d.org/index.php/ejl4d/article/view/290.

Muleya, G., Simui, F. Mundende, K., Kakana, F., Mwewa, G. & Namangala, B. (2019). Exploring learning cultures of digital immigrants in technologically mediated postgraduate distance learning mode at the University of Zambia. *Zambia Informational Communication Technology (ICT) Journal, 3*(3), 1–10. https://ictjournal.icict.org.zm/index.php/zictjournal/article/view/83.

Musingafi, M. C. C., Mapuranga, B., Chiwanza, K., & Zebron, S. (2015). Challenges for open and distance learning (ODL) students: Experiences from students of the Zimbabwe Open University. *Journal of Education and Practice, 6*(18), 59.

Ouma, R., & Nkuyubwatsi, B. (2019). Transforming university learner support in open and distance education: Staff and students perceived challenges and prospects. *Cogent Education, 6*, 1. https://doi.org/10.1080/2331186X.2019.1658934

Rahman, H. (2014). The role of ICT in open and distance education. *Turkish Online Journal of Distance Education-TOJDE, 15*(4), Article 9. https://www.researchgate.net/publication/273898 911_The_Role_Of_Ict_In_Open_And_Distance_Education. Accessed October 27, 2020.

Seely Brown, J., & Adler, R. P. (2008). Open education, the long tail, and learning 2.0. *Educause Review, 43*(1), 16–20.

Simui, F. (2018). *Lived experiences of students with visual impairments at Sim University in Zambia: A hermeneutic phenomelogical approach.* University of Zambia. Unpublished PhD Thesis.

Simui, F., Chibale, H., & Namangala, B. (2017a). Distance education examination management in a lowly resourced north-eastern region of Zambia: A phenomenological approach. *Open Praxis, 9*(3), 299–312. https://doi.org/10.5944/openpraxis.9.3.442

Simui, F., Kasonde-Ngandu, S., Cheyeka, A. M., Simwinga, J., & Ndhlovu, D. (2018a). Enablers and disablers to academic success of students with visual impairment: A 10-year literature disclosure, 2007–201. *British Journal of Visual Impairment, 36*(2), 163–174. https://doi.org/10.1177/026461 9617739932

Simui, F., Mwewa, G., Chota, A., Kakana, F., Mundende, K., Thompson, L., Mwanza, P., Ndhlovu, D., & Namangala, B. (2018b). "WhatsApp" as a learner support tool for distance education: Implications for Policy and Practice at University of Zambia. *Zambia ICT Journal, 2*(2), 36–44. https://doi.org/10.33260/zictjournal.v2i2.55.

Simui, F., Namangala, B., Tambulukani, G., & Ndhlovu, D. (2018c). Demystifying the process of ODL policy development in a dual-mode context: Lessons from Zambia. *Journal of Distance Education.* https://doi.org/10.1080/01587919.2018.1457946

Simui, F., Nyaruwata, L. T., & Kasonde-Ngandu, S. (2017). ICT as an enabler to academic success of students with visually impaired at Sim University: Hermeneutics approach. *Zambia ICT Journal, 1*(1): 5–9. http://ictjournal.icict.org.zm/index.php/zictjournal/article/view/9

Sinclair, E. (2017). A case study on the importance of peer support for e-Learners. In *Proceedings of the 9th International Conference on Computer Supported Education (CSEDU 2017)* (Vol. 2, pp. 280–284). https://doi.org/10.5220/0006263602800284.

Tunnell, D. (1975). Open Education: An expression in search of a definition. D. Nyberg (Ed.), *The philosophy of open education* (pp. 10–16). Routledge and Kegan Paul.

Walberg, H. J., & Thomas, S. C. (1971). *Characteristics of open education: Toward an operational definition.* TDR Associates Inc.

Webb, E., Campbell, D. T., Schwartz, R. D., & Sechrest, L. (1966). *Unobtrusive measures: Non-reactive research in the social sciences.* Rand McNally.

Webb, E., Campbell, D. T., Schwartz, R. D., Sechrest, L., & Grove, J. G. (1981). *Non-reactive measures in the social sciences* (2nd ed.). Houghton Mifflin.

Woo, E. H. C., White, P., & Lai, C. W. K. (2016). Impact of information and communication technology on child health: ICT and child health. *Journal of Paediatrics and Child Health, 52*(6), 590–594. https://doi.org/10.1111/jpc.13181

Francis Simui is a senior lecturer at the University of Zambia. He is an educationist with vast experience working with civil society organisations. His areas of specialisation include: (i) developing effective Open and Distance Education system and (ii) developing an effective inclusive education systems. He is a Canon Collins Trust/Chevening Alumni and a board member of Advisory Board of the Network of Open Educational Resources and Multimodal Self-Directed Learning in Southern Africa (NOMSA).

Karen Ferreira-Meyers is Associate Professor and Coordinator Linguistics and Modern Languages at the Institute of Distance Education (University of Eswatini). She has a keen interest in research on open education, open pedagogy and OER in addition to the teaching and learning of languages, distance and e-learning, autofiction and autobiography, African literatures, crime and detective fiction. She publishes regularly on these subjects, both in English and in French. Translation and interpreting are also close to her heart, in particular when they are education-related. She holds a Ph.D. in French and Francophone literatures, four Master's degrees (Romance Philology, English Linguistics for the Language Practitioner, LLM and MIDT) and strongly believes in lifelong learning.

Chapter 8
Can Open Science Offer Solutions to Science Education in Africa?

Karen Ferreira-Meyers and Amit Dhakulkar

Abstract In this chapter, we examine some international and continental challenges related to science education and science teacher training. Authors such as De Beer (J New Gener Sci 14:34–53, 2016) indicate that there is a general lack of qualified science and mathematics teachers in African primary and secondary schools. In addition to the challenge of integrating indigenous knowledge in African schools (Jegede in Int J Sci Educ 19:1–20, 1997; De Beer in The decolonisation of the curriculum project: the affordances of indigenous knowledge for self-directed learning, (NWU self-directed learning series, volume 2), AOSIS, Cape Town, 2019b), science education challenges can be classified as systemic (e.g. lack of resources, outdated curriculum, curricular change, policy reform and classroom-related aspects (e.g. class size, teacher pedagogical content knowledge and skills, relevant assessments) (Ogunniyi and Rollnick in J Sci Teach Educ 26:65–79, 2015; Tikly et al. in Supporting secondary school STEM education for sustainable development in Africa, University of Bristol, 2018). Literature review forms this chapter's main research methodology. Research questions are related to the following thematic areas: communities of practice for science teachers, contextualisation and Indigenous Knowledge Systems (IKS), and assessments. Open Science (OS), its components, benefits and general principles (openness, inclusion, fairness, equity and sharing) are used to develop a framework/model to address the issues raised. While scholars are increasingly motivated to augment the transparency of their work using the Open Science Framework (OSF) (Bezjak et al. in Open science training handbook, Zenodo, 2018; Munafò et al. in Nat Hum Behav 1:1–9, 2017; Nosek et al. in Science 348:1422–1425, 2015; Nosek et al. in Proc Natl Acad Sci 115:2600–2606, 2018; Stall et al. in Nature 570:27–29, 2019), it is not clear whether the uptake of OS is similar for science educators. The proposed model makes use of different aspects of the OSF to create a community of practice of teachers and students with a peer network of "critical friends". In our conclusion, we give recommendations in view of radically improving science teacher education on the African continent and beyond.

K. Ferreira-Meyers (✉)
Institute of Distance Education, University of Eswatini, Kwaluseni, Swaziland

A. Dhakulkar
University of the North West, Potchefstroom, South Africa

149
D. Burgos and J. Olivier (eds.), *Radical Solutions for Education in Africa*, Lecture Notes in Educational Technology, https://doi.org/10.1007/978-981-16-4099-5_8

Our proposed model offers the opportunity to extend the principle of openness to science teachers and students by fostering sharing, collaboration while also focusing on self-directed learning and constructionist pedagogy.

Keywords Science education · Open science · Teacher education

8.1 Introduction

Science education and in particular science teacher education is an area of concern on the African continent. The lack of trained science teachers (De Beer, 2016) and relevant educational resources (Ogunniyi & Rollnick, 2015; Tikly et al., 2018) have been highlighted as main challenges over the years and a few solutions have been proposed and implemented to overcome these. In this chapter, we examine challenges and identify how solutions can be potentially adapted from the principles of Open Science (OS).

The chapter starts with the observation that, while there is significant research into science teacher education and the reasons for the limited "stock" of qualified science teachers, there is hardly any study which links the issues of science education in general and science teacher education in particular with OS principles. The OS movement is the result of a long period of questioning how science is conducted and how the public finds out about and interacts with scientific research findings. It is also the result of the discovery of problems relating to the way existing scientific methods are applied. These problems include a lack of transparency, insufficient stakeholder involvement, disconnect from the public, and limited reproducibility of research findings (Gigerenzer, 2018; Owens, 2018). The OS approach to science extends principles of openness to the entire research cycle: starting from hypothesis generation and design of experiments to data collection, analysis, interpretation and dissemination. OS seeks to remove all barriers to conducting high quality, rigorous and impactful scientific research by ensuring that the data, methods and opportunities for collaboration are open to all. Emerging digital technologies and "big data" (Zook et al., 2017) have further accelerated the OS movement by creating new approaches to data sharing, connecting researcher networks and facilitating the dissemination of research findings. Seen from this perspective, OS principles have resulted in a novel and inclusive approach to the process of doing science. Our main objective in this study is to investigate whether OS principles can be applied to problems of teaching–learning science in the (virtual) classroom and to potentially transform teaching–learning practices by providing innovative and radical solutions based on appropriate use of technology.

8.1.1 Research Questions

Our research questions arise from themes identified during the review of literature on science teacher education and which can be potentially addressed through the OS framework. These are

1. *Communities of practice for science teachers*: Wenger (2011) defines communities of practice (CoP) as "groups of people who share a concern or a passion for something they do and learn how to do it better as they interact regularly". Thus, in the context of science teacher professional development, such CoPs would provide a forum for teachers to share, reflect on and analyse their classroom practices (MacPhail et al., 2014). This leads us to our first research question: *How can the OS framework help in nurturing and fostering communities of practice in the context of science teacher education in Africa?* In the OS framework, this can be achieved by teachers sharing their practices with the rest of the CoP. Thus, the teachers' CoP can identify and create best practices which take into account the teaching and learning needs and challenges. This includes, but is not limited to, resource generation in the form of low- or no-cost science laboratories, contextual simulations and resource materials within a localised context.

2. *Contextualisation and Indigenous Knowledge Systems*: In recent times, there have been several efforts to bring IKS in tune with the science curriculum. This theme forms our second research question: *How can the OS framework help in IKS contextualisation into science curricula?* There are several layers to this theme: from creation of relevant and contextual learning resources and translations to classroom implementation.

3. *Assessment*: As different studies have highlighted, the teaching–learning practices of science are geared towards summative assessments which are based mostly on rote-memorisation. On the one hand, a parallel can be drawn here to the *product* aspect of doing science, where only the end product (e.g. a research paper) is highlighted. On the other hand, the OS framework emphasises the *process* of doing science and the final *product* is just one part of the overall process. Similarly, we ask the question: what is the equivalent of such a process approach to assessing learning in science? *How can the OS framework help in designing assessment for science learning?*

8.1.2 Methodology

The main methodology adopted for this study was a desktop literature review looking at research on science education and science teacher education in the African context. This is also a useful starting point for further research. Our chapter builds on previous research linking OS principles to science education in order to increase transparency and trustworthiness (see, e.g., Cook, 2016; Cook et al., 2018; Johnson & Cook, 2019; van der Zee & Reich, 2018).

Part 1 thus looks at the literature on science education in Africa and identified challenges in this area. Part 2 focuses on OS principles and the possible benefits OS can bring to science teacher education. Finally, we link each challenge with a proposed OS solution in implementable recommendations, which include a shift in science teacher education towards heightened openness (including collaboration and self-directed learning) which in turn could lead to better qualified teachers able to accompany learners in their quest for twenty-first-century skills.

8.2 Literature Review

In this section, we look at the challenges of science education in the African context and the systemic, infrastructural, historical and socio-cultural aspects of these challenges. We then turn our focus to the OS movement and elaborate on its principles with examples relevant to our study.

8.2.1 Challenges for Science Education

The area of science education and science teacher education has been researched in the African context. De Beer (2016) identifies three major challenges in the South African context, which resonate in other African countries too. These challenges are:

> not enough well-qualified science and mathematics teachers in our schools, that affective outcomes are marginalised in an examination-driven school system, and that many schools have a lack of appropriate equipment and materials for effective teaching and learning. (p. 34)

Added to these challenges is the neglect of IKS which presents a different world and is in sync with the learners' everyday experiences (Le Grange, 2007). We therefore explore the following: (i) impact of IKS on science teaching and learning, (ii) relevant teaching–learning resources (including, but not limited to languages and contexts), (iii) quality of teachers, and (iv) assessment of science learning and related problems.

First we look at issues related to the colonial past of African nations and the indifference to IKS in existing science curricula (see Otulaja & Ogunniyi, 2017). When the African nations became independent they more or less inherited the colonial system of education which had a Western worldview and values embedded within it. Science education in African nations was no exception. Even though, since independence from the colonial past, science has been seen as a way forward to a better future, in general all African countries seem to be lacking in the area of science education. One of the main reasons is the irrelevance of the content of science education in relation to the learners' everyday contexts and socio-cultural milieu (De Beer, 2019a). The Western worldview presents a contrasting and divergent picture of understanding nature to that of the indigenous one. As Jegede (1997) remarks:

Closely related to the issue of authentic science, and of significance to the non-western cultures especially of Africa, is the issue of worldviews projected by school science. School science as currently being taught, projects only one form of worldview - the western view which holds claim to superiority over any other form of studying nature. They neither recognise the variations among people nor the different worldviews learners bring into the science classroom. (p. 4)

Some of the major differences between the Western worldview and IKS are given by Jegede (1997).

African mode of thought	Western science
Anthropomorphic, monistic-vitalistic and metaphysical based on cosmology interwoven with traditional religion orally communicated the elders' repository of knowledge is truth which is not to be challenged learning is a communal activity	Mechanistic, exact and hypothesis-driven seeks empirical laws, principles, generalisation and theories public property, divorced from religion primarily documented via print truth is tentative and challengeable by all learning is an individual enterprise

Thus we see a basic incompatibility between the two modes and a conflict in the models that learners experience in their schools and societies. The science being delivered in only one mode–the Western—presents a decontextualised view and alienates the learners. Since the identification of the importance of IKS, there has been a sustained effort to "decolonise" the curriculum and produce coherent approaches which combine the two views (e.g. see De Beer (2019b) and Le Grange (2016)).

Given this background, the curricula and the classroom practices which have been developed in European contexts will not work as expected in the African contexts. For example, there was a direct "import" of many curricula such as *Nuffield Science* from the developed countries without recognising the worldview of the learners and therefore it did not work (Jegede, 1997).

Another reason for a possible mismatch has to do with language use. The dominance of European languages (English in particular) in academia has led not only to the reduced importance of languages from the Global South in communication, but also to the quiet demise of ways of thinking and knowing inherent to a given language. This aspect of language dominance in communication and ways of thinking has been termed as *epistemicide*—the killing of knowledge systems (Hall & Tandon, 2017; Santos, 2015).

As already identified, the lack of quality teaching–learning resources adds to this. To overcome this challenge, several projects have been creating and disseminating Open Educational Resources (OER) in various languages across Africa. These include: OER Africa, Siyavula, Teacher Education in Sub-Saharan Africa (TESSA), OpenUCT (University of Cape Town), Saide's African Storybook, MATSS programme (Malawi Access to Teaching Scholarship Scheme), OpenLearn, African Health OER Network, AgShare Initiative and AfriVIP (African Veterinary Information Portal). Some of these projects have teaching–learning resources for science, for example, TESSA (http://www.tessafrica.net/) provides a comprehensive resource list for science teachers at different grade levels, in multiple languages, produced by Africans and suited to various African countries. Nevertheless, the nature of such resources in relation to the IKS perspective is not clear. Also, even though the potential of teachers remixing or adapting OERs to their needs is viable due to their licence conditions, there are personal, cultural and psychological challenges preventing this (Harley, 2011). Overall, OER repositories play a crucial role in our envisaged approach using the OS framework for improved science teacher education.

As remarked in the 2007 McKinsey report (Barber & Mourshed, 2007), "[t]he quality of an education system cannot exceed the quality of its teachers", the state of school education is a reflection on the quality of its teachers. Science education in Africa is no exception to this. One of the necessary requirements for any educational programme to succeed is that it should have a robust teacher professional development programme aligned with the objective of the overall educational policy in a particular country. In their study of pre-service science teachers of 12 African countries, Ogunniyi and Rollnick (2015) remark the need for both long-term pre-service professional development along with short courses for in-service teachers; they suggest continuous support for in-service teachers: "Even the in-service programmes for the practising science teachers would need more attention in terms of school-based support and mentorship activities" (p. 77). Ramnarain and Schuster (2014) point to the lack of in-service teacher support for addressing curricular reforms and implementing student-centred pedagogical practices.

Similarly, a critique of programmes for pre-service teachers is the theoretical emphasis on ideas such as constructivism, inquiry, group work and practicals, and the lack of application of these in the "real" classrooms (Stutchbury & Katabaro, 2011, p. 3). Stutchbury and Katabaro (2011) point to the importance of teacher peer networks after listing the following major challenges: making resources available in all the institutions when there is a lack of Internet access or printing resources, assuming teachers can perform given activities and complete the syllabus as well, practical modelling of theoretical ideas during teacher education programmes and supporting pre-service teachers in schools.

Likewise, the most common mode of in-service teacher professional development are disjointed and ineffective workshops, while better learning for teachers happens within their CoPs and through "critical friends" (De Beer & Mentz, 2019; McCarthy & Bernstein, 2011). In addition to these aspects, self-directed learning should be emphasised during teacher professional development sessions, and inputs are needed from partners and other stakeholders to make teacher professional development effective (Sebotsa et al., 2019).

Finally, we note, with Ogunniyi and Rollnick (2015), that formative assessments mimic the way science teaching/learning occurs. As the examinations are heavily rote-memorisation-based, the science teaching itself involves mainly facts and is strongly reliant on memorisation and regurgitation of facts by the students (Jegede, 1997). This emphasis on memorisation in turn changes the pedagogy where teacher-centred knowledge transfer is preferred to the constructivist student-centred mode (Ramnarain & Rudzirai, 2020). Thus, *if assessments are left untouched in any educational reforms, they will severely undermine any innovative teaching–learning processes.* To ensure radical science teacher education transformation, assessment must be reformed along with other systemic changes in education.

8.2.2   Principles of Open Science: Need and Implications

In this section, we define OS and discuss the core principles of the OS movement and their implications for doing science and for science education. The OS movement arose out of limitations in the process of doing science traditionally.

8.2.2.1   Defining OS

The idea of OS is not new; it is based on Mertonian norms of science (Merton, 1973), namely communalism, universalism, disinterestedness, originality, and scepticism (CUDOS). OS is a movement that aims at making scientific research, including publications, data, software, physical samples, accessible to everyone. However, suitable frameworks for its implementation could only be developed in the last two decades or so. Other than the theoretical framework and infrastructural issues, the need for OS is amplified by the social impact of science on society at large and, more recently, due to the Covid-19 pandemic.

OS as a movement can be seen as an umbrella term for many associated practices which rest on the basic principle of sharing work under inclusive licences (see Fig. 8.1, FOSTER taxonomy, below). After many decades with no commonly accepted and formal definition (European Commission, 2016; Kraker et al., 2011; OECD, 2015; Pitrelli & Arabito, 2015), today, there are several approaches and definitions of OS; any given definition will emphasise some aspects of the movement.

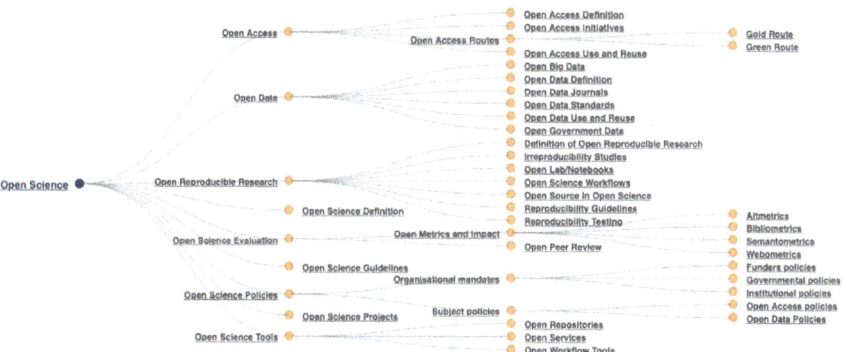

Fig. 8.1 OS FOSTER taxonomy showing the various inclusive categories, from (OECD, 2020; Pontika et al., 2015). The image is released with a Creative Commons 4.0 by NC ND licence

Vicente-Saez and Martinez-Fuentes (2018) proposed the following: "Open Science is transparent and accessible knowledge that is shared and developed through collaborative networks". More recently, Gomes-Diaz and Recio (2020) proposed this: OS is "a political and legal framework where research outputs are shared and disseminated in order to be rendered visible, accessible, reusable is developed, standing over the concepts enhanced by the Budapest Open Science Initiative (BOAI), and by the Free/Open Source Software (FOSS) and Open data movements". We use the term OS as discussed by the public consultation on Science 2.0 Science in Transition (European Commission, 2015) which popularised it (also see Burgelman et al., 2019). For this particular chapter, our focus is on the traditional acceptance of a science teacher, namely that person who teaches physics, biology, chemistry, geography, mathematics and ICT.

Another definition of OS is indicative of the processes involved: "Open science is about the way researchers work, collaborate, interact, share resources and disseminate results. A systemic change towards OS is driven by new technologies and data, the increasing demand in society to address the societal challenges of our times and the readiness of citizens to participate in research" (Netherlands EU Presidency, 2016, p. 2). Broadly speaking, OS is research conducted in a way that allows others to collaborate and contribute (OECD, 2020) which includes diverse elements which are visible in the FOSTER taxonomy (Fig. 8.1).

While there are references to opening up science information and protocols to the general public as early as the sixteenth century (David, 1994, 2008; National Research Council, 2003), it is generally accepted that making complete sets of raw data collected as part of a research project open to the public only became acceptable in the late 1940s, through the start of repositories or archives for social sciences research data (Bisco, 1966). In education too, researchers expressed concern about the closed nature of research practices throughout the twentieth century. For example, Peterson et al. (1982) asked for more details in descriptions of independent variables. In the early 2000s, as a response to the lack of transparency and the limited ability to evaluate research based on published reports only, the need to establish indicators of research quality for correlational, group design, single case and qualitative research was felt (see, e.g., Brantlinger et al., 2005; Gersten et al., 2005).

The relatively recent OS movement is linked to the Open Education movement and the focus on OER. This is not often highlighted in research on OS, but the link is made explicit in this excerpt: "Open Science opens up new ways in which research/education/innovation are undertaken, archived and curated, and disseminated across the globe" (Ayris et al., 2018, p. 4). As such, and as the word "open" implies, it refers to giving open access to information to anyone. The main elements of OS can be summarised broadly in these categories: Open Data, Open Analysis, Open Materials, Preregistration and Open Access. In other words, OS processes are related to open access to research data, open discussion and analysis of research results and open communication with society. According to Van Dijk et al. (2020), OS in educational research provides opportunities to increase the transparency and therefore replicability of research. Transparency, reproducibility and reusability are major components of OS (Wilkinson et al., 2016).

We now explicate the components of OS as seen in Fig. 8.1. The first component, Open Data (OD), refers to the practice of making all raw data used in an analysis publicly available (Nosek et al., 2012; Nuijten, 2019), as opposed to presenting only summary data in a scientific publication, usually in the form of means and standard deviations. Sharing data in an open manner allows researchers to use (part of) these datasets for additional analysis under inclusive open licences. In order for data to be considered open, it must meet the requirements of availability and accessibility (often this is expressed as data being available at a reasonable reproduction cost and, if possible, downloadable from the Internet), reuse and redistribution (this includes that the data can be intermixed with other datasets), universal participation (meaning there should be no discrimination when it comes to accessing data).

OD can also lead to other research based on the same datasets: "A second benefit of Open Science methods is they can serve as a catalyst for research. While data are often collected with a particular hypothesis in mind, it is likely other research questions could be answered using different models with the same data" (Van Dijk et al., 2020). This aspect can have significant implications for classroom practices. Another benefit of OD is the potential of combining different datasets to "ask novel questions, combining data can help answer questions that researchers were not able to answer in their own sample due to low numbers of participants, or low numbers of behavioural occurrence" (Bainter & Curran, 2015).

A related aspect to OD is a data science laboratory, which, according to Hollaway et al. (2020), refers to a cloud-based, collaborative and tailorable platform enabling users with different requirements and expertise to find data-driven solutions to a wide range of challenges. Online, open labs are a key factor in the acquisition of knowledge for sciences because the lack, cost, maintenance of traditional laboratories are contributing factors to inadequate teacher education in Africa (De Beer, 2016). They provide remote, Internet access, by one or many users simultaneously, to real equipment or virtual experiments located elsewhere (Zapata-Rivera et al., 2020).

OS's second component, Open Analysis, means that the public can view and use the different steps undertaken to analyse the open data (Klein et al., 2018). This aspect has important implications for the reproducibility crisis that science is facing. Open Materials is another important feature of OS: all materials used in a study are shared openly (Klein et al., 2018). These materials might include objects such as research-created assessments, questionnaires, intervention protocols and implementation fidelity checklists. Van Dijk and her colleagues (2020) note that the fourth element is Preregistration, which refers to the situation whereby the parameters of a study (i.e. hypotheses, data collection methods, data analysis plan) are delineated (Nosek & Errington, 2019) and uploaded in an online registry which the public can freely download.

The fifth, and arguably most important, element is that of Open Access (OA). OA, by making scientific work accessible outside academia, could produce better informed, less ignorant social actors—including science teachers, which would be beneficial to the common good (Masnick, 2015). OA also means access to publications, realised through a number of current OS instruments such as the use of open licences (e.g. Creative Commons or GNU FDL), open data repositories, preprints, alternative publishing platforms, international infrastructures of scientific information such as Google Scholar, social networks such as ResearchGate, Academia.edu, Unpaywall, Sci-Hub and others aiming to make broader access to scientific knowledge possible. Related to Open Access is the concept of Open Scholarly Communication (Bykov & Shyshkina, 2018) which refers to open peer-review services, provided by electronic journals, use of altmetric platforms, discussion using the open data and publication, and open evaluation of research results.

Finally, we also note the broader inclusive aspects of OS in terms of *citizen science*: "Open scientific collaboration refers to the forms of collaboration in the course of the scientific process that do not fit under open data and open publications. It includes different types of outputs such as open code, open hardware, the use of collaborative platforms between scientists and the 'citizen-science' phenomenon" (Open Science Monitor, 2018). Other researchers include principles relating to Open Methods in OS. The main idea here is to document and make research methodology and methods freely available and thus enhance the scientific process.

In addition, there are Open Education (OE) and Open Educational Practices (OEP), OER and Open Textbooks. We have briefly outlined Africa-specific OER projects in the previous section. According to Hryhorova et al. (2020), such open educational or training portals (such as MIT OpenCourseware, edX, Coursera) provide a new means to prepare scholars and already established teachers to form an educational professional community using the online mode. Ideally, such portals improve the links between existing resources, ensure exchange of information and observance of copyright and intellectual property, share information such as "best online course" competitions, and vacancies (Hryhorova et al., 2020), and allow content to be updated automatically.

In addition to Open Portals, the International African Institute (IAI) lists African Digital Research repositories from 28 countries, also noting that there are no known repositories in 24 African countries (https://www.internationalafricaninstitute.org/repositories). During the pilot phase of the African Open Science Platform additional information was gathered in view of mapping these types of repositories (http://africanopenscience.org.za/). Selected African Research and Education Networks (NRENs) are working together to prepare a framework for the operation of a sustainable, shared OA repository and a research data management platform, as part of the AfricaConnect3 (Oaiya, 2020a). The mission statement of Open Science Africa also lists in its principles IKS and contextualisation (Oaiya, 2020b). Thus we note a growing awareness about the significance of OS and systemic large-scale efforts towards providing the infrastructural facilities for supporting an OS framework within the African contexts. This is a promising development for our own envisaged model of science teaching–learning.

Finally, we note that, in addition to the other "Open" aspects mentioned as core principles of OS, the use of Free and Open Source Software (FOSS) for infrastructural and communication platforms, data storage and analysis, modelling and pedagogical aspects becomes an imperative. Without the use of FOSS, scaling and free use of software resources by all the stakeholders becomes an additional challenge.

In summary, the ability to make discrete connections across the entire research life cycle from start to conclusion and to critically identify sources of bias underpins OS principles and practices. Thus we see that OS includes a variety of elements and practices to bring about universal access to all aspects of the process, which is in contrast to traditional science which only focuses on the end products. In the next section, we discuss the roles each of these categories of OS can play in the teaching–learning practices of science.

8.3 The Proposed Model

In the preceding sections, we have seen some of the challenges to science education in the African context and discussed the core principles of OS and some of their implications. In this section, we outline the model based on the OS framework for addressing some of the identified challenges. The model has two levels of operation: the teacher and the learner level. We set the context of problems a particular level addresses and then proceed to show how these can be solved. Each level has some unique processes, while some of the processes are overlapping or replicated in both levels. Due to the scale and nature of the data, discourse and resources use of digital cloud-based services is necessitated. A cloud-based approach to store and share data provides an opportunity for open learning as it allows broader access to quality learning resources, supports collaborative learning in a learning environment available for the user practically from any place and at any time (Popel et al., 2017). Next we describe the major components and processes of the levels with some relevant explanatory examples. Figure 8.2 shows the overall conceptual structure of the proposed model with its various components, their interlinkages, inputs and outputs.

Teacher Level: As identified in the literature one of the major challenges facing African nations is the lack of qualified science teachers. This lack is both qualitative (overall quality of teachers is inadequate to handle science teaching–learning) and quantitative (there are less teachers than required in the African education systems). The quality aspect can be further categorised into content knowledge, pedagogical knowledge (or even further, as in the Koehler and Mishra's TPACK model: Technological Content Knowledge, Pedagogical Content Knowledge, Technological Pedagogical Knowledge and Technological Pedagogical Content Knowledge), awareness about various resources (both contextual and non-contextual), and classroom practices and management (Koehler & Mishra, 2009).

One of the recurring issues identified with pre-service teacher education is the lack of practical contexts for the theoretical ideas that teachers learn: *the practice that they learn is dissociated from the theory*. And for in-service teachers, the problem has been to find relevant and continuous support for their daily practice. As has been noted, the most common approach to professional support to teachers is disjointed unsuccessful workshops (De Beer & Mentz, 2019; McCarthy & Bernstein, 2011). Thus, in both pre- and in-service training, there is an acute need of continuous and appropriate teacher support.

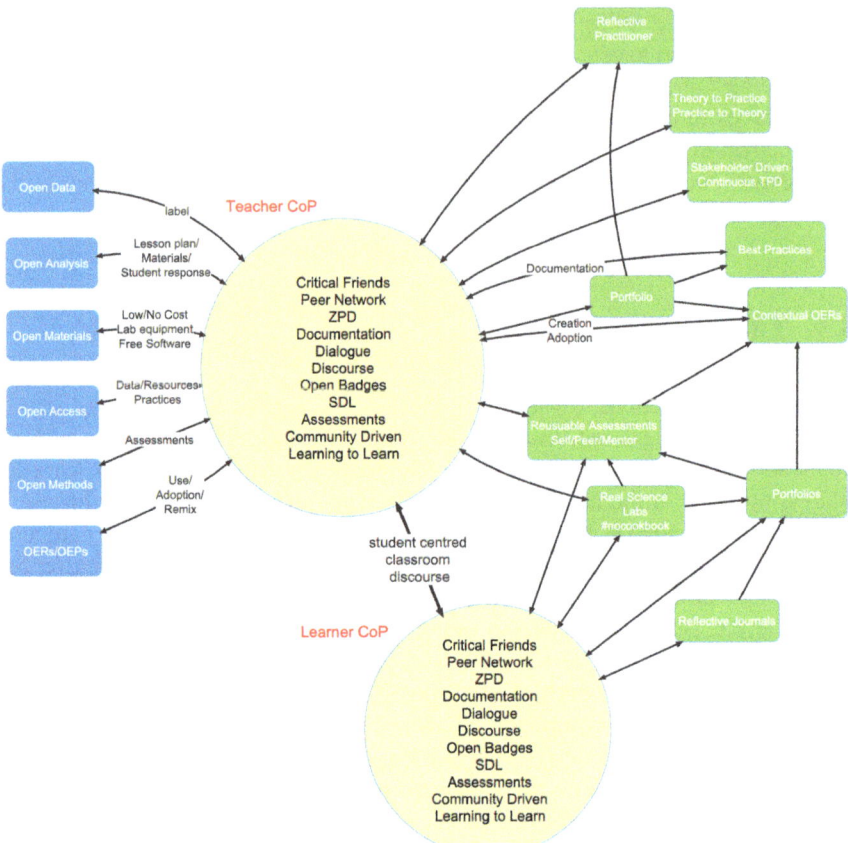

Fig. 8.2 Proposed science education model using OS principles. The major CoP processes and components are indicated inside the circles. The dual arrows represent the two-way traffic of the different categories of inputs and outputs, and the CoPs. The generic inputs are in blue; they are mediated to the students via classroom discourse. The generic outputs are in green; they are interdependent and also feed back to the CoPs

Student Level: The student level of the model is similar to the teacher level but is addressed locally, at the school level. The CoP will be largely limited to the interaction space of the students in the school, with a possibility of connecting with other students of other schools/countries through ICT.

Communities of Practice: To address the concerns identified with regard to science teacher education we propose the formation of *communities of practice* (CoP) of teachers supported by the OS framework. CoPs are defined as "groups of people who share a concern or a passion for something they do and learn how to do it better as they interact regularly" (Wenger, 2011, p. 1) (see also Lave, 1991; Wenger, 1998; Patton & Parker, 2017). We envision the CoP to be a vibrant place where both pre-and in-service teachers can exchange ideas and converse freely. The CoP will be teacher-driven, addressing the problems the teachers face and supporting the synergy between IKS and Western science. Such a forum can be at the cluster (or block) level where a group of schools from a certain geographical area can converse. This can perhaps lead to super- and sub-groups depending on the situation and the number of participants.

The modality of the CoP will be in the form of an online forum where teachers post their reflections on practice and issues important to them and will thus be community-driven. The CoP can be anonymised if needed because of privacy concerns. The CoP might need some mentoring to create the user-base for effective participation. The mentors can be proactive teachers, teacher trainers. An Open Badge system, such as that found in collaborative online fora such as Wikipedia and StackExchange, can promote active participation in the forum activities (see, e.g., Kidwell et al., 2016).

Built based on the OS framework the CoP will be an umbrella structure to cover various facets of teaching and learning science—from the contextual discussion of theoretical ideas to the creation of relevant resources, their implementation and feedback. And, as the theory of diffusion innovation states, there are five stages of any adoption process; there will be always a small group of people who will take initiative in creating and implementing novel ideas in any given population (Rogers, 2003). This has important implications for the spread of innovative ideas developed by teachers in the context of their own classroom that can be shared with other teachers to reuse, adapt and modify to suit their own needs. In addition, Robinson (2009) argues for the importance of peer conversation in the spread of innovations. Kaminski (2011) further points to the concept of peer networks as key in the diffusion of innovation. Peer networks with their internal conversations can be seen as the critical mass of innovators, early adopters and opinion leaders who are capable of initiating the innovation adoption process. Similarly, Valente (2005) demonstrates the substantial influence of peer networks on people's behaviour: "networks are important influences on behaviour because most people acknowledge that they receive information and influence via their social networks and that they model the behavior of others" (p. 113). Thus the support provided by such peer networks will allow innovations to spread in the network and reach all participating teachers.

Peer network of Critical Friends: The concept of a "critical friend" has been an important medium for fostering collaborative learning among teachers (Costa & Kallick, 1993; Wennergren, 2016). The online CoP will provide a larger number of such critical friends than in a physical setting. These critical friends will provide the necessary feedback for resolving challenges and improving the quality of the teaching–learning process. Such a process of providing positive feedback and critique will take time and concerted efforts, in particular from the mentors and more experienced teachers. As in any other CoP or peer network, a *critical mass* of active members will be needed to sustain and grow the community.

Flexible Zone of Proximal Development (ZPD)—Everyone has a role to play: A ZPD, as first posited by Vygotsky (1978), entails the tasks that can and cannot be done by learners with the help of more able peers or mentors. Generally speaking, a ZPD can be seen as the metaphorical distance between the actual developmental level and the potential level that can be achieved with the help of a more able peer or mentor.

Usually, knowledge transfer is seen as *asymmetrical* as the flow of knowledge occurs from a higher to a lower potential. For example, in a classroom situation, the flow of knowledge would be from teachers to students. If the situation is *symmetric*, it would mean the learners are at the same level (Newman et al., 1989). The use of ZPD in teacher education has been explored earlier (Warford, 2011). In our proposed model, the teachers will be at different levels of expertise for various skills which will create an ideal environment for ZPD. But it would be a *flexible* ZPD (Dhakulkar et al., 2018), meaning that the learner identities are not fixed as more or less able peers. A teacher who is a learner (less able peer) in one situation might be a mentor (more able peer) in another, thus the role of learner or mentor is flexible. For example, a learner might need help (less able peer) to understand a complex theoretical idea, while the same learner can be an expert (more able peer) in using a particular application. This aspect has particular significance for IKS as it will help bring such knowledge to the fore in contextual applications and will situate it within the CoP. Such a network, where everyone has something to contribute, creates vibrant opportunities for participation for all and can thus be inclusive.

Sharing of experiences, practices and more—Open Data, Open Analysis, Open Methods: One of the core principles in OS is the sharing of all the processes while doing scientific work, including aspects of Open Data, Open Analysis and Open Methods. Seen in the context of a CoP such data and methods can include innovative practices, classroom logs, reflective notes, student work (e.g. to indicate typical alternative conceptions) or demonstrations and use of equipment. Similarly, the transparent analysis done by the critical friend peer network on a lesson plan or teacher performance in the classroom can help teachers improve their practice. The CoP can also lead to documentation of best practices that have worked well or have not worked as planned in a given context. Any innovation done by a teacher which worked well in the classroom can be included. This is an important aspect of the teaching–learning process to be documented as there is no guarantee that a particular practice will also work in another context. Traditionally, if one were to share these practices, there is no network by which such practices would directly go from one teacher to another with some form of support. The quick feedback on such shared content in an OS-based CoP will entail faster improvement cycles at the grassroots level.

OERs and OEPs—Resources and contextualisation: In one sense the OERs and associated OEPs situated in the CoP are the essence of the proposed model. The OS provides an overall framework which brings together the different components. The major output of the model is in the form of linguistically and culturally contextualised OERs and OEPs to implement them. The 5Rs of OER make such use, adaption, remix and distribution possible. Some aspects of the overlap and the linkages between OS and OE are detailed in Bykov and Shyshkina (2018). Continuous CoP support will also allow the OERs to collaboratively evolve at much faster rates. There are already many OER development projects that work with teachers (e.g. TESSA) but they do not make full use of the OS principles (e.g. continuous sharing of data or practices).

In our model, such OER creation and implementation using OEP is supported by the CoP composed of critical peers and covers all aspects of the teaching–learning processes. Similarly, the IKS can be brought to the fore within the OERs to contextualise the learning by different stakeholders. The standard printed textbooks are based on print technology. Frequent reviews, revisions, contextual (cultural and linguistic) adaptations, and subsequent distribution are not always possible and can be expensive. In this sense, OERs present a potentially perfect solution for such aspects.

Assessments—Self, Peer, Mentor and Standardised: As we have remarked earlier, assessments present the crux of the teaching/learning problem. The entire educational system is geared towards preparing students for year-end examinations. As noted in several studies, these year-end exams are based mostly on memorisation of content (facts) and its reproduction by the students. This issue is equivalent to the *process vs. product* view of doing science. The teaching–learning process is the process, while the score in the final examinations is the product. And, as in traditional science, there is an overemphasis on the product. *Unless this overemphasis is changed no fundamental reform in science education is possible.* These remarks about the assessments apply equally to teacher education and to learners in the various schools.

In our proposed model, we tackle this problem by making the most of the affordances given by the technology-supported OS framework. Broadly we can categorise assessment into four types: self, peer, mentor and standardised. We integrate these four aspects of assessment in the model. The online platform where the learners will participate in the CoP plays a crucial role in this respect. Many aspects of self-assessment can be embedded within the platform (e.g. using simple questions or self-evaluation rubrics). Peer and mentor assessment can be in the form of critical and transparent feedback on the different categories of artefacts posted in the CoP. This will also allow the learners to incorporate the feedback in the next version of the artefact. This idea of versioning in the assignments by the learners after receiving feedback is missing from the current system in both schools and teacher education institutions, but a similar approach is routinely used in other "open" situations (e.g. this chapter itself underwent several revisions). Such assignment revisioning can be done well using suitable platforms and thus is a record of the activities done by the learner. The assignments given to the learners can be personalised and based on a variety of approaches (e.g. inquiry method, project-based learning); the main point here is to document the entire process of doing the assignment (replicating the *process* aspect of doing science).

Also, in this context, giving assignments where all the answers are the same will be of little use (e.g. "Write down Newton's law of gravitation".). We refer here to the concept of "renewable assignments/assessments": "A 'renewable assessment' differs in that the student's work won't be discarded at the end of the process, but will instead add value to the world in some way" (Wiley, 2016, n.p.; also see Jhangiani, 2016; Wiley et al., 2017). This conception of an assignment as work in progress which will lead to an artefact of value at the end of its cycle is completely in line with our proposed model and also fits well within the 5Rs of OERs. This approach can have an outcome which is not possible in the traditional model: students can create and remix the OERs that they will use. For example, they can suggest new demonstrations or (re)write a textbook. Perhaps they might also discover new ways of using IKS and thus make original contributions to the larger body of knowledge. In this sense, the "cookbook" approach to learning science will not be of use. De Beer and Petersen (2016) suggest that #cookbooksmustfall; we agree with them and add that it will work even better when all aspects of the teaching–learning processes are shared in a CoP (just as in the case of OS) and supported by a peer network of critical friends. This will provide contextual assignments which can be approached in a variety of inclusive ways with feedback and assessments from the peer network and will consequently address some important challenges identified above.

When it comes to assessment, *portfolios* also offer an excellent opportunity for providing process-based assessment. Both teachers and students can create public portfolios which contain their relevant contributions and ideas or questions and assignments. These public profiles can themselves be a resource for other teachers and students and serve as an indicator of self-assessment. In addition, they can also be used to appraise the performance of the portfolio holder while bringing transparency to the process.

Reimagining pre-service teacher education: With the proposed CoP in place, the nature and implementation of pre-service teacher education can be reimagined as practice-based and emerging from the real challenges and best practices in the field with concrete connections to the theoretical frameworks underpinning them. In such a scenario education can be learner-driven and will have a strong inclination towards self-directedness. A maxim in teacher education says that most teachers will teach in the manner in which they themselves were taught. We posit that many teaching challenges arise from this fundamental discord of practice and theory: pre-service teachers are not taught in the manner they are supposed to teach. Changing the entire approach to pre-service teacher education to a practice-based approach in which there is a continuous support and mentoring will have a long-term impact on the way science is taught and learned in the schools. This can be based on the concept of micro-credits which the pre-service teachers can earn while they are engaged with practice.

8.4 Discussion: «Let's Speed Up Science Education by Embracing Open Science»[1]

In this section, we briefly discuss the various highlighted points in the previous sections. The quote from Wilder and Levine (2016) was about practices of science, but, as our proposed model shows, it can be equally adapted to science education. The modified quote, where we added "education" can be seen as a one-line summary of the chapter. Clearly, traditional approaches to grassroots- and policy-level problems of science education have not been successful. OS principles can give us a novel approach to potentially solve the issues relating to quality teachers, to the lack of

---

[1] Our title is a variation of Wilder and Levine's (2016) "Let's speed up science by embracing open access publishing".

infrastructure and resources in African schools and, more broadly, education systems, because OS gives stakeholders as participants a voice rather than seeing them as just passive recipients. Student and teacher agency gets a central role in this proposed model, as the (online) CoP is implemented by a network of peers in the form of critical friends. We envision that in these CoPs the student-centred (including pre-service teachers) pedagogical discourse leads to documentation and discussion on the issues most important to the stakeholders. The OS framework with its default open licences for all the shareable content makes the legal spread, use, adaptation and remix of the innovations easier in the network. This aspect is crucial for a free dissemination of knowledge in any particular network. Similarly, the oft contrasting worldview (IKS and Western) can be synthesised to provide a multifaceted approach to do science, with the African contexts, cultures and languages taken into account. This way the stakeholders can create, contribute and change the content, methods, practices as required. This approach allows for a large number of pre-service teachers to access resources with the support of a large peer network of critical friends and addresses our first research question. In this manner, a large cadre of science teachers can be created, who are qualified and will also be continuously improving their practice by being part of the CoP.

Similarly, due to the nature of agency given to the stakeholders for resource and practice creation and adoption, IKS integration will be accomplished from within the community. Here again, the CoP and its peer network will play a crucial role, and, as already indicated, a *flexible* ZPD will make use of the different stakeholder capacities. Thus IKS, along with contextual adaptations for culture and language, will be the stakeholders' responsibility. This addresses our second research question, which looked at how it could become possible to create an environment for integrating IKS and local contexts within the teaching and learning of science.

Finally, for the third research question, which examined assessments, we note that the traditional practice of memorisation-based examinations will have to go. We propose a shift from *product-driven* approaches (national examinations that focus on facts and are often "disposable" in nature) to *process-driven* approaches (contextualised, reusable assessment types, such as portfolios or real project/laboratory-based assignments) which are aided by self, peer and mentor-based (including teacher trainers, head-teacher, inspectors, administrators) transparent feedback and evaluation. Such a change in approach represents a major shift in pedagogical paradigm and power structures/hierarchies and, subsequently, will have far-reaching systemic impact, including, but not limited to, teaching–learning practices, classroom/online discourse and teacher education. The process-driven approach with proper documentation will allow learners to look at their work at different points, which will entail an insight in how they learn. The transparency at each stage of the process with associated feedback from a peer network of critical friends will also create a better contextual understanding. The proposed assessments, reflective journaling and participation in the peer network all have a strong learner-centred (both teachers and students) component and will thus also entail self-directed learning (SDL). For SDL to take root in the CoP more agency should be explicitly given to the learners as a part of the strategy (Bosch et al., 2019; Brockett & Hiemstra, 2019; Knowles,

1975). Similarly, the proposed model includes influence of constructionist pedagogy espoused by Seymour Papert who emphasises construction of public artefacts which are personally meaningful (Noss & Hoyles, 2017; Papert, 1980). Finally, we note that the peer network of critical friends will help fulfil the most crucial requirement in learning as per constructionist pedagogy: "The kind of knowledge that children most need is the knowledge that will help them get more knowledge" (Papert, 1993, p. 139). In our model, the "children" are both teachers and students. How the proposed model entails SDL and constructionist pedagogy needs to be articulated in detail and is not our current focus.

The overall output of the model in terms of contextual OERs, best practices, documentation of classroom discourse and creation of CoP for both teachers and students can influence a wider research culture and environment, including reward and recognition for OS practices and contributions to the global ecosystem. It is established that the OS approach has its benefits and is generally seen in a positive light (Harle & Warne, 2019). But the implementation of the proposed model will lead to systemic changes which are not peripheral in nature. In this sense, the model we propose is highly disruptive, which will redraw many boundaries between the different stakeholders and the roles that they play. Nevertheless, such a restructuring is necessary if we have to create a suitable and sustainable environment for implementing such a novel and radical solution.

8.4.1 Recommendations

We now list some of the broad recommendations that are warranted by the proposed model.

1. Systemic policy-level changes at national and institutional level to help create:

    (a) Digital infrastructure for the OS framework and its maintenance.
    (b) CoP for both teachers and students.
    (c) Standard Operating Procedures for data sharing.
    (d) Enabling environment for creating, sharing and adapting OERs and OEPs with IKS.

2. Sustained effort at the grassroots level to:

    (a) Engage various stakeholders in the CoP in a positive manner.
    (b) Help create an enabling environment for creating, sharing and adapting OERs and OEPs.
    (c) Assimilate IKS within the OERs and OEPs.
    (d) Raise awareness about OS and its implications.

3. A revamp of the science teacher education programmes from the grassroots level upwards based on the CoP.

4. More agency given to teachers and students to decide classroom discourse and assessment.
5. A radical change to the science education assessments which focus on self, peers and mentors and which are highly contextualised and personalised.

8.4.2 Challenges

One of the crucial challenges to the proposed model is the presence of digital infrastructure to turn it into reality. Universal access to connected computing devices, online platforms and associated services are a must (Gomes-Diaz & Recio, 2020). Digital literacy is a prerequisite for the proposed model to work. A synergy of such OER and OS existing or proposed projects and their experiences in the field will be crucial in implementing the proposed model. Also, it is important to note that, just because resources are Open Access, does not mean that they have no associated costs. The proposed model further needs to look at the financial aspects in the local ecosystems for an economically sustainable implementation.

The other major challenge is the cultural shift in some of the standard practices in the traditional school environment and in teacher education. Further, many of the traditional power hierarchies will get challenged in the proposed model, as it allows for transparency at all levels. For example, mentors will have to give reasons publicly for their evaluation of a learner. In addition to this, the creation of the synergy between IKS and some of the scientific principles might not always be easy to achieve. Further, there are other challenges to OS acceptance and implementation: not everything can be open (certain data is inaccessible for reasons of privacy, security and safety) and there needs to be a system of checks and balances to ensure that data is ethically shared. These challenges which look at the infrastructural, ethical and cultural aspects warrant further detailed studies.

Affirmative changes at policy level (institutional and national) which will help the implementation of the proposed model are needed, with a focus on setting up the infrastructure and environment for the OS framework (Gomes-Diaz & Recio, 2020). Harle and Warne (2020) note the existence of (draft) national policies—or the strongly worded intention to have such—on open data/OS in Ethiopia, Zambia, Botswana, Uganda, Namibia, Kenya, Burkina Faso, Côte d'Ivoire and Senegal. It remains a task to make institutional policies on science education which embraces the nascent OS framework as per our proposed model.

8.5 Conclusion

The chapter sought to respond to the challenge thrown at the academic and scientific community by Vicente-Saez and Martinez-Fuentes (2018), namely that it would be interesting to explore the links among Open Learning, OS and Open Innovation, and to find out how these contribute to the creation of a new Open Society. Our focus in this chapter was on OS and science education. Krishna (2020) proposed the development of the ideals of OS and a social contract between science and society. This can be done through improved science teacher education, continued teacher professional development and change in teaching and learning practices. This is especially relevant in the light of the Covid-19 pandemic, when science teacher education will have to be drastically revised.

Our research design based on an exploratory qualitative study through literature review and informal discussions with science teacher educators has allowed us to unearth a number of important challenges and avenues for solutions, relating to the use of OS principles in science education and particularly in science teacher education.

We formulated three research questions which focused on CoPs for science teachers, contextualisation of IKS within the resources and teaching–learning processes, and the nature and implementation of assessments. We proposed a model based on the OS principles to address these challenges. We recognise that this is a theoretical model, which might need long-term efforts and investment to be implemented, especially given the infrastructural and cultural challenges in the African context. This remains an obvious limitation of the study. Other limitations are related to mapping the detailed influence of the different components of the CoP, their interactions and their pedagogical aspects.

Using the OS framework requires a culture of change that prepares future citizens, teachers and researchers. It is a fairly novel (and at times radical) way of organising scientific processes based on collaboration and knowledge sharing through the use of digital technologies. While OS scholars and researchers mostly focus on how the movement prompts transformation in the way research is conducted and disseminated, our stance is related to pedagogy and how science teacher education and its challenges on the African continent can be addressed. If, during teacher education, we can demonstrate and encourage future teachers to become early adopters of OS practices, they can go on to explore opportunities for OS collaborations in consortia or research networks and connect with other teachers and researchers to build OS communities.

OS principles also "open up" borders, meaning that, as educational stakeholders, we can access data, methods, methodologies, evaluations, scholarly communication and publications that are available throughout the world. We are no longer limited to what happens within our continent. While unilaterally importing solutions from outside the African continent will continue to augment Western bias, participating on an equal footing via an OS platform will give us an opportunity to include principles of IKS specific to our teaching and learning environments. We need to adapt the OS framework to our needs and problems.

References

Ayris, P., López de San Román, A., Maes, K., & Labastida, I. (2018). Open science and its role in universities: A roadmap for cultural change. *Leuven: LERU Office*. Retrieved November 20, 2020.

Bainter, S. A., & Curran, P. J. (2015). Advantages of integrative data analysis for developmental research. *Journal of Cognition and Development, 16*(1), 1–10.

Barber, M., & Mourshed, M. (2007). *How the world's best-performing schools systems come out on top*. McKinsey & Company.

Bezjak, S., Clyburne-Sherin, A., Conzett, P., Fernandes, P., Görögh, E., Helbig, K., Kramer, B., Labastida, I., Niemeyer, K., Psomopoulos, F., Ross-Hellauer, T., Schneider, R., Tennant, J., Verbakel, E., Brinken, H., & Heller, L. (2018). *Open science training handbook*. Zenodo.

Bisco, R. L. (1966). Social science data archives: A review of developments. *The American Political Science Review, 60*(1), 93–109.

Bosch, C., Mentz, E., & Goede, R. (2019). Self-directed learning: A conceptual overview. In E. Mentz, J. De Beer, & R. Bailey (Eds.), *Self-directed learning for the 21st century: Implications for higher education* (pp. 1–36). AOSIS.

Brantlinger, E., Jimenez, R., Klingner, J., Pugach, M., & Richardson, V. (2005). Qualitative studies in special education. *Exceptional Children, 71*(2), 195–207.

Brockett, R. G., & Hiemstra, R. (2019). *Self-direction in Adult learning: Perspectives on theory, research and practice*. Routledge.

Burgelman, J. C., Pascu, C., Szkuta, K., Von Schomberg, R., Karalopoulos, A., Repanas, K., & Schouppe, M. (2019). Open science, open data and open scholarship: European policies to make science fit for the 21st century. *Frontiers in Big Data, 2*(43).

Bykov, V. Y., & Shyshkina, M. P. (2018). The conceptual basis of the university cloud-based learning and research environment formation and development in view of the open science priorities, нформаційні технології i засоби навчання *(Information Technologies and Learning Tools), 68*(6), 1–19.

Cook, B. G. (2016). Reforms in academic publishing: Should behavioral disorders and special education journals embrace them? *Behavioral Disorders, 41*(3), 161–172.

Cook, B. G., Lloyd, J. W., Mellor, D., Nosek, B. A., & Therrien, W. J. (2018). Promoting open science to increase the trustworthiness of evidence in special education. *Exceptional Children, 85*(1), 104–118.

Costa, A. L., & Kallick, B. (1993). Through the lens of a critical friend. *Educational Leadership, 51*, 49–51.

Curran, P. J., & Hussong, A. M. (2009). Integrative data analysis: The simultaneous analysis of multiple data sets. *Psychological Methods, 14*(2), 81.

David, P. A. (1994). Positive feedbacks and research productivity in science: Reopening another black box. In O. Grandstand (Ed.), *Economics and Technology* (pp. 65–89). Elsevier.

David, P. A. (2008). The historical origins of 'open science': An essay on patronage, reputation and common agency contracting in the scientific revolution. *Capitalism and Society, 3*(2).

De Beer, J. (2016). Re-imagining science education in South Africa: The affordances of indigenous knowledge for self-directed learning in the school curriculum. *Journal for New Generation Sciences, 14*(3), 34–53.

De Beer, J. (2019a). Glocalisation: The role of indigenous knowledge in the global village. In J. De Beer (Ed.), *The decolonisation of the curriculum project: The affordances of indigenous knowledge for self-directed learning, (NWU Self-directed Learning Series Volume 2)* (pp. 1–23). AOSIS.

De Beer, J. (Ed.) (2019b). *The decolonisation of the curriculum project: The affordances of indigenous knowledge for self-directed learning,* (NWU Self-directed Learning Series Volume 2), AOSIS, Cape Town.

De Beer, J., & Mentz, E. (2019). The use of cultural-historical activity theory in researching the affordances of indigenous knowledge for self-directed learning. In J. De Beer (Ed.), *The decolonisation of the curriculum project: The affordances of indigenous knowledge for self-directed learning (NWU Self-directed Learning Series Volume 2)* (pp. 87–116). AOSIS.

De Beer, J., & Petersen, N. (2016). Decolonisation of the science curriculum: A different perspective (#Cookbook-Labs-Must-Fall). In *Proceedings from ISTE International Conference on Mathematics, Science and Technology Education: Towards Effective Teaching and Meaningful Learning in Mathematics, Science and Technology*.

Dhakulkar, A., Shaikh, R., & Nagarjuna, G. (2018). Zone of proximal development in the era of connected computers. In S. Ladage & S. Narvekar (Eds.), *Proceedings of epiSTEME 7 International Conference to Review Research on Science, Technology and Mathematics Education* (pp. 214–221). Ed. by. CinnamonTeal Publishing.

European Commission. (2015). *Validation of the results of the public consultation on Science 2.0: Science in Transition*. Retrieved October 25, 2020 from https://ec.europa.eu/research/consultations/science-2.0/science_2_0_final_report.pdf.

European Commission. (2016). *Open innovation, Open Science, open to the world. A vision for Europe*. Brussels: European Commission, Directorate-General for Research and Innovation.

Gersten, R., Fuchs, L. S., Compton, D., Coyne, M., Greenwood, C., & Innocenti, M. S. (2005). Quality indicators for group experimental and quasi-experimental research in special education. *Exceptional Children, 71*(2), 149–164.

Gigerenzer, G. (2018). Statistical rituals: The replication delusion and how we got there. *Advances in Methods and Practices in Psychological Science, 1*(2), 198–218.

Gomes-Diaz, T. & Recio, T. (2020), *A policy and legal Open Science framework: a proposal*. Retrieved October 25, 2020 from https://arxiv.org/pdf/2010.04508.pdf.

Hall, B. L., & Tandon, R. (2017). Decolonization of knowledge, epistemicide, participatory research and higher education. *Research for All, 1*(1), 6–19.

Harley, K. (2011). Insights from the Health OER inter-institutional project. *Distance Education, 32*(2), 213–227.

Harle, J., & Warne, V. (2019). *Open Access: Challenges and opportunities for Low- and Middle- Income Countries and the potential impact of UK policy*. Retrieved November 20, 2020 from https://assets.publishing.service.gov.uk/media/5f85aa45e90e0732a2448113/20-10-05_DFID_OA_in_LMICs_-_final_report.pdf.

Hollaway, M. J., Dean, G., Blair, G. S., Brown, M., Henrys, P. A., & Watkins, J. (2020). Tackling the challenges of 21st-century open science and beyond: A data science lab approach. *Patterns, 1*(7), 100–103.

Hryhorova, T., Lyashenko, V. P., Hvozdeva, I., & Getman, I. (2020). Use of open training portals to host developed STEM courses. In *43rd International Convention on Information, Communication and Electronic Technology (MIPRO)* (pp. 622–625). IEEE.

Jegede, O. J. (1997). School science and the development of scientific culture: A review of contemporary science education in Africa. *International Journal of Science Education, 19*(1), 1–20.

Jhangiani, R. (2016, December 7). Ditching the "Disposable assignment" in favor of open pedagogy. https://doi.org/10.31219/osf.io/g4kfx.

Johnson, A. H., & Cook, B. G. (2019). Preregistration in single-case design research. *Exceptional Children, 86*(1), 95–112.

Kaminski, J. (2011). Diffusion of innovation theory. *Canadian Journal of Nursing Informatics, 6*(2), 1–6.

Kidwell, M. C., Lazarević, L. B., Baranski, E., Hardwicke, T. E., Piechowski, S., Falkenberg, L. S., & Errington, T. M. (2016). Badges to acknowledge open practices: A simple, low-cost, effective method for increasing transparency. *PLoS Biology, 14*(5), e1002456.

Klein, O., Hardwicke, T. E., Aust, F., Breuer, J., Danielsson, H., Hofelich Mohr, A., & Frank, M. C. (2018). A practical guide for transparency in psychological science. *Collabra: Psychology, 4*(1), 1–15.

Knowles, M. (1975). *Self-directed learning: A guide for learners and teachers*. Cambridge Books.

Koehler, M., & Mishra, P. (2009). What is technological pedagogical content knowledge (TPACK)? *Contemporary Issues in Technology and Teacher Education, 9*(1), 60–70.

Kraker, P., Leony, D., Reinhardt, W., & Beham, G. (2011). The case for an open science in technology enhanced learning. *International Journal of Technology Enhanced Learning, 3*(6), 643–654.

Krishna, V. V. (2020). Open science and its enemies: Challenges for a sustainable science-society social contract. *Journal of Open Innovation: Technology, Market, and Complexity, 6*(3), 61.

Lave, J. (1991). Situating learning in communities of practice. In L. B. Resnick, J. M. Levine, & S. D. Teasley (Eds.), *Perspectives on socially shared cognition* (pp. 63–82). American Psychological Association.

Law, Y.-H., (2018). Replication failures highlight biases in ecology and evolution science. *The Scientist Magazine*. Retrieved November 20, 2020 from https://www.the-scientist.com/features/replication-failures-highlight-biases-in-ecology-and-evolution-science-64475.

Le Grange, L. (2007). Integrating western and indigenous knowledge systems: The basis for effective science education in South Africa? *International Review of Education, 53*(5–6), 577–591.

Le Grange, L. (2016). Decolonising the university curriculum: Leading article. *South African Journal of Higher Education, 30*(2), 1–12.

MacPhail, A., Patton, K., Parker, M., & Tannehill, D. (2014). Leading by example: Teacher educators' professional learning through communities of practice. *Quest, 66*(1), 39–56.

Masnick, M. (2015). Don't Think Open Access Is Important? It Might Have Prevented Much Of The Ebola Outbreak. Retrieved October 9, 2020 from https://www.techdirt.com/articles/20150409/17514230608/dont-think-open-access-is-important-it-might-have-prevented-much-ebola-outbreak.shtml.

McCarthy, J., & Bernstein, A. (2011). Value in the classroom: The quantity and quality of South Africa's teachers. Centre for Development and Enterprise.

Merton, R. K. (1973). *The sociology of science: Theoretical and empirical investigations.* University of Chicago Press.

Munafò, M. R., Nosek, B. A., Bishop, D. V. M., Button, K. S., Chambers, C. D., du Sert, N. P., Simonsohn, U., Wagenmakers, E.-J., Ware, J. J., & Ioannidis, J. P. A. (2017). A manifesto for reproducible science. *Nature Human Behaviour, 1*(1), 1–9.

National Research Council. (2003). The purpose of publication and responsibilities for sharing. In *Sharing publication-related data and materials: Responsibilities of authorship in the life sciences.* The National Academies Press.

Netherlands EU Presidency. (2016). *Amsterdam Call for Action, 2016*. Retrieved October 10, 2020 from https://www.government.nl/binaries/government/documents/reports/2016/04/04/amsterdam-call-for-action-on-open-science/amsterdam-call-for-action-on-open-science.pdf.

Newman, D., Griffin, P., & Cole, M. (1989). *The construction zone: Working for cognitive change in school.* Cambridge University Press.

Nosek, B. A., Alter, G., Banks, G. C., Borsboom, D., Bowman, S. D., Breckler, S. J., Buck, S., Chambers, C. D., Chin, G., Christensen, G., Contestabile, M., Dafoe, A., Eich, E., Freese, J., Glennerster, R., Goroff, D., Green, D. P., Hesse, B., Humphreys, M., & Yarkoni, T. (2015). Promoting an open research culture. *Science, 348*(6242), 1422–1425.

Nosek, B. A., Ebersole, C. R., DeHaven, A. C., & Mellor, D. T. (2018). The preregistration revolution. *Proceedings of the National Academy of Sciences, 115*(11), 2600–2606.

Nosek, B. A., & Errington, T. M. (2019, September 10). *What is replication?* https://doi.org/10.1371/journal.pbio.3000691.

Nosek, B. A., Spies, J. R., & Motyl, M. (2012). Scientific utopia: II. Restructuring incentives and practices to promote truth over publishability. *Perspectives on Psychological Science, 7*(6), 615–631.

Noss, R., & Hoyles, C. (2017). Constructionism and microworlds. In E. Duval, M. Sharples, & R. Sutherland (Eds.), *Technology enhanced learning* (pp. 29–35). Springer.

Nuijten, M. B. (2019). Practical tools and strategies for researchers to increase replicability. *Developmental Medicine & Child Neurology, 61*(5), 535–539.

Oaiya, O. (2020, August 01). *LIBSENSE in AfricaConnect3*. Retrieved November 20, 2020 from https://spaces.wacren.net/display/LIBSENSE/LIBSENSE+in+AfricaConnect3.

Oaiya, O. (2020, September 09). *Open Science Africa: Principles and actions for global participation.* Retrieved November 20, 2020 from https://spaces.wacren.net/display/LIBSENSE/Open+Science+Africa%3A+Principles+and+Actions+for+Global+Participation.

OECD. (2015). Making open science a reality. *OECD Science, Technology and Industry Policy Papers* (Vol. 25). OECD Publishing.

OECD. (2020). *Open Science*. Retrieved November 20, 2020 from https://www.oecd.org/science/inno/open-science.htm.

Ogunniyi, M. B., & Rollnick. (2015). Pre-service science teacher education in Africa: Prospects and challenges. *Journal of Science Teacher Education, 26*(1), 65–79.

Open Science Monitor. (2018, 30 April). *Open Science Monitor Draft Methodological Note.* Retrieved November 20, 2020 from https://ec.europa.eu/info/sites/info/files/open_science_monitor_methodological_note_v2.pdf.

Otulaja, F. S., & Ogunniyi, M. B. (Eds.). (2017). *The World of Science Education: Handbook of research in science education in sub-Saharan Africa.* Springer.

Owens, B. (2018) Replication failures in psychology not due to differences in study populations. *Nature News.* Retrieved November 20, 2020 from https://www.nature.com/articles/d41586-018-07474-y.

Papert, S. (1980). *Mindstorms; Children, computers and powerful ideas.* Basic Books.

Papert, S. (1993). *The children's machine: Rethinking school in the age of the computer.* Basic Books.

Patton, K., & Parker, M. (2017). Teacher education communities of practice: More than a culture of collaboration. *Teaching and Teacher Education, 67*, 351–360.

Peterson, L., Homer, A. L., & Wonderlich, S. A. (1982). The integrity of independent variables in behavior analysis. *Journal of Applied Behavior Analysis, 15*(4), 477–492.

Pitrelli, N., & Arabito, S. (2015). Open Science training and education: Challenges and difficulties on the researcher' side and in public engagement. *Journal of Science Communication, 14*(4), C01.

Pontika, N., Knoth, P., Cancellieri, M., & Pearce, S. (2015, October). Fostering open science to research using a taxonomy and an eLearning portal. In *Proceedings of the 15th International Conference on Knowledge Technologies and Data-Driven Business* (pp. 1–8).

Popel, M., Shokalyuk, S. & Shyshkina, M. (2017). The Learning Technique of the SageMathCloud Use for Students Collaboration Support. In *ICT in Education, Research and Industrial Applications: Integration, Garmonization and Knowledge Transfer*, CEUR-WS.org, 1844 (pp. 327–339).

Ramnarain, U. D., & Rudzirai, C. (2020). Enhancing the pedagogical practice of South African Physical Sciences teachers in inquiry-based teaching through empowerment evaluation. *International Journal of Science Education, 42*(10), 1739–1758.

Ramnarain, U., & Schuster, D. (2014). The pedagogical orientations of South African physical sciences teachers towards inquiry or direct instructional approaches. *Research in Science Education, 44*(4), 627–650.

Robinson, L. (2009). *A summary of diffusion of innovations.* Retrieved November 20, 2020 from http://www.enablingchange.com.au/Summary_Diffusion_Theory.pdf

Rogers, E. (2003). *Diffusion of innovations* (5th ed.). New York.

Santos, B. S. (2015). *Epistemologies of the South: Justice against epistemicide.* Routledge.

Sebotsa, T., De Beer, J., & Kriek, J. (2019, October). Self-directed learning and teacher professional development: An adapted Profile of Implementation. In *Proceedings of Teaching and Education Conferences* (No. 9612181). International Institute of Social and Economic Sciences.

Stall, S., Yarmey, L., Cutcher-Gershenfeld, J., Hanson, B., Lehnert, K., Nosek, B. A., Parsons, M., Robinson, E., & Wyborn, L. (2019). Make scientific data FAIR. *Nature, 570*(7759), 27–29.

Stutchbury, K., & Katabaro, J. (2011). TESSA secondary science: Addressing the challenges facing science teacher-education in Sub-Saharan Africa. In *DETA Conference 2011*, 3–5 August 2011, Maputo, Mozambique.

Tikly, L., Joubert, M., Barrett, A. M., Bainton, D., Cameron, L., & Doyle, H. (2018). *Supporting secondary school STEM education for sustainable development in Africa*. University of Bristol.

Valente, T. W. (2005). Network models and methods for studying the diffusion of innovations. In P. J. Carrington, J. Scott, S. Wasserman (Eds.), *Models and methods in social network analysis* (pp. 98–116). Cambridge.

van der Zee, T., & Reich, J. (2018). Open education science. *AERA Open, 4*(3), 1–15.

van Dijk, W., Schatschneider, C., & Hart, S. A. (2020). Open science in education sciences. *Journal of Learning Disabilities*, 0022219420945267.

Vicente-Saez, R., & Martinez-Fuentes, C. (2018). Open science now: A systematic literature review for an integrated definition. *Journal of Business Research, 88*, 428–436.

Vygotsky, L. S. (1978). *Mind in society: The development of higher psychological processes*. Harvard University Press.

Warford, M. K. (2011). The zone of proximal teacher development. *Teaching and Teacher Education, 27*(2), 252–258.

Wenger, E. (1998). Communities of practice: Learning as a social system. *Systems Thinker, 9*(5), 2–3.

Wenger, E. (2011). *Communities of practice: a brief introduction*. Retrieved November 25, 2020 from https://scholarsbank.uoregon.edu/xmlui/bitstream/handle/1794/11736/A%20brief%20introduction%20to%20CoP.pdf.

Wennergren, A. C. (2016). Teachers as learners–with a little help from a critical friend. *Educational Action Research, 24*(2), 260–279.

Wilder, R., & Levine, M. (2016, December 19). *Let's speed up science by embracing open access publishing*. Retrieved November 20, 2020 from https://www.statnews.com/2016/12/19/open-access-publishing/.

Wiley, D. (2016). *Toward Renewable Assessments*. Retrieved November 25, 2020 from https://opencontent.org/blog/archives/4691.

Wiley, D., Webb, A., Weston, S., & Tonks, D. (2017). A preliminary exploration of the relationships between student-created OER, sustainability, and students' success. *The International Review of Research in Open and Distributed Learning, 18*(4).

Wilkinson, M., Dumontier, M., & Aalbersberg, I. (2016). The FAIR Guiding Principles for scientific data management and stewardship. *Scientific Data, 3*, 160018.

Zapata-Rivera, L. F., Aranzazu-Suescun, C., & Larrondo-Petrie, M. M. (2020). Teacher training plan for engineering online laboratories composition. In *18th LACCEI International Multi-Conference for Engineering, Education, and Technology: "Engineering, Integration, and Alliances for a Sustainable Development" "Hemispheric Cooperation for Competitiveness and Prosperity on a Knowledge-Based Economy"*, July 27–31, 2020, Virtual Edition.

Zook, M., Barocas, S., Boyd, D., Crawford, K., Keller, E., & Gangadharan, S. P. (2017). Ten simple rules for responsible big data research. *PLoS Computational Biology, 13*(3), e1005399.

Karen Ferreira-Meyers is Associate Professor and Coordinator Linguistics and Modern Languages at the Institute of Distance Education (University of Eswatini). She has a keen interest in research on open education, open pedagogy and OER in addition to the teaching and learning of languages, distance and e-learning, autofiction and autobiography, African literatures, crime and detective fiction. She publishes regularly on these subjects, both in English and in French. Translation and interpreting are also close to her heart, in particular when they are education-related. She holds a Ph.D. in French and Francophone literatures, four Master's degrees (Romance Philology, English Linguistics for the Language Practitioner, LLM and MIDT) and strongly believes in lifelong learning.

Amit Dhakulkar is a researcher in science and mathematics education. Amit has been working with and recommending the use of Open Educational Resources (OERs) and Free and Open-Source Software in education for last decade under various projects. His interests include graphicacy, OERs, designing and developing teaching–learning activities in science, mathematics and digital literacy, technology in education and open pedagogy. He has a Ph.D. in science education. Currently, he is working as a Post-doctoral Researcher under the UNESCO Chair on Multimodal Learning and OER at the North-West University in South Africa.

Chapter 9
Open Learning in the African Context: Challenges and Possibilities for Self-directed Learning

Moeketsi Letseka and Mmabaledi K. Seeletso

Abstract African societies have always had their traditional education. This evolved during the advent of missionary works when most societies were exposed to Western education, which sought to instil "reading of the Bible". In traditional African education, teaching and learning were done orally, through open gatherings around the fire where the elders told stories, or challenged the youngsters in myths, legends, idioms, and solution-oriented quizzes. With the arrival of European missionaries' modes of delivery changed as formal classroom setups were introduced. This chapter, which is written from an open distance learning context, looks into ways in which self-reliance and self-directness might be facilitated in an African open learning context. The chapter, which is conceptual in nature, further explores the challenges and possibilities that characterise open and distance learning (ODL). It shall be argued that ODL aims at creating autonomous and self-directed learners who can champion their own learning. The chapter shall draw on the works of Mentz et al. (2019), Mentz and Oosthuizen (2016), and Knowles (Self-directed learning. Association Press, 1975a; Self-directed learning: a guide for learners and teachers. Cambridge Adult Education, 1975b) to argue that self-directed learning (SDL) is a product of autonomous students who, on their own volition, identify their learning needs and create ways of achieving outcomes. Based on the ODL experiences, the chapter shall argue that ODL is a student-centred mode of delivery. Thus, through a convergence of ODL and SDL, students employ various interventions to create and co-create knowledge and solutions to their own learning. Against this backdrop, the chapter shall argue that SDL and ODL are pertinent modes of delivery of teaching and learning in times of global crises such as the current COVID-19.

Keywords Open and distance learning · Self-directed learning · Autonomous learners · Traditional African education

M. Letseka · M. K. Seeletso (✉)
UNESCO Chair on ODL, University of South Africa, Pretoria, South Africa

9.1   Introduction

This chapter grapples with the nexus between open distance learning (ODL) and self-directed learning (SDL) in the African context. On the one hand, the University of South Africa's *Open Distance e-Learning Policy* describes ODL as

> A multi-dimensional concept aimed at bridging the time, geographical, "economic, social, educational and communication distance between student and institution, student and academics, student and courseware and student and peers. Open distance e-learning focuses on removing barriers to access learning, flexibility of learning provision, student-centeredness, supporting students and constructing learning programmes with the expectation that students can succeed. (UNISA, 2018, p. 2)

Letseka (2015) argues that by its very nature ODL targets mature working adults who do not have the time to pursue higher education qualifications at full-time contact tertiary institutions. He argues that ODL is "marketed as an alternative mode of access to higher education for non-traditional students – mature working students" (Letseka, 2016, p. 3).

One the other hand, Knowles (1975a, b, p. 19) describes self-directed learning as "a process in which individuals take the initiative, with or without the help of others, in diagnosing their learning needs, formulating learning goals, identifying human and material resources for learning, choosing and implementing appropriate learning strategies, and evaluating learning outcomes". Knowles (1975a, b, p. 19) picks out various description that attempt to capture the deeper nuances of the notion of self-directed learning. Among these are:

- "Self-planned learning";
- "Inquiry method";
- "Independent learning";
- "Self-education";
- "Self-instruction";
- "Self-teaching";
- "Self-study";
- "Autonomous learning".

This chapter is divided into four sections. In the first section we define the key terms and concepts used, and how we understand them. These are "open and distance learning", "self-directed learning", "autonomous learners", and "traditional African education". We undertake to clarify these concepts as we understand them, and how we intend to use them in the chapter. We especially look at the various definitions of "self-directed learning" as understood by different scholars. In the second section, we explore the concepts of traditional African education and formal Western-oriented education. We submit that Africans always had their unique forms of educating young people, through orality. This was done by the elderly members of the community who passed varying pearls of wisdom through storytelling, idioms, proverbs, quizzes, and hands-on exploration of the natural habitat with the young people. Thus, traditional African education was neither formalised nor documented. There was no written curriculum. We shall argue that the introduction of Western European education was for the sole purpose of ensuring that Africans learn to read and follow the prescripts of the Christian Bible. Our view is that through the process of communal socialisation, traditional African education sought to educate young people to embrace their communities as well as their cultures.

In the third section, we discuss the prospects and challenges of SDL in the African context. We shall argue that the concept of SDL has evolved from days of correspondence education to the advent of online learning, which relies on the use of digital technology. However, our view is that challenges such as poor Internet connectivity and high costs of data remain critical impediments to SDL. We shall argue that as a component of ODL, SDL can be most effective in driving teaching and learning during times of global crises and pandemics. This view is informed by the current situation of the outbreak of the COVID-19 pandemic where almost all sectors, including education, have been rendered dysfunctional. It is worthwhile noting though that because ODL institutions are already operating at a distance, students have been able to continue with their studies despite the outbreak of COVID-19.

We consider the concepts of open and distance learning (ODL) and self-directed learning (SDL) as closely related given that both seek to produce autonomous learners, who most of the time, work alone, separated from the facilitator or instructor, but sometimes seek group or peer solidarity for support and motivation. The final section offers some concluding remarks. We now turn to the section that defines the key concepts.

9.1.1 Defining the Key Concepts

In this section, we briefly define the key concepts as used in the chapter. The concepts in question are "open and distance learning"; "self-directed learning"; "autonomous learners", and "traditional African education".

9.1.1.1 Open and Distance Learning

Open and distance learning (ODL) is a mode of delivery where the teacher and the learner are separated from one another, both in space and time. Nowadays, most institutions resort to a mix of ODL and face-to-face contact delivery in their offerings of higher education. In its *Open Distance e-Learning Policy*, the University of South Africa (UNISA) (2018, p. 2) defines ODL as

> A multi-dimensional concept aimed at bridging the time, geographical, economic, social, educational and communication distance between student and institution, student and academics, student and courseware and student and peers. Open distance e-learning focuses on removing to barriers to access learning, flexibility of learning provision, student-centeredness, supporting students and constructing learning programmes with the expectation that students can succeed.

Letseka and Pitsoe (2014, p. 1944) draw attention to literature that attempts to shed light on conceptions of ODL (Commonwealth of Learning, 2004; Holmberg, 1995; Moore & Kearsley, 1996; Perraton, 2000; Perraton et al., 2001; Peters, 1998; Rowntree, 1996; Rumble, 1997; UNESCO, 2002). It is their contention that "the concept of ODL suggests an educational approach designed to reach learners in their homes/offices/shops, etc., provide learning resources for them to qualify without attending formal classes in person, or create opportunities for lifelong learning, no matter where or when they want to study" (Letseka & Pitsoe, 2014, p. 1944). In the same vein, Redelinghuys (2017, p. 55) argues that ODL relates to a combination of distance education and open learning. While Latchem (2019) opines that:

> [O]pen and distance learning is essentially a social interactive, constructive, self-regulated and reflective process and the importance of developing autonomy, responsibility and self-efficacy in the learners and a sense of connection and engagement with their tutors and peers.

For Mnyanyi and Mwette (2009, p. 1), ODL is a viable means of "supporting attainment of academic, social and economic development". All the above narratives suggest that ODL can help reduce inequality due to increased access in higher education.

9.1.1.2 Self-directed Learning (SDL)

Self-directed learning is a multifaceted concept with multiple definitions. Self-directed learning is an approach to education which involves learners taking responsibility of their own learning. Such learners are expected to be able to choose their own learning strategies as well as identify resources they consider most suitable to help them achieve their goals. Morris (2019, p. 56) argues that "self-directed learning is a critical competence that empowers adults to adapt accordingly to fluid and complex social contextual changes".

In addition, Spencer and Jordan (1999) define SDL as a process where learners take responsibility of their own learning, at the same time determining their aims as well as learning resources so as to deal with activities. Dickinson (1992, p. 12) corroborates Spencer and Jordan (1999) as he presents SDL as "a state in which the learner is fully in control of the decision-making process regarding the learner's own learning and accepts full responsibility for it."

Robinson and Persky (2020, p. 2) define SDL as follows: "Self-directed learning can be defined as the outcome of creating an experience that empowers learners to make decisions about the information they want to become proficient in." Self-directed learning is further defined as an approach to learning in which students take charge of their learning (cf. Knowles, 1975a, p. 15). Of the many definitions of SDL provided by different scholars who wrote extensively on the concept, this chapter shall adopt one by Knowles (1975a, b, p. 18), who describes the phenomenon as:

[A] process in which individuals take the initiative, with or without the help of others, in diagnosing their learning needs, formulating learning goals, identifying human and material resources for learning, choosing and implementing appropriate learning strategies, and evaluating learning outcomes.

Knowles (1975a, b) definition depicts self-directed learners as people who can take responsibility for their own learning; identify their own learning goals and resources; as well as people who are in a position to even evaluate if they have indeed achieved what they had set out to achieve. Towle and Cottrell (1996) similarly concur that self-directed learners take initiative and responsibility for their own learning, they manage their time, manage their teaching, and do most of these out of their volition when motivated. In essence, self-directed learning provides students with a rare opportunity to teach themselves critical skills they need to develop into lifelong learners. It gives learners total independence to manage their studies.

9.1.1.3 Autonomous Learners

At a philosophical level, the notion of "autonomy" can at best be understood from the Lockean conception of excellence as rational liberty of self-direction. Autonomy refers to the capacity to form, pursue, and revise life plans in the light of our personal commitments and circumstances (Enslin, 1993; Galston, 1991). Enslin (1993, p. 6) argues that autonomy means "the individual's capacity for self-direction, for engaging in thought and activity which is her own, in the sense of not being determined by causes beyond her control". Learner autonomy refers to the principle where learners take an increasing amount of responsibility for what they learn and how they learn it. Autonomy, therefore, is the ability to take charge of one's own learning and life's trajectory. In the traditional face-to-face set-up, the delivery is teacher centred and learners remain passive recipients of whatever is being taught. Brazilian philosopher Paul Freire (1970) was critical of this approach, which called the "banking" concept of education. Holec (1981, p. 3) argues that an autonomous learner has the "ability to take charge of one's learning."

9.1.1.4 Traditional African Education

Traditional African education was based on African philosophical conceptions of what meant to educate the young people. Traditional African education emphasised learning by doing, or training on the job, respect for elders, lifelong education, which implied learning to live and living to learn. This type of education was oral. It was passed from one generation to the next through the process of socialisation and was done largely through word of mouth. At the heart of traditional African education was the importance of story-telling, recounting of legendary chronicles, as well recitation of idioms and solving of thorough context-based quizzes. As Adeyinka and Ndwapi (2002, p. 18) point out, part of the purpose of African traditional education was the development in children of a communal spirit, by which each individual saw himself/herself as part of a bigger unit, working and living together for the common good.

9.2   Insights into African and Western Education

9.2.1   Background to Traditional African Education

Africans always had their own way of teaching and training their people; both children and grown-ups. There was curricula in African societies, though not in the form that we see it as documented in modern time education. Traditional African education was largely geared towards imparting survival skills to enable everyone to be of service to their societies. Mosweunyane (2013, p. 50) argues that "… learning that occurred in Africa was necessitated to meet the exigencies of the whole society through training of its individual members, either in groups or on individual basis."

Mosweunyane (2013) further contends that Africans then, did not follow any formalised curricula, and this he observes, "… resulted in important knowledge and skills getting lost when the custodians of such knowledge and skills died or lost their cognitive abilities, such as going insane" (p. 50). In countries of Southern Africa such as Botswana, initiation schools such as Bogwera and Bojale played a great role in socialisation of young adolescents on their passage to adulthood by passing indigenous knowledge and skills on to them. The family as a unit was the first "classroom" for traditional African education, where children were taught their culture and other societal expectations by word of mouth through socialisation.

Africans had their ways of studying science, geography, and resource management. This they did by walking in and learning through interactions with their "surroundings such as river systems, the hills and forest, the type of flora and fauna …" (Mosweunyane, 2013, p. 52). Mosweunyane (2013) contends that some animals were not to be killed or eaten as they were considered sacred and respected as totems. Africans also had their own way of doing scientific experiments which in the modern world are carried out in laboratories. Mosweunyane (2013, p. 53) observes that "the fermentation of grains in the brewing of beer accorded African societies an opportunity to learn through observation and fermentation."

Schapera (1938, p. 106), one of the renowned African historians of his time, wrote that "traditional schools systematically taught young adults a number of secret formulae and songs in Botswana, admonishing them to honour, obey, and support the chief; to be ready to endure hardships … to be united as a regiment and help one another, to value cattle as a principal source of livelihood, … ungrudgingly obey old people …". This type of education endures to date and has over the years, managed to maintain the peace and tranquil that prevails even in present-day Botswana.

Letseka (2013, p. 341) argues that indigenous African education among the Basotho people of Lesotho was intimately integrated with the social, cultural, artistic, religious, and recreational life. Thus, the education that the Mosotho youth received fitted the group. Concomitantly, the expected social roles in society were learned by adulthood. He argues that the African youth's ethnic group and community were held by rules and regulations, values and social sanctions, approval, rewards and punishments, etc., into which the youth was inducted. At the heart of the educational induction among the Basotho was the pursuit of *makhabane*, or the virtues. Such virtues included industry or hard work, respect for persons, humility, perseverance, service to the nation and patriotism. Sabl (2005, p. 212) argues that the virtues can be briefly summed up as those key attributes and personal qualities that the citizenry needs "if democracies are to remain stable."

9.2.2   Remarks on Western Missionary Education in Africa

Education during the colonial era was used mainly for the purpose of converting Africans into the Christian faith. Various missionaries of the time—Anglican, Roman Catholic, Wesleyan, Paris Evangelical Missional Society (PEMS), Dutch Reformed Church, and many others built mission stations and mainly primary schools to provide basic Western education and religious teachings to Africans. Modern approaches to education such as introduction of the formal classroom system sought to transform the African way of learning, from indigenous African values to Western European values. Those that were targeted and eventually converted to Western education despised and turned against their own education which was grounded on oral literature, fables, folklores, proverbs, myths and legendary stories. With the advent of colonisation, education became the tool for the promotion of Western colonial values and cultures to the detriment of indigenous African values and cultures. The primary goal was to instil appeal and admiration of Western European values and cultures. This was said to be done to provide "Christian clerks, traders, interpreters and chiefs" (Mosweunyane, 2013, p. 51).

Modern education completely changed the way in which Africans transmitted knowledge and information. Bray et al. (1986) observed that African education reflected on values and expectations of the community while the Western European education system came with something completely different. Modern English was emphasised and highlighted as a symbol of intellectual development. The "more intelligent" individuals progressed and accumulated wealth with those perceived to be "less intelligent" working for them and helping them accrue more wealth while the rest of the people remain poor. With the Western education, accumulation of wealth was used as a measure of success and the rich started to despise the poorer members of their societies. Western education also introduced the colonisers' languages and were immediately adopted as languages of instruction in modern schools. This practice made Africans despise their languages as they attached no good to them.

9.2.3 Open Learning in African Context

Open learning has always been a common feature of traditional African education. This can be attributed to lifelong learning practices that existed from very early years until late in adulthood. Africans taught their cultures and ways of life through the process of socialisation. Open and distance learning as a concept, like the process of socialisation, is able to develop autonomous, empowered and self-directed learners given that most learning would be done individually, at times under very challenging circumstances.

Mnyanyi and Mwette (2009, p. 1) observed that "… demand of ODL is increasing due to the associated potential for new innovations and use of Information and Communication Technology (ICT)". However, it is worthwhile noting that in Africa as a whole, ICT comes with its own challenges that hinder its maximum use of ODL. Connectivity remains a challenge as well as technophobia, especially among adult learners. Use of ICT is critical for supporting ODL. But emphasis should be on equity and equality, both of use and access. ODL as a teaching and learning philosophy is also overshadowed by the high diversity of its learners. This has always been a great challenge in Africa, and remain such, to date.

We want to argue that lifelong learning has always been a characteristic feature of traditional African education, from early childhood through to adulthood when they too had to assume the role of "teacher" to the younger generation. Lifelong learning in the African context endured despite the absence of formal "classrooms". Education was distant and open, without boundaries. Access was extended to every member of the society and anybody with knowledge and experience was a teacher. All these ended with introduction of modern education where the teacher was the fountain of knowledge and information and could not be questioned.

9.2.4 Self-directed Learning (SDL)

Self-directed learning has its origins in adult learning. Some researchers view it as a skill in which one takes time to develop, or what Robinson and Persky (2020) refer to as scaffolding. Robinson and Persky (2020, p. 3) argue that "By taking the lead on their learning, the learner takes responsibility for many activities that are traditionally directed by the instructor". Boyer et al. (2014) contend that SDL de-emphases the common belief that teaching should involve an educator as the main source of knowledge and information. Instead, they view SDL as placing emphasis on knowledge construction though engagement and dialogue. In the same breadth, Knowles (1975a, 1975b) posits that SDL occurs in collaboration with others, for instance peers, mentors etc. while Bonk and Lee (2017) regard SDL as a process.

Gibbons (2002, p. 2) regards SDL as "[A]ny increase in knowledge, skill, accomplishment, or personal development that an individual selects and brings about by his or her own efforts using any method in any circumstances at any time." Sze-Yeng and Hussain (2010, p. 1913) add that SDL involves "A learner's autonomous ability to manage his or her own learning process, by perceiving oneself as the source of one's own actions and decisions as a responsibility towards one's lifelong learning."

It seems reasonable to argue, from the literature that a key aspect of SDL is motivation. Long (2000, p. 16) notes that motivation is the "… energy, drive, or desire that encourages, impels or sustains an individual to accomplish a goal or task." Once motivated, SDL students are likely to perform much better, and can even aim for more.

9.3   Self-directed Learning in Africa: Possibilities and Challenges of Self-Directed Learning in Africa

Teaching and learning today have changed, with more emphasis placed on creating environments that enable the students to take responsibility and ownership of their learning. Self-directedness requires students to display characteristics such as being innovative, autonomous, being problem solvers and solution oriented, being self-disciplined, eager to learn, willing to take risks, and most importantly, to regard failure as an opportunity to learn from the experience and mistakes and grow.

Self-directed learners take responsibility for their own learning and are lifelong learners. They are able to connect what they learn with the world around them. Collaboration is a key indicator of SDL. As Bonk and Lee (2017, p. 47) observe, "… any achievement from self-directed learning often requires some form of support or guidance." Silen and Uhlin (2008, p. 463) posit that SDL students are challenged to take responsibility of their learning, and have to "make choices and decisions about their studies." However, in order to succeed it is critical that SDL students are afforded a conducive, supportive and enabling environment.

9.3.1   Prospects for Self-directed Learning in the Africa Context

SDL students are often more confident, which helps them become more innovative in their thinking (Guglielmino, 1977; Long, 2000). It is this confidence that helps them plan, pace and take ownership of their own learning. In Africa, some contexts dictate that students, especially those from marginalised backgrounds, adopt SDL not through their will, but due to experiential circumstances such as lack of resources and facilities that are conducive to productive teaching and learning. Guglielmino and Long (2011) are of the view that SDL is a dynamic combination of attitudes and skills that are necessary for individuals that deal with various aspects of their lives. Similarly, Kidane et al., (2020, p. 1) note that "Self-directed learning is an appropriate and preferred learning process to prepare students for lifelong learning in their professions and make them stay up-to-date." It is their contention that "self-directed learners have an adequate amount of accountability to select the content to be studied, to assign time for it, and to understand the content deeply..." (Kidane et al., 2020, p. 2).

SDL is perceived to promote sharing of knowledge and ideas between peers, who can also inspire one another. Team work by peers helps to get almost everyone involved. It promotes creativity and innovation through collective discussion to solve challenges. Over and above all the highlighted possibilities that SDL can bring, it is worthwhile noting that SDL has proven to respond positively to pandemics and other crises such as the COVID-19, which is attributed to global paralysis.

9.3.2 Challenges of Self-directed Learning in Africa

Generally, Africa has enduring challenges with issues that are related barriers to implementation of open learning, and by extension SDL. The world is now caught up with and required to respond to the challenges of the Fourth Industrial Revolution (4IR). The advent of the 4IR necessitates that all sectors, including education, leverage their services and products through use of digital technology. The latter continues to be less ubiquitous in many sectors, but more so in the education sector in many African contexts. The main challenge is access to both technology hardware such as computers, tablets, smart phones, access to the Internet and signal towers. In cases where computers, tablets, smart phones are available, the litmus test becomes electricity, without which technological devices might be available, but they might be useful to leveraging the offering of open learning and SDL services. SDL is all about the autonomy and independence of the learners, who need to be able to work on their own, and/or in collaboration with their peers. Given some of the above-mentioned unintended consequences of technology, the knowledge society that is envisaged by some African protocols and conventions may never be realised.

9.4   Conclusion

This chapter discussed the view that Africans always had their own forms of education, though their curricula were never documented. As such, it is important to note that education in Africa did not only start at the advent of western education, but had always been there over the years. It is also imperative that African languages should be introduced in schools and countries need to see how they can make their languages relevant to global and emerging trends, just like European language remain languages for commerce and trade. In African countries such as Botswana, some parents can even decide that their children should not do their national language, Setswana, as one of the languages offered, and would rather opt for foreign languages such as French and Portuguese.

It is also important to note that some institutions of higher learning in some African countries such as the Botswana University of Agriculture and Natural Resources, BUAN, are calling for integration of both modern and traditional herbs to address the COVID-19 pandemic. This should not just be about herbs but a lot of other resources. Traditional education needs to be re-visited, and their best practice infused into the mainstream education.

References

Adeyinka, A. A., & Ndwapi, G. (2002). Education and morality in Africa. *Pastoral Care in Education: An International Journal of Personal, Social and Emotional Development, 20*, 17–23.

Bonk, C. J., & Lee, M. M. (2017). Motivations, achievements and challenges of self-directed informal learners in open educational environments and MOOCs. *Journal of Learning for Development, 4*(1), 36–57.

Boyer, S. L., Edmondson, D. R., Artis, A. B., & Fleming, D. (2014). Self-directed learning: A tool for life-long learning. *Journal of Marketing Education, 36*(1), 20–32.

Bray, M., Clarke, P. B., & Stephens, D. (1986). *Education and Society in Africa*. Edward Arnold.

Commonwealth of Learning. (2004). *Planning and implementing open and distance learning systems: A handbook for decision makers*. Commonwealth of Learning.

Dickinson, L. (1992). *Learners autonomy 2: Leaner training for language learning*. Authentik.

Enslin, P. (1993). Should nation-building be an aim of education? Inaugural lecture delivered at the University of the Witwatersrand, Johannesburg, September 22.

Freire, P. (1970). *Pedagogy of the Oppressed*. Continuum.

Galston, W. A. (1991). *Liberal purposes: Goods, virtues, and diversity in the liberal state*. Cambridge University Press.

Gibbons, M. (2002). *The self-directed learning handbook: Challenging adolescent students to excel*. Wiley.

Guglielmino, L. M. (1977). *Development of the self-directed learning readiness scale*. Ph.D. Thesis. University of Georgia.

Guglielmino, L. M., & Long, H. B. (2011). Perspectives: The international society for self-directed learning and the international self-directed symposium. *International Journal of Self-Directed Learning, 8*(1), 1–6.

Holec, H. (1981). *Autonomy and foreign language learning*. Pergamon.

Holmberg, B. (1995). *Theory and practice of distance education* (2nd ed.). Routledge.

Kidane, H. H., Roebertsen, H., & van der Vleuten, C. P. M. (2020). Students' perceptions towards self-directed learning in Ethiopian medical schools with new innovative curriculum: A mixed-method study. *BMC Medical Education, 20*(7), 2–10.

Knowles, M. S. (1975a). *Self-directed learning*. Association Press.

Knowles, M. S. (1975b). *Self-directed learning: A guide for learners and teachers*. Cambridge Adult Education.

Latchem, C. (2019). Independent study, transactional distance, guided conversation and adult learning. In I. Jung (Ed), *Open and distance education theory revisited. Implications for digital era*. Springer.

Letseka, M. (2013). Educating for *Ubuntu*: Lessons from Basotho indigenous education. *Open Journal of Philosophy, 3*(2), 337–344.

Letseka, M. (Ed.). (2015). *Open distance learning (ODL) in South Africa*. Nova Publishers.

Letseka, M. (Ed.). (2016). *Open distance learning (ODL) through the philosophy of Ubuntu*. Nova Publishers.

Letseka, M., & Pitsoe, V. (2014). The challenges and prospects of access to higher education at UNISA. *Studies in Higher Education, 39*(10), 1942–1954.

Long, H. B. (2000). Understanding Self-direction in learning. In H. B. Long (Ed.), *Practice and theory in self-directed learning* (pp. 11–24). Motorola University Press.

Mentz, E., & Oosthuizen, I. (eds.) (2016). Self-directed learning research, AOSIS, Cape Town. http://dx.doi.org/10.4102/aosis.2016.sdlrl14.01

Mentz, E., de Beer, J., & Bailey, R. (eds.), (2019). Self-directed learning for 21st Century: Implications for Higher Education. AOSIS, Cape Town. https://doi.org/10.4102/aosis.2019.BK1 34.07

Mnyanyi, C., & Mwette, T. S. A. (2009). Open and distance learning in developing countries: The past, the present and the future. *Gender and Behaviour, 18*(2), 15803–15812.

Moore, M. G., & Kearsley, G. (1996). *Distance education: A systems view*. Wadsworth.

Morris, T. H. (2019). Adaptivity through self-directed learning to meet the challenges of our ever-changing world. *Adult Learning, 30*(2), 55–66. https://doi.org/10.1177/10451595518814486

Mosweunyane, D. (2013). The African educational evolution: From traditional training to formal education. *Higher Education Studies, 3*(4), 50–59.

Perraton, H. (2000). *Open and distance learning in the developing world*. Routledge.

Perraton, H., Robinson, B., & Creed, C. (2001). *Teacher education through distance learning: Technology, curriculum, cost, evaluation*. UNESCO Division of Higher Education.

Peters, O. (1998). *Learning and teaching in distance education: Analyses and interpretations from an international perspective*. Kogan Page.

Redelinghuys, J. (2017). The use of interactive technology for effective teaching and learning in open distance learning. Ph.D. Thesis, Faculty of Education Sciences. North West University.

Robinson, J. D., & Persky, A. M. (2020). *Developing self-directed learners*. American Association of Colleges of Pharmacy.

Rowntree, D. (1996). *Exploring open and distance learning*. Open University.

Rumble, G. (1997). *Costs and economics of open and distance learning*. Kogan Page.

Sabl, A. (2005). Virtue for pluralists. *Journal of Moral Philosophy, 2*(2), 207–235.

Schapera, I. (1938). *A handbook of Tswana law and customs*. Munster.

Silen, C., & Uhlin, L. (2008). Self-directed learning—A learning issue for students and faculty. *Teaching in Higher Education, 13*(4), 461–475.

Spencer, J. A., & Jordan, K. R. (1999). Learner-cantered approaches in medical education. *British Medical Journal, 318*, 1280–1283.

Sze-Yeng, F., & Hussain, R. M. R. (2010). Self-directed learning in a socio-constructivist learning environment. *Procedia-Social and Behavioural Sciences, 9*, 1913–1917.

Towle, A., & Cottrell, D. (1996). Self-directed learning. *Archives of Discourse in Child School, 74*, 357–359.

UNESCO. (2002). *Open distance learning: Trends, policy and strategy considerations*. UNESCO Division of Higher Education.

UNISA. (2018). *Open distance e-learning policy*. UNISA Press.

Moeketsi Letseka is professor of philosophy of education and holder of the endowed United Nations, Educational, Scientific and Cultural Organisation (UNESCO) Chair on Open Distance Learning (ODL) at the University of South Africa (UNISA). He is Editor-in-Chief of *Africa Education Review*. He is Co-chairperson of the Finance Standing Committee of the World Council of Comparative Education Societies.

Mmabaledi Kefilwe Seeletso is Lecturer and Heads the Department of Educational Management and Leadership at Botswana Open University (BOU), formerly Botswana College of Distance and Open Learning (BOCODOL). Dr. Seeletso specialises on Open and Distance Learning content planning, online learning and research supervision. She was a recipient of the Fulbright Scholarship, during which she served at the University of Denver as a visiting scholar from August 2017 to January 2018. She is also the University of Bath Ambassador in Botswana and a member of the UKRI International Peer Review College. Dr. Seeletso served as a Post-doctoral Fellow at the University of South Africa, Pretoria, based at the UNESCO Chair on ODL from May 2019 to March 2021.

Chapter 10
Educators' Beliefs, Perceptions and Practices Around Self-Directed Learning, Assessment and Open Education Practices

Isabel Tarling and Sandhya Gunness

Abstract In the wake of a global pandemic, educators need to reflect on their practices, and deeply question whether and how they are ensuring that their teaching provides opportunities to develop 21st century skills such as adaptability, flexibility, a growth mindset and self-directed learning (SDL). Open educational practices can develop student's SDL by actively engaging them in the co-design of curriculum and assessment processes. Such co-design of assessment practices may mitigate existing stressful, high-stakes examination focussed assessments with more holistic, continuous learning approaches to democratise teaching and learning and make it more relevant to students. To achieve these ideals, current education practices were examined to identify areas where these can evolve to support SDL goals through open education practices. Following an interpretivist epistemology, this mixed-methods study surveyed educators about their assessment practices, beliefs and perceptions, to understand how this aligns to their current learning outcomes, how/whether they develop SDL, and their use of open education resources (OER) and practices (OEP). The survey was completed by 42 educators, some were lecturing in higher education contexts, and others were school teachers who had recently graduated from postgraduate education programmes. The concerns based adoption model (CBAM) was used to analyse the survey responses. Findings identify the need to encourage changes in educators' beliefs, perceptions and practices around OER and OEP, assessment and SDL competencies. It is suggested that educators be exposed to diverse assessment practices that emphasise regular, meaningful feedback toward developing students' metacognitive judgement and calibration as critical SDL competencies.

Keywords Self-directed learning · Assessment · Open education resources · Open practices · Democratisation of education

I. Tarling (✉)
Two Oceans Graduate Institute, Cape Town, South Africa
e-mail: isabel@limina.co.za

S. Gunness
University of Mauritius, Moka, Mauritius

© The Author(s), under exclusive license to Springer Nature Singapore Pte Ltd. 2021
D. Burgos and J. Olivier (eds.), *Radical Solutions for Education in Africa*, Lecture Notes in Educational Technology, https://doi.org/10.1007/978-981-16-4099-5_10

10.1   Introduction

Opportunities for self-directed learning (SDL) have expanded exponentially in the last few decades through the Internet, Web 2.0 meet-read-write-produce affordances and the increased use of smart technologies. Against a backdrop of economic, environmental and social challenges, organisations like the World Economic Forum and many others call for a multiplicity of skill sets and competencies to innovate, create, solve complex problems in collaboration with many others, and to think critically. However, education contexts across Africa may not always prioritise such skills and competencies.

In developing countries like Mauritius, Malawi and South Africa, the COVID-19 pandemic has exacerbated existing uncertainty, fluctuating markets, and political and socio-economic instability, leading to even greater unemployment and the social challenges that accompany this. Within this context, and against the backdrop of the vast potential of education, educators need to reflect on their practices, and deeply question whether and how they are ensuring that the education system provides for adaptability and flexibility, equity, a growth mindset and eventually sustainable development through self-directed learning practices for all people.

This study presents a glimpse of current practices and reflects on changes in the education system to become more adaptable and flexible, and to develop open democratic education processes. Firstly, it seeks to understand current practices regarding open educational resources (OER) by educators across Africa and in different contexts and capacities. With this understanding, the aim is to develop recommendations for a change plan to create awareness and foster use of OER, and understanding and adoption of open licencing approaches by those involved in education. Secondly, it uncovers perceptions and practices regarding SDL to identify ways in which student-directed activities can be embedded within the curriculum practices. Since assessment typically drives teaching and learning, the third research question ties these two strands together, seeking to understand educators' beliefs, perceptions and practices around different types of assessment and how, if at all, these support SDL and the use of OER towards establishing open education practices (OEP).

The intent of this study is to identify to what extent open practices are used to mitigate the stressful high-stakes examination focus with a more holistic, continuous learning approach where students' voices are part of assessment design, and develop their competencies as self-directed learners. The chapter presents a review of discourses regarding assessment and how current assessment models are designed to challenges these discourses, providing a means to imagine how this could be changed. Using an interpretivist epistemology, we explore educators' perceptions, practices and beliefs around assessments, OER and SDL. In the discussion section, findings from this exploration are interrogated to inform the design of future change processes.

10.2 Literature Review

The literature review sets the stage and develops the rationale of questioning existing practices, beliefs and perceptions around assessment. Employing a future-orientation, it extracts ideas of how credit-bearing assessment models can evolve to encourage self-directed paths to learning, propelled by students' sense of curiosity and creativity, and the use of OER and open education practices in this process.

Assessment and evaluation are often used as synonyms, but it may be more useful to clearly articulate the difference. The process of gathering evidence of the knowledge, skills and capacities students develop through the teaching and learning process is referred to herein as assessment. Through assessment, educators can measure what students can do and what they have learnt. Evaluation follows the assessment process and involves the interrogation and analysis of data produced from learners' assessment and reflection on the analysis process (Baranovskaya & Shaforostova, 2017). Insights gained from such data evaluation and analysis, commonly referred to as learning analytics, are then used to guide teaching and learning decisions or plan remedial interventions.

Educators at all levels of the system assess students for a variety of reasons using either informal or formal assessment. Compared to formal assessment, informal assessment is often less planned or predetermined, may be impromptu and regards learning in-the-moment using a range of procedures to gauge progress in learning (Baranovskaya & Shaforostova, 2017). The quality and use of informal assessment is often based on the educator's experience and intuition (Black & Wiliam, 1998, 2018), the results of which may not always be recorded. Formal assessments are planned in advance and conducted at predetermined times using specific instruments to collect evidence of learning. A form of formal assessment, diagnostic assessments, provides a basis point of a students' prior knowledge, skills and capacities at the start of a learning section. As learning progresses, different methods of formal assessments are used to measure learning (Black & Wiliam, 2018), including self-, peer- or group-assessment, observation-, test- or task-based assessments. The results of formal assessments are recorded and evaluated, and the interpretation of this informs educational plans and strategies to address the teaching and learning needs identified through the assessment.

Formal assessments are often categorised as assessments *of*, *for* and *as* learning, or as summative or formative assessments. Black and Wiliam's (1998) review of assessment literature tracked the development of a distinction between summative and formative assessment. Drawing on such research, a distinction between assessment *of* learning and *for* learning, and later assessment *as* learning, emerged (Black & Wiliam, 1998; Charteris et al., 2016; Gardner, 2009; Hargreaves, 2005). As such, assessment *of* learning refers to a measure of the extent to which students have met learning outcomes, assessment *for* learning refers to the extent to which teachers and students use assessment evidence to inform the learning process, and assessment *as* learning relates to learning that takes place while students monitor and direct their own learning.

Instead of such prepositional permutations, Black and Wiliam (2018) propose an emphasis on the types of inferences drawn from the assessment. Inferences that are drawn from assessment of student's status or potential, are functionally summative. Functionally formative assessments provide information about the kind of practices that would best support the learner in their learning process. Hence, a term test showing learners' achievement at a given time can be used to draw summative inferences about their grasp of the knowledge, skills and competencies developed during that period. Equally, formative inferences can be drawn from the test results suggesting where the student is experiencing learning challenges and giving the teacher and student insight into areas to improve teaching and learning (Black & Wiliam, 2018). Following this argument, it may therefore be more productive to distinguish between assessment types as having a formative or summative function, rather than formative or summative assessment per se, or assessments *of*/*for*/*as* learning.

The quality of assessment types can be measured in terms of among other, reliability, validity, educational impact, objectivity and trustworthiness (Schuwirth & Van Der Vleuten, 2011). Reliability of assessment refers to the consistency with which the instrument will yield similar results, for instance whether a test, task or observation will receive similar results when administered by different people at different times. The validity of an assessment refers to the extent to which it achieves the purpose for which it was designed. A tension may result between reliability and validity when an assessment may achieve high reliability even though it does not measure what it was intended to, or it may achieve its purpose but produce unreliable results. Ideally, assessments also need to be devoid of personal bias and secure consistency of educators' judgements to make it objective and trustworthy, even though this is not always possible especially with informal assessments (Schuwirth & Van Der Vleuten, 2011).

Discourses around assessment may be changing, albeit slowly. In higher education, Boud (2007) argues that increasingly dominant discourses emphasise the summative function of assessment, to the detriment of its formative function. A primary and secondary focus to assessment can be distinguished in such discourses (Boud, 2007). Primarily assessment is viewed in terms of quality assurance, measurement of outcomes and means to ensure confidence in the standards and procedures of teaching and learning at the institution. A secondary outcome of assessment is the need to provide feedback to students and educators towards improving teaching and learning processes (Black & Wiliam, 1998, 2009, 2018). Using discourse analysis of assessment texts in higher education, Boud (2007) found that learning often takes a subordinate position to the procedures devoted to the primary focus: rules and regulations for examination, mechanisms for marking and scoring, avoiding plagiarism, etc. Not surprisingly, Boud (2007) found that educators' time-to-task mirrors this priority, with educators spending much of their time marking assignments and examinations, while less time is spent on shaping the learning process for students.

The discourse emphasizing the summative function of assessment has been challenged in different respects. Hattie's (2009) seminal study on the factors that support learning achievement placed feedback along with positive relationships with teachers at the top of the list. Emphasizing measurement, quality assurance processes, results and achievement, distracts from a focus on feedback that may improve the learning process. A summative focus may also not develop students' metacognitive skills to judge their perceived understanding, capability, competence and preparedness with their actual achievement. These skills are referred to as calibration, the ability to make metacognitive judgements of perceived and actual achievement (Alexander, 2013; Hadwin & Webster, 2013). Calibration is a critical metacognitive skill as it guides learning processes in terms of task execution and planning, performance outcomes and strategic adaptation (Hadwin & Webster, 2013). Where students display poor calibration, they may misjudge their decisions and learning efforts, believing erroneously that their efforts to complete a task are adequate or that they had spent sufficient time studying, even studying the wrong content because they misjudged the importance thereof. Their performance in assessments may also be compromised, since their perception of what is required and what the actual requirements of a question are, are misaligned. Regular, in-time formative feedback provides the student with tools to better calibrate their perceived judgements with their actual performance.

Providing students with strategic and regular feedback within the learning process, a formative function of assessment, is critical (Black & Wiliam, 1998, 2009, 2018) to developing SDL skills as various studies have found. Feedback improves students' calibration of learning since it develops their ability to metacognitively judge their performance, self-regulation and self-assessment (Hattie, 2013), foundational skills needed to develop SDL. SDL, Knowles (1975) argues, is a learning process through which students take initiative whether assisted by others or not, to diagnose their learning needs, develop appropriate learning goals and goal-directed behaviours, to choose appropriate learning strategies and resources, and to assess their learning outcomes. Poor calibration often results in learners setting poor learning goals, misdiagnosing their learning needs or the resources they may require, and implementing inappropriate learning strategies (Hadwin & Webster, 2013). They are often unable to break down larger academic tasks into smaller achievable sub-tasks, or to systematically analyse the learning process to identify where or how they made learning mistakes. Regular and strategic feedback on the learning process helps students to break down tasks, analyse mistakes and prioritise how to correct this. Innovations that strengthen the formative function of assessment and especially feedback are therefore critical to develop students' metacognitive judgement and calibration, towards developing the SDL competencies, and, as Black and Wiliam already in 1998 indicated, improving learning yields.

Discourses around assessment are also changing in terms of access and equity. The ever-growing number of open education resources (OER) and particularly open courseware (OCW) available on the Internet offer students an alternative pathway to life-long, SDL (Friesen & Wihak, 2013). OER are simultaneously an emerging technological innovation and educational tool which blurs the distinction between formal and informal learning (Ehlers, 2011). In an era where the ability to access and use knowledge is directly linked to economic advantage, OER offer the prospect of radically redistributing how knowledge is shared and who can access this (Conrad & McGreal, 2012; Ehlers, 2011; Karunanayaka et al., 2015). Through OER, students who cannot access learning through formal higher education institutions can access learning, while some OER courses even offer degree credentialing at no or minimal cost (Conrad & McGreal, 2012; Friesen & Wihak, 2013). The assessment and subsequent credentialing of such OER courses does not readily align with dominant discourses, especially with regard to the emphasis on quality assurance, measurement and outcomes.

In African education contexts, OER offer a radical solution to provide non-traditional students with access to learning, the economy and social capital. Disturbing numbers of students across African contexts fail to reach secondary education with only the smallest percentage accessing higher education (Barnett, 2018; Department of Basic Education, 2017; Lehohla, 2016). High dropout rates are often related to a disconnect between the knowledge, skills and capacities taught in schools and those needed for participation in the economy, meaning what students learn in schools may not be valued by potential employers. Moreover, potential employers may struggle to understand transcripts provided by education institutions or to match achieved grades with their economic requirements (Friesen & Wihak, 2013). As an alternative to such mark schedules, OER and particularly OCW increasingly uses badges to represent students' achievement of specific learning outcomes, skills or competencies. These badges are designed to give potential employers a visual, easy-to-understand symbol of the students' achievement (Friesen & Wihak, 2013) and are therefore easier to decipher by potential employers. Friesen and Wihak (2013) further argue that students can choose which badges they want to share and can link the badge to digital artefacts they created, providing potential employers with actual evidence of their competencies. In this way, badges as part of OER, challenge the dominant discourse since, compared to formal course exit-grades, these are neither standardised nor representative of course-level achievements. However, since anyone on the Web can issue a badge, it is difficult to credential the achievement and competencies they signify.

OER also challenge dominant discourses related to assessment with its greater inclusion of the recognition of prior learning (RPL). RPL provides an alternate form of assessment, giving non-traditional students access to higher education. Mature students who have participated in economic activities have gained knowledge, skills and capacities through work, experience, informal training and life experiences (Conrad & McGreal, 2012). In an effort to provide such non-traditional students access to higher education, institutions offer the RPL (also referred to as PLAR: Prior Learning Assessment and Recognition) route (Conrad & McGreal, 2012; Conrad et al., 2013; Friesen & Wihak, 2013). Students typically submit a portfolio and/or complete an exam to provide evidence of their experiential learning, but may also be interviewed or asked to complete skills tests. RPL may also include OER badges, acknowledging the validity of students' prior knowledge and how this contributes to their self-fulfilment, status and social capital (Conrad & McGreal, 2012). In this way, RPL offers non-traditional students a flexible pathway to higher education institutions, formal assessment and accreditation.

A further challenge to the dominant discourse regards the focus of assessment. Education leaders and practitioners are increasingly moving towards learning content and experiences that promote 21st century skills such as creativity and innovation, collaboration, communication and critical thinking, the so-called *soft* skills. However, while teaching and learning may increasingly include such *soft* skills, assessment practices tend to prioritise the *hard* skills of recalling factual knowledge or mastering the skills needed in languages, Mathematics and/or the Sciences (Valtonen et al., 2017). OER and particularly badges challenge this practice, offering badges for *soft* skills and linking these badges to a students' created artefacts as evidence of such skills.

The education crisis that emerged from the COVID-19 pandemic offered educators a chance to re-evaluate and reflect on existing assessment practices. As learning moved from inside to outside the classroom, the need to evolve assessment practices became critical. Previously, modalities of learning assessment had been strongly dependent on students' physical presence, either for administration or to observe their daily progress. Lockdowns and school-closures forced educators around the world to review assessment processes and the provision of feedback to continue and shape the learning process for students. Formative feedback, once the domain of teachers, needed to become a community-driven activity where parents and important others were equipped to gauge whether students were understanding content or how learning was developing. Students themselves had to rapidly become self-directed, to set goals, gauge their learning needs and choose appropriate learning strategies and resources, and to assess their learning outcomes.

Countries and education systems responded differently to the need for assessment review following school-closures; while some embraced the change, others remained resolute in their pursuit of the status quo. A survey carried out by UNESCO (2020) demonstrated different countries' response to assessment due to COVID-19 and lockdowns: 58 out of 84 surveyed countries postponed or rescheduled exams, and 11 cancelled exams altogether; 23 introduced alternative methods such as online or home-based testing, but 22 maintained the end-of-year exams as planned. Some countries, specifically those in Latin America, faced less pressure with a long tradition of classroom-based assessments rather than standardised high-stake exams. In other countries like Uganda, South Africa and Hong Kong exams are considered the 'ultimate outcome' of the education sector, and their postponement was avoided at all costs. Even where learners had missed a significant number of school-days and learning opportunities, they were forced to take the end-of-year exams. The end of year exams is a stressful period for students, their parents and teachers, educational institutions, administrators and education ministries, exacerbated by the COVID-19 pandemic. In South Africa, for instance, the school-leaving exams at the end of 2020 were made all the more challenging when 195 students were found to have cheated in the Mathematics and Physics paper. Subsequently, the Department of Basic Education wanted all students to rewrite these papers which was only prevented when a court ruled that such action would be unnecessary. Against the backdrop of an emotional roller-coaster of their last year of schooling, the pressure to return and rewrite an exam when many students had already gone on holiday was immense. The insistence of the DBE for students to rewrite these papers reflects their resolute view of the final school-leaving exams as the 'ultimate outcome' of schooling. Their reliance on this final formal exam process, and forcing schools to continue with end-of-year exams for the other grades, despite major losses of learning time, may also indicate resistance to alternate assessment approaches and methods.

As this example illustrates, assessment practices are often impervious to change. Where alternate models have been used, like moving exams to online spaces, the actual assessment process has remains largely unchanged. Using emerging technologies to conduct assessment process may appear to affect change, but the power-relations between students and teachers remain unchanged. Even when using technologies to conduct assessment, the teacher mostly remains dominant, setting tasks and deciding on normative standards that the student should achieve. The student generally is not included in these decisions, and their voice remains unheard when learning outcomes or assessment criteria is decided. Students are also allowed little if any agency in the choice of assessment, or given an opportunity to display *soft* skills as those developed through SDL, from goal-oriented behaviours to assessing their own learning. While the current crisis has in many ways accelerated the development of students' SDL competencies, assessment practices have not largely remain stable. In most cases, assessments remain inflexible, undemocratic and institutionalised, and unresponsive to students' exposure levels, inequalities regarding gender and access for instance.

Efforts to change beliefs, perceptions and practices regarding assessment have been numerous. International agencies such as the United Nations Educational, Scientific and Cultural Organization (UNESCO) and the Organization for Economic Co-operation and Development (OECD) have for many years worked to develop new approaches to teaching and learning in order to democratise education. Such a democratisation process is intended to foster quality education that may contribute to the eradication of poverty, and considers factors of coverage, timeliness, easiness and relevance of education (Semenov, 2005). Democratising education also involves changing teaching-centric approaches to learning-centred processes (Tarling, 2018; Tarling & Ng'ambi, 2016) in which assessment requires new dimensions (Mainali & Heck, 2017; Weimer, 2002). Such new dimensions recognise students' voices in the design of assessment and negotiates flexibility and choice into assessment, ultimately creating customised assessment experiences. Opening assessment practices may hold the key to this democratisation process. Open assessment of learning is understood as a process of learning verification and feedback that takes place collaboratively, mediated by freely available digital tools. Teachers participating in open assessment of learning produce or adapt assessment resources, and students adapt and reshape these resources for the purpose of generating for themselves an assessment that meets their personal needs, learning styles and context (Chiappe, 2012).

Merely changing the means and tools of assessment to include technological resources does not change the nature of learning assessment (Redecker & Johannessen, 2013; Voogt et al., 2013). A paradigm shift is required to democratise not only assessment but teaching and learning processes. It is questionable whether education systems and educators in particular are ready for such a democratisation process. In the next section, we discuss how we sought to understand the assessment and open education practices of educators in higher education and those who recently graduated from teacher preparation programmes; and whether they purposefully develop SDL competencies as part of this, with the goal of understanding their readiness for change to existing practices, perceptions and beliefs.

10.3   Methodology

Guided by an interpretivist epistemology, this mixed-methods study used a self-completed online survey to ask educators from select African states about their assessment practices, beliefs and perceptions, how this aligns to learning outcomes, how/whether they develop SDL and their use of OER in this process. The content is embedded in five African states (Mauritius, South Africa, the Seychelles, Uganda and Zambia) where low-bandwidth and low-connectivity is common, and resistance to changing pedagogical approaches often pose significant challenges to online learning and assessments.

Ethics approval for this study was obtained from the Two Oceans Graduate Institute. The goals of the study and its purpose were stated at the start of the questionnaire to inform potential participants of all the processes and questions involved in the research. Participants were assured at the start of the online questionnaire that their participation was anonymous and voluntary, and that they could withdraw at any time should they wish. They were also asked to provide consent to participate in the study, for the information they provided to be shared and whether they would consider participating in a follow-up interview should this be required. This was done to limit feelings of coercion and to ensure that participants provided informed consent. Participants were also assured of the confidentiality of their responses and that all information they provided would be processed in accordance with the university's data and subjects rights, and that data would remain secure and not be shared with third parties.

10.4   Data Production and Analysis

Sampling for the data production was intended to include probability and cluster sampling, but due to different challenges and poor responses, this approach was adapted. Cluster sampling is particularly useful when a study population is dispersed across a wide geographical area as in this study, and economises time and costs incurred. The intention of the study was to randomly select participants by approaching education department officials in the ministries of education in the African states, and requesting that the online survey be shared electronically with the education and teaching college/university staff in their respective countries. However, when the survey was being distributed, many of the countries were coming out of lockdown, meaning education ministries and educators were overwhelmed with post-lockdown challenges. Although the ministry officials were willing to share the survey and wanted to participate in the study, the challenging times as schools and higher education institutions were reopening, resulted in surveys either not reaching educators or them not returning the surveys. At this point, we realised that returning and catching-up with months of lost teaching-time, placed too much pressure on educators and we did not want to add to their burden. Subsequently, the researchers shared the survey with educators in their circle of influence using social media and direct emailing. This resulted in 42 responses compared to a few hundred that they had hoped for. Participants completed the survey between August and September 2020 using an online Google Form (GForm).

The data collected from the different questions on the online GForm was analysed using quantitative as well as thematic analysis. The GForm responses were converted to Google Sheets (GSheets), and data prepared for analysis. The first round of analysis used Power BI, wordcloud.com, the data studio on Google, and the data analysis tools in GSheets for the quantitative data analysis. The qualitative data produced from longer paragraph-type answers were analysed using thematic analysis after coding the data first to identify trends and then comparing it to answers from the quantitative data. Findings from this data analysis process are discussed.

10.5   Findings

The concerns-based adoption model (Hord et al., 1987) was used to analyse participants' levels of use (Fig. 10.1) and stages of concerns (Fig. 10.2) about technologies in Education, hereafter referred to as eLearning. This was important to note considering the digital nature of open education resources and practices, eLearning as part of SDL and eAssessment. There appeared a significant difference between participants' personal/private use of devices and their levels of use of devices for eLearning. Only one participant indicated that they used their device once or twice a month, two used it once or twice a week, and the rest can be considered frequent users. Frequent users indicated that they used their devices '*almost every waking moment*' (32%), '*a few times a day*' (49%) or '*at least once a day*' (12%), meaning 93% of participants frequently use their devices for personal use. Since most participants were frequent users of devices, we wondered whether their levels of use for eLearning could be at a similar level.

Participants' personal use mostly paralleled their levels of use for eLearning and stages of concern on the CBAM. The participants who only used their personal devices once or twice a month, also indicated that they were at Level (1) Orientation regarding eLearning. The same participants indicated that they were concerned with how the technologies would affect their students. This suggests a much higher personal level of use, and trying to find ways to use technologies with students. Similarly, most users (85%) who indicated a high frequency of personal use ranked themselves at a relatively high level of use for eLearning, indicating a Routine (8),

Refinement (11), Integration (7) or Renewal (7) level. Their stages of concern were similarly at the top end of this scale. This would suggest that high personal use may positively impact high levels of use of technologies for teaching and learning. However, a few users (17%) who indicated high frequent personal use, noted that their use of technologies for eLearning ranked relatively lower on CBAM's Levels of Use, either at Level (1) Orientation and one user was on (0) Non-Use; these users indicated a much higher stage of concern, registering mostly on the collective impact stage (green). The data thus suggests that personal use of technologies in most cases positively aligns with high levels of use of technologies for eLearning and high stages of concern, but this is not predictive.

Open education resources (OER) and open education practices (OEP) are typically digital in nature and support eLearning goals. Respondents indicated that they used OER in different ways, as indicated in Fig. 10.3. The OER most frequently used were online textbooks, images and exercises for different subjects, followed by music, newspaper articles and movies. Almost half of respondents indicated that they also used OER journals and journal articles, reference works and related materials. Other OER like simulations, blogs, digital maps and open datasets were used less frequently. However, when OER are understood as merely resources with an open licence, this question could be interpreted differently. Although the questions stated that these digital resources were OER, participants could have merely indicated the types of digital tools they used frequently, rather than correlating this to OER. To understand whether they correlated OER to digital tools, we probed their levels of use of OER as an innovation.

The popularity of certain OER suggested that OER as an innovation was generally at a high level of use on CBAM, especially considering the general high level of personal use among participants. The data, however, indicated a different reality.

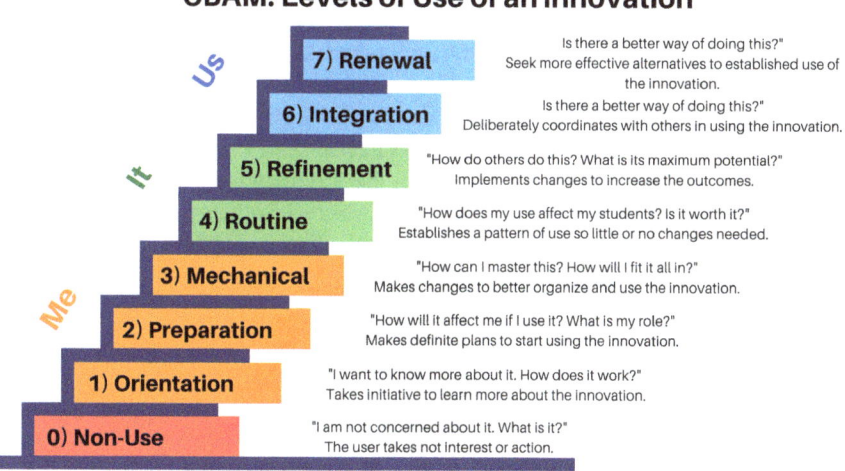

Fig. 10.1 CBAM levels of use

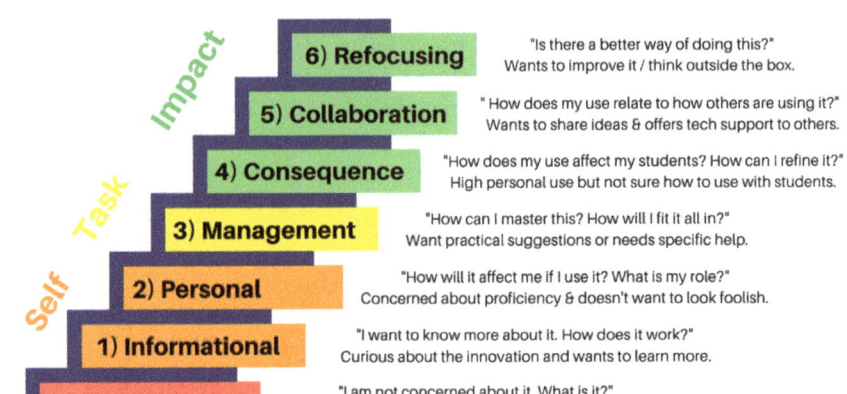

Fig. 10.2 Stages of concern form the concerns based adoption model (CBAM)

Although respondents indicated a high personal level of use of digital devices, the level of use for OER as an innovation rarely correlated to this. We compared their personal use of technology with those who had not heard of OER or did not use it (22%); with participants who had used it at least once (32%); and those who were regular users (46%). The regular users of OER did not correlate to the levels of personal use. One (1) respondent's personal use was at a level (0) Non-Use and three (3) at a level (1) Orientation (thinking of using technology), but they indicated that they regularly use OER. Similarly, non-correlation between higher personal use was noted by the group who only used OER once. Compared to the stages of concern, those who had never used OER ranged from 2 at stage (1) Orientation, 1 each at stages (4) Management, (5) Consequence and (6) Collaboration, with 6 at level (7) Refocusing. The data thus suggests that high personal use does not correlate to high levels of use of OER, or to the stages of concern on the CBAM.

If educators were not keen on using OER and 54% either never or only ever used it once, we wondered if this low use correlated to their open education practices (OEP). Evidence for OEP was derived from the way they planned their curriculum delivery, and how likely they were to share their work with others (see Fig. 10.4). Most respondents displayed a low use of OEP: 9 (22%) of respondents preferred to create all their teaching resources from scratch while almost half (44%) mostly used their own material but also used OER from time to time or borrowed from colleagues. Only 12% of respondents regularly used OER for assignments, activities and/or assessments displaying open education practices. The low use of OER generally was thus confirmed as only a small minority regularly used it for eLearning generally or as part of OEP to create teaching and learning resources. It was encouraging to note that although a little more than half of participants were willing to use OER or borrow from colleagues, most participants (93%) said they would likely share their

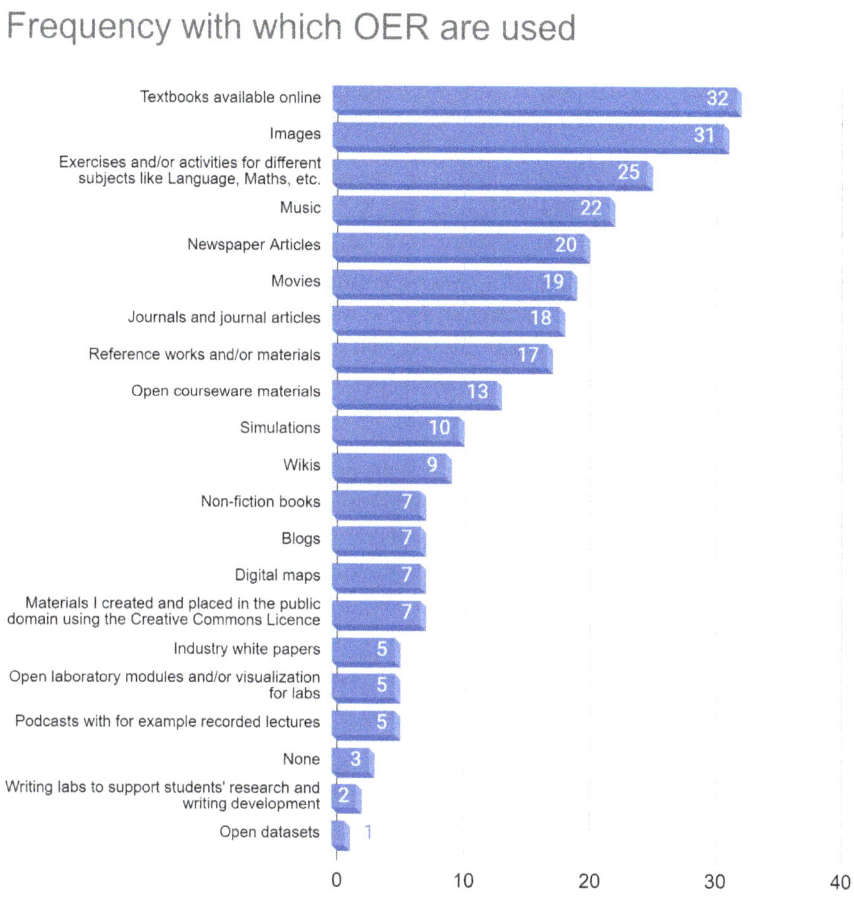

Frequency with which OER are used

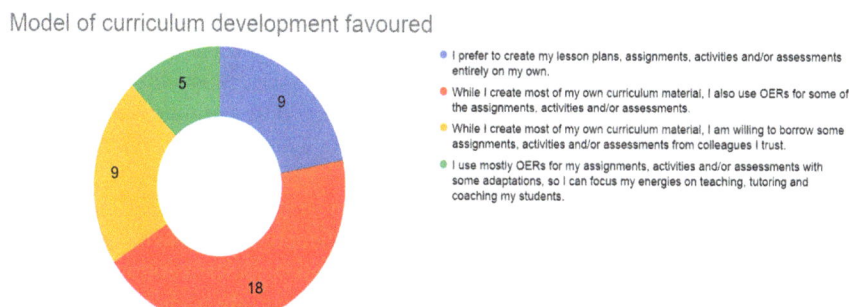

Fig. 10.3   Frequency with which participants use OER

Model of curriculum development favoured

Fig. 10.4   Model of curriculum developed favoured by educators

own resources, displaying an openness to OEP. With the relatively low level of OER and OEP use, we questioned which barriers may have contributed to the low use.

Different barriers to the use of OER were identified that limit its potential value to teaching and learning. We identified general barriers to OER use from literature and experience in the field, and asked participants to indicate which applied to them. Only a few participants (15%) identified no barriers, while the others identified a few first and many second-order barriers (Ertmer, 1999). First-order barriers refer to external factors, while second-order barriers are internal or specific to the user. Far fewer first-order barriers to OER were identified, ranging from institutions not permitting its use (5%), some colleagues (5%) or students (5%) being critical of it, and the institution failing to recognise those who used it (22%). Another first-order barrier is the relevance of OER, with participants noting that the OER that were available were not relevant to their teaching and learning needs.

Second-order barriers to OER were more frequently identified than first-order barriers. Second-order barriers are internal to the individual and mostly relate to their beliefs, perceptions or practices. Participants repeated noted a concern relating to the legal ramifications of using OER, with 41% of respondents being afraid of infringing on copyright or committing plagiarism, while a further 37% were concerned about ownership of the material. This may relate to the few who were sceptical about using OER or critical of the resources produced, with one person stating:

> I am critical of many resources available as OER as my philosophy is to think creatively and to solve problems in my own unique way. I want to encourage this in my students and urge them not to comply to the opinions of others.

It appears this educator may labour under the assumption that reusing, repurposing or remixing OER are forms of intellectual dishonesty, or that they may not understand the creative commons licencing of OER. As with this lecturer's comment, it may also indicate a mistrust of OER or the perception that OER are of a lower quality than the work they can produce themselves. Lastly, educators were concerned that the search for OER would be too time-consuming (41%) or would require too much data (27%). Data-use in low-bandwidth areas where data costs are considerable and time equates to data usage, means ineffective searching not only wastes time but also money in terms of data. The data thus indicated that respondents' perceptions and limited knowledge and understanding around the creative commons licencing of OER, and their inability to quickly locate appropriate and relevant OER posed the greatest barriers to its use.

In light of the different barriers to OER use, most notably the frequently cited second-order barriers, we asked respondents which benefits they considered to using OER. When seeking to change educators' practices, beliefs and perceptions, it is often beneficial to let them identify a rational reason to support their changed practices (Heath & Heath, 2010; Tarling, 2018), and to identify the benefits that OER provide. Respondents rated different benefits of using OER with the scale: strong, fair, weak and no benefit. The strongest benefits of using OER were identified as enhancing the user's knowledge of a subject, and achieving greater equity by increasing access to resources for students and their access to knowledge. Another strong benefit was identified as publishing and also using OER which encourages the sharing of best practices. The publication and use of OER in supporting developing nations and communities and subsequent development of networks was a further strong benefit. More respondents than for any other item, indicated that the potential cost and/or time saved to develop OER were of *weak* or *no* benefit. Despite respondents clearly understanding the benefits of using OER, both personally and at a national scale, these rational reasons appear to have limited impact to increase the use of OER.

The potential of OER to support SDL was also probed. Respondents were first asked to define SDL and then to rate examples as having either strong, fair, weak or no relation to SDL to compare their definitions and applications thereof. When defining SDL, two respondents quoted Knowles' (1975) definition while another stated:

> It is a technique where someone chooses to set the learning objectives to meet his or her requirements, looking for appropriate resources and learning methods to bring about the necessary results without the support of others.

The remaining descriptions of SDL were thematically analysed and compared to the ratings of the various examples. A common theme that emerged as with the example above was self-determinism of learning, where the student can decide on the learning goals and direction of learning to control the process. SDL was also associated with independence in the learning process where the student takes responsibility for their progress and assessment, one participant stating, for example: It is '[t]*aking charge of your own learning, resources and outcomes*'. The independent theme also correlated to the rating of examples, where: '*Independent academic study on a topic that the student is passionate about*' was rated as the strongest example of SDL. Students taking the initiative to learn was a further theme that emerged and three respondents associated this with active or discovery-based learning. The role of teacher ranged from no involvement, to fringe-involvement as a facilitator or guide, to taking control and deciding the learning outcomes to teach students how to work independently. Typically, respondents from schools emphasised the role of the teacher to develop students' independence while those from Higher Education focused on the independent nature of SDL.

What educators prioritise for inclusion is reflected in their planning. Educators rated the priority they assign to different competencies which support the development of SDL. They could choose from a range of activities based on Knowles' (1975) competencies for SDL, including among other diagnosing and formulating learning needs in the form of learning goals, identifying the required resources to support learning, choosing appropriate strategies and assessing the outcomes of learning. Educators indicated the priority they assign to the different activities using the scale (a) *I make every effort to include it in my plans*; (b) *If I can, I include it in my plans*; and (c) *It's great but I don't think about it when I plan*. The least prioritised activity was students learning self-efficacy to manage how and when they access the Internet. Developing students' competencies to set goals and self-assess was also prioritised by fewer educators, followed by a lower priority placed on information literacy to search for, evaluate and use information. Although some participants indicated that they made every effort to include these activities in their planning, more did not, suggesting that even if educators supported SDL, they did not prioritise the development of competencies to achieve this.

SDL competencies involve among other the ability to self-assess learning outcomes in order to set goals for future learning and choose appropriate strategies and resources to achieve this. Hattie (2009, 2013) found that feedback as a formative function of assessment serves to develop students' metacognitive judgement skills and through this, to calibrate their perceived and actual achievement. We therefore asked educators about the types of assessments they used, wondering if their assessment practices supported the development of SDL competencies. More than half of respondents (61%) frequently used assessment to diagnose students' prior skills, competencies and knowledge at the beginning of a course or session. A similar group (63%) used the formative function of assessment throughout a term or course while almost 70% only used assessment to summatively assess learning between 1 and 4 times per term or course. This data was compared to educators' preferences regarding different types of assessment (see Fig. 10.5). Group work, worksheets and workbooks, and standardised test were used most frequently by most respondents, followed by role plays, dramas and scenarios, observations and projects or assignments. 61% of respondents never used portfolios, and 56% never used case studies as part of assessments. Crosswords, word searches and written submissions such as diaries, letters, blogs or experiments, and simulations were either never used by between 34 and 40% of respondents, or used at least once or twice a term or in a course by 20–40% of respondents. Standardised tests, marking worksheets and workbooks, often serve a summative function, and were regularly used by most educators (this group included educators from primary to high school, higher education to district office officials). Other assessment types may more readily align with the formative function of assessment such as assessing essays and paragraphs (and particularly drafts of this), group work and tasks that require teachers to use observation techniques for example role plays, dramas, debates, discussions etc. Such types of assessment can serve both a formative and a summative function. For example, a student may have to submit drafts of their work over the course of a term or semester, which are either assessed by the educator or peer-assessed, as a formative function of assessment, and lastly assessed summatively when the final product is submitted.

10.6 Discussion

The data indicated that there are many challenges to the dissemination and integration of OER in education institutions. Almost half of participants indicated a lack of knowledge about plagiarism, ownership and creative commons licencing. Similarly, many were unsure how to search for or where to find relevant OER, worrying about time and data wasted in the process. At an organisational level, participants faced different challenges, with institutions either not encouraging nor recognising the

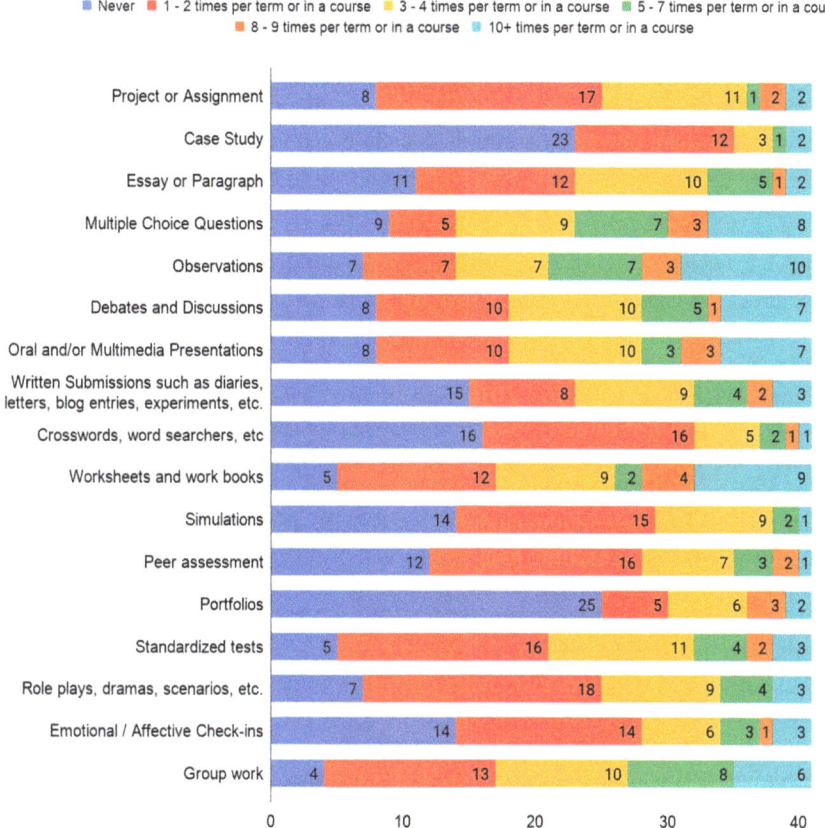

Fig. 10.5 Frequency with which different assessment types of used

use of OER. OER and OEP have the potential to significantly address multiple challenges at education institutions in Africa, and it would be beneficial to embark on a greater awareness campaign to expand the knowledge base of individual educators and increase the cultural capital associated with its use from an institutional and individual perspective.

SDL although originally defined in terms of adult learning appears to be more widely appropriated as a learning strategy in schools as well. Descriptions of SDL are frequently related to students being aware of their learning needs, taking responsibility and initiative in the learning process, and assessing the outcome (Knowles, 1975; Sumuer, 2018). Similarly, educators from higher and basic education participating in the study defined SDL in terms of students' self-determinism, independence and control of the learning process. Those in basic education described the role of the teacher as gradually teaching learners to be more independent while still actively structuring the learning process, while those in secondary and higher education saw the educator as increasingly detached from the learning process, either as a facilitator or guide, or not involved at all. The data thus suggests that while SDL may once have been associated with andragogy, it is no longer the case and those in basic education are appropriating this strategy as well. It may relate to the blurring between adult and children's learning, raising fundamental questions about such a distinction. Is there a magical age when one stops learning as a child and at the stroke of midnight on one's 18th birthday for instance, start learning in a different way? Or is learning just learning and different strategies are more appealing to different individuals regardless of their age?

The development of students' self-efficacy regarding online communication and computer-use is significantly mediated by Web 2.0 tools (Sumuer, 2018). The low priority given to the development of students' self-efficacy by educators is concerning, especially since self-efficacy is a vital skill need to develop self-regulation (McLoughlin & Lee, 2010) and in turn develop self-regulated learning. Similarly, since SDL is directly reliant on goal-setting and goal-directed behaviours, as well as self-assessing learning outcomes, it is concerning that these two competencies were not prioritised by most teachers. This contrasts the priority almost all educators placed on developing students' independence and the responsibility they take for their learning. Teaching goal-setting and goal-directed behaviours, and self-assessment are crucial competencies to develop independence and responsibility and should be prioritised (Knowles, 1975; Sumuer, 2018) to develop students' SDL towards becoming life-long learners. It suggests that as with OER, it would be beneficial to embark on a greater awareness campaign to develop teachers' knowledge around the competencies that are needed to develop SDL and underlying skills they can encourage towards achieving this.

Regarding assessment strategies, few educators appear to be shifting their practices towards goals of self-assessment, inclusion and the democratisation of assessment practices. Using portfolios is a useful strategy to develop students' goal-directed behaviours and ability to self-assess, yet almost two thirds of participants did not use this. This was also evident when educators identified the priorities, they place on developing SDL competencies, with half of respondents not prioritising self-assessment. Instead, the greater emphasis for this group of educators was on developing students' competencies to become independent and to take responsibility for their learning, to nurture a love for learning and creativity and innovation. These priorities, coupled with the higher frequency of use for assessments that are teacher-dependent and which serve summative functions (standardised tests, workbooks and worksheets), suggest two things. It firstly suggests that most of the educators in the group did not prioritise SDL but elements of this, and particularly independence in completing tasks set by the educator. Such an emphasis does not develop SDL as there is no self-determinism on the part of students to pursue learning interests, identify learning goals and resources to support this. Secondly, based on the data indicating low levels of use for OER and OEP, it appears that educators are also not democratising assessment practices using OEP or delving into existing OER to support assessment. OER and particularly OEP have the potential to improve and democratise assessment practices if used and published, as acknowledged by educators in the survey. However, since few are using these, the potential of OER and OEP cannot be realised.

10.7 Conclusion

The study addressed three research questions. Firstly, it asked what current education practices are used across African education contexts that rely on OER. OER use was shown to be limited, and open education practices were not widely adopted. The limited adoption of OER and OEP suggests greater awareness campaigns are required to encourage its use and relevance. The study also probed educators' perceptions and practices regarding SDL. Educate prioritised the development of students' independence and responsibility over competencies that support the development of SDL. Thirdly, we explored educators' assessment practices and priorities, noting that they widely focus on teacher-driven and designed assessments that do not typically include students' voices or choices. As such, it was found that assessment designs do not widely adopt open education practices towards democratising education and assessment.

The chapter firstly reviewed literature to uncover dominant discourses regarding assessment and how open education resources and practices may address these discourses. Guided by an interpretivist epistemology, a relatively small-scale study with 41 participants across 5 African states was conducted to explore educators' perceptions, practices and beliefs around assessments, OER and SDL. Although the focus for the study was on higher education practices, educators who had recently graduated from a university's postgraduate programme were also included to understand to what extent their experiences at the university had equipped them to employ OER and OEP in their classes. Using quantitative and thematic analysis, survey data provided by educators from primary and higher education, and education district offices, were interrogated and findings discussed.

While digital learning practices may slowly be changing, assessment practices appear to have remained stagnant. Most educators prioritised assessment practices that are designed by and rely heavily on the teacher, and mainly focused on developing students' abilities to take responsibility for and work independently to achieve the goals set by the teacher. Both formal and informal assessment provide evidence of learning, and potentially open dialogue between the educator and student to strengthen learning across the curriculum. If such practices were democratised, and students' voices included in their design, there is potential for such open assessment practices to address the contextual challenges and learning priorities of students, and for students to customise their assessment experience. This may evolve education and assessment from its heavy reliance on high-stakes exams that measure outcomes, to assessment that is focused on improving the learning process. However, the low use of OER and OEP by educators suggest that its potential remains untapped to effect change to practices, perceptions and beliefs.

The competencies that educators prioritised did not suggest that current teaching practices focus on the development of SDL competencies. Instead, the data indicates that while educators support the goals of SDL, that they do not actively develop student's competencies to achieve this. Educators prioritised skills such as fostering creativity and innovation in students, guiding them to become independent learners, to take responsibility for their learning and nurturing a love for learning. These skills, though important, do not readily align with the competencies needed to develop SDL such as goal setting and developing goal-oriented behaviours, identifying the need for and choosing different learning strategies and resources, or self-assessment. Accurate calibration is critical if students are to accurately judge appropriate learning goals and decide on goal-directed behaviours, or to judge the resources they may need for different activities. In short, accurate calibration is critical to effectively develop SDL processes. Emphasizing the competencies needed for SDL, and through focused, strategic and regular formative feedback developing students' calibration may hold the key to unlocking the potential of OER for traditional and non-traditional students.

Findings indicate the need for ongoing professional development at scale to change and democratise classroom practices towards constructively aligning learning outcomes, assessment and learning tasks to democratise education, develop SDL competencies and encourage open education practices. OER and open courseware have the potential to open learning for non-traditional and traditional students across Africa who would not ordinarily have accessed this. Research has indicated that SDL has been practiced in the past and continues to be used in Sub-Saharan Africa by indigenous knowledge-builders, so it is not a foreign concept in Africa. Students who have developed as life-long learners draw on SDL competencies to do so, and educators have an important role to play in developing these. Hence, the need for professional development at scale to encourage change to educators' beliefs, perceptions and practices around OER and OEP, assessment and SDL competencies.

Findings from this study may also inform changes to education policy and institutional practices to encourage and support greater use of OER generally for eLearning and OEP to develop eAssessment. There is a need to develop cultural capital around open practices which would include acknowledging and rewarding those who display OEP, and addressing criticism towards OER in a transparent and honest manner. In particular, the perceptions around ownership and plagiarism should be acknowledged and an awareness for creative commons licencing developed to address incorrect perceptions and beliefs. The greater OER community may also gain insight from such awareness campaigns, in order to address the challenges educators from African education contexts experience when searching for relevant OER. While there are certainly many OER repositories available, the content is often relevant to education contexts in the Global North where they were produced. Greater awareness campaigns may lead to more relevant OER being developed.

The findings also suggest that the educators who graduated from university did not appropriate OER or OEP any more than counterparts in other African states. This suggests that teacher education programmes may need to prioritise their curriculum to not only support the use of OER and open practices, but to also equip educators at graduate and postgraduate level to develop open education resources. Much can be learnt from existing programmes aimed at this, such as UNESCO's project, Open Education for a Better World (OE4BW), which both the authors have participated in. Through the project, scholars who produce OER mentor those wanting to learn how to do so. Not only does this equip a greater section of society to create open resources, but it also models open practices that mentees can emulate. Such projects as OE4BW could potentially address the lack of OER use and limited open practices in university teacher education programmes, but more widely prepare a greater section of society to create relevant, quality OER that address the direct needs of educators across Africa.

References

Alexander, P. A. (2013). Calibration: What is it and why it matters? An introduction to the special issue on calibrating calibration. *Learning and Instruction, 24*(1), 1–3. https://doi.org/10.1016/j. learninstruc.2012.10.003

Baranovskaya, T., & Shaforostova, V. (2017). Assessment and Evaluation Techniques. *Journal of Language and Education, 3*(2), 30. https://doi.org/10.17323/2411-7390-2017-3-2-30-38.

Barnett, E. (2018). *Education quality in Malawi: What role for decentralisation?* (Issue May) [London School of Economics and Political Science]. http://etheses.lse.ac.uk/3746/1/Barnett__ education-quality-in-malawi.pdf. Retrieved 18 Nov 2020.

Black, P., & Wiliam, D. (1998). Assessment and classroom learning. In *Assessment in education: Principles, policy and practice* (Vol. 5, No. 1). Routledge, Taylor Francis Group. https://doi.org/ 10.1080/0969595980050102.

Black, P., & Wiliam, D. (2009). Developing the theory of formative assessment. *Educational Assessment, Evaluation and Accountability, 21*(1), 5–31. https://doi.org/10.1007/s11092-008-9068-5

Black, P., & Wiliam, D. (2018). Classroom assessment and pedagogy. *Assessment in Education: Principles, Policy and Practice, 25*(6), 551–575. https://doi.org/10.1080/0969594X.2018.144 1807

Boud, D. J. (2007). Reframing assessment as if learning was important. In D. J. Boud & N. Falchikov (Eds.), *Rethinking assessment for higher education: Learning or the longer term* (pp. 14–25). Routledge.

Charteris, J., Quinn, F., Parkes, M., Fletcher, P., & Reyes, V. (2016). e-Assessment for learning and performativity in higher education: A case for existential learning. *Australasian Journal of Educational Technology, 32*(3), 112–122. https://doi.org/10.14742/ajet.2595.

Conrad, D., Mackintosh, W., Mcgreal, R., Murphy, A., & Witthaus, G. (2013). *Report on the assessment and accreditation of learners using OER.*

Conrad, D., & McGreal, R. (2012). Flexible paths to assessment for OER learners: A comparative study. *Journal of Interactive Media in Education, 2*, 1–10. https://doi.org/10.5334/2012-12. Retrieved 27 Nov 2020.

Department of Basic Education (2017). *The SACMEQ IV project in South Africa: A stufy of the conditions of schooling and the quality.* http://www.sacmeq.org/sites/default/files/sacmeq/public ations/sacmeq_iv_project_in_south_africa_report.pdf.

Ehlers, U.-D. (2011). From open educational resources. *ELearning Papers, 23*, 1–8. https://www. oerknowledgecloud.org/archive/media25161.pdf. Retrieved 27 Nov 2020.

Ertmer, P. A. (1999). Addressing first- and second-order barriers to change: Strategies for technology integration. *Educational Technology Research and Development, 47*(4), 47–61. https://doi.org/ 10.1007/BF02299597

Friesen, N., & Wihak, C. (2013). From OER to PLAR: Credentialing for open education. *Open Praxis, 5*(1), 49–58.

Gardner, J. (2009). *Assessment for learning: A practical guide* (p. 108).

Hadwin, A. F., & Webster, E. A. (2013). Calibration in goal setting: Examining the nature of judgments of confidence. *Learning and Instruction, 24*(1), 37–47. https://doi.org/10.1016/j.learninstruc.2012.10.001

Hargreaves, E. (2005). Assessment for learning? Thinking outside the (black) box. *Cambridge Journal of Education, 35*(2), 213–224. https://doi.org/10.1080/03057640500146880

Hattie, J. (2009). *Visible learning: A synthesis of over 800 meta-analyses relating to achievement.* Routledge, Taylor Francis Group.https://doi.org/10.1017/CBO9781107415324.004.

Hattie, J. (2013). Calibration and confidence: Where to next? *Learning and Instruction, 24*(1), 62–66. https://doi.org/10.1016/j.learninstruc.2012.05.009

Heath, C., & Heath, D. (2010). Switch: How to change things when change is hard. In *New York* (No. 1). Broadway Books. http://www.amazon.com/dp/0385528752.

Hord, S. M., Rutherford, W. L., Huling-Austin, L., & Hall, G. E. (1987). *Taking charge of change.* Southwest Educational Development Laboratory.

Karunanayaka, S. P., Naidu, S., Rajendra, J. C. N., & Ratnayake, H. U. W. (2015). From OER to OEP : Shifting practitioner perspectives and practices with innovative learning experience design. *Open Praxis, 7*(4), 339–350.

Knowles, M. S. (1975). *Self-directed learning: A guide to learners and teachers.* Associated Press.

Lehohla, P. J. (2016). *Education series volume III: Education enrolment and achievement: Vol. III.*

Mainali, B. R., & Heck, A. (2017). Comparison of traditional instruction on reflection and rotation in a Nepalese high school with an ICT-rich, student-centered, investigative approach. *International Journal of Science and Mathematics Education, 15*(3), 487–507.

McLoughlin, C., & Lee, M. J. W. (2010). Personalised and self regulated learning in the Web 2.0 era: International exemplars of innovative pedagogy using social software. *Australasian Journal of Educational Technology, 26*(1), 28–43. https://doi.org/10.1523/JNEUROSCI.4255-09.2010.

Redecker, C., & Johannessen, Ø. (2013). Changing assessment—Towards a new assessment paradigm using ICT. *European Journal of Education, 48*(1), 79–96.

Schuwirth, L. W. T., & Van Der Vleuten, C. P. M. (2011). Programmatic assessment: From assessment of learning to assessment for learning. *Medical Teacher, 33*(6), 478–485. https://doi.org/10.3109/0142159X.2011.565828

Sumuer, E. (2018). Factors related to college students' self-directed learning with technology. *Adult Education Quarterly, 34*(4), 29.

Tarling, I. (2018). *Transforming teaching through the transformative integration of emerging technologies in the ePlay MakerSpace: a critical socio-cultural design-based study* (Issue February) [University of Cape Town]. https://open.uct.ac.za/bitstream/handle/11427/28367/Tarling;_Isabel_Transforming_teaching_2018.pdf?sequence=1.

Tarling, I., & Ng'ambi, D. . (2016). Teachers pedagogical change framework: A diagnostic tool for changing teachers' uses of emerging technologies. *British Journal of Educational Technology, 47*(3), 554–572. https://doi.org/10.1111/bjet.12454

Valtonen, T., Sointu, E., Kukkonen, J., Kontkanen, S., Lambert, M. C., & Mäkitalo-siegl, K. (2017). TPACK updated to measure pre-service teachers' twenty-first century skills. *Australasian Journal of Educational Technology, 33*(3), 15–31.

Voogt, J., Knezek, G., Cox, M., Knezek, D., & ten Brummelhuis, A. (2013). Under which conditions does ICT have a positive effect on teaching and learning? A call to action. *Journal of computer assisted learning, 29*(1), 4–14.

Weimer, M. (2002). Learner-centered teaching: Five key changes to practice. John Wiley & Sons. Retrieved from https://goo.gl/WRoZWO.

Dr. Isabel Tarling is an ICT Integration specialist, holds a PhD in Education Technologies and Teacher Professional Development from UCT, and is director of Limina's learning design division. Her extensive experience working with teachers from all phases, subjects and backgrounds, directly impacts the hands-on and change-driven teacher professional development courses she develops. In 2019 she was selected by the UNESCO chair at the Josef Stefan Institute, Slovenia, to create an online course for teachers as part of the Open Education for a Better World program. As an author, she is widely published and her research on teacher change is included in the national Professional Development Framework for Digital Learning. In July 2020 her adaption of the book, Teachers Discovering Computers: Integrating Technology in the South African Classroom, was published for teachers and teaching students. Dr. Tarling passionately believes that the key to transforming teaching and learning lies in empowering all educators to create and innovate with technologies and to plan and manage change. This belief drives her to inspire all those in education to create and innovate with technologies, and to inspire others to do the same. Her research interests focus on Technology Integration in Discipline-Specific areas, design thinking and developing socially embedded transformative programmes to support community-based innovation.

Mrs. Sandhya Gunness is a senior lecturer in Open and Online learning and the Programme coordinator for the MSc Educational Technologies and the MA Educational Leadership programmes at the University of Mauritius (UoM). She has conducted many workshops with COL, UNESCO, COMESA and the SADC on numerous e-learning projects and is currently pursuing her PhD studies in the field of Horizontal Collaborative Networks and development of T-Shaped graduates. She was consulted by the Ministry of Education for conducting a national survey on the use of Digital Tablets in Primary schools in Mauritius in collaboration with the World Bank and has contributed to the drafting of the National Open Educational Resources policy for Mauritius. Her research interests include Open Educational Practices, transdisciplinary skills and collaborative networking.

Chapter 11
Bala Wande—Foundation Phase Mathematics OER: Collaborative Development and Use

Sihlobosenkosi Mpofu, Permie Isaac, Tobeka Ndamase, Luleka Sonjica, and Ingrid Sapire

Abstract The TIMSS-Numeracy Study of 2015 tested a nationally representative sample of Grade 5 students and found that 61% could not do basic mathematics such as adding and subtracting whole numbers or solving simple word problems. Studies have shown that this is in large part because students have not built the foundations of early numeracy in Grades R to 3. In response to this, Bala Wande, a Foundation Phase mathematics project was established to develop and trial materials for Grades R-3. The greater project consists of three randomised control trials in three different provinces in South Africa which will be piloted and evaluated over a period of four years (2019–2023). The student materials developed for the project are all OER, and although they are aimed at very young students, the designers aim to make them user friendly so that these students can use them independently. Teacher support is clearly needed in this phase, and Teacher Guides have been developed that align with the student material, also as OER. The evaluation at the end of the project term will produce rigorous evidence to show 'what works' in the field of early numeracy. In this empirical case study, the collaborative development and early take-up of the materials are used to shed light on good practice for OER development, take-up and dissemination. Findings show that teachers value and are able to implement the lesson activities suggested in the Teacher Guide and students worked well in the independent activity book.

S. Mpofu
University of Kwazulu Natal, Durban, South Africa

S. Mpofu · I. Sapire (✉)
University of Witwatersrand, Johannesburg, South Africa
e-mail: ingrid.sapire@wits.ac.za

P. Isaac
Rhodes University, Grahamstown, South Africa

T. Ndamase
SANTS, Pretoria, South Africa

L. Sonjica
Varsity College, Sandton, South Africa

Keywords Foundation Phase mathematics materials · Take-up of OER ·
Independent learning · examples and pictures in mathematics materials

11.1   Introduction

Mathematics learning in South Africa has been in the doldrums for some time now as evidenced by low competence levels at the Foundation Phase (Grades R-3) for mathematics in the Annual National Assessments (Department of Basic Education, 2014). Bertram et al. (2015) found that Foundation Phase teachers' low subject content and pedagogic content knowledge is responsible for poor performance in mathematics. The issue of early grade teachers with challenges in both subject content and pedagogic knowledge is not limited to South Africa (World Bank, 2019), and it needs to be addressed in order to improve mathematics learning outcomes (Venkat & Spaull, 2015). The potential of open educational resources (OER) to impact on educational change is huge. Good quality, freely accessible materials that could be used to support teaching and learning could be part of the solution to the mathematics education problem. One problem that restricts the potential impact of OER is the extent to which available materials are taken up, but collaboration in the OER development process has been shown to improve the take-up of OER (Sapire & Reed, 2011). The Bala Wande project, a mathematics intervention seeking solutions to the country's education crisis, is currently being evaluated in two randomised control trials in two different provinces of South Africa. The long-term goal of the project is to develop high-quality OER materials to support early grade mathematics teaching and learning. The project established a large collaborative reference team with representatives from the universities, the Department of Basic Education and non-governmental organisations working in Foundation Phase mathematics to inform the materials development process in order to maximise both the quality and the potential for take-up of the materials. To leverage funding the project builds on already existing Foundation Phase mathematics material and has developed a high-quality set of learner workbooks aligned to easily accessible teachers' guides that are supported by video footage which offers further assistance to teachers in their take-up of the material. Videos have an effect of activating mental process involved with knowledge and comprehension as they are easier to follow than written texts (Pai, 2014). The Bala Wande videos are a very useful tool for teachers because they allow teachers to listen to how activities are modelled and to view both teacher and learner behaviour in action. Watching model videos prepares teachers for real-life situations as they can view learner struggles and activity transitions (Pai, 2014). Key ideas from the literature of mathematics education in the Foundation Phase (Anthony & Walshaw, 2009; Askew, 2012, 2016) have informed the materials development process. These are presented in the theoretical orientation, and they informed the analytical framework of this chapter.

11.2   Mathematics Teaching and Learning in South Africa: Theoretical Orientation

A major challenge noted by Hoadley (2012) is that Foundation Phase students exit the phase without adequately developing number sense which may result in their exiting the phase with arithmetic deficiencies that prejudice them in higher grades. Evidence of these deficiencies is mentioned in Chikiwa et al. (2019) where Grade 2 students resorted to using their fingers or drew sticks for counting when they counted or performed additive operations. Number sense is defined as a person's ability to use and understand number (Chikiwa et al., 2019). Development of number sense means among other things that students are able to understand how numbers relate to each other, apply the use of number in real-world situations, do mental calculations with ease and to use mathematical strategies in solving mathematical problems (Chikiwa et al., 2019). Number sense grows gradually as students engage in mathematical activities (Burns, 2005) and become more able to reason abstractly. At the abstract stage, students use numbers and other symbols efficiently. The Bala Wande OER introduce numbers and symbols at an early stage. Concrete objects and representations are used to support students to overcome one of the challenges of early grade learning, which is the writing of number symbols (Munn, 1998; Zhou & Wang, 2004). In the Bala Wande OER, there are lessons that are dedicated developing students' number sense while simultaneously proving time for developing writing skills. By the time concrete objects and representations are withdrawn, students should already be familiar with number symbols and operations (Sowell, 1989). Active learning is promoted in the Bala Wande OER through the inclusion of games, many of which are played with manipulatives which help students to visualise and explore numbers in a variety of contexts. The use of manipulatives in the development of number sense is discussed next.

Manipulatives are tools that aid students to think during a learning process (Askew, 2012) because concrete objects engage students and make learning more interesting. Students must be motivated to learn mathematics, and one way of doing this is through providing engaging activities during lessons—manipulatives play a big role in creating the excitement. Students enjoy playing with manipulatives, and at the same time, they are consolidating their conceptual understanding of mathematics. Manipulatives also help students to express mathematical problems in a variety of ways (Sebesta & Martin, 2004). For example, when students use manipulatives when doing addition, they can see the physical increase in quantity which helps develop their number sense. Manipulatives help students to do mathematics with confidence as they provide another mode of representation which helps them to achieve generalisations which form the substance of abstract learning (Sebesta & Martin, 2004).

Manipulatives can be used at any stage of learning, whenever it is necessary, but at some point, students need to stop using manipulatives and do problems without concrete objects (Chikiwa et al., 2019). While Sowell (1989) encourages long-term use of manipulatives and argues their benefits, teachers ultimately will need to move from focused use of manipulatives to the use of representations and symbols. Chikiwa et al. (2019) noticed in their research that some students were stuck on manipulatives and struggled to do mathematical calculations without the use of fingers and other manipulatives. Once students have grasped number concept, a move from concrete to iconic representations is essential; they should not be held at the concrete level. Iconic representations in mathematics are pictures or images to which mathematical meaning is attached. Mathematical representations help illuminate mathematical concepts that would otherwise be difficult to comprehend in abstract form. They help students organise their mathematical thinking. Representations are useful because they can build students' understanding and enable them to demonstrate reasoning (Askew, 2016). The use of representations should always aim to lead to abstraction of concepts. The Bala Wande OER have applied this theory and is richly illustrated to further support the move to abstract learning.

The purpose of tasks which lead to abstraction is to produce new historic facts for the learner (Lavie et al., 2019). The Bala Wande learner material has activities that have been planned to support abstraction on the part of students. In the materials, there are contextualised and decontextualised activities, storytelling, questions and games. All of these are designed to lead students along the path to abstraction. Number sense (the goal of Foundation Phase learning as discussed above) develops over time based on repeated meaningful exposure to and exploration of numbers, opportunities to visualise numbers in different contexts and to reason about numbers in ways that are not limited by traditional algorithms (Sood & Jitenda, 2007). The use of language in the reasoning process is critical and is discussed next.

Number sense develops when students are given opportunities to make sense and reason about number (Anthony & Walshaw, 2009). Storytelling helps students to refine their own thinking and to consolidate their understanding of mathematical strategies. In multilingual contexts, it is good if students use both their main language and the dominant language (e.g. English) for the development of their mathematics vocabulary and their understanding (García & Wei, 2014). Bilingual classrooms become an important tool to overcome language inadequacies as described by Hoadley (2012) where students had one tenth of the vocabulary needed for them to succeed. In the process of storytelling, the use of explanation and justification improves fluency and enhances mathematical reasoning. Storytelling is not only powerful for the speaker but creates vivid and powerful images in the listener's mind (Haven, 2014). Storytelling is a powerful tool for the development of number sense because it enables this development in a way that is not bound by traditional algorithms (Haven, 2014). One of the sometimes underrated (or under-utilised) but highly useful means of teaching is the use of games in the learning of mathematics. Games are a regular feature in the Bala Wande OER.

Playing games in a mathematics class does not only improve attitudes but also develop problem solving skills (Bragg, 2012). Mathematics games are important because discussions that take place while students are playing the games develop number sense. Games encourage strategic mathematical thinking as students use different strategies for solving problems while playing. Games also present an opportunity for practice and consolidation of concepts. According to Stein and Bovalino

(2001), games make students think and reason in a more meaningful way. Students are likely to notice patterns as they play games. For example, they can notice number doubles—2 fours move you to 8, 2 threes move you to 6; if you are at 7, you need 3 to get to 10 and so on. Mathematics learning is a result of experiences that take place in the classroom. Deliberate steps must be taken in order for students to be presented with rich opportunities to learn (Yeh et al., 2019). It is against this background that the Bala Wande OER were produced. They aim to be user friendly and to support active learning which could help students to bridge gaps that have been identified in the development of their number sense.

11.3 The Use of Examples and Pictures in Teaching Mathematics

Mathematics is a subject where examples play an important role in concept development. Watson and Mason (2002) argue that learning of mathematics is a process through which generalisation comes from specific examples. Giving examples in class equips students with tools that can be used to solve problems (Bills, et al., 2006). While there are many different ways in which examples can be used, for the purpose of this chapter, we focus on examples for concept development in a Grade 1 class. This established the analytical framework for the study. Worked examples are very important in explaining the content and concepts that the teacher conveys in class (Leinhardt, 2001). Unlike in other subjects where reading a book or giving notes can take the centre stage, in mathematics, examples (and counter-examples) are the drivers of communicating concepts to students (Peled & Zaslavsky, 1997). Exemplification does not only come from the teacher as books that students use can also be a good source of procedural and conceptual communication. While Watson and Mason (2002) argue that examples are chosen from a wide range of possibilities, at the Grade 1 level, content has to be mediated gradually so as to accommodate novice students. The Bala Wande OER were developed bearing in mind that the number and type of examples are affected by the concept to be taught and the teacher knowledge of the associated content (Ng & Dindyal, 2015).

Teacher knowledge in selection of examples is important because it is in these examples that students' understanding of concepts is achieved (Askew, 2012). Teachers need to choose examples carefully because some examples lead to misconceptions. For example, when introducing multiplication, using the example $2 + 2 = 4$ and $2 \times 2 = 4$ (rather than $2 + 2 + 2 = 6$ and $2 \times 3 = 6$) may lead students to unintended misconceptions. Teachers using the Bala Wande OER benefit from having access to pre-selected examples for both teachers and students. Teacher agency should always be supported (and developed) by a programme for effective take-up (Priestley et al., 2015). Bala Wande presents material that teachers are free to use, on their own or supplemented by other examples, according to their professional discretion. How the examples will be used is largely dependent on teachers' knowledge of mathematics. The extent to which teachers are able to use materials independently (and to promote independent learning on the part of students) bears evidence of their capacity to support teacher agency. Examples on their own may not be adequate to promote independent learning, and diagrams and pictures are very important for students especially at the Grade 1 level.

Although the use of pictures and diagrams in mathematics learning is sometimes dominated by numeric and symbolic calculation activities, it is one of the most effective and least expensive ways of driving concepts home, especially in Grade 1 where many students cannot read on their own. Park and Brannon (2013) argue that learning is most effective when different areas of the brain are triggered and that symbols, for example, addition signs, number symbols, pictures and diagrams use different area of the brain. Park and Brannon also found that exposing students to visual representations helped students' performance in numerical mathematics tasks. One of the principles of the Realistic Mathematics Education (RME) is that learning of mathematics must start with familiar context that makes sense to students and that pictures can provide this context and stimulate mathematical thinking (van den Heuvel-Panhuizen et al., 2009). Diagrams, illustrations and game cartoons all aim to provide a contextual base for young students of mathematics. Pictures linger longer in students' mind, and this triggers new thoughts and enhances understanding of mathematical concepts (Askew, 2016). The Bala Wande OER are highly visual—it is full of diagrams and illustrations that support independent learning.

The case study reported on in this chapter sets out to answer the following research questions in order to shed light on the take-up of the Bala Wande OER.

a. In what ways are the Bala Wande OER accessible, useful and supportive of the teaching of mathematics in Grade 1 classes?
b. What can be learned from the use of the Bala Wande OER by young students?
c. Do the Bala Wande OER support independent learning and if so to what extent?

The case study methodology is discussed next.

11.4 Methodology

The research site for this study (De Vos et al., 2011) was the 29 Bala Wande intervention schools located in three districts (Nelson Mandela Bay, Buffalo City Municipality and Sarah Baartman Municipality) of the Eastern Cape Province of South Africa. The Eastern Cape Province is the lowest ranking province in terms of GDP (Stats SA, 2019).[1] In addition to this, educational outcomes in the province are very low (Department of Basic Education, 2014), and thus, the Bala Wande intervention has been located there to test innovative ways of enabling changes in the system. The randomised control trial that determines the overall project design has been set up to

---

[1] The other intervention site is in the Limpopo Province of South Africa, another low-ranking province in the country.

determine the extent to which the intervention is able to transform the system. This case study was designed to investigate the extent to which the OER materials were taken up and enabled independent learning in the early stages of the intervention.

11.4.1 Research Design

The research design was a mixed-methods study incorporating qualitative and quantitative data collection and analysis. Qualitative and quantitative data were collected in order to achieve the research objectives of the case study (De Vos et al., 2011). The combined qualitative–quantitative (triangulated/mixed-methods) approach was beneficial to this study for purposes of complementing explanations, predictions, descriptions and association between variables in order to construct a credible basis for the generalisability of the study's findings (Leady & Ormrod, 2013; Creswell, 1994).

Qualitative research is characterised by data that is not numerical in nature, and the findings are arrived at without the use of statistical procedures (Creswell, 1994). From a qualitative perspective, this study incorporated descriptive and interpretive perceptions that emerged in discussions based on the elements of OER that the users (teachers and coaches) of the resources found meaningful and useful. One of the strengths of a descriptive–interpretive research design is the connection between the goal (end) and the path (means) taken to achieve the stated goal (Mouton, 2013) as well as the capacity to enhance the generalisability of the study's findings (Leady & Ormrod, 2013). The interpretive aspect was necessitated because the authors needed to interpret the views of the users of the OER in relation to user-friendliness for both teachers and coaches.

On the other hand, the quantitative (statistical and numerical) approach entailed a more objective analysis of coding of the use of the material by the students. The objective and controlled quantitative data collection process is not prone to manipulation by the researcher for purposes of 'aligning' to some research interests or agendas (Creswell, 1994). While the qualitative data collection strategies were fundamentally discussion-oriented, the quantitative data collection variants were mainly non-descriptive, quantifiable and measurable (De Vos et al., 2011). The collection of the study data is discussed next.

11.4.2 Data Collection

The qualitative data was collected in the three educational districts where the project is based. The project office invited teachers to participate in the interview, and 14 teachers from across the three districts agreed to be interviewed. All nine of the project coaches participated. The coaches are the facilitators of the Bala Wande OER, and the teachers are the users of these resources. We informed participants that no information from the study would be shared in such a way that it may adversely or otherwise affect them. They were also informed that they could withdraw from the study at any time and with no consequences.

The data collected for quantitative analysis was a set of student books identified by teachers as 'good student' books from 25 out of the 29 project schools. Four schools were inaccessible due to COVID-19 restrictions[2], and in all schools, selection of books was slightly limited because students had been allowed to take home the books at the commencement of the lockdown but had never returned them to school. Purposive sampling (selection of 'good student' books) was carried out based on the judgement of the research team that this would produce the best possible data relevant to the research questions (Black 2010). Altogether 72 learner books were collected from the 25 schools and 13 pages that focused on mainly the concepts of ordering numbers, more than, less than and number bonds were scanned for the coding analysis. The data sample and analysis are now discussed. Participation in the research was voluntary.

11.4.3 Data Sample and Analysis

The qualitative data sample was in the form of five focus group interviews which provided perceptions and social realities, from which meaningful and intelligible conclusions could be drawn (Wiersma, 2000). The focus group interviews were guided by an open-ended interview schedule in order to allow the voice of the partic- ipant to be heard more clearly (Assad, 2015). Participants were allowed to express themselves freely in their language of choice. While the interview questions were posed predominantly in English, most of the participants responded in isiXhosa (the local language widely used in the Eastern Cape), using very little English. Allowing the use of the local language enhanced participants' voice (Vyncke, 2012). The researchers probed further when responses were unclear or to seek further detail in given explanations. All focus group interviews were recorded and transcribed to facilitate analysis which was carried out through conducting a thematic content anal- ysis (Creswell, 1994). All the data collected in this study has been kept as evidence and as a true record of the research process.

The quantitative data was derived from coding independent written exercises from scans of selected pages from the Bala Wande Learner Activity Book (LAB). Codes were recorded in Excel sheets for analysis. Reliability of the coding (Kumar, 2012) was ensured through consensus discussions prior to the coding and validity checks that were conducted across at least 60% of the codes by one of the senior research team members (close to 90% agreement was achieved). Analysis of the data was carried out using comparisons of summative counts of the codes which could point to the accessibility/user-friendliness of the student OER or potential pitfalls in its

[2] South Africa went into hard lockdown on 26 March 2020, this was lessened over time, but the country is still officially in a 'state of emergency' due to COVID-19.

presentation. In this way, the quantitative data supported the triangulation of the findings emerging from the qualitative data. The research findings are presented next.

11.5 Findings

Interviews with the coaches and teachers gave insight into the ways in which the Bala Wande OER support mathematics teaching in Grade 1. Firstly, we discuss the ways in which the OER were used by teachers and coaches and experienced as accessible, useful and supportive. This also speaks to ways in which the materials facilitated independent use by teachers and coaches. Secondly, the analysis of activities from the scanned pages of the Learner Activity Book revealed that the OER could be taken up for independent use by young students. The extent of this independent use (according to data from this case study) was limited, but this limitation cannot be generalised to the full OER set of materials since the context of the study (schools under COVID-19 restrictions) did not allow for adequate representation of the general usefulness of the OER.

11.5.1 Take-Up and Perceptions of Usefulness of the Bala Wande Materials

As mentioned above, nine Bala Wande coaches and 14 Grade 1 teachers participated in the interviews that focused on the materials. Both coaches and teachers commended the high quality of the Bala Wande OER, and across the board, there was agreement that the materials (Teacher Guide, videos, manipulative box and Learner Activity Book) were accessible and useful. There was also evidence of the ways in which the strength of the Bala Wande material, resulting from careful, collaborative development and drawing on the theory of mathematics education and learning design supported more effective use on the part of teachers and coaches.

11.5.1.1 The Teacher Materials and Manipulatives

The different components of the Bala Wande materials combine to give general support to teachers (and coaches in support of teachers), and findings show that these different facets of support were all appreciated. Teachers and coaches made comments in relation to the Teacher Guide, the videos, the manipulatives box and the Learner Activity Book. Generally, teachers showed great appreciation for the materials, and many said that they had shared or would like to share the materials with colleagues from other schools—one said *I have already recommended the use of Bala Wande resources that are online to friends. Bala Wande material explains what you must do to teach giving each and every step you must do to teach. I would recommend Bala Wande to all teachers* (Teacher 3). We first discuss the findings in relation to the Teacher Guide.

The Teacher Guide contains project background information, general curriculum and assessment planning, weekly overviews of the sequenced lesson activity series and daily support for the core daily lesson activities. The aim of the programme is to support teachers to teach in a way that develops students' mathematical understanding and number sense which will ultimately enable them to calculate with confidence. Each week is introduced with two pages of guidance for the week's lessons. The first page gives an overview that provides a summary of the mental maths, games and lesson content for the five days of the week. The overview indicates the resources teachers need to prepare for each day's activities. The resources are listed and shown using thumbnails to motivate teachers to find and prepare them for the lessons. Objectives that should be achieved as a result of the planned teaching for the week are listed with a space for teachers to give an indication of which objectives were achieved in the week. Finally, assessment for the week is noted on this page. Rubrics/checklists are provided in the weeks where oral and practical assessment is recommended and a prompt relating to the written assessment for the week is given (the written assessment tasks are included in the Learner Activity Book). Daily planning includes guidance for the mental maths lesson starters, whole class activities, games and learner independent work. The first four days of each week follow the same routine of teaching, while day five provides an opportunity for consolidation and assessment of the work covered in the week. Aligned with good practice for teaching and learning (Askew, 2012, 2016), teachers are encouraged each day to engage interactively with their students as a whole class (or in groups) to a point where they feel students are ready to work independently, at which point they continue to engage interactively with the students by circulating amongst them.

All of the teachers involved in the study expressed confidence that they could use the Teacher Guide without outside assistance from the coach or anyone else although one said *Well I needed a coach at the beginning but now I can work independently* (Teacher 9). The coaches affirmed that the Teacher Guide could be used by teachers, once they gained confidence, *The Teacher Guide is detailed in such a way that it can support teachers* (Coach 2). The teachers' confidence came from their experience of using the Teacher Guide and the support it offers. A novice teacher said, *The TG helps a lot; this is my first year. At University we did a lot of theory but less practice. Pictures and weekly previews help the teacher to prepare for teaching. Each day is clearly broken down.* (Teacher 3). Other teachers also commented on the value of the daily support, *The TG guides me on what to do daily.* (Teacher 5) and that this support enables them to be independent, *I can use the TG without a coach because the TG is clear. We can work using the TG without a coach.* (Teacher 6). Teachers also commented on the value of the examples provided in the material, *It is with class work, examples and clear instructions and assessment* (Teacher 1). The Teacher Guide is highly visual, with the lesson activities presented using sequences of photo stills. One coach mentioned the stills saying *They can also* look *at the pictures as they would tell them what to do* (Coach 4).

Teachers felt supported by the Teacher Guide because it helps them with their daily work, but in addition to this, teachers experienced additional support from the videos. The Bala Wande videos capture live classroom footage of master teachers mediating the planned lesson activities in project schools. Some videos include instances where students ask questions and grapple with concepts and show how teachers help these students overcome their difficulties. Teachers seemed especially pleased to have the video support in cases where they experienced confusion as to how to interpret the Teacher Guide. The essence of what they said is summed up in the following comment: *Videos help us a lot as we go to them in instances where there is doubt. After watching the videos, you have a picture of how the lesson must go. First lesson became clearer when I looked at the video than TG. We normally use them (videos) after failing to understand the TG* (Teacher 1). Five of the teachers specifically mentioned the videos as useful when there was some confusion about what to do, and in addition to this, one teacher commented that the *Videos help you to reflect on how you teach* (Teacher 6). This view was emphasised by a coach who said *Videos help me a lot when I do afternoon lessons … because teachers observe the model from the video … videos make the concept you teaching to be visible…* (Coach 4). The coach did however add a proviso that teachers needed to make time to watch the videos: *The Bala Wande videos also help teachers if they can give themselves time to watch them* (Coach 4). Finally, another teacher mentioned specific content where the videos gave useful support saying that *Videos help us simplify how we play games. They also help us with Mental Maths* (Teacher 9).

The Teacher Guide is presented in a bilingual format running one of the official languages together with English.[3] In the Foundation Phase in South Africa, students should be taught in their home language according to curriculum policy, but this presents certain challenges in the classroom. Teachers and coaches spoke about the value of the bilingual support in the materials. One teacher said *I like that it is bilingual, if I don't understand in one language, I try the other to make meaning. (Teacher 6)*, and a coach comment that aligns with this comment was *Maths is in two languages is necessary, when some of the things are not clear in isiXhosa. For me [bilingualism] is an advantage because these days students are familiar with both languages, they use both languages at home* (Coach 2).

The manipulatives provided for use in the classwork activities were seen as highly useful, and teachers appreciated that the Teacher Guide gave support in the use of the manipulatives. Teacher 2 said *When I use a resource, students can refer to their own resource each and touch them. I like these resources because they open students' minds. We do not just use these in isolation, the Teacher Guide guides us on how to use the resources.* This was echoed by several other teachers. Teacher 8 was particularly enthusiastic, saying *I get everything I need for teaching from the box.* The manipulatives are provided for both teachers and students, and another thing

---

[3] The Bala Wande OER have been produced in three of the 11 official South African languages to date. The aim is to develop the material in all of the official languages over time.

that teachers found very useful was the Learner Activity Book, which is discussed next.

11.5.1.2 The Learner Activity Book[4]

In the interviews, coaches and teachers also gave their views on the usefulness, supportiveness and accessibility of the student workbook—a full colour workbook, aligned to the planned lesson activities, of which every project student receives a copy of every term. The quality of the workbook was highly commended by the teachers and coaches. The richly visual presentation of the workbook including many pictures (diagrams) was seen as highly useful as were the worked examples which were seen as supportive and enabling of independent work. Perceptions were mixed as to whether or not students could use the workbook independently—this based on students' inability to read because of their age (Grade 1s). Teacher examples selected to illuminate the examples in the workbook were posited as useful enablers, especially for those who could not read. These findings are now discussed in more detail.

Firstly, the issue of young students not yet being able to read the activity instructions was seen as problematic, mentioned explicitly by one coach who commented that *My observation [was that] they could not work on the [workbook] on their own...* (Coach 1). This coach was concerned about how students could respond to questions in the workbook when they could not read the text. While this a valid consideration, the other coaches and most of the teachers did not think that inability to read text was an insurmountable problem, especially considering all the visual support given in the workbook. As one teacher said, *Learners[5] cannot read, they need you to explain but the [workbook] has pictures that help learners understand what they need to do* (Teacher 1). This teacher is referring to one of the three key supportive elements in the workbook that emerged in the findings. These three elements are pictures (diagrams), worked examples and teacher examples. These findings are in line with the literature. Park and Brannon (2013) speak about the use of pictures in learning mathematics, Ng and Dindyal, (2015) highlight the use of examples, and Askew (2016) emphasises the need for teachers to provide meaningful examples for their classes and to engage actively with students as they work through these examples. Manipulatives were also found to be supportive of independent work, and although these are not directly a component of the OER, it is mentioned since this also aligns with the literature (Chikiwa et al., 2019). For example, one teacher said that *For addition questions, if there is a picture it is easy for students to add but if there is no picture, we give them manipulatives and they work successfully* (Teacher 1). The findings in relation to the supportiveness of pictures (diagrams) are discussed first.

---

[4] The student workbook of which each student received a copy is called the Learner Activity Book. In this discussion, we will refer to it as the student workbook.

[5] In South Africa, students are generally referred to by their teachers as 'learners'.

Coach 4 was of the view that the pictures (diagrams) in the workbook are good enough to enable students to work independently. She said *there are some good activities that some students can do on their own… because there are pictures that they see.* Coach 4's view was supported by six teachers who were of the view that pictures in the workbook played a role in enabling independent learning. Teachers said things such as *Some learners are aided by the pictures, yet others are able to add even questions without a diagram* (Teacher 7), *Bala Wande has made our work easy by including pictures* (Teacher 2), *Even the pictures in the book are much help* (Teacher 6). Teacher 1 emphasised the need for the teacher to support the students to read the activities, but once that was done, the pictures were there for further support: *The teacher needs to read questions for the learner but even though text must be read for the learner the book itself helps learner understand what has been read to them through pictures or diagrams that emphasise what has been read.* Teacher 6 said that *Pictures say a lot in teaching, once you give an example, students can learn very fast* which emphasised that while pictures are very important in supporting learning, they can have even better effect if used together with examples. The use of examples to aid independent learning in the Bala Wande workbook is discussed next.

Five out of nine teachers expressed their appreciation of the examples that Bala Wande workbook provides as they help students work independently. In the Bala Wande workbook, every exercise starts with a worked example of how students can respond to the question. Examples in the workbook are very important because they afford students problem-solving techniques and approaches which are tools that equip them to respond to questions (Bills et al., 2006). Examples are a very important component in creating an environment where students are able to work with less guidance from the teacher Watson and Mason (2002). Teachers appreciate the examples in the textbook, and they believed that they are partly responsible for students working independently. Understanding of concepts is the cornerstone for teaching mathematics, and exemplification is one of those ways of achieving this goal (Watson & Mason, 2002). Teacher 3 was of the view that sometimes students can learn without a teacher by merely viewing the examples and pictures in the workbook: *In some parts learners can learn without much support from the teacher for example, in subtraction and some learners look at the picture and an example and they get the concept. I know that because when I go around checking students' work you find that some students would have gone further ahead.* Teacher 4 said that *The workbook teaching examples are good—we only do two examples and they do the rest of the work without further help. The last group [of learners] need[s] me to go through [the activities] with them slowly.* Here, we see that the examples in the workbook are not all that is needed—active explanations from the teacher prior to learners doing activities in their workbooks are also an enabler of independent work. This is the final finding that is now discussed.

All of the teachers who were interviewed were of the view that examples that teachers give prior to students doing classwork are important in fostering independent learning. Teacher 2 spoke about giving examples in a way that got the activity going *When you say give students one more or two more questions, they just need a few examples and thereafter are able to work with little help.* In a different approach,

Teacher 1 spoke about giving examples when students struggled with the work saying *In instances where students struggle, I give an example.* At Grade 1 level, the idea is not to have students work entirely independently but to have them work with little assistance from the teacher, and the teaching of mathematics is more often than not accompanied by examples. Teacher 8 expressed this view saying *If we do an activity together as a class, students are able to proceed without much help,* Teacher 5 concurred with this saying *I agree students cannot do classwork without an example. Once an example is done learner can proceed with the work. Clever students are always ahead of the teacher probable because their parents help them.* Teacher 5's view is that there is need for modelling how activities should be done, without which it is not possible for students to do classwork. Coach 2 made the point that a*bout 20% of the students can work own their own depending—some students are generally gifted … and sometimes there is parental involvement, it depends on the child's background and how parents help the learner. The rest depends on the teacher and how he interacts with students…so that students can work without the teacher's assistance.* Firstly, we see here that gifted students have been observed to be having the ability of working independently but key to students working independently largely depends on teacher interaction with students. This interaction is not so that the learner continually depends on the teacher but rather has an end result of independent learning. The teacher helps the learner understand and interpret pictures and examples in the workbook.

As mentioned above, Teacher 3 advocated for the use of the Bala Wande materials without being prompted to do so. Eight other teachers indicated that they had also done so because of the value that teachers had found in the materials and also that these materials can be used independently without support. Teachers have thus shown confidence in the way that the students they are teaching are beginning to use the Bala Wande materials constructively. The Bala Wande project, supported by the OER that have been developed for use in the intervention, aims to enable students to develop number sense (Burns, 2005). In the next section, the analysis of selected learner independent work gives insight into the way in which this goal is being achieved.

11.5.2   Student Independent Work in the Bala Wande Workbook

As was shown in the previous section, teachers found the Bala Wande materials useful, and many agreed that the workbook enabled students to work independently (at least to an extent). The usefulness of the materials to students was thus evident; however, it was seen to depend largely on the presence of a knowledgeable other (the teacher and to a lesser extent the parent/guardian) because of the age of the students and the time that they have spent in active formal school. The focus of the quantitative part of this case study was to analyse scans of student work from 72 Grade 1 students' books from 25 schools. For this purpose, 13 pages of student work were scanned from each book. The work covered in these pages included the following topics: numbers to five; one more and two more; one less and two less; bonds of five; more than and less than; comparing numbers. Codes were developed by the team, and consensus on the manner in which the codes should be assigned was achieved through discussion. First a general code was assigned to each question. These codes were as follows:

- Correct—All responses on that page were correct and complete.
- Incorrect—All responses on that page were incorrect.
- Incomplete—Some of the responses were missing on the page.
- Partially correct—Some responses were correct, while others were incorrect.
- Blank—Students did not attempt this page at all.

The counts for general completion of the scanned student work are summarised in Table 11.1.

It can be seen from Table 11.1 that students were able to respond with a certain degree of success to the majority of activity questions in the scanned pages. There are some counts that stand out and which we discuss here. As it can be seen in row two of Table 11.1 (**Correct**), page 34 presented the greatest challenge to students (Fig. 11.1).

Page 34 had an activity which called for students to say how many items could be seen and then to compare counts of items. The challenge that affected students on page 34 came in the second part of the activity question. While students may have responded correctly to the first part of the question where they were required to 'Write how many objects each animal has', they did not respond to the second part where they were asked to 'Circle the animal that has more'. More detailed coding (not shown in this table) revealed that 36 students did not circle the animal with more elements. One of the reasons that may have contributed to students not responding to the second part of the question was that students may have struggled to cope with more than a single instruction. While this may have been the reason for the students' failure to complete page 34 correctly, there were other activities where students had to deal with three instructions and they did so successfully, for example, on page 42 where 27 students managed to respond correctly, the activities contained multiple instructions. Possible reasons for students' poor achievement on page 34 could be that when the teachers were mediating this activity they may have neglected

Table 11.1 Summary general completion of workbook pages ($n = 72$)

Page	34	41	42	44	45	54	55	56	86	87	89	90	91
Correct	0	37	27	22	36	15	46	18	33	29	38	36	26
Incorrect	2	4	0	2	6	1	2	10	1	1	0	0	4
Incomplete	25	1	14	11	2	2	1	6	2	5	4	2	7
Partially correct	18	23	22	26	17	42	12	21	16	24	17	20	19
Blank	6	7	9	11	11	12	11	17	20	13	13	14	16
Correct–Incorrect	− 2	33	27	20	30	14	44	8	32	28	38	36	22

① Bhala ukuba isilwanyana ngasinye sinezinto ezingaphi.

Write how many objects each animal has.

② Biyela isilwanyana esinezinto ezininzi.

Circle the animal that has **more**.

okanye
or

Fig. 11.1 Summary of the general completion of Bala Wande workbook pages ($n = 72$)

to mention or emphasise the second instruction, it may have been the layout of the activity that confused them, or another possibility is that they may have circled using a faint pencil that could not be seen after some time.

The bottom row of Table 11.1 shows that when we consider the difference between pages where students got everything correct and those where all of the answers written on the page were incorrect, there is a positive difference for most pages that we analysed. This shows that generally, students must have been comfortable working in the workbook because they did so with greater success than failure. We shall zoom on pages 54, 55 and 56 because these pages contain a series of three activities which are all about the bonds of five. On these pages, the difference between correct and incorrect is lower for pages 54 and 56. On page 54, the questions were linked to a concrete activity with blocks. On page 55, the activity was linked to a pictorial (diagrammatic) representation of the bonds of five, and lastly, on page 56, the activity involved completing bond diagrams that were more abstract. Evidently, the more abstract activity was more difficult for students than the one linked to the pictorial representation, which makes sense since at this stage students are still moving from a concrete to a more abstract understanding. The activity linked to the pictorial representation was completed by most students successfully which aligns with the finding that teachers and coaches felt that the pictures in the Bala Wande material provide good support to students. The Bala Wande material seeks to enable students to move from concrete activities to abstract understanding. Even though the work was abstract in the final activity, 18 students managed to respond correctly to all the questions. The low success rate on page 54 (concrete activity) could be a result of the learners' difficulty in recording what they had done concretely, even if they did perform the activity successfully. The high success rate on page 55 may indicate that some understanding had been gleaned through learners doing the concrete activity and thus being more prepared to do the pictorially linked activity (even though they were not very successful in recording their findings from the concrete activity). In the following section, we discuss the implications of our findings.

11.6 Discussion and Conclusion

Teachers in the study appreciated the Teacher Guide that Bala Wande provided to them with. What they liked was the structure of the book, the suggested sequenced planning and the support this gave them in their preparation for teaching. The Teacher Guide is a complete guide for the teaching of mathematics in Grade 1, and novice teachers found the guide particularly useful because it provides teaching ideas, examples for teaching, suggests and explains how manipulatives are to be used, classwork for students and even assessment. Teachers also appreciated the video support because it models the way in which all aspects of a mathematics lessons could be conducted—the mental mathematics, whole class activities, games and independent student work. It also gives support with regard to the examples used in the classroom. Findings showed that teachers felt conformable using the Teacher Guide independently, which means that it is well suited as an OER for more general use.

Pictures in mathematics books are part of the mathematical reform (van den Heuvel-Panhuizen, et al., 2009). Children and adults alike are generally attracted to pictures, and pictures have the power to engage an audience straight away. Both the teacher and student Bala Wande books are filled with pictures. The visual presentation of lesson activity planning in the Teacher Guide (photo stills sequences) was found useful by teachers and coaches. The speech bubbles are a powerful tool in the Bala Wande OER because they give teachers suggestions of the language that she could use. The learner book is full of attractive diagrams and illustrations. Students specifically would seek to make sense of what is in the pictures and attempt to respond to the activities in the book. Teachers in the study observed that students are able to do activities that they have not yet mediated—hence independent work was also supported by the OER.

Examples are one of the most powerful ways of conveying mathematical concepts (Bills et al., 2006). Examples develop students' experiences and improve their development of number sense. Both teachers and coaches attributed students' successful independent work to the presence of examples in the workbook. Examples communicate mathematical thought between teachers and students, but in the case that a worked example communicates this thought, the knowledgeable other in the workbook. This cannot hold for all activities for students at such a young age, but this case study suggests that learning design can support independent learning, at least to an extent. The fact that students could mediate mathematical concepts using examples in the book shows how powerful examples are in the learning of mathematics. Examples in the Bala Wande Books enhance mathematical thinking of students and enable them to work independently.

The results from the analysis of learner activities indicate that students were comfortable using the workbook. The pages that were analysed contained core Grade 1 concepts, and there were activities where concrete objects were used, representations were given and abstract work was posed. The scans of learner work produced rich evidence of student work. Learner interviews would be useful to follow up on these findings which are speculative based on the quantitative counts, and even more pages of the workbook need to be analysed in order to inform the OER development going forward.

Although this study of take-up was carried out during a period where access to schools was not easy due to COVID-19, the findings show that the Bala Wande OER did facilitate independent use (forced upon teachers and students to a greater extent during the lockdown than would normally have been the case). This bodes well for further use of the materials over time as they are revised and refined in response to feedback and evaluative findings from the project over the coming years during which the project will be active.

The problem of poor mathematics education at the Foundation Phase level (Grades R-3) is not restricted to South Africa (World Bank, 2019). Materials development is an iterative process—the Bala Wande OER are being and will continue to be refined over the following three years so that when the project term ends, materials of the highest possible quality will be available as an OER that could be taken up by any users who choose to do so. The project will run for a further three years, and over this time further data collection and materials review processes with be carried out so that more can be learned from the field and the materials can be refined and enhanced. The findings of this interim case study indicate that the Bala Wande materials, developed as OER, have the potential to support teachers and students as they aim to improve mathematics learning outcomes.

References

Anthony, G., & Walshaw, M. (2009). Characteristics of effective teaching of mathematics: A view from the west. *Journal of Mathematics Education, 2*(2), 147–164.

Askew, M. (2012). *Transforming primary mathematics*. Routledge.

Askew, M. (2016). *A practical guide to transforming primary mathematics—Activities and tasks that really work*. Routledge.

Assad, D. A. (2015). Task-based interviews in Mathematics: Understanding student strategies and representations through problem solving. *International Journal of Education and Social Science, 2*(1), 17–26. Available from: http://www.ijessnet.com/wpcontent/uploads/2015/01/2.pdf.

Bertram, C., Christiansen, I., & Makurdi, T. G. (2015). Exploring the complexities of describing foundation phase teachers' professional knowledge base. *South African Journal of Childhood Education, 5*, 169–190. https://doi.org/10.4102/sajce.v5i1.355

Bills, L., Dreyfus, T., Mason, J., Tsamir, P., Watson, A. & Zaslavsky, O. (2006). Exemplification in mathematics education. Prague, Czech Republic: PME. In J. Novotna (Ed.), *Proceedings of the 30th conference of the international group for the psychology of mathematics education*. PME.

Bragg, L. A. (2012). Testing the effectiveness of mathematical games as a pedagogical tool for children's learning. *International Journal of Science and Mathematics Education, 10*(6), 1445–1467.

Burns, A. (2005). Action research. In E. Hinkel (Ed.), *Handbook of research in second language teaching and learning* (pp. 241–256). Lawrence Erlbaum.

Chikiwa, S., Westaway, L., & Graven, M. (2019). What mathematics knowledge for teaching is used by a Grade 2 teacher when teaching counting. *South African Journal of Childhood Education, 9*(1), a567. https://doi.org/10.4102/sajce.v9i1.567

Creswell, J. W. (1994). *Research design: Qualitative and quantitative approaches*. Sage Publications Inc.

Department of Basic Education (South Africa). (2014). *Report on the annual national assessment of 2014 grades 1 to 6 and 9*. Department of Basic Education.

De Vos, A. S., Strydom, H., Fouche', C. B. & Delport, C. S. L. (2011). *Research at grass roots: For the social sciences and human service professions* (4th edn.). Van Schaik.

García, O. & Wei, L. (2014). *Translanguaging: Language, bilingualism and education*. Palgrave Macmillan.

Haven, K. (2014). *Story smart: Using the science of story to inspire, persuade, influence, and teach*. Libraries Unlimited

Hoadley, U. (2012). What do we know about teaching and learning in South African primary schools? *Education as Change, 16*, 187–202.

Kumar, R. (2012). *Research methodology: A step-by-step guide for beginners* (3rd ed.). MPG Books Group.

Lavie, I., Steiner, A. & Sfard, A. (2019). Routines we live by: From ritual to exploration. *Educational Studies in Mathematics, 101*(2), 153–176. https://doi.org/10.1007/s10649-018-9817-4.

Leady, P. D., & Ormrod, J. E. (2013). *Practical research planning and design* (10th ed.). Pearson Publishers.

Leinhardt, G. (2001). Instructional explanations: A commonplace for teaching and location for contrast. In V. Richardson (Ed.), *Handbook of research on teaching* (4th edn.) (pp. 333–357). American Educational Research Association.

Mouton, J. (2013). *How to succeed in your master's and doctoral studies. (18th impression).* Van Schaik.

Munn, P. (1998). Symbolic function in pre-schoolers. In C. Donlan (Ed.), *The development of mathematical skills* (pp. 48–71). Hove.

Ng, L. K. & Dindyal, J. (2015). Examples in the teaching of mathematics: Teachers' perceptions. In M. Marshman, V. Geiger, and A. Bennison (Eds.). *Mathematics education in the margins (proceedings of the 38th annual conference of the mathematics education research group of Australasia)* (pp. 461–468). MERGA.

Pai, A. (2014). A picture worth a thousand words? Making a case for video case studies. *Journal of College Science Teaching, 43*(4), 1–6. https://doi.org/10.2505/4/jcst14_043_04_63

Park, J. & Brannon, E. (2013). Training the approximate number system improves math proficiency. *Association for Psychological Science, 24*(10). https://www.ncbi.nlm.nih.gov/pmc/articles/PMC3797151/.

Peled, I., & Zaslavsky, O. (1997). Counter-examples that (only) prove and counterexample that (also) explain. *FOCUS on Learning Problems in Mathematics, 19*(3), 49–61.

Priestley, M, Biesta, G. J. J., & Robinson, S. (2015). Teacher agency: What is it and why does it matter? In R. Kneyber and J. Evers (Eds.), *Flip the system: Changing education from the bottom up.* Routledge.

Sapire, I. & Reed, Y. (2011). Collaborative design and use of open educational resources: A case study of a mathematics teacher education project in South Africa. *Distance Education, 32*(2), 195–211.·https://doi.org/10.1080/01587919.2011.584847.

Sebesta, L. M., & Martin, S. R. M. (2004). Fractions: Building a foundation with concrete manipulatives. *Illinois Schools Journal, 83*(2), 3–23.

Sood, S., & Jitendra, A. K. (2007). A comparative analysis of number sense instruction in reform-based and traditional mathematics textbooks. *Journal of Special Education, 41*(3), 145–157.

Sowell, E. (1989). Effects of manipulative materials in mathematics instruction. *Journal for Research in Mathematics Education, 20*, 498–505.

Stats SA (Statistics South Africa). (2019). Four facts about our provincial economies. http://www.statssa.gov.za/?p=12056.

Stein, M. K., & Bovalino, J. W. (2001). Manipulatives: One piece of the puzzle. *Mathematics Teaching in Middle School, 6*(6), 356–360.

van den Heuvel-Panhuizen, M., van den Boogaard, S., & Doig, B. (2009). Picture books stimulate the learning of mathematics. *Australian Journal of Early Childhood, 34*(3), 30–39.

Venkat, H., & Spaull, N. (2015). What do we know about primary teachers' mathematical content knowledge in South Africa? An analysis of SACMEQ 2007. *International Journal of Educational Development, 41*, 121–130.

Vyncke, M. (2012). The concept and practice of critical thinking in academic writing: An investigation of international students' perceptions and writing experiences (Published MA Dissertation. King's College, London).

Watson, A & Mason, J. (2002). Extending example spaces as a learning/teaching strategy in mathematics. In A. Cockburn and E. Nardi (Eds.), *Proceedings of the 26th conference of the international group for the psychology of mathematics education, 4* (pp. 377–385). PME.

Wiersma, W. (2000). *Research methods in education: An introduction* (7th ed.). Allyn and Bacon.

World Bank (2019). *Ending learning poverty: What will it take?* World Bank. http://hdl.handle.net/10986/32553.

Yeh, C. Y. C., Cheng, H. N. H., Chen, Z., Liao, C. C. Y., Chan, T. (2019). Enhancing achievement and interest in mathematics learning through Math-Island. *RPTEL, 14*(5). https://doi.org/10.1186/s41039-019-0100-9.

Zhou, X., & Wang, B. (2004). Preschool children's representation and understanding of written number symbols. *Early Child Development and Care, 174*, 253–266.

Sihlobosenkosi Mpofu has been involved in mathematics education since 1995. He was a mathematics teacher for 16 years. He has worked in several teacher development programmes since 2012. Sihlobosenkosi was involved in mathematics script writing for mindset learning channel during the transition from NCS to CAPS. He has a Ph.D. in Mathematics Education from the University of Kwazulu Natal and University of Witwatersrand. He is a senior mathematics specialist on the Bala Wande Foundation Phase Mathematics Programme team.

Permie Isaac is Foundation Phase trained and has 8 years of teaching experience in Grade 2 and 3. She has been a part-time lecturer at Rhodes University for the past 4 years, lecturing IsiXhosa method for BEd FP and PGCE FP as well as Education Environment. She is also part of a team that lectures Foundation Phase Literacy Teaching short courses at Rhodes University. Permie has participated in the development of the Bala Wande videos and print materials, and she is the lead of the Eastern Cape intervention of Bala Wande Foundation Phase Mathematics Programme.

Tobeka Ndamase has been teaching mathematics since 1990. She has taught mathematics in Foundation Phase, Intermediate Phase and Senior Phase. At present, she is tutoring SANTS Grade R Diploma students. Tobeka has been on the Bala Wande Foundation Phase Mathematics Programme team since 2019 first as a literacy and then as a mathematics specialist coach. She has also supported the versioning (English/IsiXhosa) of the Bala Wande Mathematics material. She is currently enrolled for a Masters in Developmental Studies.

Luleka Sonjica has been a Foundation Phase educator for 21 years. She has a JPTD (1992—Algoa College of Education), a B.Ed. degree (Foundation Phase) (2008—NMU) and B.Ed. Honours (2010—NMU). She presently lecturers for the Varsity College B.Ed. Foundation Phase and tutors for the SANTS B.Ed. Foundation Phase. She is a mathematics specialist coach on the Bala Wande Foundation Phase Mathematics Programme team and has participated in the materials development. She is currently enrolled for a Masters in Developmental Studies.

Ingrid Sapire has been involved in mathematics teacher education for 27 years and is based at the University of the Witwatersrand. Since 2012, her focus has been on the development of materials at scale for Foundation Phase mathematics teachers and students both at a provincial and national level. She is currently heading the multilingual Bala Wande (Calculating with Confidence) Foundation Phase Mathematics Programme and working on her Ph.D., in multilingualism in Mathematics in the Foundation Phase.

Chapter 12
The Adoption of Open Educational Practices to Support Practical Work at Moroccan Universities

Khadija El Kharki, Khalid Berrada, Faouzi Bensamka, and Daniel Burgos

Abstract One of the grand challenges of education is to provide free and open access to high-quality educational content, which is addressed by the open educational resources (OER) movement since their first emergence at UNESCO's 2002 forum. The use of OER is increasingly being recognized as one of the most significant educational movements in the twenty-first century. Indeed, the value and pivotal importance of OER for education have become evident. Nowadays, OER are commonly used, adapted, remixed, and shared. The concept of open educational practices (OEP) refers to practices that include the use of OER in education. Laboratory experiences are a critical part of science education. Given the cancelation of physics practical work from the first-year program of scientific bachelor's degrees in Moroccan universities, universities and instructors have increasingly been expected to offer alternatives to traditional face-to-face laboratories. However, virtual laboratories are an institutional OER initiative and appear to have great potential to provide laboratory experiences in a virtual educational environment, as an alternative to the face-to-face laboratory. In this work, we present the EXPERES project as an OEP aimed to build an OER repository, containing virtual experiments mapped to the physics curriculum for the first year of the bachelor's degree. This chapter presents our experience in adopting OEP, for developing virtual laboratory, then sharing it as OER. The main results of this OER initiative are: (1) the publication of the conceptualization and scripting manual, which is available online under an open access license; (2) the development

K. El Kharki · F. Bensamka
Trans ERIE, Faculty of Sciences Semlalia, Cadi Ayyad University, BP.: 2390, Marrakech, Morocco
e-mail: bensamka@uca.ac.ma

K. Berrada (✉)
Faculty of Sciences, Mohammed V University, Rabat, Morocco
e-mail: k.berrada@um5r.ac.ma

D. Burgos
Research Institute for Innovation & Technology in Education (UNIR iTED), Universidad Internacional de La Rioja (UNIR), Avenida de la Paz, 137, 26006 Logroño, La Rioja, Spain
e-mail: daniel.burgos@unir.net

Research Unit Self-Directed Learning, Faculty of Education, North-West University (NWU), Potchefstroom 2531, South Africa

of a virtual laboratory and its implementation using a Moodle platform to offer open and massive access to the virtual practical activities.

Keywords Open education · OER · OEP · OER mainstreaming · OEP adoption · Virtual laboratories · Simulations · EXPERES project · Educational platform · Higher education · Cadi Ayyad University · Moroccan Universities

12.1 Introduction

Article 26 of the Universal Declaration of Human Rights declares that everyone has the right to education, that education shall be free, and technical and professional education shall be made generally available and higher education shall be equally accessible to all based on merit (United Nations, 1948). As well, the role of education cannot be underestimated, so that, education is indispensable for every human being, it is a boon to human life. Indeed, education is a process by which an institution provides systematic instruction and enables a person to better contribute to human civilization (Bhardwaj, 2016).

More specifically, higher education systems play major roles in social development. However, they face immense challenges in meeting rising enrollment demands worldwide. Forecasts suggest that the total number of learners in higher education is expected to reach nearly 380 million by 2030, 472 million by 2035, and more than 594 million by 2040, all up from roughly 216 million in 2016 and 250 million in 2020 (Calderon, 2018; ICEF Monitor, 2018). However, this growth is unlikely to be accompanied by equivalent increases in the human and financial resources available to the higher education sector.

Meanwhile, education is a key issue of the 2030 Agenda for Sustainable Development, being both directly connected to the 17 goals of the agenda and at the core of Sustainable Development Goal 4 (SDG4), which aims to ensure inclusive and equitable quality education and promote lifelong learning opportunities for all (United Nations, 2015).

While open education is a concept of opening access to education to all, it is based on the belief that education and knowledge are public goods and that everyone has the right to access quality education (Belawati, 2014). The rapid evolution of open education has been influenced and accelerated by the advancement of information and communications technologies (ICTs) and their integration into the educational system. Also, open education is defined broadly as encompassing resources, tools, and practices (Tlili et al., 2019) such as open educational resources (OER) and open educational practices (OEP) to improve educational access, effectiveness, and equality worldwide (Lane, 2009).

Furthermore, the concept of OER is becoming increasingly prominent in education. Shear et al. (2015) stated that OER are one of the most significant teaching forms of the twenty-first century. Otto (2019) affirmed that OER can by no means be ignored in the context of teaching and learning in a digital world. In addition, the creation and dissemination of OER should, therefore, be a key focus for educational institutions, because they have great potential for reducing the cost of expanding quality education (Marcus-Quinn & Diggins, 2013). Lately, the impact of OER on educational systems has become a pervasive element of educational policy. Because OER can contribute to solving the education challenges related to learning for the twenty-first century, for instance: fostering teachers' professional development, containing educational costs, continually improving the quality of educational resources, widening the distribution of high-quality educational materials, and breaking down the barriers to high-quality learning opportunities (Orr et al., 2015). Besides, many studies show that learners achieve the same or better learning outcomes when using OER (Hilton, 2019).

On the other hand, for scientific and technical discipline programs, laboratory experiences play an important and essential role. Furthermore, science cannot be meaningfully taught to learners without hands-on experiences in laboratories (Hofstein & Lunetta, 2004).

In Moroccan universities, laboratory practical activities of physics were unfortunately eliminated from the first year program since 2012, due to the problems of the massification of learners in faculties of sciences that provide open access. Indeed, the continuous growing evolution of new learners enrolled in scientific and technical training required thinking about alternative means to provide training in the laboratory. The adoption of OEP and OER provides virtual laboratories, as an inexpensive alternative to physical and real laboratories, and may bring several material benefits to institutions. Virtual laboratories are a technological innovation that provides new learning environments for learners, based on simulations, to allow learners to study, learn, and investigate on their own.

The purpose of this article is to present the Moroccan OEP initiative that aimed to promote an OER repository, by creating, developing, and implementing a virtual laboratory holding virtual experiments mapped to the physics subjects taught in the first year of the bachelor's degree. In addition to sharing it as an OER, for the benefit of all scientific learners. The chapter is organized as follows. The second presents a general background of OER and OEP in higher education, the barriers that face their adoption, and the current state and initiatives of OER in Morocco. The third section describes the Moroccan OEP initiative in developing virtual laboratories. The subsequent section presents the results and discussion. The last section is for the conclusion and perspectives.

12.2 OER and OEP in Higher Education

Open education, including the use of OER and the adoption of OEP, has the potential to challenge educators to change their practice in fundamental ways (Kaatrakoski et al., 2017). In addition, the concepts of OER and OEP are regarded as two pillars of the broader open education movement (Tlili et al., 2019). While in 2012, the World OER Congress, which was attended by governments and educational and

OER experts, emphasized using OER as a means of providing equal access to knowledge. The Congress led to the adoption of the Paris OER Declaration, which calls on governments worldwide to license publicly funded educational materials openly for public use (UNESCO, 2012a, 2012b). OER have achieved global recognition and, at least in principle, mainstream acceptance (Hoosen et al., 2019). In particular, OER and OEP have the potential to lower costs and increase participation in higher education. Results from Murphy's (2013) study indicated that although higher education institutions are aware of and interested in, OER and OEP, several challenges need to be overcome to achieve their potential (Murphy, 2013).

12.2.1   What Are OER and OEP?

The term OER was created in 2002 at a United Nations Educational, Scientific, and Cultural Organization (UNESCO) Forum on the impact of open courseware for higher education in developing countries to describe a new global phenomenon of openly sharing educational resources. Participants at the forum defined OER as "technology-enabled, open provision of educational resources for consultation, use, and adaptation by a community of users for non-commercial purposes". They are typically made freely available over the Internet. Their principal use is by teachers and educational institutions to support course development, but they can also be used directly by learners (UNESCO, 2002). The motivation behind OER is to provide more equal access to knowledge and educational opportunities, and for educational resources to be available to all (Hoosen et al., 2016). Since then, many other definitions of OER have been espoused in literature. Downes (2011) developed a definition of OER that focused on the intended use of OER, rather than on the essential components. OER are materials used to support education that may be freely accessed, reused, modified, and shared by anyone. Guo et al. (2015) believed that OER is the bundle of learning resources that can be used and adjusted by the user without any legal and economic restrictions. Jung and Hong (2016) defined OER as study materials with an intellectual property license that permits repetition in use and distribution. Additionally, OER include full courses, programs, syllabi, curricula, teachers' guides course materials, modules, learner guides, teaching notes, textbooks, e-texts, research articles, videos, audio tracks, assessment tools and instruments, interactive materials such as simulations and role plays, experiments, demonstrations, databases, software, apps (including mobile apps), and any other materials that have been designed for use in teaching and learning used to support access to knowledge that is openly available for use by educators and learners, without an accompanying need to pay royalties or license fees (Atkins et al., 2007; Butcher, 2015; Hylén & Schuller, 2007; UNESCO, 2002; UNESCO & Commonwealth of Learning, 2011). In addition, to be more specific, the word open in OER indicates that these materials are licensed with copyright licenses that provide permission for everyone to participate in the 5R activities: retain, reuse, revise, remix, and redistribute. According to Nipa and Kermanshachi (2019), all of the definitions agree that:

- OER must be free and available through ICT;
- OER must be open, accessible legally with minimum licensing and copyright;
- OER materials must be able to be adapted and customized by the user, based on their needs;
- OER materials must be permitted to be retained, reused, revised, remixed, and redistributed by the user.

Otherwise, OER has emerged as a concept with great potential to support educational transformation. While its educational value lies in the idea of using resources as an integral method of communication of curriculum in educational courses, its transformative power lies in the ease with which such resources, when digitized, can be shared via the Internet. Importantly, there is only one key differentiator between an OER and any other educational resource: its license. Thus, an OER is simply an educational resource that incorporates a license that facilitates reuse, and potentially adaptation, without first requesting permission from the copyright holder (Butcher, 2015). In addition, OER has the potential to make a significant contribution to SDG4. UNESCO recognizes the vital role of innovations such as OER in achieving SDG4, in order to foster inclusive and equitable quality education (Hoosen et al., 2019).

The term OEP refers to the use of OER for teaching in an innovative and collaborative environment (Zhang et al., 2020). OEP are a set of activities around instructional design and implementation of events and processes intended to support learning (Andrade et al., 2011). They are described as collaborative practices that support the creation, the use, the reused, and the management of OER through institutional policies, promote innovative pedagogical models, and respect and empower learners as co-producers on their lifelong learning paths (Andrade et al., 2011; Cronin, 2017; Ehlers, 2011). These practices can help enhance learning quality, access, and effectiveness in universities (Weller, 2014).

12.2.2 Use and Creation of OER in Higher Education

The OER initiative has been underway for almost two decades now, and higher education institutions are adopting OER. In addition, the use of OER has changed the landscape of higher education (Atkins et al., 2007). According to McKerlich et al. (2013), the use and creation of OER are important aspects of adoption and both are needed for the benefits of OER to be fully realized. Indeed, OER offer opportunities for broadening participation in higher education, reducing course development and study costs, and building open collaborative partnerships to improve teaching and learning practices, they have yet to gain significant mainstream traction. Research surrounding open education has focused on adoption at the institutional level, identifying key enablers and barriers to practice, but the practicalities of engagement with open resources are not often addressed (Stagg, 2014). Besides, OER can help to turn the passive learning environment into an interactive one (Yoon, 2017). However, OER materials ensure an interactive environment by encouraging interaction and collaboration between learners (Hoosen et al., 2016). Further, some of the attractive characteristics of OER for enabling the potential transformation of higher education include their equity, quality, and efficiency: OER may provide more equal access to knowledge to many traditionally disadvantaged potential users who, due to geographical, demographical, financial, or cultural reasons, may not otherwise have such opportunity (Bossu et al., 2012; Conole, 2012; Hockings et al., 2012).

12.2.3 Barriers to Adopting OER and OEP in Higher Education

OER and OEP have already had a significant impact on higher education and have great potential for providing further positive transformation. However, OER and OEP adoption have not been universal, with several obstacles and barriers still hindering their wider influence (McKerlich et al., 2013; Wang & Towey, 2017), for example, multimedia skills, knowledge of intellectual property, copyright and licensing practices, and research capacity (Nie, 2012), time, organizational culture, and availability of resources (Murphy, 2012). As the OER movement is global, there are also cultural differences (Nie, 2012). Besides, Cox and Trotter (2017) found that language barrier, low level of technological advancement, and lack of consideration in the institutional policy for OER materials copyright are the major barriers in adopting OER materials for lecturers in South Africa. Also, in developing instructional activities for a course, the instructional designer finds it challenging to incorporate OER in the activities when the faculty who is responsible for providing the material is not an expert in the field of the course (Wright & Reeves, 2019). In addition, Wang and Towey (2017) listed instructors' lack of awareness of potential advantages of OER, teachers' lack of experience in finding and choosing OER materials while developing a course, lack of institutional policies encouraging development and inclusion of OER materials in course syllabus with reward and incentives as major challenges in adoption of OER in higher education. Further, the major issues regarding the sustainability of the OER materials are the lack of proper acknowledgment and academic awareness, absence of incentives, insufficient proof of effectiveness, the dearth of technical tools, and few, if any, policies about openness (de Carvalho et al., 2016).

12.2.4 OER and OEP in Morocco

The concepts of OER and OEP were introduced in Morocco in 2016, following the OER Morocco declaration (OpenMed Morocco, 2016), during the Morocco OER

Strategy Forum hosted by Cadi Ayyad University in Marrakesh. This declaration calls the Moroccan authorities to support enhancing and developing open education in higher education by promoting the integration of OER and OEP to educational systems, also expanding access to lifelong learning at all levels. After that, many institutional initiatives heading toward this orientation have arisen. In particularly to encourage all universities in Morocco, to contribute to producing online resources in various fields, for ensuring and improving the learning quality, a national institutional platform (https://www.mun.ma/) named MUN (Morocco Digital University) was implemented in 2019 by the Ministry of National Education, Professional Training, Higher Education and Scientific Research. A panoramic overview concerning the current state of OER in Morocco was presented in Zaatri et al. (2020). Besides, at Cadi Ayyad University, another initiative of OEP adoption entitled UC@MOOC (Mooc of Cadi Ayyad University), trying especially to face the massiveness in higher education, for open access faculties has been created, since 2013 (Idrissi et al., 2018, 2020; Zaatri et al., 2019).

All of these initiatives are fine examples of academic collaboration in developing educational content for higher education; they focus exclusively on improving the quality and accessibility of the course (theoretical part) by creating and offering Massive Open Online Courses (MOOC) and neglect the important laboratory experiences. However, for scientific education all educational content including laboratory practical work requires support, to enhance the quality of the teaching and learning process. In addition, research evidence on the diffusion and adoption of OER for virtual laboratories in Morocco is not founded. It is in this context that the EXPERES project was set up, whose objective is to support practical laboratory activities for scientific disciplines. It is an OEP initiative aimed to provide open online physics laboratory activities, which is presented in the following section.

12.3 The Adoption of OEP to Support Practical Laboratory Work in Moroccan Universities

12.3.1 Obstacles to Practical Scientific Education Based on the Face-to-Face Laboratory

In scientific and technical discipline programs, laboratory experiences play a major role to understand theoretical lectures. The benefits of physical laboratories are in providing environments for learners to apply theoretical knowledge presented in the theoretical courses and to acquire new practical skills. In addition, they have a strong impact on learners' learning outcomes (Clough, 2002). However, since 2012, Moroccan universities especially open access faculties have been facing one of the biggest challenges during this decade which is the problem of learners' massification. Consequently, it has become impossible to arrange for all learners enrolled in the first year to carry out physics practical activities in laboratories. This situation led to eliminating laboratory practical work of physics from the first-year program of the bachelor's degree in faculties of science. Scientific subjects cannot be understood effectively without practical activities in the laboratory. With the new situation, it is being increasingly expected from university educators and curriculum developers at Moroccan universities to provide alternatives to traditional face-to-face laboratories by incorporating OER into their laboratory teaching, for providing virtual laboratories as an alternative solution to traditional laboratories.

12.3.2   The Adoption of OEP to Offer an Alternative to Traditional Face-to-Face Laboratory

To overcome the situation described above, Moroccan universities have decided to employ information technologies and adopt open educational practices and resources, to reintegrate practical laboratory activities into the first-year program. As we said previously in this chapter, the use of OER and the adoption of OEP in higher education provide important opportunities to offer equal and democratic access to knowledge. In addition, due to the influence of information technologies and the Internet in the field of education, new forms of laboratories that support distance and online education have emerged, such as virtual and remote laboratory, virtual reality, augmented reality.

Based on all these data, the solution proposed was to build an OER repository, containing virtual experiments by the development of a virtual laboratory where the physical system is virtualized through a series of simulations, which are used to emulate the experiments. This solution was the main goal of the EXPERES project, an Erasmus+ CBHE (Capacity Building in the field of higher education), implemented in 2018, by the twelve Moroccan universities, the Ministry of National Education, Professional Training, Higher Education and Scientific Research, and with the help of six European partners.

The virtual laboratory implemented is an institutional OER and OEP initiative, focused on developing laboratory experiments that are mapped to the physics curriculum of the first year for scientific and technical disciplines, the introduction and use of a virtual laboratory to do practical works is a paradigm shift in an educational system that is slow to change. However, the main purpose to utilize virtual laboratory is because it is the appropriate tool among other types to address educational needs for laboratory activities no longer met by universities in the traditional face-to-face laboratory teaching due to the phenomenon of massification. Results from Raman et al.'s (2014) study indicated that using OER such as virtual laboratory on desktops and tablets had similar effects in learner performance to using physical laboratory. Also, this has interesting implications for education policy-makers who are looking to reduce the digital divide (Raman et al., 2014).

To set up the EXPERES project, from the preparation until implementation and testing of the platform, a set of activities has been designed in 12 work packages and were performed by the working group that was composed of the Moroccan universities and the European partners under the coordination of the University of Murcia (Spain) and Abdelmalek Essaadi University (Morocco), in order to exchange expertise and competencies that have been needed for the development of the scheduled actions of the project.

12.3.3   Methodology

The methodology adopted for the creation of the virtual practical activities and the development and the implementation of this virtual laboratory is composed of five steps (El Kharki et al., 2018, 2020), as shown in Fig. 12.1.

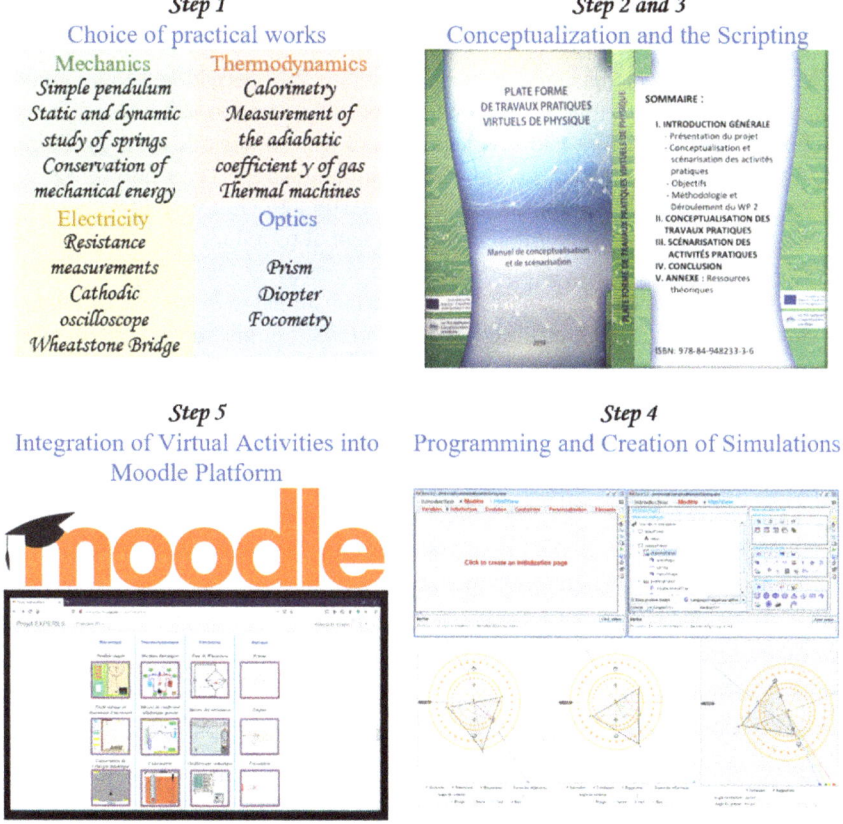

Fig. 12.1 Methodology adopted for the development of the virtual laboratory of the EXPERES project

The first step consisted of the choice of the practical work to be developed; the decision taken was to start first with the same 12 practical works presented in the face-to-face laboratory. The second and third steps are concerning the preparation of the conceptualization and the scripting sheets for the 12 practical activities chosen. The conceptualization sheet describes in detail the learning activity, and the scripting sheet is prepared to facilitate the programming step. A manual including the 12 conceptualization and scripting sheets has been published, and it is available online under an open access license. The fourth step is about the development of virtual simulations by using Easy JavaScript Simulations (EJSS), an open-source software, and using JavaScript programming language to create the simulation. The fifth step concerns the implementation of the Moodle platform, for hosting the simulations developed (Thc EXPERES platform).

12.4   Results and Discussion

OER and OEP have increasingly been recognized by the international community as innovative tools for meeting the challenges of providing lifelong learning opportunities for learners from diverse levels and modes of education worldwide. In addition, they have emerged as concepts with great potential to support educational transformation. One of the main purposes for OER is to support education; they do so with heightened accessibility, and they have the potential to reduce barriers to learning through enhanced attention, motivation, and engagement of learners (Sclater, 2011).

At Moroccan universities, an OEP initiative that aimed to develop a virtual laboratory as an OER has been achieved, in order to offer an institutional alternative to the traditional face-to-face laboratory, which was eliminated due to their weakness to afford the large numbers of learners. The main outcome of this initiative is the implementation of a virtual laboratory and its integration into a Moodle platform. The virtual experiments developed are according to the physics curriculum of the first year, three virtual activities for each physics subject taught during semesters 1 and 2 (mechanics, thermodynamics, electricity, and optics). The virtual laboratory is available online through the Internet for all the learners, to offer them the possibility to do the virtual activities at any time and any place, which is an important point in providing access to knowledge. Besides, the preliminary results obtained from the exploitation of the EXPERES platform indicated that the use of virtual laboratory has the potential to increase learners understanding of fundamental scientific concepts and phenomena, which improve the quality of learners learning and enhance the learning outcomes because they can repeat the experiment as many times as necessary and also increase flexibility, engagement, and motivation.

Even if the platform has not yet been officially adopted by the Ministry of National Education, Professional Training, Higher Education, and Scientific Research many Moroccan HE institutions have adopted it for their learners for the first year curriculum of the license degree.

In order to facilitate and promote the accessibility for learners and to ensure the proper functioning and management of the platform, each university has duplicated the same platform developed in its server.

At Cadi Ayyad University, since it was launched online in November 2018, the EXPERES platform (http://www.tpexperes.uca.ma) has been employed by 1450 users, about 40 teachers and 1410 learners, from faculty of science, and other higher education institutions, as is shown in Table 12.1.

The learners and teachers who experimented with the platform during the two years after its implementation are very satisfied with this experience; also, they recommended developing and add other virtual activities to cover the entire physics course (El Kharki et al., 2021).

As the program of physics is almost the same for faculties of science, faculties of sciences and technologies, multidisciplinary faculties, engineering school, and other scientific institutions, the online virtual laboratory created has been shared over the web and between institutions (Fig. 12.2).

For the dissemination and the exploitation of the platform, other public or private schools and universities with regular access could also benefit and use the platform, either they can ask for an installation package if they want to install the platform in

Table 12.1 Number of users enrolled in the EXPERES platform between 2018 and 2020

Year	The number of enrolled users
2018	244
2019	307
2020	899

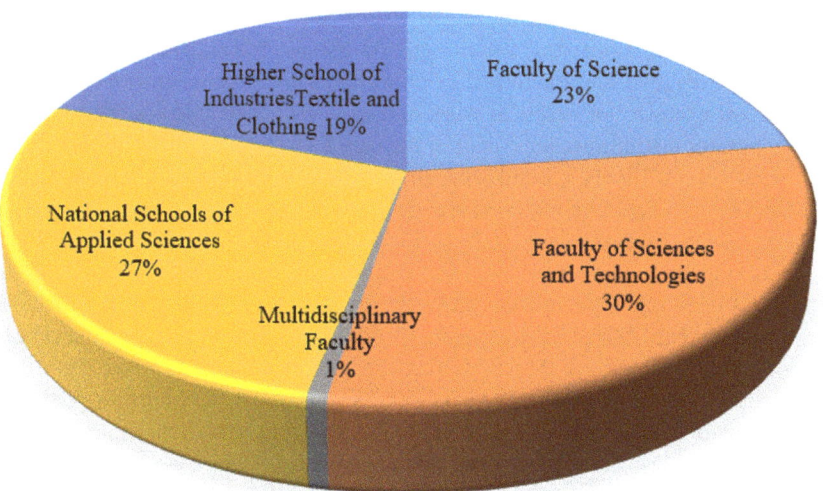

Fig. 12.2 Institutions user of the EXPERES platform of Cadi Ayyad University between 2018 and 2020

their server, or they can prepare a sheet of learners and teachers information, who want to have accounts on the platform; then, they ask a university among the twelve universities to create their accounts and offer them access.

Another product of the OEP initiative is the manual of conceptualization and scripting. It presents a reference with high-quality that can help and support the conceptualization and the scripting of other practical activities in various scientific disciplines. It was published online under an open access license, in order to let educators get the benefit from it when they want to develop other virtual experiments.

The platform developed is considered as an OER, because it supports open access and offers equal access to educational opportunities without barriers. Also, it provides open learning by offering the possibility to study and learn at any time and anywhere.

12.5   Conclusion and Perspectives

This chapter presented a Moroccan experience of adopting OEP and providing OER, which was the development of a virtual laboratory as an online learning experimental tool. This laboratory provides open access for all Moroccan university teachers and learners. All universities have duplicated the same platform in their server, to facilitate and promote the accessibility for learners and to ensure the proper functioning and management of the platform.

The manual of conceptualization and scripting, in addition to the implemented platform, which are the main results of the EXPERES initiative has been shared under the open license "CC BY-NC-SA" that allows their share and modification.

The first results of the exploitation of the EXPERES platform indicate that both learners and teachers were ready to use virtual laboratories hosted in the Moodle platform as an educational tool, which supports distance learning for scientific education. This alternative solution to real laboratories in institutions with an open access stay a good exercise for practical work and can be considered as a pre-laboratory preparation for institutions that can offer the face-to-face laboratory with limited and controlled access. For the second case, virtual laboratories may be very effective for complementing education methods and teaching material for teachers and learners who have limited access to a real laboratory in their institutes (Diwakar et al., 2015).

There is evidence that open education, including the use of OER and the adoption of OEP, is encouraging a shift in educational practice (Littlejohn & Pegler, 2014; Masterman & Wild, 2012). OEP provide full benefit from freely and easily accessible and reusable resources. For that, an educational culture must be fostered, that is built on the sharing of resources for, and experiences from, OEP. Furthermore, promoting open educational practices and resources is a key measure educational policy-makers, and funding bodies can adopt to bring education and lifelong learning closer to the demands of the knowledge society (Geser, 2007).

At the end of the project, Moroccan universities have signed a charter aimed to sustain results, by maintaining the collaboration between the team project for the future development of the platform and to support the extension of the platform to other practical work in other disciplines.

Acknowledgements The authors would like to thank the European Commission for funding the EXPERES project. Our thanks also to all the participants and collaborators of the EXPERES project for their contribution and involvement. The authors would like to thank also the Francophone University Agency (AUF) for supporting the adoption of OER at Cadi Ayyad University.

References

Andrade, A., Ehlers, U.-D., Caine, A., Carneiro, R., Conole, G., Kairamo, A.-K., Koskinen, T., Kretschmer, T., Moe-Pryce, N., Mundin, P., Nozes, J., Reinhardt, R., Richter, T., Silva, G., Holmberg, C. (2011). *Beyond OER-shifting focus to open educational practices: OPAL report 2011.* Retrieved from https://nbn-resolving.org/urn:nbn:de:hbz:464-20110208-115314-6.

Atkins, D. E., Brown, J. S., Hammond, A. L. (2007). *A review of the open educational resources (OER) movement: Achievements, challenges, and new opportunities.* Creative Common Mountain View.

Belawati, T. (2014). Open education, open education resources, and massive open online courses. *International Journal of Continuing Education and Lifelong Learning, 7*(1), 1. Retrieved from https://search.informit.com.au/documentSummary;dn=805233669063317;res=IELHSS.

Bhardwaj, A. (2016). Importance of education in human life: A holistic approach. *International Journal of Science and Consciousness, 2*(2), 23–28. Retrieved from http://www.ijsc.net/docs/issue4/importance-of-education-in-human-life.pdf.

Bossu, C., Bull, D., & Brown, M. (2012). Opening up down under: The role of open educational resources in promoting social inclusion in Australia. *Distance Education, 33*(2), 151–164. https://doi.org/10.1080/01587919.2012.692050.

Butcher, N. (2015). In A. Kanwar & S. Uvalić-Trumbić (Eds.), *A basic guide to open educational resources (OER).* Retrieved from http://hdl.handle.net/11599/36.

Calderon, A. (2018). *The higher education landscape is changing fast.* Retrieved July 20, 2020, from University World News, the global window on higher education website: https://www.universityworldnews.com/post.php?story=2018062208555853.

Clough, M. P. (2002). Using the laboratory to enhance student learning. *Learning Science and the Science of Learning*, 85–94.

Conole, G. (2012). *Fostering social inclusion through open educational resources (OER).* https://doi.org/10.1080/01587919.2012.700563.

Cox, G., & Trotter, H. (2017). Factors shaping lecturers' adoption of OER at three South African universities. In C. Hodgkinson-Williams & P. B. Arinto (Eds.). Retrieved from https://www.idrc.ca/en/book/adoption-and-impact-oer-global-south.

Cronin, C. (2017). Openness and praxis: Exploring the use of open educational practices in higher education. *International Review of Research in Open and Distributed Learning: IRRODL, 18*(5), 15–34. https://doi.org/10.19173/irrodl.v18i5.3096.

de Carvalho, C. V., Caeiro Rodríguez, M., Escudeiro, P., & Llamas Nistal, M. (2016). *Sustainability of open educational resources: The eCity case* (pp. 479–484). Retrieved from http://hdl.handle.net/10366/131586.

Diwakar, S., Kumar, D., Radhamani, R., Nizar, N., Nair, B., Sasidharakurup, H., & Achuthan, K. (2015). Role of ICT-enabled virtual laboratories in biotechnology education: Case studies on blended and remote learning. In *International Conference on Interactive Collaborative Learning (ICL), 2015* (pp. 915–921). https://doi.org/10.1109/ICL.2015.7318149.

Downes, S. (2011). *Open educational resources: A definition.* Retrieved from https://www.downes.ca/cgi-bin/page.cgi?post=57915.

Ehlers, U.-D. (2011). Extending the territory: From open educational resources to open educational practices. *Journal of Open, Flexible, and Distance Learning, 15*(2), 1–10.

El Kharki, K., Bensamka, F., & Berrada, K. (2020). Enhancing practical work in physics using virtual Javascript simulation and LMS platform. In D. Burgos (Ed.), *Radical solutions and eLearning* (pp. 131–146). https://doi.org/10.1007/978-981-15-4952-6_9.

El Kharki, K., Bensamka, F., Berrada, K., El Hajjaji, K., El Kbiach, M. L., & Bounab, L. (2018). Vers un laboratoire virtuel des TP en Sciences physiques: cas du projet EXPERES. *International Journal of Applied Research and Technology, 1*(December). Retrieved from http://www.ijartech.com/lirePDF2.php.

El Kharki, K., Berrada, K., & Burgos, D. (2021). Design and implementation of a virtual laboratory for physics subjects in Moroccan Universities. *Sustainability, 13*(7). https://doi.org/10.3390/su13073711.

Geser, G. (2007). *Open educational practices and resources.* OLCOS Roadmap, 2012. Retrieved from https://files.eric.ed.gov/fulltext/ED498433.pdf.

Guo, Y., Zhang, M., Bonk, C. J., & Li, Y. (2015). Chinese faculty members' open educational resources (OER) usage status and the barriers to OER development and usage. *International Journal of Emerging Technologies in Learning, 10*(5). https://doi.org/10.3991/ijet.v10i5.4819.

Hilton, J. (2019). Open educational resources, student efficacy, and user perceptions: A synthesis of research published between 2015 and 2018. *Educational Technology Research and Development,* 1–24. https://doi.org/10.1007/s11423-019-09700-4.

Hockings, C., Brett, P., & Terentjevs, M. (2012). Making a difference—Inclusive learning and teaching in higher education through open educational resources. *Distance Education, 33*(2), 237–252. https://doi.org/10.1080/01587919.2012.692066.

Hofstein, A., & Lunetta, V. N. (2004). The laboratory in science education: Foundations for the twenty-first century. *Science Education, 88*(1), 28–54.

Hoosen, S., Butcher, N., & OER Africa. (2019). Understanding the impact of OER: Achievements and challenges. In S. Knyazeva & UNESCO Institute for Information Technologies in Education (Eds.). Moscow, Russia: UNESCO Institute for Information Technologies in Education. Retrieved from https://iite.unesco.org/wp-content/uploads/2019/04/Understanding_the_impact_of_OER_2019_final.pdf.

Hoosen, S., Moore, D., & Butcher, N. (2016). *Open educational resources (OER) guide for students in post-secondary and higher education.* Retrieved from http://hdl.handle.net/11599/2093.

Hylén, J., & Schuller, T. (2007). Giving knowledge for free. *OECD Observer.* https://doi.org/10.1787/9789264066021-ja.

ICEF Monitor. (2018). *Study projects dramatic growth for global higher education through 2040.* Retrieved July 20, 2020, from Market intelligence for international student recruitment from ICEF website: https://monitor.icef.com/2018/10/study-projects-dramatic-growth-global-higher-education-2040/.

Idrissi, A. J., Berrada, K., Bendaoud, R., Machwate, S., Miraoui, A., & Burgos, D. (2020). Starting MOOCs in African University: The experience of Cadi Ayyad University, process, review, recommendations, and prospects. *IEEE Access, 8,* 17477–17488. https://doi.org/10.1109/ACCESS.2020.2966762.

Idrissi, A. J., Margoum, S., Bendaoud, R., & Berrada, K. (2018). UC@MOOC's effectiveness by producing open educational resources. *IJIMAI, 5*(2), 58–62. https://doi.org/10.9781/ijimai.2018.02.007

Jung, I., & Hong, S. (2016). Faculty members' instructional priorities for adopting OER. *The International Review of Research in Open and Distributed Learning, 17*(6). https://doi.org/10.19173/irrodl.v17i6.2803.

Kaatrakoski, H., Littlejohn, A., & Hood, N. (2017). Learning challenges in higher education: An analysis of contradictions within Open Educational Practice. *Higher Education, 74*(4), 599–615. https://doi.org/10.1007/s10734-016-0067-z.

Lane, A. (2009). The impact of openness on bridging educational digital divides. *International Review of Research in Open and Distributed Learning, 10*(5). https://doi.org/10.19173/irrodl.v10i5.637.

Littlejohn, A., & Pegler, C. (2014). Reusing resources: Open for learning. *Journal of Interactive Media in Education, 2014*(1). https://doi.org/10.5334/2014-02.

Marcus-Quinn, A., & Diggins, Y. (2013). Open educational resources. *Procedia-Social and Behavioral Sciences, 93*, 243–246. https://doi.org/10.1016/j.sbspro.2013.09.183.

Masterman, L., & Wild, J. (2012). *OER impact study: Research report*. JISC Open Educational Resources Programme.

McKerlich, R. C., Ives, C., & McGreal, R. (2013). Measuring use and creation of open educational resources in higher education. *The International Review of Research in Open and Distributed Learning, 14*(4). https://doi.org/10.19173/irrodl.v14i4.1573.

Murphy, A. (2012). *Benchmarking OER use and assessment in higher education*. Retrieved from https://eprints.usq.edu.au/21968/.

Murphy, A. (2013). Open educational practices in higher education: Institutional adoption and challenges. *Distance Education, 34*(2), 201–217. https://doi.org/10.1080/01587919.2013.793641.

Nie, M. (2012). *EVOL-OER: The evolution of OER. SCORE fellowship final report*. Retrieved from https://web.archive.org/web/20151124055713/http://www.open.ac.uk:80/score/evol-oer-evolution-open-educational-resources.

Nipa, T. J., & Kermanshachi, S. (2019). Assessment of open educational resources (OER) developed in interactive learning environments. *Education and Information Technologies*, 1–27. https://doi.org/10.1007/s10639-019-10081-7.

OpenMed Morocco. (2016). *Déclaration du Maroc sur les Ressources Educatives Libres-OER Morocco Declaration*. Change.org. Retrieved February 18, 2020, from https://openmedproject.eu/wp-content/uploads/OER-Morocco-Declaration.pdf.

Orr, D., Rimini, M., & Van Damme, D. (2015). Open educational resources: A catalyst for innovation. *Educational Research and Innovation*. https://doi.org/10.1787/9789264247543-en.

Otto, D. (2019). Adoption and diffusion of open educational resources (OER) in education. *The International Review of Research in Open and Distributed Learning, 20*(5), 122–140. https://doi.org/10.19173/irrodl.v20i5.4472.

Raman, R., Achuthan, K., Nedungadi, P., Diwakar, S., & Bose, R. (2014). The VLAB OER experience: Modeling potential-adopter student acceptance. *IEEE Transactions on Education, 57*(4), 235–241. https://doi.org/10.1109/TE.2013.2294152.

Sclater, N. (2011). Open educational resources: Motivations, logistics and sustainability. In *Content management for e-learning* (pp. 179–193). https://doi.org/10.1007/978-1-4419-6959-0_10.

Shear, L., Means, B., & Lundh, P. (2015). *Research on open: OER research hub review and futures for research on OER*. Menlo Park, CA, USA: SRI International.

Stagg, A. (2014). OER adoption: A continuum for practice. *International Journal of Educational Technology in Higher Education, 11*(3), 151–165. https://doi.org/10.7238/rusc.v11i3.2102.

Tlili, A., Huang, R., Chang, T.-W., Nascimbeni, F., & Burgos, D. (2019). Open educational resources and practices in China: A systematic literature review. *Sustainability, 11*(18), 4867. https://doi.org/10.3390/su11184867.

UNESCO. (2002). *Forum on the impact of open courseware for higher education in developing countries*. Retrieved from https://unesdoc.unesco.org/ark:/48223/pf0000128515.

UNESCO. (2012a). *Open educational resources congress passes historic declaration*. Retrieved from http://www.unesco.org/new/en/communication-and-information/resources/news-and-in-focus-articles/in-focus-articles/2012/open-educational-resources-congress-passes-historic-declaration.

UNESCO. (2012b). *The Paris OER declaration 2012*. Retrieved from https://unesdoc.unesco.org/ark:/48223/pf0000246687.

UNESCO, & Commonwealth of Learning. (2011). *OER Policy Guidelines to be Launched at the UNESCO General Conference*. Retrieved from http://www.unesco.org/new/en/media-services/single-view/news/unescocommonwealth_of_learning_oer_policy_guidelines_to_be/.

United Nations. (1948). Universal declaration of human rights. *UN General Assembly, 302*(2). Retrieved from https://www.un.org/en/universal-declaration-human-rights/.

United Nations. (2015). *Transforming our world: The 2030 agenda for sustainable development*. Retrieved from https://sustainabledevelopment.un.org/post2015/transformingourworld.

Wang, T., & Towey, D. (2017). Open educational resource (OER) adoption in higher education: Challenges and strategies. In *2017 IEEE 6th International Conference on Teaching, Assessment, and Learning for Engineering (TALE)* (pp. 317–319). https://doi.org/10.1109/TALE.2017.8252355.

Weller, M. (2014). *Battle for open: How openness won and why it doesn't feel like victory*. https://doi.org/10.5334/bam.

Wright, R. E., & Reeves, J. L. (2019). Open educational resource (OER) adoption in higher education: Examining institutional perspectives. *FDLA Journal, 4*(1), 9. Retrieved from https://nsuworks.nova.edu/fdla-journal/vol4/iss1/9.

Yoon, J. (2017). Developing a list and a rubric of interactive open education resources (OER) for science teacher candidates of diverse students. *TEM Journal, 6*(3), 512–524. Retrieved from https://www.ceeol.com/search/article-detail?id=560173.

Zaatri, I., El Kharki, K., Bendaoud, R., & Berrada, K. (2019). The use of open educational resources at Cadi Ayyad University: State of art review. In *2019 7th International Conference on ICT & Accessibility (ICTA)* (pp. 1–4). https://doi.org/10.1109/ICTA49490.2019.9144857.

Zaatri, I., Margoum, S., Bendaoud, R., El Malti, I. L., Burgos, D., & Berrada, K. (2020). Open educational resources in Morocco. In *Current state of open educational resources in the "Belt and Road" countries* (pp. 119–134). https://doi.org/10.1007/978-981-15-3040-1_7.

Zhang, X., Tlili, A., Nascimbeni, F., Burgos, D., Huang, R., Chang, T.-W., Jemni, M., & Khribi, M. K. (2020). Accessibility within open educational resources and practices for disabled learners: A systematic literature review. *Smart Learning Environments, 7*(1), 1. https://doi.org/10.1186/s40561-019-0113-2.

Khadija El Kharki is a Ph.D. student at Cadi Ayyad University (UCA). She is a holder of a master's degree in Engineering and Technology of Education and Training. She is developing research on virtual laboratories based on digital simulation with the JavaScript programming language with Trans ERIE research group at UCA.

Khalid Berrada is currently professor of physics at Mohammed V University in Rabat (UM5R). He was professor and Director of the Centre for Pedagogical Innovation at Cadi Ayyad University in Marrakech since 1996. He was also a UNESCO Chairholder on "Teaching physics by doing". He has been a member of many national and international conferences and meeting committees. He is also one of the developers of the successful French program of UNESCO Active Learning in Optics and Photonics. He is coordinating the UC@MOOC project created in 2013 at UCA. He has led a group of researchers on educational innovation at UCA (Trans ERIE) and the Morocco Declaration on Open Education since 2016.

Faouzi Bensamka is professor of physics at Cadi Ayyad University (UCA). He member of Trans ERIE and was the Director of Material Sciences Laboratory at UCA. He is involved in many aspects of research on pedagogy and training trainers. He was the responsible of the Mathematics and Physics Sciences Curricula at Faculty of Sciences Semlalia. He has participated in many programs and projects around pedagogy and has been member of many scientific committees. He is developing research on assessment using LMS platforms, JavaScript simulations and Microcomputer-based laboratory.

Daniel Burgos works as Vice-rector for International Research (https://research.unir.net), UNESCO Chair on eLearning and ICDE Chair in Open Educational Resources, at Universidad Internacional de La Rioja (UNIR, https://www.unir.net). He is also Director of the Research Institute for Innovation & Technology in Education (UNIR iTED, https://ited.unir.net). He is an Extra-ordinary Professor at North-West University (South Africa). His work is focused on Adaptive, Personalized and Informal eLearning, Learning Analytics, Open Education and Open Science, eGames, and eLearning Specifications. He holds degrees in Communication (Ph.D.), Computer Science (Dr. Ing), Education (Ph.D.), Anthropology (Ph.D.), Business Administration (DBA), Theology (Ph.D.), Open Science & STEM (Ph.D.), Management (Ph.D.) and Artificial Intelligence & Machine Learning (postgraduate, at MIT).

Chapter 13
Self-directed Learning: Readiness of Secondary School Students in Mauritius

Vandanah Gooria, Perienen Appavoo, Upasna Bhunjun, and Abheenaye Chauhan Gokhool

Abstract Open education and technology are transforming the journey of schooling. The way students prepare themselves for learning is becoming more challenging in the global educational environment. In the wake of technology integration in the learning process and the current trend to embrace online learning, self-directed learning (SDL) skills have drawn the attention of many researchers in the field. Technology-savvy students are ready to embrace new techniques for learning but how far are they inspired to learn on their own, acquire the necessary skills and take initiatives when they are still young and lack experience? This chapter unveils the findings of a study on the levels of SDL skills of upper secondary school students in Mauritius. A mixed-method approach collected data from 108 students involving both genders of varying learning performance. Primary data was collected using a validated questionnaire based on the four constructs—self-discipline, self-motivation, self-management and collaboration. A Cronbach's alpha test was used to test the reliability of the 32-items in the questionnaire. It was revealed that the mastery of SDL skills was not gender biased and did not depend on the learning performance of students, but was found to be significantly dependent on the level of computer skills, thus purporting that those who were proficient users of computing tools were well-poised to embrace self-directed learning. Additionally, students with higher learning performance and those who had prior exposure to online courses demonstrated high collaborative skills. And thus, these students were found to be more apt and motivated to adopt self-directed learning.

Keywords Self-directed learning · Collaborative skills · Young students · Mauritius

V. Gooria (✉) · P. Appavoo · U. Bhunjun · A. C. Gokhool
Open University of Mauritius, Réduit, Moka, Mauritius
e-mail: v.gooria@open.ac.mu

© The Author(s), under exclusive license to Springer Nature Singapore Pte Ltd. 2021
D. Burgos and J. Olivier (eds.), *Radical Solutions for Education in Africa*, Lecture Notes in Educational Technology, https://doi.org/10.1007/978-981-16-4099-5_13

13.1   Introduction

When our grandparents went to school, it consisted largely of memorisation and rote learning. There was very little scope for them to think creatively or work outside the box. Now, we often cannot control the experience that children have once they attain the age of compulsory education, but we can influence their learning experience. These early years of schooling are critical in order to empower students to become self-directed individuals. At the secondary level, how they will be inclined to view their learning experience would certainly be different to that of primary school with the use of technology. The educational environment has experienced quite a lot of changes since the past few years and one element which has pushed these changes is technology. And nowadays the beauty of technology allows people, mainly students, to learn on their own. This has resulted in an increase in students taking control of their learning, together with the formal educational context. Authors such as Hussey and Smith (2010) put forward that SDL allows students to have more control on their learning needs and what they want to learn on their own. Students can study on their own or can seek help from their peers or teachers to assist them in their learning process. To make SDL successful, there are several elements attached to it such as being aware of the concept, being ready to implement it, to be self-disciplined and self-motivated, to be able to manage his/her own work and also be able to integrate technological tools in their self-directed learning activities.

13.2   Research Objectives

The aim of this chapter is to investigate students' self-directed learning skills, especially in the context of e-learning and to determine the underpinning variables leading to the adoption of SDL among young students. Self-discipline, self-motivation, collaboration and self-management of upper secondary students in Mauritius were examined in order to see whether they are effective self-directed students and can thus make use of technology to achieve their learning goals. It further investigates how self-directed skills and readiness may support increased individualised and autonomous learning of young students.

13.3   Theoretical Framework

This research is anchored to a theory which marks issues of motivation of young students, i.e. self-determination theory (SDT) by Deci and Ryan (2000) as the entire discussion revolves around autonomy, self-discipline, self-motivation and self-management of students. Literatures from Ryan and Deci (2004), Black and Deci (2000), Palmer (2007) viewed that when students are motivated they begin working immediately, ask questions, volunteer answers, pay attention and be eager to learn new things. Therefore, students will exert energy and optimise effort to do their best if they are motivated. Their learning experiences are more meaningful and they intend to go deeper into the topic on their own to fully understand it. Hence, the need for autonomy is vital for the student to carry out a task of his/her own choice. It is not forced or coerced in any way (Deci & Ryan, 2000). Further, SDT when applied to the realm of education is focused primarily on promoting in students' own interest in self-directed learning, a valuing of education and confidence in their own capacities and attributes (Deci & Ryan, 2000). This implies that their satisfaction of having the feeling of making their own decisions (need for autonomy), of experiencing mastery (need for competence) and of feeling connected and belonged (need for relatedness) will tell their level of interests and willingness in doing such academic tasks. The model of "collaborative constructivist" has broadened the application of SDL into three main components: self-management, self-monitoring and motivation (Garrison, 1997).

13.4 Literature Review

Student Engaging with Technology, Information from Web and Self-directed Learning

Since the emergence of the Internet, the volume of information has been growing exponentially and students are consuming too much information from over 1.8 billion websites and on top of this on average 571 new ones are created every minute (Oksana, 2018). Therefore, it is no wonder that information overload has become an issue for our young students to learn on their own. On one hand, digesting loads of free data, and on the other hand, lack of quality information can be both problematic for young students and is beyond their control. Given this kind of situation, it is not surprising that young people are suffering from information overload and feel an urgent need on how to detox these information and focus on relevant, reliable learning materials that meet their educational needs in reality. Therefore, empowering young people with SDL readiness and skills is pivotal in their educational endeavour.

Online courses help students in becoming more proficient in using technological tools and applications. For the moment, 1.8 billion young people between the ages of 10 and 24 are studying, working and finding their own ends (Lei, 2020). They are blooming at a time when the world is at a critical crossroad with challenges in many sectors. The present youth is a generation who is brought up in a well-to-do digital environment and captivated in a world diffused with various types of information and communication technologies (ICTs). Their usage of technologies is termed and categorised into various names: Millennials or Gen Y (Dimock, 2019), e-Gen, N-Gen, young students of the digital era (Rapetti & Cantoni, 2010). Digital learning, OER and online education have led the way in schools during the start of the COVID-19 pandemic. Does the engagement with technology facilitate or hamper their own learning capabilities and performance? Tabassum and Hanan (2016) proved that the use of technology has a direct positive relationship with students' engagement and SDL, but no significant direct effect was found between technology use and academic performance. On one end of the spectrum, it is believed that digital technology does increase and transform the teaching and learning process (Beetham & Sharpe, 2012) while on the other end, it is perceived that various technologies act as "disruptive" (Losh, 2014) and a challenge for students, schools and universities to cope with. Given the fact that technology affordances are in concurrence with the learning environment, it is likely that young are using them to enhance their academic knowledge and meeting their own educational challenges. Nevertheless, the young are often trapped in dilemmas when they use different methods of technologies on their own and randomly in education, like, When did learning take place? What to learn? Where did learning take place? How did learning happen? What kind of technology tools to use in order to learn? It is further reported by Drain et al. (2012) that students who "intelligent use" electronic devices have improved their academic performance. Kuh and Hu (2001) found that students who heavily indulge in their own online recreation, are closely linked to impaired academic performance. Since many of these learning technologies are interactive, it is easier to create an environment where learning is fun.

13.5 Self-directed Learning Awareness, Readiness and Collaboration

SDL helps students to be more autonomous in their learning (Gibbons, 2002; Hussey & Smith, 2010), especially in this new era of open learning. According to Kleden (2015), students participating in SDL found that they learnt better than the conventional way of learning in classrooms. SDL helped students to become aware of their learning needs and reduce their dependence on classroom learning. SDL also enabled the students to acquire critical thinking skills. When students acquire these skills, they have a different mindset and also become independent and do share their ideas with their peers or teachers. Xuan et al. (2018) stated that awareness is a fundamental component in the SDL process as if students are not aware of the processes of SDL, they will not be able to proceed with their own learning. Students should be aware that their own efforts will contribute to their learning process and teachers need to emphasise on the importance of SDL and make students aware of the processes towards SDL.

Brookfield (2009) stated that students need to be aware of what they want to learn, how they will proceed to learn, where to look for materials and finally how to evaluate their learning outcomes. This will enable students to proceed with their SDL without any barriers and attain their objectives successfully. Therefore, being aware of several elements as mentioned by Brookfield is a key factor in SDL. This is supported by Brandt (2020) who mentioned several elements of SDL awareness such as the students need to be aware of the choices available for learning and also evaluate their tasks. Students must set their goals, plan their learning, choose the resources they will use and finally evaluate their progress. They can either work independently or from time to time, consult other people. The peers or teachers can provide feedback to the students in order to improve their learning process. Furthermore, Benson (2001) emphasised on the fact that students need to know how they will proceed with their learning. Teachers should also be encouraged to provide support and feedback to students so that SDL is successful. Teachers should show that they are in favour of SDL and Thornton (2010) supported this view. In his research paper, he stated that teachers have the capability of developing independent learning among students and teachers should convince their students to adopt the SDL technique. Although teachers do have a busy schedule, they should provide ways for students to become independent and develop their own learning strategies. He also stated that students should also be encouraged to share their knowledge, and this can result in better problem-solving. The guidance of teachers is also important for young people to take ownership of their learning with the necessary ICT tools. However, in modern educational technology, the idea of student autonomy also jerks on the importance of collaborative learning (CL). The sphere of learner autonomy requires that learners to be independent and become lifelong learners (Appavoo et al., 2019). In one sense, CL is promising to move students away from their dependence on their teachers and do their learning on their own (Lin, 2015).

Additionally, Kapur (2018) stated that students need to work in collaborative teams from time to time with others such as classmates or teachers or both, to achieve their objectives when engaging in SDL. They will be able to get guidance and support and most important, feedback. Students need to be told whether they are on the right track or not. Furthermore, teachers are required to create awareness among students about how to deal with SDL. Teachers normally instil skills such as cognitive and intellectual in their learning and also provide opportunities to their students to work on their own. For example, Kapur (2018) mentioned that in some schools, educators allow their students to participate in workshops and to research on their own, around a specific topic. This encourages students to work independently, self-assessed themselves and also receive feedback from their peers. When the students have acquired adequate awareness, they can easily participate in debates and can improve their self-management skills in future. Students should also be encouraged to express themselves in class. As Kapur (2018) stated, teachers should encourage their students to raise questions or give ideas about the teaching and learning methods so that the students are satisfied or improvement can be brought forward. As mentioned by Gibbons (2002), students should be aware of their strengths and weaknesses and look for choices to solve these problems in order to improve their process of SDL. Interactions with peers will enable students to gather more ideas into how to better improve their SDL.

On the other hand, Sumuer (2018) stated that for students to benefit from the opportunities of SDL, they should be ready to be self-directed. One of the oldest definitions put forward by Wiley (1983) is that SDL readiness is about the abilities, personality traits and attitude that are needed to conduct SDL. Lasfeto and Ulfa

(2020) defined SDL readiness as students being ready to learn on their own. Several studies from Shaikh (2013) and Guglielmino and Guglielmino (2005) have shown that SDL readiness is a fundamental factor in making students learn on their own. When students are ready to learn independently, they are able to portrait positive behaviours towards SDL. This applies also in the context of online courses. If students are ready for online learning, they will be able to conduct their learning positively else they will have difficulties to cope with online courses. This is supported by Broadbent (2016) who found that SDL readiness is significant in making online learning successful. The more the level of SDL readiness among students, the more they will be able to engage with online learning. Chu and Tsai (2009) found that the more a student is ready to embark in SDL, the more he or she will be using technology to support his or her learning. In his research, Piskurich (2003) found that there are several components of student readiness in the online context. Many students are becoming online users due to the trend for the past few years and in order to be well-versed with the technological tools, the author found that although technical skills are important, readiness for SDL is more important. Therefore, technical readiness and SDL readiness are two major elements for the student readiness. In terms of technical readiness, the student needs to have the required skills, knowledge and aptitudes in technology so that he/she is ready to adapt to online learning. On the other hand, Piskurich (2003) explained that if students are to be ready for SDL, they need to understand their own learning, develop an attitude towards SDL, that is the students need to have a strong desire to learn on their own, and willing to learn new things. Students also need to be confident and see problems as challenges instead of barriers to learning and discuss their problems with their peers or teachers to obtain feedback. Students who do not seek feedback are eventually developing barriers to their learning. The author added that SDL readiness also includes skills such as reading and writing, the ability to plan their learning by having time management skills and defining properly their learning goals. In order to measure the readiness for SDL, Fisher et al. (2001), produced a reliable and valid scale and observed that students will benefit from technology for SDL, the more they want to learn, are able to manage and control their learning. Other authors such as McLoughlin and Lee (2010) stated that technologies in terms of mobile devices and the Internet have hugely contributed to SDL activities where students have the ability to communicate, search and share information. These technologies also enable students to seek support from peers in order to guide them in their process of SDL. Students should be aware of the technologies available so as to benefit from the opportunities derived from these tools in order to facilitate the process of SDL (Sumuer, 2018). In several studies conducted by Callaghan and Bower (2012) and Hamid et al. (2015), it was observed that students using online social network sites had the opportunity to complete certain tasks collaboratively and also to incorporate new knowledge independently or with the help of their peers. This indicates that if students are aware and ready to use technology in the process of SDL, they can benefit from several opportunities. Using technological tools allows students to share various information with their peers or teachers. According to Song et al. (2004), the students should be able to manage their learning with the resources available, like, for example, information resources, students can share information when conducting online learning with their peers or teachers through technological tools such as Zoom or WhatsApp. In terms of information, students should ensure that the information being obtained is reliable and still valid. Technology, on the other side, improves the learning experiences, and then students have recourse to SDL. Technology enables students to plan, implement and evaluate their own learning (Lee et al., 2014). Through technology, students are able to create a learning community with their peers or teachers and collaborate with them and also to have access to information available worldwide.

It is said that while entering school, girls perform equal to or better than boys on nearly every measure of achievement, but by the time they graduate high school or college, they have fallen behind (Sadker & Sadker, 1994). However, discrepancies between the performance of girls and the performance of boys in elementary education lead some critics to argue that boys are being neglected within the education system. Chapman (1997) highlighted that girls are becoming more academically successful than boys, but in this study, there is the absence of gender biasness whereby both boys and girls demonstrated the same level of SDL skills.

13.6 Self-discipline, Self-motivation and Self-management

Motivation and engagement play an important role in student's learning and academic performance. Closely related to motivation is self-discipline. Self-discipline is the ability of students to monitor their own behaviours. Self-discipline is a key skill which influences students and allows them to achieve their learning outcomes. Discipline creates good students and lifelong students. Students who are highly self-disciplined show a more positive outlook to long-term goals and academic achievement. According to Duckworth and Seligman (2005), individuals having low levels of self-discipline are confronted with diverse problems in their social and personal life. However, as per Hofmann et al. (2012), students having high levels of self-discipline drive success and are better at achieving their goals which in turn have a positive impact in improving their moods and make them happier. According to Cho and Heron (2015) and Kauffman (2004), studies in advanced technologies indicated that self-regulatory strategies might aid the use of cognitive strategies, metacognitive processing and motivational beliefs. Sasson and Dori (2012) stated that self-discipline is closely related to self-control. It is the ability to control things which may have negative outcomes. Additionally, Sasson and Dori (2012) emphasised that self-discipline manifests itself in different forms such as endurance, perseverance, thinking before acting and the ability to perform despite any inconvenience, adversities and difficulties. Self-disciplined students are more focused towards their studies and other areas of their life. Discipline helps to create eagerness in students. As such, students are able to experience a disciplined life characterised by success and better academic performance. Online courses provide students with the possibility of teaching themselves essential skills about how to become lifelong students. They can become more responsible and collaborate with peers during the learning process.

Motivation is essential in every aspect of life be it in a professional sphere or as a student studying at high school. According to McIsaac and Gunawardena (1996), online courses offer many advantages and several factors have been recognised as being crucial to the success of online education. Motivation is one such factor (Bekele, 2010). Schunk et al. (2008) define motivation as "the process whereby goal-directed activity is instigated and sustained" (p. 4). According to Schunk et al. (2008), students who are motivated are more likely to actively engage themselves, start any challenging activities and embrace a deep approach to learning. Self-motivation is an important skill in online education. Self-motivation drives students to keep going in their studies and achieve their goals. Self-motivation defines whether or not a student will undertake a task, even if it is a challenging task. Self-motivation has been recognised as an important skill in shaping students as well as helping students to learn and achieve their goals in online contexts. However, as stated by Muilenburg and Berge (2005), high dropout rates from online courses is closely related to poor motivation. Self-motivation guides students towards a particular goal but according to Garrison (1997), this has questioned the underlying assumptions that view online students as independent, self-directed and intrinsically motivated. According to Lepper (1988), students who are intrinsically motivated enjoy the learning process for their own sake and the feeling of achievement it brings to them whereas students who are extrinsically motivated are those who learn and expect a reward or just learn to avoid certain punishment. Motivation is an important indicator and predictor of learning and student academic achievement. Students who are more engaged in their studies are more motivated to learn deeply and perform better. According to Brophy (2010), there is a collaborative relationship between a student and the learning environment. Modern views link motivation of students to their cognitive and affective characteristics such as beliefs, views and opinions.

Self-management skills refer to approaches, policies and skills that individuals use to achieve their goals and objectives. Self-management skills help students to plan and organise their work and control their thoughts and feelings. According to Zimmerman and Martinez-Pons (1988), students who have a high level of self-management skills are better able to set their goals and are problem solvers. Additionally, they have a positive outlook when faced with academic challenges. Self-management skills help students to become successful students. Strong self-management skills help students to set goals independently and manage their own time.

13.7   Research Methodology

In order to meet the objectives of this study, the authors adopted a mixed quantitative and qualitative approach whereby an online questionnaire was designed and administered to students. The online questionnaire was designed with the main objective of understanding the students' level of SDL skills at the upper secondary level in Mauritius. A pilot test was conducted among 10 randomly identified students from two schools and no changes were undertaken, based on the feedback of the students.

A pilot test was conducted among 10 students, and the teachers had the opportunity to go through the questions as well and no changes were identified.

Once the online questionnaire was finalised, it was sent to the teachers from the identified groups of schools in Mauritius. The teachers had the responsibility to disseminate the online questionnaire among students from the upper level and the respondents were students aged 15–19 years old. The questionnaire was designed using a 5-point Likert scale and consisted of 51 items divided into six sections and the items were developed based on the different components in the literature review. The survey was conducted over a period of 3 weeks with only 108 respondents. SPSS software and word clouds were used to analyse the responses quantitatively and qualitatively.

Since ethical considerations is one of the most important elements in research, several aspects were taken into consideration while carrying out the survey among students. A careful attention was given in data collection, and we sought the collaboration of teachers on a voluntary basis. The teachers were contacted and briefed about the research being undertaken so that they could disseminate the information voluntarily to their respective students. The teachers play a vital part of recruitment and administering this survey. However, the researchers remained present via WhatsApp to clarify any confusion to them. The teachers were encouraged to assist the researchers and report of any issues or feedback from the students. A link of the online survey was sent to teachers for onwards submission to their students to partake in the study on voluntary basis. The participants involved are from the target group identified in the previous section.

No students were forced to take part in the research. Each student was required to provide their consent to participating in the study, by completing the first section in the online questionnaire. Those who did not give their consent were automatically directed to the end of the questionnaire. Since it was an online survey, students were free to withdraw from it at any point in time if they believed they could not answer the questions.

Confidentiality was also considered during the study. At the start of the questionnaire, the authors clearly mentioned that all the data would be kept confidential and anonymous will only be used for this study. The protection of the privacy of the participants was ensured, and there were no questions related to personal details such as their names or surnames. Data obtained would only be used for this research. The aim of the study was also mentioned in the questionnaire to remind students of its purpose.

13.8 Results and Findings

13.8.1 Descriptive Analysis

The objective of this study is to investigate students' self-directed learning skills, especially in the context of e-learning. After data cleaning, 108 responses were retained for analysis. The sample comprised secondary school students of varying learning performance of which 61.6% females. The majority of the respondents were above 17 years demonstrating a rather high level of computer skills, and being very familiar with computing tools like laptop, Internet and mobile phone. More than 80% of them reported that they spent a lot of time online, shopping and social networking. Moreover, most students had average or high experience with online courses. This description of the respondents confirms that respondents represented a fair sample of the student population, in terms of gender, learning performance and level of computer skills.

Inferential Analysis

Inferential analysis was carried to investigate the relationship between SDL skills index and the different variables. The index was computed based on the 32 items of the questionnaire which captured respondents' SDL skills. The Mann–Whitney test ($U = 1074, p = 0.913$) revealed the absence of gender biasness, revealing that both boys and girls demonstrated the same level of SDL skills. However, a study conducted among undergraduate students revealed that female students had significantly higher self-directed learning skills than male students (Askin Tekkol & Demirel, 2018). This calls for further investigation to better understand as to why this difference exists between secondary and undergraduate students.

A Kruskal–Wallis test revealed that there is a statistically significant difference in level SDL skills among the different levels of computer competency (X^2 (2) = 7.667, $p = 0.022$). The difference was mainly between those having a low level and those having an intermediate (X^2 (1) = 6.160, $p = 0.013$) or high level ($p = 0.015$) of computer proficiency. Therefore, it can be deduced that students who had a good mastery of computer skills were better positioned for self-directed learning. Given the strong relationship between the levels of computer competency and experience with online courses (X^2 (2) = 0.252, $p = 0.008$), it was not a surprise to see that students with more experience in online courses were those who had higher scores on the SDL index.

This study also revealed that there was no significant effect of learning performance on students' SDL index (X^2 (2) = 2.264, $p = 0.322$). This finding appears to differ from the studies of Stewart (2007) and Chou and Chen (2008) who reported that students' self-directed learning skills and learning performance are positively related.

The 32 items of the questionnaire were grouped under four constructs, namely self-discipline, collaboration, self-motivation and self-management. To ensure that the items were reliable to measure each construct, a Cronbach's alpha test was carried out and the results were found to be greater than 0.70, hence showing that all items appropriately measured the different constructs. Figure 13.1 compares responses across the four constructs, showing significant differences between the positive (agree and strongly agree) and negative ones (disagree and strongly disagree). It can be observed that three constructs—self-discipline, collaboration and self-motivation had relatively high percentages of positive responses around 60%, whereas self-management had 46% positive responses. Under the constructs, self-discipline, and collaboration, the statements to which the majority of the respondents responded favourably were "*I need to keep my learning routine separate from my other commitments*", and "*I am open to new ideas*", respectively. The item which received the highest number of positive responses from the self-motivation construct was "*I find both success and failure inspire me to further learning*", whereas for the self-management construct it was "*I am able to plan and set my learning goals*". These findings revealed that a significant majority of secondary school students in Mauritius, independent of gender, demonstrated adequate SDL skills and were thus poised to embrace a new learning paradigm, necessitating the acquisition of such skills, like online learning or the flipped classroom concept (Tan & Koh, 2014).

To explore the deeper connections between each of the four constructs and the level of *computer competency* and *experience with online courses*, a Kruskal–Wallis test was conducted. It was found that self-motivation was significantly different across the different levels of computer competency (X^2 (2) = 8.422, p = 0.015). Importantly, there is also a strong link between students' self-motivation abilities and experience with online courses (X^2 (2) = 23.60, p = 0.001). According to this result, it appears that frequent use of computers and familiarity with online courses develop self-directed learning skills among students who are thus more motivated

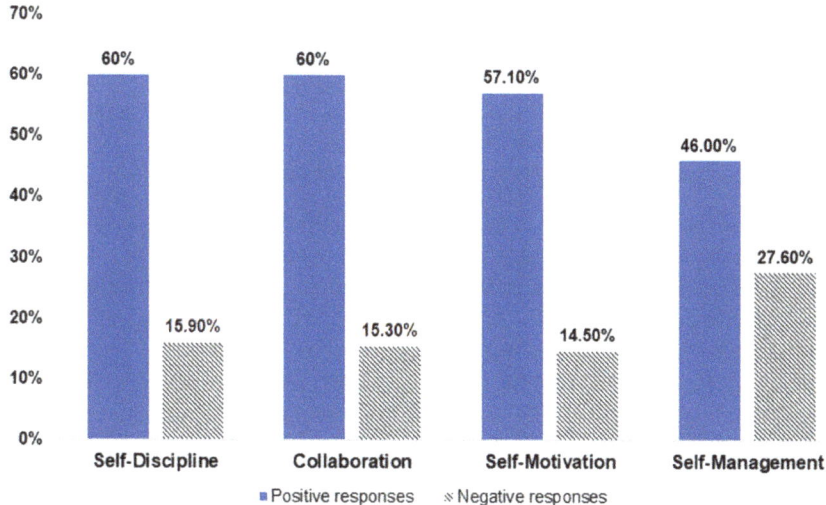

Fig. 13.1 Responses to the constructs of SDL

to learn on their own, which is a key characteristic of self-directed students (King, 2011). This is probably an iterative process which shows that the integration of technology in education and the development of SDL skills are closely intertwined. Appavoo et al. (2015) revealed the high uptake of computers in secondary schools in Mauritius, thus leading to conclude that this integration cannot but boost SDL competencies among students to higher levels.

Another finding of this study was the strong relationship between students' *learning performance* and *collaboration* (X^2 (2) = 8.984, p = 0.011). It shows that the higher the learning performance of students, the higher were their collaborative skills. Analysis of the responses also revealed a positive association between *experience with online courses* and *collaboration* (X^2 (2) = 18.951, p = 0.001); hence, testifying that students who had greater experience with online learning was those who also demonstrated collaborative skills. This corroborates with the findings of Wang and Hwang (2012, cited in Fakomogbon & Bolaji, 2017) who mentioned that collaborative learning promotes learning performance. Since collaborative skills form part of the set of SDL skills, we conclude that those with higher learning performance are more apt to adopt self-directed learning. It is thus highly opportune for teachers to incorporate collaborative learning activities where students of average ability can benefit more from having the opportunity to collaborate with high-ability students as suggested by Sears and Reagin (2013). For example, strategies like group work and peer tutoring can be promoted in our schools.

13.8.2   Measures to Improve SDL

Figure 13.2 shows that young students can improve their self-directed learning by setting learning goals, planning schedules, devoting more time to their studies, deliberate practice and less distractions. Excerpts from students' responses include:

> Keep away from distractions like mobile phones and social media and try to plan a schedule to dedicate time to each subject and working past papers.
>
> Striking the right time balance between entertainment and studying

Despite several roadblocks to self-learning, students should be ready to learn. This is possible when they set self-discipline movements such as having a timetable, focusing on the learning goals and changing their mindset to be more motivated individuals. According to Pink (2011), there are three main internal motivations for SDL: *Autonomy*, freedom to determine your path; *Mastery*: the chance to grow competency; *Purpose*: connection to some greater good. Furthermore, deliberate practice is the hard work of SDL and with the world going digital, young people need to be more disciplined at studying independently and better at managing their own time.

From the data collected, it can be observed that students have provided several elements in order to improve their self-directed learning skills. One frequent factor which many students have mentioned is *motivation*. Many students stated that due to

Fig. 13.2 Measures for students to improve SDL

the fact they were not motivated, they did not maximise their self-directed learning skills. Some extracts from students' responses include: *"there should be new motivating techniques of learning, or students nowadays lack motivation to study or even there should be more motivating words and encouragement"*. This is supported by Schunk et al. (2008) who stated that self-motivation is an important skill in online education and it makes students more engaged in their learning activities. Therefore, both schools and teachers should identify ways to motivate their students to improve their self-directed learning skills. When students are motivated, they will be more willing to learn by themselves, set and achieve their goals.

When analysing the data, there were other responses from students concerning the recommendations. Students mentioned that teachers should provide more assistance in helping them to improve their self-directed learning and also encourage this activity among students and additionally provide feedback. Some students stated *"teachers should guide them properly on how to self-learn, give scores, provide some guidelines and provide feedback"*. Brandt (2020) stated that teachers or even peers should provide feedback so that students improve their learning process. Teachers should also encourage participation during the online sessions so that students are guided towards the right path. Benson (2001) explained that a teacher, during self-directed learning, has the role of clarifying goals, shaping learning activities and assessing learning outcomes. Therefore, in such cases, teachers should be provided proper training in order to guide and assist students or regularly check on the students to ensure they are not facing any difficulties. Moreover, Thornton (2010) stated that teachers have the capability of developing independent learning among students and teachers should convince their students to adopt the SDL approach. Hence, based on the responses obtained from students, teachers should be able to inspire and communicate the benefits of SDL to students.

Beetham and Sharpe (2012) mentioned that digital technology does contribute to SDL but can also be a challenge for students. Many students expressed their concerns that they had difficulties to use technological tools during their SDL activities and that more training should be provided. They stated that "*there should be the necessary facilities available, students should be encouraged to use technological tools, and also give training on how to use them*". Schools and teachers should provide adequate training concerning technological tools so that students are able to communicate, search and share information when undertaking SDL. Students should be aware of the technologies available so as to benefit from the opportunities derived from these tools in order to facilitate the process of SDL (Sumuer, 2018). A better planning in terms of online sessions should be provided as well.

13.8.3   Covid-19 Impact on Students' SDL Skills

In this study, it has been observed that online learning has positively impacted on the self-learning skills of students. It has enabled students to improve their time management skills and learn according to their schedule and convenience. For instance, students stated that "online courses have encouraged self-learning as the Internet was easily accessible for in-depth research and Zoom allowed for discussions". As stated by Kleden (2015), students participating in SDL found that they learnt better than the conventional way of learning in classrooms. It can be concluded that online learning has enabled students to become more responsible towards their studies and manage their time effectively (Fig. 13.3).

However, despite the various benefits, online learning also brings some disadvantages. The present study showed that students found online learning very challenging. Many students felt distracted and stated that online learning did not prove to be beneficial for them. For instance, one student stated that "it has had a bad impact on my studies as the conditions we are studying have changed". According to Muilenburg and Berge (2005), high dropout rates from online courses is closely related to poor motivation. It can be concluded that the shift from traditional learning to online learning has left students with a lack of self-motivation. Moreover, in collaboration with students, teachers are also accountable for creating a sense of control to ensure that there are meaningful outcomes and a continuous effort to learn. However, students stated that there was "the lack of guidance from their teachers during online teaching". As a result, students felt stressed and this has negatively impacted on their learning abilities.

Fig. 13.3 Impact of COVID-19 on students' SDL

13.9   Conclusion

Online learning has gained more popularity in the twenty-first century. The integration of technology with education has transformed education. The aim of this research was to assess students' self-directed learning skills in the context of e-learning and the study revealed some interesting findings. It can be observed that most students do have recourse to SDL directly or indirectly. However, it should be pointed out that those students who have good computer skills or online experiences are more at ease with the concept of SDL. This implies that technology is a crucial element in SDL. The research further evinced an absence of gender biasness, revealing that both boys and girls showed the same level of SDL skills.

Additionally, to be self-directed, students need to be self-motivated and the study indeed laid emphasis on the fact that students were not really into SDL as they were not motivated. The research proposed ways for students to be self-motivated, which will contribute to the success of SDL. A key element in motivating students is the support from teachers, and they have a crucial role to play in the SDL process. They should be able to provide adequate support and guidance to the students and also provide feedback to ensure that the students are on the right path. Other elements which also contribute to the success of SDL are self-disciplined, collaboration and self-management, that is the ability to set goals and work towards them. Although SDL has many positive impacts and on the other side, challenging, the research revealed that students are willing to adopt the concept of SDL in order to improve their learning process, provided the necessary resources are available. Fostering SDL in the curriculum setting or instructional practices for young students whereby they can perform self-assessment activities and create strong convictions for self-directed students.

13.10   Future Research

The opinions of teachers on SDL approach need to be studied in future and how their guidance can be a motivating factor in assisting self-directed students. From the above, there is also a call for future research to better understand why there is a difference between secondary and undergraduate students whereby female students have higher SDL skills than male students. This research can be extended to university students where they are involved in independent learning.

13.11   Limitations

There were several limitations related to the current study. The major one is the COVID-19 pandemic which affected every sector of the world, thus have to face the new normal in the education sector. It had a massive impact on the school calendar, which resulted in students to be under pressure for both their semester and examinations and schools to be closed and resumed not in their normal period. This constraint therefore had a direct impact in data collection with only 108 responses. Students were more focused in their studies with a new mode of teaching and learning and had little or did not spare time to fill the questionnaire. The authors also had another limitation in terms of time constraints. Since the school calendar had experienced some changes due to the pandemic, it became difficult for the authors to meet the deadline for the research work.

Acknowledgements   We would like to thank the educators who helped in the collection of data. A note of thanks is also due to Ms. S. K. Heerah Aisha for her assistance in the data analysis.

Appendix: Survey

Dear participants (students)

You are invited to participate in this survey being carried out by a group of Academics at the Open University. Please spare some few minutes of your precious time to fill this survey. You may rest assured that all the information provided will be kept confidential and anonymous and shall be used only for the purpose of this study. The aim of this study is to gauge students' experience of self-directed learning* at the lower/upper secondary level.

Please give your consent: Yes ☐   No ☐

Self-directed learning is a process in which a student takes the initiative and is in charge of his own learning process (with or without the help of others).

Section A: Demographics details

1. Gender   Female ☐   Male ☐
2. Grade:
3. Age   15 and up to 16 ☐   17 and up to 18 ☐ Above 18 ☐
4. Your SC aggregate   6–15 ☐ 16–24 ☐   More than 25 ☐
5. Rate how often you use each of the following tools? *0 (never) -1 (rarely) -2 (often) -3 (very often)*

   Tablet/PC/Laptop ☐ Internet ☐ Social networking ☐ Mobile phone ☐   Online shopping ☐
6. What is your level of computer competency?

   Beginner ☐ Intermediate ☐ High ☐
7. What is your level of experience with online courses?

   Beginner ☐   Average ☐ High ☐

		Strongly disagree	Disagree	Neutral	Agree	Strongly agree
1	**Section B: Awareness and readiness**					
1.1	I identify my own learning needs					
1.2	I keep up to date on different learning resources available online					
1.3	I am responsible for identifying my areas of deficit					
1.4	I find interactive teaching–learning sessions more effective than just listening to lectures					

(continued)

(continued)

		Strongly disagree	Disagree	Neutral	Agree	Strongly agree
1.5	I rehearse and revise new lessons					
1.6	I like to ask question(s) to the teacher					
1.7	I self-assess before I get feedback from teachers					
1.8	I stick to my teachers' explanation and notes only for my learning					
1.9	I find both success and failure inspire me to further learning					
1.10	My interaction with others helps me to develop the insight to plan for further learning					
2	**Section C: Self-directed learning skills**					
	Self-discipline					
2.1	I am responsible for my own learning					
2.2	I need to keep my learning routine separate from my other commitments					
	I set specific times for my study online					
2.3	I arrange my self-learning routine in such a way that it helps develop a permanent learning culture in my life					
2.4	I keep annotated notes or a summary of all my ideas, reflections and new learning					

(continued)

(continued)

		Strongly disagree	Disagree	Neutral	Agree	Strongly agree
2.5	I identify the need for interdisciplinary links for maintaining social harmony					
2.6	I am not distracted by other online activities (e.g. instant messages, Internet surfing) when learning online					
	Self-motivation					
2.7	I always need people to motivate me					
2.8	I enjoy exploring information beyond the prescribed course objectives					
2.9	I feel that I am not learning when the teacher is not around					
2.10	My inner drive directs me towards further development and improvement in my learning					
2.11	I seek assistance to address problems I face when learning online					
	Self-management					
2.12	I am able to plan and set my learning goals					
2.13	I am able to monitor my learning progress					
2.14	I make sure I complete all homework and coursework					
2.15	I often get confused between time for learning and time for entertainment					
2.16	I like to evaluate what I do					

(continued)

(continued)

		Strongly disagree	Disagree	Neutral	Agree	Strongly agree
2.17	I dedicate adequate time for each subject					
3	**SDL—technology use**					
3.1	I am able to use information technology effectively					
3.2	I find modern educational interactive technology enhances my learning process					
3.3	I am confident in using online tools					
3.4	I rarely discuss technological matters with my friends					
4	**Openness and other supports for the SDL process**					
4.1	I consider teachers as facilitators of learning rather than providing information only					
4.2	I often initiate online group discussions					
4.3	I keep an open mind to others' point of view					
4.4	I am open to criticism if it can improve my learning					
4.5	I do not appreciate when my work is peer-reviewed					
4.6	I am able to identify my role within a group					
4.7	I am open to new ideas					
4.8	I find easy to work in collaboration with others					

(continued)

(continued)

		Strongly disagree	Disagree	Neutral	Agree	Strongly agree
4.9	I find it challenging to pursue learning with peers coming from different cultural backgrounds					

8. Do you have any recommendations on how you may improve your self-directed learning?
9. How far has the pandemic COVID-19 impacted on your self-directed learning skills?
10. What should be done to encourage students improve their self-directed learning skills?

References

Appavoo, P., Soyjaudah, K. M. S., & Armoogum, V. (2015). Assessing young learners' readiness to embrace ICT for pedagogical gain. *International Journal of E-Learning and Educational Technologies in the Digital Media, 1*(3), 154–166.

Appavoo, P., Sukon, K. S., Gokhool, A. C., & Gooria, V. (2019). Why does collaborative learning not always work even when the appropriate tools are available? *Turkish Online Journal of Distance Education, 20*(4), 11–30.

Askin Tekkol, I., & Demirel, M. (2018). An investigation of self-directed learning skills of undergraduate students. *Frontiers in Psychology*, 2–5.

Beetham, H., & Sharpe, R. J. (2012). *Rethinking pedagogy for a digital age: Designing for 21st century learning* (2nd ed.). Routledge.

Bekele, T. A. (2010). Motivation and satisfaction in internet-supported learning environments: A review. *Educational Technology & Society, 13*(2), 116–127.

Benson, P. (2001). *Teaching and researching autonomy in language learning.* Pearson.

Black, A. E., & Deci, E. L. (2000). The effects of instructors' autonomy support and students' autonomous motivation on learning organic chemistry: A self-determination theory perspective. *Science Education, 84*(6), 740–756.

Brandt, C. W. (2020). *Measuring student success skills: A review of the literature on self-directed learning. 21st Century success skills* (pp. 1–31). National Center for the Improvement of Educational Assessment.

Broadbent, J. (2016). Academic success is about self-efficacy rather than frequency of use of the learning management system. *Australasian Journal of Educational Technology, 32*(4), 38–49.

Brookfield, S. D. (2009). Self-directed learning. In R. Maclean & D. Wilson (Eds.), *International handbook of education for the changing world of work: Bridging academic and vocational learning* (pp. 2615–2627). Springer.

Brophy, J. (2010). *Motivating students to learn* (3rd ed.). Routledge.

Callaghan, N., & Bower, M. (2012). Learning through social networking sites—The critical role of the teacher. *Educational Media International, 49*(1), 1–17.

Chapman, A. (1997). *Gender bias in education. Critical cultural in pavilion.* Retrieved February 16, 2021 from http://www.edchange.org/multicultural/papers/genderbias.html.

Cho, M.-H., & Heron, M. L. (2015). Self-regulated learning: The role of motivation, emotion, and use of learning strategies in students' learning experiences in a self-paced online mathematics course. *Distance Education, 36*(1), 80–99.

Chou, P.-N., & Chen, W.-F. (2008). Exploratory study of the relationship between self-directed learning and academic performance in a web-based learning environment. *Online Journal of Distance Learning Administration, 11*(1), 6–8.

Chu, R. J. C., & Tsai, C. C. (2009). Self-directed learning readiness, Internet self-efficacy and preferences towards constructivist internet-based learning environments among higher-aged adults. *Journal of Computer Assisted Learning, 25*(5), 489–501.

Deci, E. L., & Ryan, R. M. (2000). The "what" and "why" of goal pursuits: Human needs and the self-determination of behavior. *Psychological Inquiry, 11*(4), 227–268.

Dimock, M. (2019). *Defining generations: Where Millennials end and generation Z begins.* Pew Research Center. Retrieved February 15, 2021 from https://www.pewresearch.org/fact-tank/2019/01/17/where-millennials-end-and-generation-z-begins/.

Drain, T., Grier, L., & Sun, W. (2012). Is the growing use of electronic devices beneficial to academic performance? Results from archival data and a survey. *Issues in Information Systems, 13*(1), 225–231.

Duckworth, A. L., & Seligman, M. E. P. (2005). Self-discipline outdoes IQ in predicting academic performance of adolescents. *Psychological Science, 16*, 939–944.

Fakomogbon, M. A., & Bolaji, H. O. (2017). Effects of collaborative learning styles on performance of students in a ubiquitous collaborative mobile learning environment. *Contemporary Educational Technology, 8*(3), 268–279.

Fisher, M., Jennifer, K., & Tague, G. (2001). Development of a self-directed learning readiness scale for nursing education. *Nurse Education Today, 21*(1), 516–525.

Garrison, D. R. (1997). Self-directed learning: Toward a comprehensive model. *Adult Education Quarterly, 48*(1), 18–33.

Gibbons, M. (2002). *The self-directed learning handbook.* Jossey-Bass, Wiley. ISBN 0-7879-5955-3.

Guglielmino, L. M., & Guglielmino, P. J. (2005). *Reliability & validity information.* Learning Preference Assessment. Retrieved from www.lpasdlrs.com.

Hamid, S., Waycott, J., Kurnia, S., & Chang, S. (2015). Understanding students' perceptions of the benefits of online social networking use for teaching and learning. *The Internet and Higher Education, 26*, 1–9.

Hofmann, W., Baumeister, R. F., Förster, G., & Vohs, K. D. (2012). Everyday temptations: An experience sampling study of desire, conflict, and self-control. *Journal of Personality and Social Psychology, 102*, 1318–1335.

Hussey, T., & Smith, P. (2010). Transitions in higher education. *Innovations in Education and Teaching International, 47*(2), 155–164.

Kapur, R. (2018). *Significance of self-directed learning.* Retrieved February 12, 2021from https://www.researchgate.net/publication/335096519_Significance_of_Self-Directed_Learning#fullTextFileContent.

Kauffman, D. F. (2004). Self-regulated learning in web-based environments: Instructional tools designed to facilitate cognitive strategy use, metacognitive processing, and motivational beliefs. *Journal of Educational Computing Research, 30*, 139–161.

King, C. (2011). Fostering self-directed learning through guided tasks and learner reflection. *Studies in Self-Access Learning Journal, 2*(4), 257–267.

Kleden, M. A. (2015). Analysis of self-directed learning upon students of mathematics education study. *Journal of Education and Practice, 6*(20), 1–7.

Kuh, G. D., & Hu, S. (2001). The relationships between computer and information technology use, selected learning and personal development outcomes, and other college experiences. *Journal of College Student Development, 42*, 217–232.

Lasfeto, D. B., & Ulfa, S. (2020). The relationship between self-directed learning and students' social interaction in the online learning environment. *Journal of E-Learning and Knowledge Society, 16*(2), 34–41.

Lee, K., Tsai, P. S., Chai, C. S., & Koh, J. H. L. (2014). Students' perceptions of self-directed learning and collaborative learning with and without technology. *Journal of Computer Assisted Learning, 30*(5), 425–437.

Lei, P. (2020). *Transforming our world by 2030.* UNDP. https://undp.medium.com/17-ways-youth-are-changing-the-world-505a489e91dc. Accessed on November 22, 2020.

Lepper, M. R. (1988). Motivational considerations in the study of instruction. *Cognition and Instruction, 5*(4.00), 289–309.

Lin, L. (2015). Exploring collaborative learning: Theoretical and conceptual perspectives. In *Investigating Chinese HE EFL classrooms* (Vol. XXVII, pp. 11–28). Springer.

Losh, E. (2014). *The war on learning: Gaining ground in the digital university.* MIT Press.

McIsaac, M. S., & Gunawardena, C. N. (1996). Distance education. In D. H. Jonassen (Ed.), *Handbook of research for educational communications and technology* (pp. 403–437). Simon & Shuster Macmillan.

McLoughlin, C., & Lee, M. J. W. (2010). Personalized and self-regulated learning in the Web 2.0 era: International exemplars of innovative pedagogy using social software. *Australasian Journal of Educational Technology, 26*(1), 28–43.

Muilenburg, L. Y., & Berge, Z. L. (2005). Student barriers to online learning: A factor analytic study. *Distance Education, 26*(1), 29–48.

Oksana, T. (2018). *Are we consuming too much information?* https://medium.com/@tunikova_k/are-we-consuming-too-much-information-b68f62500089. Accessed on December 5, 2020.

Palmer, D. (2007). What is the best way to motivate students in science? Teaching science. *The Journal of the Australian Science Teachers Association, 53*(1), 38–42.

Pink, H. D. (2011). *Drive: The surprising truth about what motivates.* New York Times.

Piskurich, G. M. (2003). *Preparing students for e-learning* (1st ed.). Pfeiffer.

Rapetti, E., & Cantoni, L. (2010). "Digital Natives" and learning with the ICTs. The "GenY @ work" research in Ticino, Switzerland. *Journal of E-Learning and Knowledge Society, 6*(1), 39–49.

Ryan, R. M., & Deci, E. L. (2004). Autonomy is no illusion: Self-determination theory and the empirical study of authenticity, awareness, and will. In J. Greenberg, S. L. Koole, & T. Pyszczynski (Eds.), *Handbook of experimental existential psychology* (pp. 449–479). Guilford Press.

Sadker, D., & Sadker, M. (1994). *Failing at fairness: How our schools cheat girls.* Simon & Schuster Inc.

Sasson, I., & Dori, Y. J. (2012). Transfer skills and their case-based assessment. In B. J. Fraser, K. G. Tobin, & C. J. McRobbie (Eds.), *The second international handbook of science education* (pp. 691–710). Springer.

Schunk, D. H., Pintrich, P. R., & Meece, J. L. (2008). *Motivation in education* (3rd ed.). Pearson Merrill Prentice Hall.

Sears, D. A., & Reagin, J. M. (2013). Individual versus collaborative problem solving: Divergent outcomes depending on task complexity. *Instructional Science, 41*(6), 1153–1172.

Shaikh, R. B. (2013). Comparison of readiness for self-directed learning in students experiencing two different curricula in one medical school. *Gulf Medical Journal, 2*, 27–31.

Song, L., Singleton, E. S., Hill, J. R., & Koh, M. H. (2004). Improving online learning: Student perceptions of useful and challenging characteristics. *Internet & Higher Education, 7*(1), 59–70.

Stewart, R. A. (2007). Investigating the link between self-directed learning readiness and project-based learning outcome: The case of international masters students in an engineering management course. *European Journal of Engineering Education, 32*(4), 453–465.

Sumuer, E. (2018). Factors related to college students' self-directed learning with technology. *Australasian Journal of Educational Technology, 34*(4), 29–43.

Tabassum, R., & Hanan, M. A. (2016). Technology use, self-directed learning, student engagement and academic performance: Examining the interrelations. *Computers in Human Behaviour, 63*, 604–612.

Tan, L., & Koh, J. H. (2014). *Self-directed learning: Learning in the 21st century*. Ministry of Education.

Thornton, K. (2010). Supporting self-directed learning: A framework for teachers. *Language Education in Asia, 1*(1), 158–170.

Wiley, K. (1983). Effects of a self-directed learning project and preference for structure on self-directed learning readiness. *Nursing Research, 32*(1), 181–185.

Xuan, Y. L., Razali, A. B., & Samad, A. A. (2018). Self-directed learning readiness (SDLR) among foundation students from high and low proficiency levels to learn English language. *Malaysian Journal of Learning and Instruction, 15*(2), 55–81.

Zimmerman, B. J., & Martinez-Pons, M. (1988). Construct validation of a strategy model of student self regulated learning. *Journal of Educational Psychology, 80*(3), 284–290.

Vandanah Gooria is a Programme Manager and Lecturer in Management and Marketing at the Open University of Mauritius. She holds a master's degree in Business Administration and is currently doing her Doctor of Philosophy in Special Education Needs Management. She has 13 years of experience in public administration of the education sector and has over 7 years of professional and academic experience encompassing development of course materials/programmes, authoring courses, university teaching, market research and surveys. She is a member of the Advisory Board of NOMSA. She published research papers in well-known journals and other International Conference proceedings (10th and 11th Annual University Teaching and Learning Higher Education Conferences, ICCS and e-MIG, UNISA 8th TEIR). She co-authored one international book chapter in September 2018 *"Technology for Efficient Learner Support Services in Distance Education—Experiences from Developing Countries"*, published in Springer. Her academic interest areas are mainly Marketing Relationship, Tourism, Customer behaviour, Online marketing, Marketing planning, Open Educational Resources (OER), Special education needs Management, Technology and Open Distance Learning.

Dr. Perienen Appavoo is Head of the Research Office at the Open University of Mauritius. He holds a Ph.D. in Educational Technologies. His academic interest areas include the integration of technology in education, open and distance learning, online education and educational leadership. He has over the last six years published more than twelve research articles in peer-reviewed journals and two book chapters. He has also co-authored two books in Information Technology. He has more than twenty years of experience in the design and production of educational video programmes.

Upasna Bhunjun is a lecturer in Human Resource Management at the Open University of Mauritius. She holds a B.A. (Hons.) Business Administration with specialisation in Human Resource Management and a master's degree in Business Administration. She is a member of the association of Human Resource Professionals in Mauritius. Her main roles as an academic include teaching, supervision and moderation of dissertation, conducting research, programme development and manual writing. As an academic, she is actively involved in the designing and planning of programme of study at different levels in her disciplinary area. Besides being an academic, she is also the Programme Manager of several undergraduate and postgraduate programmes at the Open University of Mauritius. Her area of interest includes talent management, training and development, performance management, human resource development, quality assurance and open and distance learning.

Abheenaye Chauhan Gokhool is a lecturer in Marketing and Management at the Open University of Mauritius since 2013. He holds a master's degree in Global Business Management and is also a certified Digital Marketing Professional. As an academic, he is involved in teaching, supervision and moderation of dissertations, setting and moderation of examination papers, developing curriculum and manuals, research and chairing of board of examiners. He has also been involved with different stakeholders in the development of customised courses for specific audiences. His academic interest areas include marketing and management, digital marketing, marketing communications, international marketing, consumer buyer behaviour, advertising, gender stereotyping, leadership and open and distance learning. Besides being an academic, he is also the programme manager of several courses and the liaison person between the CILT (UK) and the Open University of Mauritius.

Chapter 14
A Progressive Approach to OER Adoption in Development of Short Online Courses by University Lecturers

Pauline Ngimwa and Wanjira Kinuthia

Abstract The adoption of OERs by educational content developers is a progressive process that follows four distinct phases starting from initial scepticism and resistance, through appreciation phase, followed by adoption and eventual transition to creators of OERs. This is what was established in a three-stage process of creating online research methods short courses that were followed by university lecturers. A blended learning approach was implemented to extend what was previously primarily face-to-face delivery of research methods courses. Face-to-face instructional design and blended learning training were convened to initiate the blended learning project, which was executed virtually over several months. The lecturers, who are subject matter experts in research methods, were trained and supported in the design and development of blended learning to incorporate digital learning resources, including OERs. These lecturers were introduced to the benefits of OERs in designing courses and were taught how to search for OERs and use them in the course of course design. Using content analysis of the developed courses and interviews with the lecturers, we report findings of how these progressive phases played out and what factors influenced each phase. The findings can be used to accelerate the adoption of OERs among education content developers in African higher education and hence contribute to the practice of OERs adoption.

Keywords OERs adoption · African higher education OERs · Educational content development · Blended learning development

14.1 Introduction

It is nearly two decades since the term Open Education Resources (OERs) was coined at the UNESCO's 2002 Forum on Open Courseware (UNESCO, 2002), to

P. Ngimwa (✉)
Partnership for African Social and Governance Research, PASGR, Nairobi, Kenya
e-mail: pngimwa@pasgr.org

W. Kinuthia
Hamdan Bin Mohammed Smart University, Dubai, UAE

mean 'teaching, learning and research materials in any medium, digital or otherwise, that reside in the public domain or have been released under an open license that permits no-cost access, use, adaptation and redistribution by others with no or limited restrictions' (UNESCO, 2012, p. 1). At the core of this definition is the notion that education content is accessible for use by all at no cost. For resource-constrained environments, it means that lecturers can freely download content and repurpose it to suit their learners' needs without requiring permission to do so (de Oliveira Neto et al., 2017). OERs also make it possible for lecturers to express their creativity in content development and share their content widely for others to benefit from it, thus boosting their professional profiles (Cox & Trotter, 2017). At the same time, OERs enable these lecturers to take what others have created and remix it to create something new. This flexibility and ease of access, creation, use and exchange of educational content are made possible by an inherent feature in the open licensing that gives five rights defined in Wiley's '5Rs' framework. These are: 'the right to make, own, and control copies of the content (Retain); the right to use the content in a wide range of ways (Reuse); the right to adapt, adjust, modify or alter the content itself (Revise); the right to combine the original or revised content with other open content to create something new (Remix); and the right to share copies of the original content, your revisions, or your remixes with others (Redistribute)' (Wiley, 2014).

The benefits of OERs are therefore enormous. Besides enhancing access to knowledge and educational opportunities through sharing of educational content at no cost (Torres, 2013), they are crucial towards the achievement of the fundamental right of access to education in the UNESCO's Universal Declaration of Human Rights (UNESCO, n.d.) and SDG 4 (UNDP, n.d.). They contribute to a positive impact on the quality of learning and students' outcomes as confirmed in a study by Magro and Tabaei (2020) where students enrolled in courses that used OERs performed better than those who were in the same course but using commercial books. OERs are also a means of dealing with the rising costs of textbooks (McGreal et al., 2013). They also advance opportunities for collaboration and open sharing of teaching practices that empower lecturers to learn best practice and ideas from each other (Hennessy et al., 2016).

These benefits explain why there has been an increase in the interest around the OER movement globally. In Africa, the participation of the OER movement was strengthened by two OER declarations: the 2007 Cape Town Declaration on Open Education and the 2009 La declaration de Dakar sur les REL supported by the UNESCO, COL, l''Agence Universitaire de la Francophonie (AUF) and the Organisation Internationale de la Francophonie (OIF). Both declarations encouraged accelerated efforts in the promotion of OERs in education. OERs were seen as a means of contributing to social justice by widening access, particularly in higher education especially by the marginalised population. As a result, several initiatives have emerged in Africa such as the TESSA project, FLOSS4Edu project, OER Health Alliance, Siyavula and OER Africa. The OER movement in Africa has also received a boost from intergovernmental agencies, i.e. UNESCO, Commonwealth of Learning, and the Hewlett Foundation (Hodgkinson-Williams & Arinto, 2017).

Despite this positive impetus towards fortifying the OER movement on the continent, there appears to be no concrete evidence of substantial impact and effective adoption, especially in higher education. A recent publication has also claimed that despite the campaign around the OER movement especially, challenges of OERs awareness, a lower rate of adoption and the digital divide due to socio-economic disparities persist (Ossiannilsson et al., 2020). This observation agrees with Kanwar et al. (2010) that despite OERs being a significant breakthrough in expanding access to education in the global South, bridging the digital divide and supporting capacity building, this promise of OERs has often not translated into concrete and tangible results. Further, there is apprehension about Africans being spectators and consumers of the OER developed elsewhere, and hence the movement is seen as an opportunity for neocolonialism (Ngugi, 2011). The need to translate all this action into tangible impact is more urgent with the outbreak of the COVID-19 pandemic that has forced a paradigm shift in how learners access learning. The pandemic has also widened the digital divide further.

The above demands empirical evidence, especially around OER impact and adoption in Africa. However, Hodgkinson-Williams and Arinto (2017) note that most of this research has taken place in the Global North rather than in the South. OERs research in Africa has mainly been about the evaluation of OER projects on resource creation, reuse and sharing (Butcher, 2015). We need to understand how lecturers in African higher education go about adopting OER development, what influences their decisions to participate or not participate, and how they engage through the different stages of OER lifecycle (Beaven, 2018) that comprises five key practices: finding, composing, adapting, reusing and sharing. This chapter discusses the findings of a study that explored how university lecturers adopt OERs in the development of teaching and learning resources. The study identified the process from how they become aware of the resources through to adoption and ultimately becoming creators, and what influences the decisions to adopt or not to adopt. The study is based on a short professional development training programme where existing face-to-face learning materials were converted into a blended learning model, which provided a platform for adopting OERs. A review of related studies is first presented, followed by theoretical framing and the methodology that was adopted. Next, the findings are presented and then discussed. Finally, recommendations and conclusions are presented.

14.2   Review of Related Studies

A review of the existing literature suggests that there are only a few studies on OERs adoption and usage by lecturers in African higher education. Most of what is documented is mostly anecdotal, with limited empirical evidence as noted by Hodgkinson-Williams (2010). Nonetheless, some studies have evaluated existing OER projects (Butcher, 2015), but the focus is mostly on basic education. The TESSA OER project, one of the successful African projects, has provided a testing ground for some of the evaluation studies. For example, a study by Murphy and Wolfenden (2013) on the 'Extending and Embedding TESSA OER' project established how OERs were being used by teachers to broker pedagogical change among their colleagues and institutions. This resulted in increased access and enhanced learning experiences for learners. Another study on embedding TESSA materials also found out the need for advocacy work to support teachers (Wolfenden et al., 2010). They found out that teachers needed the endorsement of stakeholders, including school administrators, district officials and parents.

Studies on the usage of OERs have converged around the need for adaptation and localisation of OERs to make them relevant, essentially because most of them are developed outside this context. For instance, a study by Wilson (2008) on the suitability of UK's OpenLearn OER in a South African' university found that these resources needed to be localised to a South African language since English is not the only official language in South Africa. Such language adaptation has been highlighted in similar studies in other developing contexts. An example is a study by Hatakka (2009) which established that culturally embedded issues in the style of English language in Western developed OERs presented comprehension difficulties to learners. Jimes et al. (2013) in their case study of open textbooks by South African teachers also confirmed that OERs are useful when they are developed and evaluated through a process that draws on the local context for which they are created to be used. Studies on the TESSA project have also validated these findings on the need for adaptation and localisation to fit local systems and cultures. For instance, Wolfenden et al. (2012) reported on a highly structured and supported process of adaptation of TESSA OER for nine country settings across sub-Saharan Africa. They identified certain factors in this process that supported the adaptations of the resources. What is characteristic of these studies is that they are based on OERs that are primarily foreign or designed with a Western perspective and therefore have to be adapted to the African context. This confirms the concern raised earlier about Africans being consumers of OERs content developed elsewhere.

Generally, studies on lecturers' adoption and usage of OERs have tended to focus on enabling factors. For example, studies carried out by Luo et al. (2010) and Ngimwa and Wilson (2012) established that OERs adoption among African lecturers is hampered by technological, institutional and national policies, social as well as cultural and personal barriers. Ngimwa and Wilson's study, in particular, found that lack of incentives weakened the rate of adoption where academics' participation in the development of OERs was not recognised as an intellectual contribution when it came to promotion. Hodgkinson-Williams et al. (2017) also found that full participation required structural factors, i.e. infrastructural support, permission to share, as well as institutional and government support to be in place to enable uptake. These findings have also been corroborated by Cox and Trotter (2017) in their study on factors that influenced faculty in three South African universities to adopt OERs. The study found that infrastructural support, legal permissions as well as cultural and social variables determined whether and how adoption takes place. It also identified an important aspect of institutional and personal volition, suggesting that an institution or a lecturer can choose to participate or not to participate. This agrees with de Oliveira Neto et al. (2017)'s study which established that faculty members with PhDs were less likely to use OERs because they could create their teaching materials.

Other studies have established that adoption is confined to a few converts (champions) working either collaboratively or independently and privately (Beaven, 2018; Harold & Rolfe, 2019). These early adopters have intrinsic motivations for getting involved. Wolfenden et al. (2017)'s study established that these champions were teachers whose values and beliefs about effective teaching resonated with what OERs offer, i.e. opportunities for participatory pedagogy. Another motivation is the open nature of OERs that allows teachers to add their content (Belikov & Bodily, 2016; Magro & Tabaei, 2020).

Studies that have focused on barriers to adoption have established low awareness and appreciation of the OER concept and open licensing (Pete et al., 2018), inability to discover OER repositories and inability to differentiate between digital resources and OER (Belikov & Bodily, 2016).

Regarding the actual creation, reuse or sharing by lecturers, evidence remains scanty as noted by Beaven (2018). However, this study records that reuse happens in private spaces referred to as 'dark reuse' and recommends a further investigation to understand invisible practices around 'dark reuse'. The study reported in this chapter has investigated this complex OERs ecosystem to uncover what motivates lecturers in the African context to use or not use and reuse, create and share OERs and how this happens.

14.3 Theoretical Framework

This study was framed within social constructivist and communities of practice perspectives. Social constructivism and communities of practice highlight the structures and processes that scaffold learning in informal environments (Panke & Seufert, 2013). Social constructivism views learning as a situated activity, and it emphasises the role and importance of social contexts that learners bring to a learning environment. The social constructivism theory stresses a learner's role in knowledge acquisition by organising information into individually meaningful constructs. As noted by Mayer (1996), learning is the process of knowledge construction, and the teacher is the cognitive guide for academic tasks, whereas the learners are sense makers (Mayer, 1996). Learning is supported when learners can probe their construction of meaning against others' understandings. Hence, meaning and knowledge are socially negotiated and are supported through collaborative, authentic activities.

While constructivist approaches can serve as a theoretical projection screen for various group learning methods, open learning settings which are based on peer-to-peer interaction allow for the enhancement of a community of practice (CoP) paradigm. In a community of practice, 'learning means becoming or belonging differently than we do at the moment' (Lee & Roth, 2003). Regardless of whether it is face-to-face, 'finding one's place' or 'belonging' is not much different. Instead, communities usually develop characteristic activity patterns or 'orientations'.

Communities learn together in various ways, whether meeting regularly, sharing documents or conversing online. They have different orientations towards the process of learning together. Orientation is a pattern of activities and connections through which members experience being a community (Wenger et al., 2009). A researcher who looks at open learning from a CoP perspective will try to identify the community's characteristic activity pattern. She/he might also be interested in the different roles the community offers and how it supports a certain level of reciprocity while maintaining the idea of 'legitimate peripheral participation'. Reciprocity can take place in a mode of 'generalised exchange', so that 'a benefit given to a person is reciprocated not (necessarily) by the recipient but by someone else in the group' (Kollock, 1999).

Another potential research focus is the process of identity formation. Identity for the community as a whole involves discussing boundaries between one community and another; it implies positioning a given community within a constellation of other communities. 'Building identity consists of negotiating the meanings of our experience of membership in social communities' (Wenger, 1998). Learning together in a CoP does not require or produce a homogenous group of members with identical goals. Instead, the activity level, learning aspirations, and needs vary by each member.

The use of technology contributes to the tension between the individual and the community. While a tool may be designed for groups, it is mainly used individually, often when one is alone. Technology also increases the complexity of the group/individual polarity (Wenger et al., 2009). In communities of practice, everyone has something to contribute or to learn. Users can create their content or courses or subscribe to existing courses either as active participants or as followers.

Though not all open, informal learning happens in the context of communities of practice, many websites are examples of successful open learning. However, today's open learner is not only a member of the virtual community but also of various other social communities (Panke & Seufert, 2013).

14.4   Methodology

In this study, blended learning was defined as an approach that combines online learning resources and engagement with face-to-face learning content that requires the physical presence of the learner and the facilitator. Several blended learning models are used depending on the instructional goals. Some models include face-to-face, rotational, flex, labs, self-blend, and online driver (Friesen, 2012). Even blended learning models can be blended, and the models are not mutually exclusive. Many components comprise a blended learning model, including instructor-delivered content, e-learning, webinars, conference calls, live and online sessions with the instructors, and social media.

Blended learning allows for the personalisation of learning, flexibility and convenience. The method allows for the integration of innovative technology-enhanced learning (TEL) resources and tools, including digital learning resources, e-assessment, e-portfolios, among others. The project reported in this study sought to integrate relevant TEL strategies and resources such as eCases, video, and audio, PowerPoint presentations, and PDF documents using the Moodle learning management system (LMS).

At its conception, the training programme began as a face-to-face (classroom learning) delivery method. Over time, it moved to technology-enabled learning. It has been continuously introducing various aspects of blended learning. Each delivery begins with online engagement in Moodle for 2–3 weeks that precedes the face-to-face delivery. The discussion forum is used to engage participants in reflecting on assigned readings, discussion questions, and videos. The face-to-face component is also supported by digital resources such as PowerPoint presentations, e-cases, video and audio clips, and animations, lectures, small and large group discussions, group activities, among other strategies. In the last year and a half, the programme has moved more towards blended learning. The first goal was to enhance the learning experiences and outcomes. A second goal was to explore ways to cut down costs of face-to-face delivery, including travel costs and time and accommodation. Figure 14.1 illustrates the e-learning spectrum and the focus of this project.

The purpose of this study was to document and analyse the process that the lecturers, who are subject matter experts in research methods, were trained and supported in the design and development of blended learning to incorporate digital learning resources, including OER. The study aimed to provide insight into the following questions:

1. How do course writers adopt open educational resources when developing content for blended learning delivery?
2. What are the opportunities and challenges when adopting open educational resources when developing content for blended learning delivery?

A combination of processes was followed to obtain data that have been used to provide reported findings. In the first instance, a three-stage process was applied to

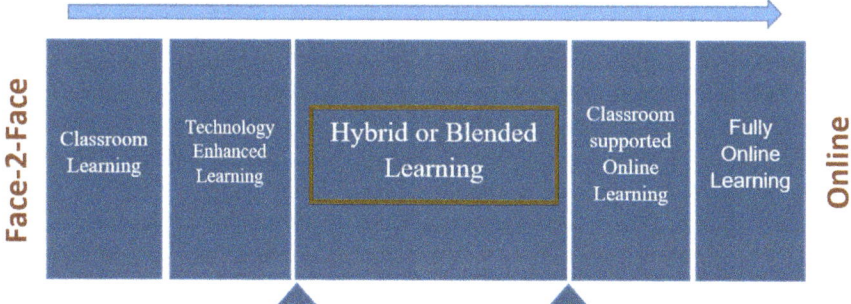

Fig. 14.1 Blended learning project. *Attribution* Murray (2004)

convert pre-existing face-to-face courses into an online format in which OERs were adopted. These are courses that are used in a short professional development training programme for early and mid-career researchers and delivered through an innovative pedagogy that is interactive and learner-centred. The process of converting the courses to blended format involved heavy reliance on technology-enhanced learning (TEL) strategies and resources such as the use of multimedia contents in the form of Word and PDF documents, PowerPoint slides, video and audio clips, electronic cases studies, games and simulations, images, web pages, social media links, process diagrams and checklists. Most of this was obtained from OERx and Creative Commons license multimedia.

The first stage focused on training content developers on how to convert learning content for TEL. These content developers are also the programme's instructors who usually are university lecturers, most of them lacking TEL strategies and were not conversant with OERs. Therefore, an instructors' retreat was organised to launch the project and provide training on how to engage with TEL strategies and resources, especially introducing OER concept and how to locate or create OERs needed in the content development process.

The second stage comprised the actual course design and development process. This was carried out virtually where course teams worked remotely. The instructional designer guided them through an interactive process that lasted six months for the first round of course design and development. They were provided with different templates (i.e. blueprint template, course plan template and course development template). These templates forced them to critically make decisions about what multimedia resources they were going to use. They were also encouraged to locate suitable existing OERs or create their own as they saw fit. The Instructional Designer and Programme Manager made participant observations and recorded virtual communication between the teams and the Instructional Designer. Course feedback was provided iteratively throughout the process. Upon completion of the initial development, internal peer-reviews were completed with other content developers. Revisions were made, and the courses were then sent out for external review. After the external review, copyediting was completed for all the courses before they were implemented into the learning management system (LMS).

The emergence of the COVID-19 pandemic ushered in the third stage. The need to deliver training online forced the conversion of the blended courses into fully online formats where again adoption of OERs was encouraged. Several courses from the first round were identified for redesigning, to transform further and create more multimedia and identify additional OER where possible. Working remotely in course teams and under the guidance of the instructional designer and the Programme Manager, the content developers identified or developed appropriate digital instructional materials and strategies to create interactivity and learner-centeredness in the courses. These resources included OERs. As in the second stage, the Instructional Designer and the Programme Manager collected further participants' observations and recorded all the virtual communications between the teams and with the instructional designer. All data obtained from participants' observations and virtual communication were analysed through content analysis, for adoption of OER, noting decisions made to use or not use OERs, and obstacles encountered.

A questionnaire (Appendix provides questions that were converted to a Google Forms for ease of online data collection) was later administered to collect qualitative data from the content developers. The questions centred around their understanding and perception of OERs in general. More specifically, the questionnaire probed the extent to which the participants utilised OERs in the blended learning project and whether they have continued to use OERs in their teaching career. In addition to the questionnaire, a virtual focus group discussion (FGD) was also used to obtain triangulating data. This also provided an opportunity to clarify or follow up on data obtained during participant observations. Data was analysed by the two researchers individually and then collectively to ensure trustworthiness of the data analysed. Finally, a critical reflection of the entire process by the two researchers, both of whom are enthusiasts of the OER movement, provided an analytical lens for further sense-making and interpretation of the findings in the light of the existing body of knowledge concerning OERs adoption by African higher education lecturers.

14.5   Participants

Fourteen content writers participated in developing fourteen courses, although some content writers developed more than one course under the direction and supervision of an experienced instructional designer. There were eight male and six female participants. The writing was mainly completed in teams of two. In some cases, depending on the content, the course was completed by one writer and in a few cases by three writers depending on the required area of expertise. The content writers were subject matter experts primarily in the social sciences and humanities from African countries. They were mainly university-based academics and researchers, researchers from think tanks, research and policy institutes, knowledge-producing civil society organisations and governments. Their experience and knowledge of educational technology ranged from novices to highly experienced. Their interest too varied from those who had a low interest to those who were very keen and wanted to learn more. The latter spent more time learning how to integrate digital technologies and even experimented using different applications and resources.

Participants were recruited through purposive sampling. All of them had been involved in the blended learning project and were the focus of the study. They were initially explained the objective of the study and the process. All accepted to participate except one who felt that she had not actively participated in the blended learning project. Informed consent to participate in this study was then obtained. Participants were informed that they could opt out of the study anytime if they felt they wanted to withdraw their participation. Permission to record the virtual focus group discussion was also obtained before the session began. All participants were assured of confidentiality and data from the questionnaire and focus group discussions anonymized and securely stored.

14.6   Results of the Study

This section summarises the results of the project, organised by theme. Observations, existing gaps and challenges that were identified are summarised below. The ultimate goal was to find practical ways to address each one during the course development process and for future development and course revisions.

Variations in Blended Learning Course Outputs
In general, most courses were written with a good structure and flow and were aligned to the course objectives, learning outcomes, and learning activities. The underlying logic, flow (structure), and coverage of material were sound. However, some courses were more robust than others. For example, based on the purpose and content of the course, some were mostly text-based while others more readily integrated multimedia resources. The content writers who integrated multimedia did so in the form of PowerPoints, YouTube videos and visual information in the form of images, charts, graphs, illustrations and tables, as noted by one participant: '*I used video in the preparation of the blended learning content for CPER, and in the course of revisions like the ethics modules … I also recommended a couple of OER materials*'.

Where available and practical, eCases were integrated as learning activities. In some instances, the case studies were developed by the content writers, while in other cases, they used existing cases. Nonetheless, the examples used to illustrate the learning points were helpful, practical, localised and customised to the learning outcomes.

For those courses that were detailed, most were well-organised, and content was broken down into smaller, more easily digestible chunks. In other cases, some depth and content were recommended to make the courses more comprehensive. In several courses, the lists were quite extensive, and in some instances, the required or recommended readings could not be accessed without subscriptions to the journals or purchasing the books. In other courses, required and suggested readings were indicated but not utilised. In several instances, required links and reading were no longer available as they had been removed or redirected from the source. Some courses had ample learning activities, while others did not build in enough formative learning and assessment items.

The final implementation of each course in the LMS varied depending on the content organisation in the provided course development templates. Different tools were used to present different types of content. These were mainly in the form of forums, assignments, HTML pages and PDF documents. Courses varied in their level of interactivity and learner engagement based on the developed and selected resources and the learning activities.

Iterative feedback, internal and external review, and copyediting were built into the development process. Even though they were considered tedious and repetitive, ensuring that the courses underwent multiple rounds of feedback, the process helped to enhance the final deliverables. There is still room for improvement, but the process supports the improvement of the final outputs.

The Learning Curve in Blended Learning Course Development

There was an initial learning curve in the process of developing content for blended learning delivery. Even with training on best practices, ongoing support and supporting materials, the transformation for some happened gradually. Initially, for some course writers, who had not previously developed online or blended courses, it was somewhat challenging to visualise the process, i.e. what final deliverable would look like, and what content was best designed for online delivery versus that which was to be facilitated either face-to-face or virtually synchronously.

For example, course writers were introduced to the use of templates as a way of helping them make decisions of what digital resources, including OERs to use. However, despite there being flexibility in how the templates guide the process, some course writers found the templates constraining and sometimes deviated from them, affecting the final implementation in Moodle. In several courses, the writers opted not to use and the first and the second templates and worked directly on the final course template, due to time constraints. This affected the quality of the final deliverables. For instance, when it came to the selection of readings and development or identification of OER and multimedia resources which was guided by the second template, the course writers were less likely to include them in the course.

There were, however, those who got it right from the start. After the training, they went back and studied the templates further and engaged the instructional designer where they needed help. This category found the process easy and fun. They completed their courses ahead of the others and their final deliverables were of quality standard. An FDG participant from this category of course writers commented on his usage of the template in deciding what resources to use: '*are they relevant to the point I am trying to make or the thing I am trying to teach. And this is where my agency comes in, in midwifing, what gets to my, my, learners, and what, what does not*'.

Limited Available OERs and CC License Resources

The use of OERs was built into the process from the onset, and guidance and support were provided throughout. Due to the high cost of proprietary instructional materials, OERs are a feasible option when they are available and appropriate for a course. To the extent, possible OERs and readily available resources were integrated into some courses. However, in some cases, it was more challenging to locate and vet the resources, yet there were no appropriate substitutes.

In some courses, there was variance in the understanding of what constitutes open versus copyrighted material as one FGD participant expressed:

> Sometimes you have access but you are not too sure if it is really open. Suppose you can cite it [or] if you cannot use it for training. And if you also require to acknowledge them. … to be so explicit that this is really free, and you can use it without very much acknowledgement. So actually, that is one of the challenges I have some time, having to use it in training. It's also sceptical that are you sure you are not infringing into some copyrights issues. That is one of just something I wanted to highlight as one of the major challenges.

In situations where the Intellectual Property Rights were not appropriately incorporated, content authentication software was used to identify issues and to provide support in addressing issues as they arose.

Understanding of what constitutes OERs

The understanding and perception of OERs to the course writers were relatively consistent in their definition of OERs being resources that are available for everyone for research and teaching that are available at no cost. Those materials may be textual, audio, visual or digital images. Participants understood that depending on the license, OERs are available for use by anyone, anytime, but under certain conditions. For instance, one FGD participant indicated that '...*you can use some and modify, you can use and not modify, you can use them for commercial or non-commercial services. Others are for education purposes. So those are the conditions*'.

Scepticism in Adoption of OERs

While the idea of creating and sharing resources and knowledge was encouraging, a degree of scepticism in the adoption of OERs into the courses was observed among some course writers. These were suspicious of creating and putting one's content 'out there' with the possibility of losing its ownership. A course writer expressed:

> … because I have always felt very suspicious about OER…, why is it that the Global North has suddenly decided that we can open resources or make resources accessible. Basically, helping the South, because it is most of the time we are the people who are unable to access those resources…I get into feeling very cautious about OER.

This is an example of possible bottlenecks to expect in OER development projects. It also raises the issue of monopolisation of educational resources and the role of African academics in developing and sharing educational resources as observed by another participant:

> … what could be happening is the monopolisation of the process of knowledge degeneration. If you look at the various OER, very rarely do you find those on African perspectives… Africa is consuming their [Western] OER, but it is not part of creating. So what implications does this have for us? In the long run, what does this mean for us? …. Even though I appreciate that the onus is on us to upload….

Project Timeline Challenges

The projection was designed with ample time to locate OERs or develop a variety of multimedia, review and submit all courses before the end of the proposed timeline. However, it was challenging to maintain deadlines and manage milestones while working remotely. This was especially true when the work teams were smaller or when other constraints arose, such as scheduling, other competing workloads, i.e. teaching, and connectivity or power challenges.

Capacity Building: Evolving Project Perspective

Certain assumptions were made about how the project would be guided and supported. Course writers were encouraged to include in each course ample e-learning, OERs and multimedia resources to support the written content. However, during the content development process, it was discovered that more support was needed in certain areas that were not anticipated; for example, the use of open vs copyrighted content. This somewhat changed the scope of the project beyond course writing to support capacity building. The project morphed into a multi-phase process: (1) develop the written content primarily; (2) continue to develop the written content further; and (3) develop multimedia content and learning activities and resources.

14.7   Discussion and Recommendations

By its very nature, the open knowledge and OER movements are all about developing communities of practice. This project was framed around 'communities of practice', which offers a logical view of the social processes of knowledge creation. This did not begin with the project under discussion. This notion of communities of practice has been evident in the training programme where the course instructor pool is made up of a cohesive group of social science researchers that share knowledge and collaborative learning. This has in turn contributed to the training programme remaining successful for over a decade. For this project, the stage was set during the initial workshop where OERs, among other project details and guidelines, were introduced. More learning was moved to the virtual space where course writers shared among themselves their new content, peer-reviewed each other's work and shared ideas for improvement. Taking a social constructivist view of teaching, learning and course development, the goal was to create an experience that would allow for the individuals and small teams to together in course development. In this process, they would end up with a coherent blended learning programme that is seamless, and one that creates a standardised structure for course participants through the guidelines use of templates.

To attain success in a blended learning project that aims to incorporate OER and multimedia resources, the correct strategies for developing and delivering online content should be embraced. The course development project morphed into a three-part process where gaps were recognised. With the first part (content development) being complete, it was necessary to continue to improve on the content and proposed delivery. This was done on a smaller scale with a select number of courses. It is therefore essential to build in flexibility in the process where possible, based on specific courses depending on such factors as the discipline or topic, subject matter experts' levels of expertise, and the flexibility of the timeline and available budget.

As supported by the literature and best practices, the purpose of the templates is to serve as a guide in the general thinking about how and why content should be organised and also in terms of visual design and organisation (Holcomb & Greer, 2020). It guides how the content is eventually implemented online in terms of content organisation and visual display of menus and multimedia. The templates should demystify for course developers the task of designing for the online and blended learning environment, thus making the development less laborious (McAlpine & Allen, 2007). Templates also help to create a consistent learner experience from one course to the next. Essentially, learners should focus on the content rather than the design of the course. The template is also an opportunity to encourage the identification and development of OER and other digital resources. From the findings of this study, it is evident that those who were consistent in their usage of the templates found the process easy and enjoyable than those who did not.

Course development should be viewed as a process rather than as an event. This allows for suggestions and recommendations both from participants and peer-reviewers to be addressed. During this process, it is also essential to continuously identify and incorporate OERs and Creative Commons license learning resources. In some instances, hyperlinks to external readings become inactive over time. Thus developing or adopting OER and embedding them in the courses is a feasible way of reducing the dependency on external resources that may be either open or proprietary. Reviewing resources to identify copyrighted content and replacing them with materials that are more readily accessible over time helps to gradually create a balance in the resources selected for the courses, and also to build in a mechanism for selecting and adopting open journal articles and OERs that are current and relevant.

Ongoing course evaluation is essential, regardless of the blended learning model or approach in place. After piloting the courses, and early during the programme offering, it is advantageous to create or adopt rubrics to evaluate the quality of the courses on an ongoing basis. This rubric should be designed to check for, evaluate, and recommend OERs where possible, thus making it an integral part of blended learning development.

Capacity building and training are necessary to continue enhancing the courses by giving course developers and instructors strategies for content development and delivery. This could be considered in a series of learning opportunities that: (1) support training in online and blended learning facilitation to instructors and subject matter experts with the ultimate goal to enable them to become experts who can deliver the courses using best practices in the blended learning format. This can be done through workshops that support the development of multimedia resources such as video and audio recording, basic e-learning authoring, creation of instructional graphic, eCase development, Creative Commons and OERs content identification; (2) Enhance information and knowledge on ideal blended learning models; (3) offer best practices for developing online and blended courses including writing resources, and fundamentals of Intellectual Property Rights (IPR); (4) support identification and use of OERs and Creative Commons license resources. The training would introduce or enhance their knowledge of use and reuse of OERs, license types, how to locate OERs and other pertinent information; and (5) identification of digital resources that meet the needs of different types of learners.

The dilemma is often one of why ownership is claimed even though the content developer has compiled the content from existing resources. Some organisations design clear contracts for their writers—so that the issues of IPR and content ownership are clarified from the beginning. The study by Straumsheim (2014) showed that most instructors know little about OERs, and an even smaller number both use OERs in their courses and make their course material available to peers. In this study, some of the course writers had not heard about OERs before they participated in the project while a smaller number were aware of OERs but had never reviewed any type of open content. Of importance however is that while initially sceptical, once they became more familiar and comfortable with what OERs are all about, they embraced the concept and objectives of the OER movement as providing quality resources and positive learner outcomes.

The development of online and blended learning can be costly, especially at the inception stages, and when OERs are less available. To develop and maintain the blended courses, funding could be sought to support subscription to instructional resources such as journals, articles and eBooks in content areas where OER and Creative Commons license resources are limited until they are readily available. The courses should be viewed as 'living' resources. As newer materials become available, periodic review and updating of content are recommended.

Quality assurance is a broad concept that encompasses many of the above recommendations. However, quality assurance must be built in from the inception of the blended learning programme and become integral to continuous development and improvement. Quality assurance strategies should consider the quality of the program, the courses and the delivery of the content. Quality Matters (2013), for example, provides broad standards in the Quality Matters Rubric that includes, among other criteria, instructional materials.

It is not unusual to hear broad terms of 'good' or 'bad' blended learning courses, yet they do not specify the attributes that contribute to the designation. Rather than label a course as good or bad, it is more useful to identify the course elements that are working or not working. With guiding standards in place, a review is more likely to identify areas that require attention. The use of rubrics is relatively easy to implement for instructors, designers, and administrators who are already pressed for time. Reviewing an online or blended course with a rubric and producing 'to-do list' that one can focus on makes the revisions more seamless.

14.8 Conclusion

The study reported here was based on the process and outputs of a three-phase multi-year blended learning project. The work continues, as more short courses are developed or revised to integrate more digital resources and use innovative strategies in design and delivery. As noted, the engagement began with the programme offering and an exploration of the potential of multimedia and OERs to add quality and save time in updating the short courses. However, it evolved into a broader project with the changing and immediate needs and circumstances of partner higher education institutions on the African continent. There is a growing demand for capacity building and alternatives to costly instructional resources and subscription journals. This suggests that using OERs is a viable alternative. A key finding of this study is that there are opportunities to consider other multimedia such as eCases and animations which can later be turned into OERs. For the text-heavy content, there are opportunities for alternative presentation modes and multimedia development now that the materials have been written and implemented into the LMS. Implementing the blended learning approach should be a gradual learning process with opportunities for continuously examining the courses and revising to demystify the process. It also offers an opportunity to support course developers as the process is evolving. New content is available all the time. Hence, there is a need to search continuously for OERs and update the courses. Finally, it is important to encourage the use of the course development templates to support the course writers throughout the journey.

Acknowledgements This study is based on a project of the Partnership for Social and Governance Research (PASGR). We also would like to acknowledge our study participants, peer-reviewers, and external reviewers of the modules. The authors would also like to dedicate this chapter in memory of the late Prof. Stewart Marshall who provided insights into the framing of this chapter and passed on before it was published.

Appendix: Questionnaire Questions

1. What do you understand by Open Education Resources?
2. What is our perception of them in supporting learning in Africa?
3. To what extent did you apply them in the blended learning project?
4. What informed your utilisation or lack of utilisation?
5. What challenges did you experience?
6. What impact did the training you received at the beginning of the project have on your determination of whether to use OER or not?
7. How have you continued to use them in your teaching career?
8. Would you consider yourself as a creator…describe…

References

Beaven, T. (2018). 'Dark reuse': An empirical study of teachers' OER engagement. *Open Praxis, 10*(4), 377–391.

Belikov, O., & Bodily, R. (2016). Incentives and barriers to OER adoption: A qualitative analysis of faculty perceptions. *Open Praxis, 8*(3), 235–246.

Butcher, N. (2015). *A basic guide to open educational resources (OER).* Report for the Commonwealth of Learning and UNESCO.

Cox, G., & Trotter, H. (2017). Factors shaping lecturers' adoption of OER at three South African universities. In C. Hodgkinson-Williams & P. B. Arinto (Eds.), *Adoption and impact of OER in the Global South* (pp. 287–347).

de Oliveira Neto, J. D., Pete, J., Daryono, C., & Cartmill, T. (2017). OER use in the Global South: A baseline survey of higher education instructors. In C. Hodgkinson-Williams & P. B. Arinto (Eds.), *Adoption and impact of OER in the Global South* (pp. 69–118).

Friesen, N. (2012). *Report: Defining blended learning.* Retrieved from http://learningspaces.org/papers/Defining_Blended_Learning_NF.pdf.

Harold, S., & Rolfe, V. (2019). "I find the whole enterprise daunting": Staff understanding of Open Education initiatives within a UK university. *Open Praxis, 11*(1), 71–83.

Hatakka, M. (2009). Build it and they will come? - Inhibiting factors for reuse of open content in developing countries. *The Electronic Journal of Information Systems in Developing Countries, 37*(5), 1–16.

Hennessy, S., Haßler, B., & Hofmann, R. (2016). Pedagogic change by Zambian primary school teachers participating in the OER4Schools professional development programme for one year. *Research Papers in Education, 31*(4), 399–427.

Hodgkinson-Williams, C., & Arinto, P. B. (2017). *Adoption and impact of OER in the Global South.* African Minds, International Development Research Centre & Research on Open Educational Resources.

Hodgkinson-Williams, C., Arinto, P. B., Cartmill, T., & King, T. (2017). Factors influencing Open Educational Practices and OER in the Global South: Meta-synthesis of the ROER4D project. In C. Hodgkinson-Williams & P. B. Arinto (Eds.), *Adoption and impact of OER in the Global South* (pp. 27–67).

Holcomb, J., & Greer, T. W. (2020). Standardisation of forms, templates, and processes for implementing an e-learning program with a decentralised instructional design team. *The Journal of Applied Instructional Design, 9*(2).

Jimes, C., Weiss, S., & Keep, R. (2013). Addressing the local in localization: A case study of open textbook adoption by three South African teachers. *Journal of Asynchronous Learning Networks, 17*(2), 73–86.

Kanwar, A., Kodhandaraman, B., & Umar, A. (2010). Toward sustainable open education resources: A perspective from the global south. *The American Journal of Distance Education, 24*(2), 65–80.

Kollock, P. (1999). The economies of online cooperation. Gifts and public goods in cyberspace. In M. Smith & P. Kollock (Eds.), *Communities in cyberspace* (pp. 220–239). Routledge.

Lee, S., & Roth, W. M. (2003). Becoming and belonging: Learning qualitative research through legitimate peripheral participation. *Forum: Qualitative Social Research, 4*(2).

Luo, A., Ng'ambi, D., & Hanss, T. (2010). Towards Building a Productive, Scalable and Sustainable Collaboration Model for Open Educational Resources. In *Proceedings of the 16th ACM International Conference on Supporting Group Work (Group '10)*, Association for Computing Machinery, New York, 273–282.

Magro, J., & Tabaei, S. (2020). Results from a psychology OER pilot program: Faculty and student perceptions, cost savings, and academic outcomes. *Open Praxis, 12*(1), 83–99.

Mayer, R. E. (1996). Learners as information processors: Legacies and limitations of educational psychology's second metaphor. *Educational Psychologist, 31*(3/4), 151–161.

McAlpine, I., & Allen, B. (2007, December). Designing for active learning online with learning design templates. In *ICT: Providing choices for learners and learning. Proceedings ASCILITE Singapore 2007.*

McGreal, R., Kinuthia, W., Marshall, S., & McNamara, T. (2013). *Perspectives on open and distance learning: Open educational resources: Innovation, research and practice.*

Murray. R. B. (2004). *eLearning Tech: What's on the horizon.* https://www.slideshare.net/rodbrent/asbmb-2014murray?from_action=save.

Ngimwa, P., & Wilson, T. (2012). An empirical investigation of the emergent issues around OER adoption in Sub-Saharan Africa. *Learning, Media and Technology, 37*(4), 398–413.

Ngugi, C. (2011). OER in Africa's Higher Education Institutions. Distance Education. *August, 32*(2), 277–287.

Ossiannilsson, E., Zhang, X., Wetzler, J., Gusmão, C., Aydin, C. H., Jhangiani, R., Glapa-Grossklag, J., & Makoe, M. (2020). From open educational resources to open educational practices: For resilient sustainable education. *Distance and Mediation of Knowledge, 31.*

Panke, S., & Seufert, T. (2013). What's educational about open educational resources? Different theoretical lenses for conceptualising learning with OER. *E-Learning and Digital Media, 10*(2), 116–134.

Pete, J., Mulder, F., Oliveira, Neto, J., & Omollo, K. (2018). Differentiation in access to, and the use and sharing of (open) educational resources among students and lecturers at technical and comprehensive Ghanaian Universities. *Open Praxis, 10*(4), 405–421.

Quality Matters. (2013). *Higher ed program rubric.* Retrieved from https://www.qualitymatters.org/rubric.

Straumsheim, C. (2014). "Open, but undiscovered". *Inside Higher Ed* (November 4), at https://www.insidehighered.com/news/2014/11/04/open-educational-resources-perceived-high-quality-even-though-faculty-awareness-lags.

Torres, N. P. M. (2013). Embracing openness: The challenges of OER in Latin American education. *Open Praxis, 5*(1), 81–89.

UNESCO. (2002). *Forum on the impact of open courseware for higher education in developing countries*, Paris. Retrieved from https://unesdoc.unesco.org/ark:/48223/pf0000128515.

UNESCO. (2012). 2012 Paris OER Declaration: 2012 World Open Educational Resources (OER) Congress UNESCO, Paris, June 20-22, 2012. Retrieved from http://www.unesco.org/new/filead min/MULTIMEDIA/HQ/CI/CI/pdf/Events/Paris%20OER%20Declaration_01.pdf

UNESCO. (n.d.). *Universal declaration of human rights*. Retrieved from http://portal.unesco.org/en/ev.php-URL_ID=26053&URL_DO=DO_TOPIC&URL_SECTION=201.htm.

UNDP. (n.d.). *Sustainable development goals*. Retrieved from https://www.undp.org/content/undp/en/home/sustainable-development-goals.html.

Wenger, E. (1998). *Communities of practice: Learning, meaning, and identity*. Cambridge University Press.

Wenger, E., White, N., & Smith, D. (2009). *Digital habitats: Stewarding technology for community*. CPSquare.

Wiley, D. (2014). *The access compromise and the 5th R*. Retrieved from https://opencontent.org/blog/archives/3221.

Wilson, T. (2008). New Ways of Mediating Learning: Investigating the implications of adopting open educational resources for tertiary education at an institution in the United Kingdom as compared to one in South Africa. *International Review of Research in Open and Distance Learning, 9*(1), 1–19.

Wolfenden, F., Umar, A., Aguti, J., & Abdel G. (2010). Using OERs to improve teacher quality: emerging findings from TESSA. In *Sixth Pan Commonwealth Forum on Open Learning*, 24-28 Nov 2010, Kochi, India.

Wolfenden, F., Buckler, A., & Keraro, F. (2012) OER Adaptation and Reuse across cultural contexts in Sub Saharan Africa: Lessons from TESSA (Teacher Education in Sub Saharan Africa). *Journal of Interactive Media in Education*

Wolfenden, F., Auckloo, P., Buckler, A., & Cullen, J. (2017). Teacher educators and OER in East Africa: Interrogating pedagogic change. In C. Hodgkinson-Williams & P. B. Arinto (Eds.), *Adoption and impact of OER in the Global South* (pp. 251–286).

Pauline Ngimwa is the Programme Manager for the Professional Development and Training Programme at the Partnership for African Social and Governance Research. She has extensive work experience in the African higher education sector where she has led capacity strengthening programmes and technology-enhanced learning initiatives. Her research interests include design and use of digital educational resources including Open Educational Resources (OERs) in African higher education. She has published in this area and peered reviewed for international journals. She holds a Ph.D. and Masters of Research in Educational Technology; and B.Sc. and Masters in Information Science. She is also a fellow with the African Science Leadership Programme, University of Pretoria.

Wanjira Kinuthia holds a Ph.D. in Instructional Design and Development. She served as an Associate Professor with Tenure taught for many years at Georgia State University. She is also involved in various learning design projects in Africa, the Caribbean, the USA and the UAE. Professional activities include consulting work with NGOs on e-learning design and curriculum development, and mentoring Ph.D. students. Current service activities include Editorial Board membership on the International Journal of Education and Development using Information and Communication (IJEDICT) and e/Merge Africa mentorship program. Ongoing projects include use of OER and mobile technologies for e-learning. She has edited several books and published many articles based on her work in these areas.